STEPHEN J. FIELD

CRAFTSMAN OF THE LAW

THE COURT AND THE CONSTITUTION

A Series Edited by *Philip B. Kurland*

Carl Brent Swisher

STEPHEN J. FIELD
CRAFTSMAN OF THE LAW

With an Introduction by
Robert G. McCloskey

Phoenix Books
THE UNIVERSITY OF CHICAGO PRESS
CHICAGO AND LONDON

The University of Chicago Press, Chicago 60637
The University of Chicago Press, Ltd., London W.C. 1
Copyright 1930 by The Brookings Institution
Introduction © 1969 by The University of Chicago
Phoenix Edition published 1969
Printed in the United States of America

CONTENTS

	INTRODUCTION BY ROBERT G. McCLOSKEY	vii
	AUTHOR'S ACKNOWLEDGMENTS	xxi
	INTRODUCTION	1
I.	YOUTH AND ITS HERITAGE	5
II.	EARLY DAYS IN CALIFORNIA	25
III.	PROBLEMS OF FRONTIER LIFE	52
IV.	FROM THE BAR TO THE BENCH	73
V.	JUDICIAL ENVIRONMENTS	105
VI.	THE SUPREME COURT AND SECTIONALISM	130
VII.	GREENBACKS IN THE SCALES OF JUSTICE	166
VIII.	CHINESE IMMIGRATION	205
IX.	THE OCTOPUS	240
X.	THE GAME OF POLITICS	268
XI.	GROOMED FOR THE PRESIDENCY	283
XII.	MORE POLITICS	300
XIII.	THE TERRY TRAGEDY	321
XIV.	THE PUBLIC INTEREST	362
XV.	THE INCOME TAX	396
XVI.	WELLSPRINGS OF JUSTICE	413
XVII.	THE CLOSING YEARS	435
	INDEX TO CASES CITED	453
	GENERAL INDEX	459

INTRODUCTION

There is, as every schoolboy knows, a somewhat shop-worn question about whether historical movements are determined by salient men or by more impersonal and ineluctable "forces." No definitive resolution of the general issue is very probable and none will be offered here. But it does seem arguable that the story of American constitutional development provides qualified but solid support for Thomas Carlyle's side in the old debate. The history of our Constitution is not only "the biography of great men." Certain enabling conditions must be present in order for a creative change to occur. The national political and ideological environment must be receptive; the relevant constitutional texts and precedents must be flexible enough to tolerate growth. But even when such circumstances exist, their potentialities must be translated into deeds and doctrines by a man. And because of the peculiar status and function that America has devolved on the Supreme Court of the United States, it is likely (I do not say certain) that the man will be one of the nine judges of that court. Those judges have, to an unusual degree, the power to shape the code that binds us and our governments. The result is that their characters, their wills, their values, are stamped on the history of the nation.

No doubt some such considerations as these help account for the proliferations of "judicial biography" in America during the past fifty years. In earlier times biographers paid comparatively little attention to members of the Supreme Court except for towering figures like John Marshall or men like Salmon P. Chase who had attained celebrity in other branches of government. According to the prevailing mythology, judges were impersonal vehicles of revealed truth, not statesmen. It was the Constitution, not they, who imposed commands on America; and their personal qualities were therefore of small historical interest. But in the twentieth century the realization has grown that these judges, far from merely transmitting constitutional verity, played a part in fashioning it. It has become clear that they are thus in an almost unique position to affect the course of events, and the study of their lives has taken on a new relevance. In ever increasing numbers, scholars have turned to that study.

Carl Swisher's biography of Stephen Field was one of the first to reflect this modern preoccupation, and it remains one of the most valuable contributions to the genre. This is partly because of the author's balanced and authoritative scholarship. But it is also partly because of his subject's importance in our national chronicle. Field's tenure on the Supreme Court (1863–97) spanned what turned out to be one of the great creative eras in American constitutional history. The enabling conditions for such a development were present, and they seem, in retrospect, obvious. In these years after the Civil War, America was confronting a problem new in degree if not in kind: the relationship of a swiftly expanding capitalist economy to the political system. The public temper of these decades was at least hospitable to a solution that protected business against unfriendly government intervention—a policy of judiciously qualified laissez-faire. The due process clauses of the Fifth and Fourteenth Amendments, the tax clauses, and the commerce clause were ready to hand; and they were not so frozen either by their language or by previous interpretation as to be unadaptable to this solution. Yet the precise form and pace of the solution, the nature and degree of the adaptations, had still to be determined. And although many shared in the work, Field was probably the most important of the judges who performed this feat of constitutional alchemy in the latter half of the nineteenth century. Both the nature of this achievement and Field's importance in bringing it about are explainable only through an understanding of his life and character.

Professor Swisher's biography provides rich material for such an understanding, and each reader can make what he will of the life that is thus laid before him. Perhaps the best thing for a preface-writer to do is to draw together some threads, add certain items and interpretations that have been garnered by scholarship since Swisher wrote, and offer some observations of his own about Field's qualities and significance. What manner of man was he? What made him the man he was? What was his impact on constitutional history, and what explains that impact?

The first word that comes to mind when one sets out to describe Field is "willful." There are other, related words that might be chosen, some commonly used pejoratively and others as terms of praise: "stubborn," "dogmatic"; "independent," "indomitable." They all fit. Whatever we call it, the attribute is a main theme in the story of his life. It appears in his decision to leave his brother's law firm in New York and to seek an ampler scope for his independent spirit in the California of gold rush days. It appears in his reaction to that turbulent and, to him, exhilarating new environment. We can see it in the role he played as alcalde of Marysville, which he helped to found; in his role as a California legislator;

and later as a state judge. In each of these offices he faced
novel legal problems that called for boldly innovative
talents. The nascent state needed men who had the
self-confidence to strike out along uncharted paths, and
Field was such a man. We can see the attribute further
revealed in the quarrels he was embroiled in during those
early days and throughout his career. The affronts he
bore from Judge Turner (chap. 2) were implacably and
enthusiastically repaid, when Field became a state legislator, by a bill that sent Turner to a wilderness district
where there were "only grizzly bears and Indians"
("Reminiscences," p. 77). The Terrys, man and wife,
were a headstrong pair themselves, but no more so than
Field who faced them with his own brand of inflexible
vindictiveness (chap. 13).

Most of all and most important, we can see this quality
in the relentless way he insisted on his own legal views
even in the face of the doubts or opposition of his
brethren. Most judges, and probably most men, feel the
pressure of received group opinion. That is why lone
dissents are comparatively rare on the Supreme Court
and why a doctrine that is initially adopted by a closely
divided vote often gains later acceptance from judges
who once disputed it. Field was peculiarly insensitive to
such influences: it was hard to shake his confidence that
one man on God's side constitutes a majority. (Consider, for example, his obduracy over the legal tender
issue [chap. 7]. As late as 1884, after all other members
of the Court had conceded that the national government
had the power to control its own currency, Field had not
given an inch, nor had he flagged in his faith that righteousness, as he understood it, would triumph: "So the
question has come again, and will continue to come until
it is settled so as to uphold and not impair the contracts
of parties, to promote and not defeat justice.")

Moreover his determination was always strengthened by that abnormal vital energy that so often drives successful statesmen. In 1892, when he was seventy-six years old, Justice Gray remarked, in connection with an intramural judicial quarrel, that Field "seems to be behaving more like a wild bull than before" (Westin, p. 371). Three years later Justice Harlan said that Field had "acted like a madman" during the controversy over the Income Tax Case (Farrelly, "Harlan's Dissent in the Pollock Case, 24 *Southern California L. Rev.* 179, 1951). Field was a fighter and the kind who never gives up.

Another, perhaps kindred, character trait was vanity. Again different words, some of them less deprecatory, might come to mind. No doubt vanity is often linked with ambition, which is not necessarily a fault. Field was certainly an ambitious man. He was also a prideful one; and while pride has sometimes been called a sin, it is also sometimes thought of as a virtue.

At any rate the evidences of the quality are strewn through his biography, especially in the tale of his aspirations for high public office. From 1868 on, as Swisher says, his name was frequently mentioned as a candidate for President; and he was regarded as a reasonable prospect for Chief Justice during Cleveland's first term. He of course never attained either of these summits. Cleveland passed him over, and Field seems to have felt the rebuff deeply. As for his presidential hopes, they never had much foundation, though there is reason to believe that he nursed them nonetheless. But they were repeatedly dashed. Some of his decisions defending Chinese against persecution by nativist zealots were held against him by his fellow Californians; and when the Democratic convention of 1880 assembled, he received only sixty-five votes on the first ballot—and only six out of twelve from California. In 1884 the snub was even more decisive. The California Democratic state convention passed a resolve repudiating his candidacy by the convincing margin of 453 to 19. At the national convention his name was not even put forward, and he was left with nothing but a sense of grievance against the "radical element" that had dealt him this blow (p. 308).

The truth is that he was often tempted by vanity (or ambition) to seek popular accolades, while that same vanity (or pride) prevented him from pandering in order to win them. He had in fact a singular capacity for making enemies; and his irascibility seems to have increased as he grew older. Moreover, though he was an engaging and stimulating companion among men he thought of as his peers (e.g., railroad tycoons), his general demeanor was haughty and austere. It would be hard to fashion a more improbable prospect for elective public office.

Still another quality that stands out when we view Field is intelligence of a high, but rather special, order. None of his many rivals and calumniators has recorded any doubts about the power of Field's mind. He was thoroughly justified in his self-confidence about his abilities as a scholar-judge. The prose of his opinions is a bit oratorical and stately for modern tastes (in his more impassioned moments it took on the tone and cadence of an Old Testament prophet), but it is usually lucid and telling. There is, however, a quality about this prose— and the mind producing it—that is worthy of remark. For all its power, it is not subtle. Field's mind was not one given to recognizing that there may be two or even more plausible sides to a question, still less to acknowledging that there may be many gradations between the right and the wrong, the good and the bad. It was a mind that saw truth as a series of broad, unmistakable generalities, and that entertained few doubts.

These then were some of the predominant qualities of Field's mind and character. What were his values? More specifically, what was his attitude toward the great and absorbing question of American political life in his Supreme Court years—the relationship of government to the political order? Here the answer is clear. He was surely the most uncompromising judicial exponent of laissez-faire in his time, perhaps in American constitutional history. The point should not be overstated. Charles Fairman has called attention to a number of cases in which Field ruled against corporate privilege, these apparent anomalies being accounted for, Fairman believes, by the "syllogistic" tendency of his mind (p. 136). It is well to be reminded that no man, not even Field, is completely one-dimensional. But when that is said, the fact remains, as Swisher shows and as H. J. Graham has confirmed, that after the early 1870s Field was more consistently vigilant than any of his fellows against governmental inroads on capitalism, more willing to subject the popular will power to judicial supervision. It is not too much to say that the threat to property rights became his obsession.

When we turn to ask what influences accounted for these propensities and prepossessions, a note of caution is in order. Causation is a slippery concept at best, and modern psychology has taught us that some of the root causes of human behavior may be hidden from our view in the predawn of infancy. But perhaps we are left some leeway for conjecture about later years as well, and it is easy to find in the record experiences and factors that may have helped to form Stephen Field. His willfulness, his obduracy, his daring, can readily be traced to his life on the frontier where he learned to see himself as a man's man in a man's world, fighting for his own, and succeeding by courage and persistence where others failed. There too he may have learned to think of the law as something that can and should be molded to the needs of the times and the values of the judge. Going even farther back, we may find origins of his spirit in his family background and upbringing. His brothers, David Dudley and Cyrus, were to become, like himself, boundlessly energetic and competitive men; the household stimulated its members to stand up for themselves, and most of them evidently did.

As for vanity, that too could well have been nourished by his family background and his later career. His father's theology, which was omnipresent in his childhood, distinguished between the "elect" and their inferiors; and Field never doubted that he was one of the former. The conviction was reinforced by the successes he and his family achieved, and no doubt the opposition and criticism he suffered only reinforced it further. It was not in his nature to entertain the idea that he himself might be responsible for these slings and arrows. They were attributable to the ignorance and malignity of the multitude who questioned his title to leadership.

His basic intellectual equipment must presumably be credited to genetic factors. Environment and education cannot, even now, make silk purses out of sows' ears. But the explanation of the cast of his mind is another matter. That prose of his echoes with the tones of his father, the hell-fire-and-brimstone preacher; and the black-and-white attitude toward value issues may have had its inception there too. Nor was the frontier a setting that encouraged a taste for subtleties in a mind already disposed against them. Most of Field's life experi-

ences before he went to the Supreme Court served to
strengthen a tendency to see the world as sharply divided
between the true and the false, the bad and the good.
By that time Field was instinctively willful, self-
certain, and dogmatic. What he would be dogmatic
about, what cause his will would fasten on, was less obvious. As Swisher says, he seems not to have developed
at this point the fixed pro-business bias that distinguished
him later. Until the early 1870s he was, even in matters
affecting property rights, "a liberal, restrained judge,
tolerant of legislative innovation"; after that he was the
"arch-individualist" of the era (Graham, p. 856). One
of the primary biographical problems concerning Field is
to explain this transformation. H. J. Graham has plausibly argued that at least a partial explanation is to be
found in Field's frightened reaction to the Franco-
Prussian War and the Paris Commune. His travels as
a young man had made him more alert to European affairs
than most Americans of the day, and in 1870 he told a
friend that for months he had been thinking of almost
nothing else but the "stirring events" in Europe. Certainly it is true that a sense of alarm did spread through
educated circles in America as the news of the Commune
poured in. Certainly it is true that such an alarm, such
a fear of "a war of the poor against the rich," took an
exaggerated and sometimes almost hysterical form in
Field's mind for the remainder of his career. His ability
to believe in such a fearsome prospect may have been
ingrained by the apocalyptic doctrines of his father's
religion. The hypothesis that the Commune triggered
his forebodings is at least credible.

But whatever may be the explanation, it is clear that
about this time Field began his campaign to write a
general protection for economic rights into the American

Constitution. And the instruments for accomplishing this purpose were already at hand. The Fourteenth Amendment, ratified in 1868, was loaded with broad general phrases—"privileges or immunities of citizens," "due process of law," "equal protection of the laws." The meaning of these terms was only vaguely comprehended by the men who wrote them. Insofar as we can divine the framers' intentions, the best guess is that they had a loose idea of protecting the newly freed slaves, and an even looser idea that such clauses would provide some protection for civil rights in general. The currently prevailing interpretations of the "due-process" clause did not clearly suggest that the judiciary might use it to defend businessmen against legislative injustice. But Field seized upon it early and began urging, with characteristic persistence, that such an interpretation ought to be adopted.

And his ultimate success in bringing the Court around to his views about this and other constitutional revisions was a resounding one. As has been said earlier, his feat was by no means single-handed. Publicists, scholars, and practicing lawyers were importuning the judiciary throughout this period to save the property-owner from the outrage of government control. Field's fellow judges on the Supreme Court and elsewhere were not immune to such appeals. As a majority, they moved more slowly than Field along the doctrinal paths, but move they did: they too were infected by the pro-business bias that characterized this age in American history. Nevertheless within the Court Field was the one who pushed earliest and hardest for the result, and he must be credited with a major hand in producing it.

Its final attainment came near the end of his life, and it was doubtless facilitated, as Arnold M. Paul has argued, by the general spread in the closing years of the nineteenth century of the kind of anxieties that had been obsessing Field for twenty years. Edward Bellamy's *Looking Backward* documents the nature of these fears among men of substance. In the 1890s, the Populist party, the Homestead strike, the march of "Coxey's Army," and the passage of the Income Tax Act aggravated the sense of alarm; and this brought about with a rush the constitutional consummation Field had long espoused.

The commitment to the laissez-faire version of the Constitution, once made, was not soon to be abandoned. Field left the Court in 1897 and died in 1899, but the fruits of his labors lived on into the twentieth century. It was indeed not until 1937 that the Court divested itself of the legacy Field had done so much to bequeath. Meanwhile that legacy had played a significant part in the history of the nation.

Why was he so effective? What accounts for his impact on our constitutional development? The answer is implicit in what has already been said—in the personal qualities of the man and their relationship to the circumstances he confronted. When he came to the Court in 1863 the stage was set for the kind of performer he was. Fundamental constitutional definitions were still wanting. Even the status of the Supreme Court itself had been rendered ambiguous by the challenges to judicial authority that followed the Dred Scott decision. The constitutional situation was fluid, and the adoption of the "war amendments," especially the Fourteenth, further widened the range of the judiciary's "sovereign prerogative of choice." And as time went on the drift of "respectable" American opinion increasingly favored a choice that would grant business some shelter against menacing popular winds. Fear and a sense of righteousness combined to encourage the forging of a new constitutional order.

Field was the man for such an hour. He was bold and self-certain where others were hesitant. He thought of himself as a leader of men by natural right of superiority. Consciousness of that superiority and of the concomitant power to fabricate law in accord with the leader's notions of justice had been strengthened by his experiences as alcalde, as legislator, and as state court judge. It was almost instinctive for him to seize upon the concept of "substantive due process" while most of his brethren remained muddled for twenty more years about the meaning of that pregnant clause. The fears and the conviction of righteousness that matured slowly among his fellows was born in the mind of Field in one revelatory season. And once the object of his crusade was settled on, his whole will and his considerable intellectual talents were bent to the task of achieving it. The man who knows what he wants, who is stubborn and boundlessly energetic in fighting for it, has an advantage in most social situations. This may also be true in the small society we call the Supreme Court—especially if the temper of the times also favors his enterprise.

Justice Holmes once said: "Judges are apt to be naif, simple-minded men, and they need something of Mephistopheles." Holmes was here of course deprecating the very structure of constitutional law and judicial outlook that Field had done so much to build, the Fieldian propensity to read "conscious or unconscious sympathy with one side or another" into the law when "a vague terror went over the earth and the word socialism began to be heard." It took the space of two generations for scholars and jurists, led by Holmes, to break that structure down. Doubtless it is true that their task of critical realism

required men with a subtle and skeptical turn of mind.
Doubtless it is also true that Field was not such a man.
Neither of course was he "simple-minded" in the loose,
common usage of that term—as one dictionary puts it,
"foolish . . . having less than normal mental ability." On
the contrary, his mental ability was far above the average.
But he was (and this I take to be the meaning Holmes
had in mind) a man who thought in sweeping and grandly
simple generalities, who never doubted his premises, or
his right to impose them on his fellows. And from John
Marshall to Hugo Black the judges who have played the
primary creative parts in building our constitutional law
have been more like Field than like the Mephistophelean
model Holmes recommended. We may not always approve the structure the Fields create; and in any case their
handiwork will be refined, modified, and sometimes whit-
tled away by men of very different temperament. For
better or worse, it is judges like Field who have left the
deepest imprint on the history of the nation.

BIBLIOGRAPHICAL NOTE

Though Swisher's work remains the indispensable standard treatment, others have since made contributions to
an understanding of Field and his constitutional era.
Perhaps the most valuable of these later studies is H. J.
Graham, "Justice Field and the Fourteenth Amendment,"
52 *Yale Law Journal* 851 (1943). Charles Fairman's *Mr.
Justice Miller and the Supreme Court* (1939) is a rich
account of the constitutional period and of the judge
who, though often disagreeing with Field, most nearly
matched him in ability and contemporaneous importance.
A. M. Paul, *Conservative Crisis and the Rule of Law*

(1960), and C. P. Magrath, *Morrison R. Waite* (1963), also shed light on the Court and constitutional development in Field's time. See also Wallace Mendelson, "Mr. Justice Field and Laissez Faire," 36 *Virginia Law Review* 45 (1950); R. G. McCloskey, *American Conservatism in the Age of Enterprise* (1951); and A. F. Westin, "Stephen Field and the Headnote to O'Neill v. Vermont," 67 *Yale Law Journal* 363 (1958).

ROBERT G. McCLOSKEY

AUTHOR'S ACKNOWLEDGMENTS

In the writing of a book on almost any subject the author receives aid which deserves more than the formal acknowledgment which it is possible to make. Where the subject is biographical the indebtedness is usually heavy indeed, since many persons, including relatives, friends, acquaintances, and, perhaps, enemies, must provide much of the material which gives life to the story. For contributions without which this volume would have been incomplete I am particularly indebted to the late Mr. Irwin B. Linton, who was for many years Justice Field's secretary, and to his son, Mr. Irwin H. Linton, of Washington, D. C.; the late Mr. P. R. Stansbury, former deputy clerk of the Supreme Court of the United States; Mr. William C. Latham, of Berkeley, California; Mr. John T. Carey, of San Francisco, former United States District Attorney; Mr. Frank Monckton, of San Francisco, former clerk of the United States Circuit Court of Appeals; Miss Charlotte Anita Whitney, of Oakland, niece of Mrs. Field; and Mrs. Emelia Field Ashburner, of San Francisco, niece of Justice Field.

For the discovery of documentary material much is due to the diligent services of librarians. These services have been rendered at the Library of Congress, the California State Library, both at Sacramento and at the Sutro Branch in San Francisco, the libraries of the University of California and Stanford University, and the Henry E. Huntington Library at San Marino, California.

Although final responsibility for the material included and the conclusions expressed remains with the author, many persons have given wise and thought-provoking counsel. Professor Russell M. Story has aided in the interpretation of the political background of the California chapters. During the initial stages of the task helpful advice was given by Professor Walton H. Hamilton, and by Professor Walter J. Shepard upon whose suggestion the study was begun. Professors John Dickinson and Quincy Wright criticized many of the chapters in detail in the early drafts, and offered constructive suggestions. During the past two years Professor Leverett S. Lyon has rendered highly valued assistance through his criticisms and suggestions on matters of organization and background ideology. For innumerable helpful criticisms of ideas and of the manner in which their expression has been attempted, and for persistent encouragement, I am indebted to my wife, Idella Gwatkin Swisher. Miss Marie Butler has assisted greatly in the correction of defects of phraseology and in the clarification of ambiguous passages. Many other persons, both in the Brookings Community and elsewhere, have read and commented on part or all of the chapters, or through thoughtful discussion have aided in the development of the conclusions herein expressed. For their assistance, as well as for that of those of whom I have made specific mention, I am deeply grateful.

Finally, I wish to express like appreciation for the fellowship grants, for one year from the Robert Brookings Graduate School and for two years from the Division of Training of The Brookings Institution, which have made possible the leisure necessary for initiating this study and carrying it to completion.

CARL BRENT SWISHER

Washington, D. C.
November, 1930

INTRODUCTION

At the sound of the gavel the audience in the semi-circular room which had formerly been the chamber of the United States Senate arose and looked on respectfully while ten black-robed men, some middle aged and some elderly, filed in through the doorway. When these men had walked deliberately to their places at the bench they were greeted with the traditional cry:

"Oyez! Oyez! Oyez! All persons having business before the Honorable, the Judges of the Supreme Court of the United States, are admonished to draw near and give their attention, for the Court is now in session. God save the United States, and this Honorable Court."

At the conclusion of the greeting, at this session of the first Monday in December, 1863, nine of the justices sank into the seats which had been theirs at the preceding term, and the tenth, a newcomer, took a seat which had been specially provided for him. After certain preliminary announcements the clerk, by order of the Chief Justice, read aloud a letter which stated that Abraham Lincoln, President of the United States, "reposing special trust and confidence in the Wisdom, Uprightness and Learning of Stephen J. Field, of California," had nominated, and, by and with the advice and consent of the Senate, did appoint him to be associate justice of the Supreme Court of the United States. From another document the clerk then read the oath which the new justice had taken some months previously while still in California, in which he pledged himself to administer justice without respect to persons, to do equal right to the poor and to the rich, and

1

faithfully and impartially to discharge and perform all
the duties of his office according to the best of his abilities
and understanding, agreeably to the Constitution and
laws of the United States.

It is with this new justice, Stephen J. Field, a Democrat
from California, appointed by a Republican President to
sit as the tenth justice on the bench of the Supreme
Court, pursuant to a recent act of Congress creating the
position, that our story is chiefly concerned. He was a
trimly built man of forty-seven years. Curly, dark
brown hair covered his unusually large head, save for a
bald spot at the top; and a beard of the same color
adorned his chin. Piercing, blue-gray eyes looked out
from under heavy brows, eyes which suggested something
of the alertness of the brain which lay behind them. His
demeanor was that of solemn, judicial poise.

He had a wealth of experience already behind him—
boyhood in the home of a Congregational minister in
Puritan New England; two eventful trips to Europe;
training under Mark Hopkins at Williams College; law
practice in New York City; pioneer life in California
amid intensely dramatic scenes; service in the California
legislature; and service in the California Supreme Court.
He had now been called to Washington, at a time
when the city was a turbulent and muddy armed camp,
thronged with military men, politicians, and camp followers, and when the occasional roar of cannon on distant
hills spoke grimly of the crisis of the times.

The personnel of the Court with which he took his seat
was an odd mixture. Five of the members, including
Chief Justice Roger B. Taney, had already served long
terms on the bench, the youngest of these in point of
service having been appointed in 1846. These five had
participated in the decisions in the Dred Scott and Booth

cases, which had brought upon the Court a torrent of abuse from anti-slavery forces throughout the North. Another member had been appointed by President Buchanan in 1858. These six members were Democrats, products of the long period in which the presidential chair had been occupied almost exclusively by Democrats. Three others had, like Field, been appointed by President Lincoln. These three, however, had been chosen from the President's own political party.

With this group of men Field began his service in the Court. Some of them were his colleagues but a relatively short time, others remained longer, and one was with him for more than a quarter of a century. His own period of service lasted more than a third of a century. During that time he shared in the making of decisions which were of supreme importance in the life of the country. After the end of military operations he was active amid the combined political and legal crises when rabid politicians and over-zealous statesmen attempted to continue the subjugation of the South. A little later he played a vigorous part when he and his colleagues, as judges of the highest court in the land, had to pass upon some of the critical currency problems of the nation.

When the Fourteenth Amendment had become a part of the Constitution he worked with his usual vigor to determine the interpretation of the general phrases in the amendment, and succeeded in leaving his stamp upon them. He participated, during the decades which followed, in decisions which had to do with innumerable phases of the rapidly developing business and industrial life of the country. It was a time when, amid unprecedented conditions, the path of the law was faint indeed, and the way had to be marked out step by step by judges in the face of tremendous pressure and vociferous argument by interested parties on all sides. Inevitably the habits of thought possessed by the judges, and the conclusions derived from their past experiences, had much to do with the choices which they made. By the light of his own knowledge, experience, and beliefs, Justice Field aided in marking out the path of the law, and in so doing played his part in the solution, temporarily or permanently, of major political, economic, and social problems. Besides performing his judicial duties in Washington he made annual trips to his circuit in the far West, where he encountered dramatic experiences such as seldom fall to the lot of a judge. In addition to all this he nourished political aspirations and engaged in political activities which have been much less widely remembered in later years.

To the pages of history belongs the account of the eventful, dramatic, and strenuous career of Justice Field, interwoven as it is with the very fabric of American life. The presentation of this account, against a background of his experience and of the experience of the country, is the purpose of the following chapters.

CHAPTER I

YOUTH AND ITS HERITAGE

Stephen Field was born on November 4, 1816, in the home of David Dudley Field, a New England Congregational minister. The place was Haddam, Connecticut, a rock-ribbed little town among the granite quarries of the lower Connecticut River valley.[1] He was not a thriving infant. When Haddam women visited the mother, women who knew the menace borne by bleak New England winters for even the most robust of children, they went away remarking sagely that she would "never raise that child." Mrs. Field's staunch old Puritan father had given to his many daughters the names of the Christian graces, and to her he had given the name "Submit." During this winter she proved, as she had done before and was to do many times again, that she had been misnamed, and that there was small vestige of submission about her. With five other children at her skirts, and on the minister's meager salary of five hundred dollars a year, paid usually in such provisions as his parishioners could spare from their own larders, she brought the child through the dread season. In memory of a well-known minister they called him Stephen Johnson.

Only indirectly did Haddam ever have any significance for Stephen, save as his birthplace, for in the spring of 1819 his father accepted a call to the church at Stockbridge, a town among the Berkshire Hills of western Massachusetts. In wagons sent down from Stockbridge

[1] See description in Field, H. M., *Record of the Family of the late Reverend David Dudley Field, D. D.*, p. 17.

5

the family was moved from Haddam to the place which
was to be Stephen's boyhood home. For about three years
the Fields lived just across the Housatonic River from
Stockbridge, "a river which looked very small compared
with the Connecticut, but which was a beautiful stream,
as it flowed between banks fringed with willows, and
wound around the base of the hill on which the old house
stood." [2] Later the minister bought a house in Stockbridge. "It was a low building with a gambrel roof—a
modest manse indeed, but blessed with that contentment
which is better than great riches." [3] This house burned
down, and the people of the town aided in erecting a
structure which was thereafter the home of the family.

Stephen continued to be frail during his early childhood, and local physicians declared in their wise fashion
that he would only live until he was seventeen years of
age.[4] For one summer his father placed him on a farm
near Stockbridge, hoping that the country life would
strengthen his physique.[5] He came slowly into his own.
Long before he was seventeen he was a wiry, energetic
youngster, with dark brown hair and keen, blue-gray
eyes, who looked anything but an invalid. He and his
brothers—he now had six brothers and two sisters—in
spite of all that the parents could do, experienced many
thrilling variations from the rigorous life of Puritan
Congregationalism. He enjoyed boyish pranks, and was
not above provoking fights with his schoolmates.

[2] *Ibid.*, p. 38.

[3] *Ibid.*

[4] Field, Stephen J., *Personal Reminiscences of Early Days in California*
(manuscript), pp. 230-31. (Hereinafter cited as *Reminiscences.*) References to the *Reminiscences* when not otherwise noted are from the edition
of 1893. The manuscript is used occasionally since it contains some
unprinted material. It is filed in the Sutro Branch of the California
State Library in San Francisco.

[5] *Ibid.*

The boys could not, however, escape many of the rigid customs of the times. They heard their father deliver three sermons each Sunday, and took part in solemn devotions at home. The church at Stockbridge "was of a primeval order of architecture, standing four-square to all the winds of heaven, with tall pulpit and high-backed pews; while up aloft, perched in a kind of sentry-box, sat old Doctor Partridge, the 'tithing man,' who looked down upon the assembly below, keeping a sharp eye for the small boys who might wriggle about in their seats during the long sermon, and disturb the rigid decorum of the holy place." [6] After the morning sermon some of the worshipers went home for a cold dinner, while others ate in the pine grove on the hillside. Then they "returned to hear the second blowing of the gospel trumpet." [7]

Henry, the youngest of the boys, made record of some aspects of the home life. His account may be applied to the experience of Stephen and the other brothers, if it be kept in mind that Henry wrote as a minister, and that his conclusions may have differed somewhat from those of the other boys whose interests lay in other directions. "Our whole domestic life," he wrote, "received its tone from this unaffected piety of our parents, who taught their children to lie down and rise up in that fear of the Lord, which is the beginning of wisdom. The sweetest and tenderest moments of the day were at morning and evening prayers. We read the Bible 'in course,' beginning at Genesis and going straight through to Revelation. All sat round the fireplace in a circle. Father began, reading three verses, and we followed, from the oldest to the youngest. Sometimes my sister Mary, who had a sweet voice, sang a hymn. . . . Then the picture in Burns's

---

[6] Field, *Record of the Family*, p. 33.
[7] *Ibid.*

'Cotter's Saturday Night' was fulfilled to the letter except in one point—the 'kneeling down.' The stern old Puritans had such rigid notions that they would not kneel even to God, as if it were a sign of formality. But rising, our reverend sire took his stand behind a tall chair, as in a pulpit, and then, when all was hushed in silence, 'the saint, the husband and the father prayed.' " [8]

These scenes were sources of fond recollections for Stephen in the last years of his life.

The Sabbath, which began on Saturday evening, was observed with almost Jewish strictness. Again quoting Henry—as the sun sank on Saturday evening the father's voice was heard, " 'My sons, we are on the borders of holy time.' " Then, "for twenty-four hours it was as if the current of life had ceased to flow. The next day, as the afternoon wore on, and the Sabbath 'began to abate,' there was a painful time of waiting for the last moment to expire. How many, many times did my brother [Cyrus] and I go out in front of our door, to watch for the sun's going down! Why did it linger so long? At length it touched the rim of the hills, and slowly sank behind the ridge of pines that stood up against the western sky. Lower and lower it fell, till the orb was below the horizon. . . . Instantly, with a sense of joyous freedom [we] bounded away to play." [9]

Although Stephen, like the rest of the children, attended the common school at Stockbridge, and stood at the head of his class in spite of his love of boyish revelry, it seems evident that the major portion of his education while he remained in Stockbridge was that which he received at home. The constant drill in theological and religious matters was in itself education of a kind. Even

[8] *Ibid.*, p. 40.
[9] *Ibid.*, pp. 41-42.

though he was later to reject many of the dogmas which were taught him, his subsequent habits of thought and reasoning seem to indicate that his father's training had a tremendous influence over him. Indeed, the picture of the boy's early life would not be complete without reference to the religious, intellectual, and moral heritage which came down to him through his father, and also, in no small measure, through his mother.

The minister traced his ancestry back to the first Field who came to America, about 1630, and who, significantly, bore the biblical name of Zachariah. From this time onward the Fields, multiplying rapidly, had played a vigorous part in the rough frontier life, whether in eking out an existence from the rocky soil of New England or in defending their people from the forays of savages. They prayed earnestly, worked strenuously, and shot with unerring aim. The course of their lives was molded by their religion and by the grim struggle for existence along the frontier. In the hard life to which they were forced to accustom themselves, the fundamentals of their existence were their religious faith and creed and the material elements of property that provided food, clothing, and shelter. The struggle developed strength and power of resistance, but it left also the inevitable mark of narrowness that comes with unrelenting concentration on a few things.

David Dudley Field, of East Guilford, Connecticut, one of the large family of a former captain in the Revolutionary War, had been dedicated to the ministry. He worked his way through Yale, and distinguished himself in his studies. He received his theological training from Timothy Dwight, President of Yale, a dogmatic theologian and an extreme conservative in politics. Field demonstrated his love and admiration for his teacher by naming one of his sons Timothy Dwight. Henry once said that the family was brought up on Timothy Dwight, the Bible, and the catechism.[10] It is worth noting in the same connection that another son was named for that stern divine, Jonathan Edwards, who in the preceding century had been pastor at Stockbridge.

Field married Submit Dickinson, a descendant of another long line of New England Puritans, who also brought with her an allotment of religious devotion, strength, and perhaps the hard stubbornness which had made life possible for her ancestors. The couple moved to Haddam, where the minister served the community for more than fifteen years, and where six of the nine children were born. The family was not prosperous economically, but that was not to be expected. A more serious matter was the fact that the period was not one of prosperity for religion as such. The gradual improvement of the material prospects of the people had been followed by tragic results for religion.[11] Church attendance had fallen off, family prayers were not observed as they had once been, and the substance of religion had given way to the forms. Field's efforts were directed toward stemming the tide. His preaching, typical of that of the times and locality,[12] was largely in the form of warning his flock to avert the wrath of God by so living as to prepare themselves for the life to come. Even his secular writings, which were numerous, were thickly interspersed with such passages as the following:

"A review of the circumstances of our fathers is calculated to excite solemn and pious emotions in the mind.

[10] New York *Evangelist*, Feb. 9, 1899.

[11] See Field, D. D., *History of the Towns of Haddam and East-Haddam* (1814), p. 24, and *Statistical Account of Middlesex County* (1819), p. 30.

[12] See Adams, Henry, *History of the United States*, Vol. IX, pp. 175-76.

God cast out the heathen before them and planted them, that they might keep his statutes. The mercies and corrections visited upon them, teach us his goodness, truth and faithfulness. Their fear of his name, their observance of public and family worship, and various good works, call upon us to imitate their example; while their sepulchers remaining with us to this day, admonish us of our approaching dissolution." [13]

Of his theological beliefs his son, Henry, said: "He held the doctrines of his fathers with an acceptance which did not abate one jot or tittle from their sternness and severity, and the effect upon him was to give a stamp to the whole man. If the creed of the Puritans was an iron creed, it formed an iron character, a firmness and intrepidity which have produced the greatest effects in both Old and New England. His faith was one in which there was no enfeebling doubt. . . . To him the Bible was the word of God—the one absolute and infallible test of truth, from which there was no appeal. Like his great predecessor, Edwards, he believed that the 'Scheme of Redemption' was the key which unlocked all the mysteries of Providence and of history, from the beginning of the ages to the end of the world." [14]

Such were the thoughts, attitudes, and traditions which went to make up the conditions of home life in the midst of which the children spent their most highly impressionable years. It was perhaps inevitable that they should in some degree be molded by the conditions. Only one of them became a theologian, or in his mature years gave much attention to the problems of organized religion. Most or all of them, however, gained in the home a capacity for self-discipline which carried them

[13] Field, *History of Haddam and East-Haddam*, p. 40.
[14] Field, *Record of the Family*, pp. 35-36.

through and over obstacles later on. Stephen never became deeply interested in the application of religious doctrines. However, decades afterward, when he was an expounder of legal rather than religious principles, the lines of his reasoning and his prophecies of dire evils to come if his warnings were disregarded, bore marked resemblance to those of his father whom he then respected so profoundly. There was a resemblance, too, when he, as a judge, in his opinions and in his comments to juries, chided or scolded his fellow Californians for their deplorable conduct—conduct unworthy of a "brave and manly people."

It seems probable, in view of the fact that four of the nine children later achieved world-wide reputations, while others of them were not undistinguished, that the interplay of their own keen minds, in youth as well as later, may have had much to do with their development. Intellects of potential greatness, coming into contact with one another and with the superior reasoning powers of the father, as well as with the practical common sense and buoyant spirit of the mother, had multiple stimuli to rapid development.

Yet the educational facilities of the home were severely limited, due to the fact that it provided no library save on theological subjects. Since there was no college immediately at hand the matter of further education, out of a salary which was now only six hundred dollars a year, promised to be a cause of much worry. The minister began by sending his eldest son, named David Dudley after himself, to Williams College, at Williamstown, thirty miles north of Stockbridge. He entered in 1821 and left in 1825. He distinguished himself in his studies, but in some unrecorded incident or incidents he offended the dignity of President Griffin, and left, voluntarily or by request, without taking a degree.[15] His brother, Jonathan, entered Williams in 1828. Stephen's education included an important episode before he was ready for college. His elder sister, Emelia, was married in the fall of 1829 to a young minister, Josiah Brewer. The couple planned to leave immediately for Greece, under the auspices of the Ladies' Greek Association of New Haven, to establish schools for women. The brother, David Dudley, thought it would be wise for Stephen, then thirteen years of age, to accompany them and learn something of foreign languages, and thus to prepare himself to be a professor of Oriental languages in an American university. Stephen was delighted at the prospect, his parents consented, and the party sailed on the tenth of December. The ship which they took was bound for Smyrna. Arriving in Smyrna and finding a large population of Greeks, the Brewers decided to remain there instead of taking passage for Greece.

The opportunity of making such a change of environment was of immeasurable value to the growing boy, revealing to him as it did scenes and aspects of life of which he had never dreamed while in the narrow confines of Puritanical Stockbridge. Prominent among the experiences which he recalled in later years was the plague which broke out in Smyrna in 1831. Hundreds fell ill and many suffered sudden death. The entire population was in terror. Stephen is quoted as having given the following account of a banquet which he attended shortly after the epidemic broke out: "The guests were seated about a brilliantly lighted board. The social spirit among the guests was high. A toast was about to be drunk. The guests turned to pledge each other and saw one of the servants who was waiting upon the table fall

[15] Field, H. M., *Life of David Dudley Field*, p. 30.

dead. Instantly they all cried, 'the plague,' and in the briefest moment of time everyone fled, leaving the wine standing in the glasses, the toast undrunk. No one entered that house for a year afterward, and when they did, after employing the most powerful disinfectants, they found there the dried and decayed remnants of the feast, with the grinning skeleton of the servant who had waited upon them lying in his clothes just where he had fallen the night of the banquet." [16]

The Brewers and Stephen remained in Smyrna for two or three weeks after the beginning of the epidemic, and then concluded that it would be better to imitate the rest of the inhabitants and try to get away. They took passage on a ship bound for Malta. Upon arrival they were not allowed to land. The ship, after visiting many of the islands of the Grecian Archipelago, returned some weeks later to Smyrna, where it was discovered that the plague had passed.

In the autumn of the same year Asiatic cholera broke out. Hundreds fell sick. Brewer temporarily gave up his work of education and turned physician. Stephen, with his pockets filled with the needed medicines, went about with his brother-in-law ministering to the helpless people.

In the late autumn Mrs. Hill, the wife of an Episcopal clergyman who was in Smyrna as a missionary and teacher, wished to go to Athens. Stephen went with her. They took up their abode in what was called an old Venetian tower, and spent the winter there. He recalled as one of his most dramatic experiences the fact that he was once blown ashore from the sea, "I with a parcel of Greeks up on the hills." [17]

[16] St. Louis *Post-Dispatch*, quoted in San Francisco *Call*, May 10, 1885.
[17] *Reminiscences* (manuscript), pp. 253-54.

He made friends with American naval officers whom he met in the ports which he visited, and traveled about a great deal with them. He went to Scio, Patmos, Tenos, and other places. Once in Tenos he discovered that there were no friends near him, and that he had just one dollar and twenty-five cents in his pocket, the exact amount of the fare to Smyrna. He tucked two rolls of bread under his coat and took ship for Smyrna, where his sister was.[18] He studied the Greek language, learning it so well that, in his own words, "I used to think in it and I kept my journal in it." [19] He also learned something of Italian, French, and Turkish.

Among his most important experiences may perhaps be numbered his contacts with the Turks. His brother, Henry, recorded the following: "Of these years spent in the East, he always retained very vivid impressions. Living in a foreign country, and mingling with people of another race, language, and religion, enlarged his ideas. He formed a better opinion of the Turks. In traveling with them, he found that they were attentive to their devotions, saying their prayers in the morning, at noon, and at sunset. Often he was awakened at midnight by their rising to say their prayers. He had been educated in the strictest school of the Puritans, who, with all their good qualities, were not the most tolerant of religious opinions which differed from their own. Of course the child of a strict New England pastor was taught to look with horror upon the followers of the False Prophet; but for all this, he was profoundly impressed with what he saw, and could not but conclude that there must be something good in a religion which inspired such devotion.

[18] *Ibid.*
[19] *Ibid.*

"He found that the Turks were proverbially honest in their dealings. If he went into a bazaar to inquire if a piece of coin was good, he would be asked, 'Did you get it from a Turk?' If he said 'Yes,' that settled the point that it was good; if he said 'No,' they would ring it to test its genuineness. One day some gentlemen of his acquaintance were looking for a place in the country for the summer, and one was recommended to them as a quiet, orderly place, where the people were very moral—'for there was not a Christian within ten miles!' This was his first lesson in religious tolerance.

"Another lesson of the same kind he learned in regard to the members of the Greek church, with whom he often came in contact, and found that they were most exemplary in their religious duties. So with the Roman Catholics, of whom there were many in Smyrna; he saw in them a degree of devotion which was an example to Protestants. These things gradually opened his young eyes, and satisfied him, at least, that not all the religion in the world is to be found in Protestant Christendom." [20]

Valuable as his new experiences were for him, they could not go on indefinitely. He had to return to Stockbridge to prepare for college entrance examinations, after being away from home two and a half years. Jonathan was graduated from Williams College in September, 1832, and Stephen entered in the same month of the following year, when he was two months less than seventeen years of age. Williams had been a flourishing college in the latter part of the eighteenth century, but it had declined and it seemed at one time that a choice would have to be made between merging with Amherst and complete dissolution. A new president, however, had improved its circumstances and given it "character and standing before the public." [21] At the period when Stephen entered, the number of undergraduates varied from eighty to one hundred and twenty.[22] The faculty consisted of eight men: the president; a professor of languages and librarian; a professor of natural history; a professor of moral philosophy and rhetoric (who in 1833 was Mark Hopkins); a professor of mathematics and natural philosophy (who was Albert Hopkins); a professor of chemistry; and two tutors.

Before entering the college the prospective student had to pass examinations in geography, vulgar arithmetic, algebra, English, and a wide variety of fields in Latin and Greek. If the student passed the examinations and could provide testimonials of good moral character he was registered as a freshman. Having once entered upon his course he was subject to a rigid system of discipline. Early in the morning and again in the evening the chapel bell called him to prayers. Six hours of each day he had to remain in his room for study. On Sunday he attended church services. He signed a pledge of total abstinence, and dismissal from the college followed its violation. He was on probation until the middle of the second term, when he became a regular member by signing a pledge to observe all college laws, and "particularly that I will faithfully avoid the use of profane language, gaming, and all disorderly behavior." [23] The annual vacation of six weeks came in midwinter instead of summer, in order that students who had to work their way through college might do school teaching with a minimum of interference with their college work.

[21] Wells, D. A., and Davis, S. H., *Sketches of Williams College*, pp. 38-39.
[22] Field, D. D., *History of Berkshire* (1829), p. 170.
[23] Wells and Davis, *Sketches of Williams College*, p. 62.

Although Williams was unique in the emphasis which it placed upon studies in the natural sciences, ancient and modern languages occupied the most prominent place on the program during the first three years. Much attention was given to mathematics, and some to history and logic. Frequent themes and debates, or "disputations," were required throughout the entire four years. The fourth year differed considerably from the three preceding. The senior class was almost exclusively in the hands of the president, who, beginning in the fall of 1836, Stephen's senior year, was Mark Hopkins. . The study of languages and of the natural sciences was discontinued. The following books were studied during one or more of the three terms of the senior year: Campbell's *Philosophy of Rhetoric*; Francis Wayland's *Elements of Moral Science*; Stewart's *Elements of Intellectual Philosophy*; Richard Whateley's *Elements of Logic*; Henry H. Kaimes' *Elements of Criticism, with Lectures*; Joseph Story's *Commentaries on the Constitution*; Butler's *Analogy*; Leslie's *Short Method with the Deists*; and William Paley's *Natural Theology*. Some reading was done in political economy during the second term. Thomas Vincent's *An Explicatory Catechism*, was studied every Saturday forenoon. Public forensic disputations, by divisions, were held on the second Wednesday of each month. Original declamations were given in chapel weekly during the first and second terms.[24]

The outstanding person on the faculty was Mark Hopkins. His training had been in the field of medicine, but he had become a professor of moral philosophy and rhetoric at Williams. After six years of teaching he was made president of the college. For twenty years thereafter he taught all the studies of the senior class, corrected

[24] Curricular data compiled from the catalogs of the period.

all their literary exercises, and preached once every Sabbath.[25] He was regarded by those who knew him as one of the foremost thinkers in the country, and he combined great mental acumen with unusual ability as a teacher. He laid great emphasis upon philosophic studies. The following quotation tells much concerning the assumptions in his thinking:

"Dr. Hopkins has not been willing that metaphysics should stand for something intelligible only to the learned few, while inexplicable to the common mind. On the contrary, he has felt that the facts of the mind and the laws of its operation, it being nearest of all things to man, may be known by all with as much certainty as the facts and laws of the outer and remoter world. So he has fearlessly taken his students into this realm of study, and accustomed them to be at home with themselves, and while seeing the harmony of all knowledge, to see that the knowledge of themselves is the highest of all, and that 'The proper study of mankind is man.' So far, indeed, has he carried his views of the simplicity and intelligibility of these higher sciences, that he has been accustomed to teach them on the blackboard as he would arithmetic." [26]

The general program at Williams was evidently very similar to that which Stephen would have followed had he gone to almost any of the other colleges of his time. However, Mark Hopkins was unique. While Stephen may never have admitted that his own system of thinking was founded upon that of his teacher, there was indeed a remarkable resemblance between the Hopkins system and his own reasoning habits. Clarity, conciseness, and

[25] Hopkins, Mark, *Discourse at the Fiftieth Anniversary of His Election as President of Williams College* (1886), p. 16.

[26] Egleston. N. H., *Williamstown and Williams College* (1884), pp. 50-51. See Hopkins' system outlined in his *Outline Study of Man*.

mathematical exactness were characteristic of both, once the major assumptions for particular arguments were chosen. Furthermore, both assumed the existence of fundamental and harmonious principles permeating and explaining all the facts of life, an assumption of no little importance in the world of thought. Hopkins forced no point of view on his students. Rather, he encouraged them to question freely. His own superior reasoning powers and his popularity with his students enabled him to keep them well within bounds, however, and in most cases youthful enthusiasm for a great teacher carried them along with him. There is no reason for thinking that Stephen ever resisted.

The four years passed swiftly. Stephen distinguished himself throughout his college course. He delivered the Greek oration at the end of his junior year, and, as the student of highest rank in his class, delivered the valedictory speech at commencement in September, 1837.

Now, at the age of twenty-one, he was faced with the problem of choosing a vocation. His eldest brother, David Dudley, had studied law in the office of a friend in Albany and later in another office in New York City, and had long since established himself well enough to be able to contribute considerable sums to the Field family. Stephen, who was a vigorous young man with a good deal of aggressiveness in his disposition, was not much attracted by the thought of becoming a professor of languages. Neither did the vocation of his father appeal to him. Law, one of the most respectable and aristocratic professions, did offer attractions. In the words of De Tocqueville, written during the period when Stephen was in college: "In America there are no nobles or men of letters, and the people is apt to mistrust the wealthy; lawyers consequently form the highest political class, and the most cultivated circle of society. . . . If I were asked where I place the American aristocracy, I should reply without hesitation that it is not composed of the rich, who are united together by no common tie, but that it occupies the judicial bench and the bar." [27] The prosperity of the early thirties, followed by the panic of 1837 and the consequent entanglement of business relationships, made the practice of law increasingly profitable.[28] When David Dudley offered Stephen the opportunity of reading law in his office, the offer was accepted. Taking with him that which was the heritage of all the boys when they left home—ten dollars, a Bible, and his father's blessing—Stephen set out for New York.

He studied from 1838 to 1841, except for some loss of time due to a severe illness. While walking in the street one day he struck his knee against the hub of a cart wheel. Infection set in. The physician whom he consulted prescribed the popular cure for all ills, a dose of calomel. The supposed cure almost killed him. He was in bed for many months, during a part of which time he was with his parents, who had gone back to the old home in Haddam. Then, hoping for the improvement of his general health, he went to Albany, where he remained a year and a half. While there he read law in the office of John Van Buren, the Attorney-General of the state, and heard recitations in the Albany Female Academy—the only teaching experience he was ever to have. He returned to New York, and was admitted to the bar in 1841. Robert Sedgwick, David Dudley's partner, had retired, and Stephen took up practice with his brother. In one of the narrow streets crossing Broadway near the

[27] De Tocqueville, *Democracy in America*, Vol. I, p. 298.
[28] Field, *Life of David Dudley Field*, p. 41.

Trinity church, a strip of tin marked a door with the sign, "D. D. & S. J. Field."

The partnership lasted until 1848. During that time David Dudley was engaged in his energetic struggle for the codification of law in the State of New York, a movement which was to lead to the drafting of codes, very largely under his direction, which were to make his name known throughout the world. At the same time he carried on an extensive practice. By observing his brother, Stephen had an opportunity to learn a great deal about both law and politics. As for his own efforts at this time, however, about the only thing that can be said of them with certainty is that they in no sense won distinction for him. For all that the records tell of him, he may have done nothing more than the routine work of the office. In view of the active, rather dominating type of personality which he revealed throughout most of his life this fact seems surprising, until it is realized that David Dudley was no less dominating than he, and had the advantage of years of training and experience, and of being the senior partner. The two men were very fond of each other in their later years, but circumstances intimate that all was not as smooth in the partnership as it might have been, and Stephen once remarked that New York was not big enough to provide the right kind of opportunities for both him and his brother. Stephen was restless, and wanted a chance to strike out for himself. He often talked of going to Iowa when it was a young territory. A little later the lure of California made itself felt. David Dudley was not unwilling to have Stephen go. Indeed, in 1846 he suggested that Stephen go to California with Colonel Stephenson's regiment and get an early start in developments there, for he was sure that the war with Mexico would not come to an end until the United States had acquired the harbor of San Francisco. Stephen had little money, but David Dudley was said at this time to be worth about one hundred thousand dollars, acquired partly as the result of a remunerative practice and partly through marriage to a rich widow. David Dudley was to advance the funds with which Stephen was to make investments. Stephen was slow in making up his mind. Thus far no experiences in life had thrilled him as had those of his boyhood trip across the Atlantic, and he wanted to go abroad again. In 1848, the "Year of Revolutions," he sailed for Europe in the company of his father.

The period of more than a year which he spent traveling through Europe, with other members of his family, was charged with dramatic interest. Henry Field, who was in Europe when they arrived, met Stephen and his father in London. After spending some time there they went through Belgium and then to Paris, where they spent several weeks, and where they were joined by Mary, the youngest sister. The sons of the minister had speedily become prosperous, and the family scale of living included extensive travel and other luxuries which had had no place in a budget of six hundred dollars a year. The party found Paris very exciting. An epidemic of cholera broke out while they were there; and the government of Louis Philippe was overthrown by a revolution. Stephen and others of the party continued to travel throughout Europe, while the father returned home. In the following spring Cyrus and his wife joined the company, and all arrived in Rome shortly after French troops had taken possession. It was their good or bad fortune also to be in Vienna when hostile troops were approaching that city.[29]

[29] The account of these experiences is taken chiefly from Field, *Record of the Family*, pp. 86-87.

Stephen brought his European travels to a close in the fall of 1849. When he returned to New York on the first of October, he found the East in a tumult of excitement over California. Gold had been discovered during the preceding year. Men from all the varied walks of life were banding together to set out in search of fabulous wealth on the other side of the continent. Some were traveling overland in wagon trains or on horseback; some were taking passage to go around Cape Horn; and others were going by way of the Isthmus of Panama. Stephen lost no time in preparing to join the rush. On November 13 he was on board a steamer which was plowing its way southward through the white-capped waves of the Atlantic. He was leaving, for all time, the old life in the East, and going forward to life in a new world. He had neither wealth nor reputation, but he had health, energy, ambition, a keen mind well trained in the schools of his father and Mark Hopkins, and a heritage of richly varied experience.

CHAPTER II

EARLY DAYS IN CALIFORNIA

After a voyage of about a week, Stephen Field arrived at Chagres, an old Spanish-American town on the Caribbean side of the Isthmus of Panama, at the mouth of a river of the same name. In company with others he took a boat and was pushed up the river by Indians to Cruces, where they engaged mules and rode over the mountains, completing the sixty-mile trip to the city of Panama. The Pacific side of the Isthmus was swarming with men who were frantically eager to take ship for San Francisco. Food was poor and sanitary conditions were bad. Along with many others Field suffered an attack of cholera before he could get away.[1] He recovered sufficiently to be able to leave December 6, on the old steamer "California."

Health conditions on board the ship were no better than at Panama. Passengers were stowed in every nook and corner, and some, without berths, lay on the deck. "Many carried with them the seeds of disease, contracted under a tropical sun, which being aggravated by hardships, insufficient food, and the crowded condition of the steamer, developed as the voyage proceeded. Panama fever in its worst form broke out, and soon the main deck was covered with the sick. There was a physician attached to the ship, but he too was prostrated. In this extremity the young lawyer, just from New York and from Paris, turned himself into a nurse. . . ."[2] He went

[1] *Reminiscences* (manuscript), pp. 11-12.
[2] Field, *Record of the Family*, pp. 87-88.

about caring for his sick companions, making many lasting friends among them, including Samuel Purdy, who was to be Lieutenant-Governor of California, and Gregory Yale, who as a lawyer was later to be of assistance to Field when he needed help.

After what seemed an endless journey the ship passed through the Golden Gate into the harbor of San Francisco on December 28, 1849, and the passengers landed at eight or nine o'clock at night. Field spent seven of the ten dollars which he had with him in getting his trunks ashore. Then he set out with some of his fellow passengers to find a place to spend the night. Finally they located an adobe shack, which they agreed to pay for at the rate of thirty-five dollars a week.

The experiences of the landing in San Francisco and of that year and the years which immediately followed are chronicled in Field's *Personal Reminiscences of Early Days in California,* which he dictated to a stenographer in 1877. His account is hardly more than summarized in the pages which follow. The drama of his story is in harmony with the history of the gold rush. Men were pouring into San Francisco from all parts of the world. It was impossible to keep track of the rapidly increasing population. Only with the greatest difficulty was a semblance of order maintained, there where the riffraff of the world, part of it surfeited with gold and the rest greedy for it, was on a spree. New settlements of rough board shacks or tents grew up over night. There was little or no paving, and the muddy streets were well-nigh impassable. Teams floundered along, belly-deep in the mud, dragging loads of supplies up from the harbor. Ships brought cargoes of supplies from eastern ports, and found the wharves too crowded to land them. In hastily constructed store buildings, newly arrived merchants were selling goods at sky-high prices, taking their pay in ounces of gold. Saloons and gambling houses were crowded and doing big business, getting their share of the yellow dust brought in by the rough miners after a successful strike.

Field paid two of his remaining three dollars for breakfast the next morning, and set out to see San Francisco. In his own words: "It was a beautiful day, much like an Indian summer day in the East, but finer. There was something exhilarating and exciting in the atmosphere which made everybody cheerful and buoyant. As I walked along the streets, I met a great many persons I had known in New York, and they all seemed to be in the highest spirits. Every one in greeting me said 'It is a glorious country,' or 'Isn't it a glorious country,' or 'Did you ever see a more glorious country?' or something to that effect. In every case the word 'glorious' was sure to come out. There was something infectious in the use of the word, or rather in the feeling, which made its use natural. I had not been out many hours that morning before I caught the infection; and though I had but a single dollar in my pocket and no business whatever, and did not know where I was to get the next meal, I found myself saying to everybody I met, 'It is a glorious country.' " [3]

People who had been in California for any length of time were eager for news from the East. Field had brought a number of newspapers with him from New York, and he gave them to one of his fellow passengers to sell. In a short time the man returned and handed him thirty-two dollars. He had sold sixty-four papers at a dollar each, and had retained half the proceeds as his

[3] *Reminiscences*, pp. 6-7.

commission.[4] The money provided temporary relief
from the emptiness of his purse. He was also fortunate
in selling at a huge profit a dozen chamois skins which
his brother, Cyrus, had advised him to bring along to hold
gold dust. He had paid ten dollars for the dozen. He sold
them for an ounce of gold each. The ounce of gold was
worth from sixteen to eighteen dollars.[5]

Later he walked by a building that was being used as a
court house. He went in to watch the trial of a case. He
was surprised to see on the jury two of the men who had
arrived on the boat with him. When the trial was over
he asked them how it had happened. They replied that
they had stopped to see what was going on, when the
sheriff had summoned them to take places on the jury.
They had protested that they were strangers in the city,
but the sheriff had said that made no difference, for
nobody had been in the country three months. They
were paid eight dollars each for their services. After
that Field lingered in the court room hoping that he,
too, would be summoned for jury duty, but he was
disappointed.[6]

He had better luck in another matter. A man known
as Colonel Stevenson, who owed David Dudley Field four
hundred and forty dollars, had come to California some
years earlier. Stephen had brought the note with him,
hoping to be able to collect on it. He accidentally
discovered the man's place of business, and, without
revealing his own identity, went in and listened to the
man's stories concerning how prosperous he had become.
Then he presented the note, and the debtor, taken somewhat aback, made the payment in full.[7]

[4] *Ibid.*, p. 8.
[5] *Ibid.*, p. 9.
[6] *Ibid.*, pp. 9-10.
[7] *Ibid.*, pp. 10-11.

He rented an office for the enormous sum of three hundred dollars a month, payable in advance, hoping to begin the practice of law. With one exception, however, he found no clients. The single exception was a man who came to have a deed drawn. Field drew the deed and charged an ounce of gold, but when the client protested he reduced the charge to half an ounce. He explained his first month of legal experience in California by saying, "To tell the truth I was hardly fit for the business. I was too much excited by the stirring life around me. There was so much to hear and see that I spent half my time in the streets and saloons talking with people from the mines, in which I was greatly interested. I felt that there would soon be occasion in that quarter for my services." [8]

Life in San Francisco was so expensive that he could not long remain idle. He heard of a town called Vernon that was being established on the Sacramento River at the mouth of the Feather River. The town was expected to grow rapidly and Field thought it would be an excellent place to invest. He had little money at this time, but he expected to be able to buy on credit. Accordingly he took passage on a boat running up the Sacramento. When he reached Vernon he discovered that the winter floods had arrived before him, and had put the embryonic town almost entirely under water. He could only stay on the boat, which was going on up the Feather River. [9]

Field landed at Nye's Ranch, at the junction of the Yuba and Feather Rivers. There another town was being established, this one unaffected by the floods. Many tents had been set up, housing, in all, from five hundred to a thousand people. Outside an adobe building stood a man displaying a map of "Yubaville." It was a prospective town laid off in lots, for which people were signing at the price of two hundred and fifty dollars each. Field asked what would happen if he signed for lots and did not want them afterwards. He was told that he need not take them. Thereupon, he said, "I took his word and wrote my name down for sixty-five lots, aggregating in all $16,250. This produced a great sensation. To the best of my recollection I had only about twenty dollars left of what Colonel Stevenson had paid me; but it was immediately noised about that a great capitalist had come up from San Francisco to invest in lots in the rising town. The consequence was that the proprietors of the place waited upon me and showed me great attention." [10] The purchase gave impetus to the sale of the remaining lots.[11]

Field had with him a newspaper which contained a brief account of his departure from New York. He marked the article, and arranged that the paper should fall into the hands of the proprietors. Soon afterward one of them, a Frenchman, came up to him excitedly. "Mr. Field, are you the Monsieur Field mentioned in this paper?" [12] Field admitted that he was. He was told that a lawyer was needed to draw up the deed that was to complete the transfer of the site of the proposed town from General John A. Sutter to the promoters. Field agreed to draw the deed, and a messenger was sent to Hock Farm for General Sutter. The transaction was completed, and the land was transferred to Charles Covillaud and others for the sum of ten thousand dollars.[13]

That evening a celebration was held in a newly constructed house, the material for which had been brought

[10] *Ibid.*, p. 14.

[11] Colville's *Marysville Directory*, 1855, p. viii.

[12] *Reminiscences* (manuscript), pp. 40-41.

[13] The deed may still be seen among the Yuba County records.

up from San Francisco on the boat with Field. Two baskets of champagne were found in the settlement. These were passed around, and enthusiasm ran high.[14] Field was called on for a speech. He addressed the crowd on the merits of the locality and its glowing prospects, and ended by recommending that a government be established immediately and that a magistrate and town council be elected at once. Many agreed with him, and a meeting was called for the next morning.[15]

At the political meeting it was decided to elect a first alcalde, a second alcalde, a marshal, and an *ayuntamiento* or town council. Under Spanish law, and under normal conditions in California, the alcalde was a local judicial officer with functions similar to those of a justice of the peace. At this time, with the old central government broken down and with a new one not yet effective, the alcalde had assumed a wide range of powers. Of the election which took place Field said: "I had modestly whispered to different persons at the meeting in the new house the night before, that my name was mentioned by my friends for the office of alcalde; and my nomination followed. But I was not to have the office without a struggle; an opposition candidate appeared, and an exciting election ensued. The main objection urged against me was that I was a new-comer. I had been there only three days; my opponent had been there six. I beat him, however, by nine votes." [16]

At the time of the election it was decided to call the new town Marysville instead of Yubaville, in honor of Mrs. Covillaud, who was one of the few women in that part of the state, and a survivor of the Donner party.[17]

[14] *Reminiscences* (manuscript), pp. 43-44.
[15] *Reminiscences*, p. 17.
[16] *Ibid.*, p. 17.
[17] *Ibid.*, p. 18.

The election was something of a lark for Field. He said that with his notions of law he did not attach much importance to it, but he nevertheless made out a formal certificate of election and sent it to E. O. Crosby, prefect of the district of Yubaville. The prefect advised him to act, suggesting that in addition he should obtain a commission as justice of the peace from Governor Burnett. There was some doubt as to how long the office of alcalde would last. A constitution embodying American forms of government had been framed and adopted in the fall of 1849, but Congress had not yet accepted it and admitted California into the Union, and much of the local machinery of government had not yet been put into operation. The office of justice of the peace would, under the new government, take the place of that of alcalde. Field did as he was advised, and was sworn in as alcalde at Sacramento on January 22, 1850.[18]

With perfect confidence in himself, and with evident elation at the opportunity for exercising new powers, he took up the duties of his office. "I knew nothing of Mexican laws," he said; "did not pretend to know anything of them; but I knew that the people had elected me to act as a magistrate and looked to me for the preservation of order and the settlement of disputes; and I did my best that they should not be disappointed." [19] He went down to San Francisco to get his trunks. While there he bought, on credit, material for a frame house and several zinc houses, which were to be put up on his lots. As soon as they were erected he rented the zinc houses at high prices and fitted up the frame house as his office.[20] There he dispensed justice for the commu-

[18] *Ibid.*, p. 19.
[19] *Ibid.*, p. 22.
[20] *Ibid.*, p. 23.

nity, holding court behind a dry goods box, with tallow candles for lights.[21] He needed police assistance, but the town had made no provision for paying its officers. In order to get the necessary money, he said, "I went to the gamblers, and there were a great many there, and I said, 'Gentlemen, you are more interested than I am in having peace here because if there is trouble you will be the first sufferers. Now I want you to help me to support a police, and I am going to put a tax upon all your tables of $5.00 a week.' They cheerfully paid it, others assisted, and I had my police established." [22] The elected marshal refused to serve. Field appointed another, and directed him to appoint deputies. After that, "order and peace were preserved throughout the district, not only in Marysville, but for miles around." [23]

Of his experience as a judicial officer he said, "I tried many cases, both civil and criminal, and I dictated the form of process suited to the exigency. . . . In civil cases, I also called a jury, if the parties desired one; and in criminal cases, when the offense was of a high grade, I went through the form of calling a grand jury, and having an indictment found; and in all cases I appointed an attorney to represent the people, and also the accused, when necessary. The Americans in the community had a general notion of what was required for the preservation of order and the due administration of justice; and as I endeavored to administer justice promptly, but upon a due consideration of the rights of every one, and not rashly, I was sustained with great unanimity by the community." [24]

[21] Oral anecdote as retold in the Washington *Post*, April 10, 1899.
[22] *Reminiscences* (manuscript), p. 61.
[23] *Reminiscences*, p. 24.
[24] *Ibid.*, p. 24.

A most serious type of offense in the pioneer community was theft. There were few offenses of this kind, but when they came they were apt to be summarily punished by the people, with recourse to but little that might be called "due process of law." Two men were tried before Field for stealing a sum of money and some watches, and were convicted. There was as yet no jail in Marysville. Major Geary in San Francisco had agreed to take any convicts Field might have, if he would send with each enough money to buy a ball and chain. Marysville had no treasury to provide funds. Field knew that if the men were set free without punishment they would be lynched. He therefore ordered that they be publicly whipped—"that each of said defendants receive on his bare back one hundred lashes well laid on"—and that they be banished from the community.[25]

A few days later a man was convicted of stealing a large quantity of gold dust, which he had hidden and which he refused to surrender. The following was the order of the court: "Therefore it is ordered that the said defendant, John Barrett, be taken from this place to Johnson's Ranch, and there receive on his bare back within twenty-four hours from this time fifty lashes well laid on; and within forty-eight hours from this time fifty additional lashes well laid on; and within three days from this time fifty additional lashes well laid on; and within four days from date fifty additional lashes well laid on; and within five days from date fifty additional lashes well laid on. But it is ordered that the four last punishments be remitted provided the said defendant make in the

[25] The date of the order was April 4, 1850. The record of the case is in the *Register of Suits Before the First Alcalde*, pp. 107-8, which is filed with the recorder of Yuba County, at Marysville, Calif.

meantime restitution of the said gold dust bag and contents. The sheriff is ordered to execute this judgment." [26]
When twenty of the first fifty lashes had been inflicted the man broke down and agreed to show where the dust was hidden. After finding the dust, under the direction of the convict, the officers re-read the order of the court and discovered that there was no provision for remitting any of the first fifty lashes. Thereupon the remaining thirty were inflicted.[27]

Field referred to his method of punishment with some satisfaction, saying that "the sense of justice of the community was satisfied. No blood had been shed; there had been no hanging; yet a severe public example had been given." [28]

Field's authority in the community was strengthened by the support of a commander of United States troops on the Bear River, fifteen miles away. A soldier had committed a crime in Marysville, and had been punished by order of the first alcalde. The lieutenant in charge of the camp approved of the act, and offered Field any assistance which he might need at any time for the maintenance of order. Field allowed the promise to become known, to good effect in the community.[29]

Besides trying cases he performed many duties as an administrator. He had the banks of the Yuba River graded, to facilitate the landing of vessels. Squatters had taken up many of the more valuable lots down by the river. Field forced them to move out. He aided informally in arbitrating many disputes. On one occasion, he said, "a woman, apparently about fifty-six, rushed

[26] *Ibid.*, pp. 115-16.
[27] *Ibid.*, p. 116.
[28] *Reminiscences*, p. 26.
[29] *Ibid.*, pp. 27-28; *ibid.* (manuscript), pp. 73-75.

into my office under great excitement, exclaiming that she wanted a divorce from her husband, who had treated her shamefully. A few moments afterward the husband followed, and he also wanted relief from the bonds of matrimony. I heard their respective complaints, and finding that they had children, I persuaded them to make peace, kiss and forgive; and so they left my office arm-in-arm, each having promised the other never to do so again, amid the applause of the spectators. In this way I carried out my conception of the good Cadi of the village, from which term (Al Cadi) my own official designation, Alcalde, was derived." [30]

He summarized his achievements by saying: "To make a long story short, until I was superseded by officers under the United States government, I superintended municipal affairs and administered justice in Marysville with success. Whilst there was a large number of residents there of high character and culture, who would have done honor to any city, there were also unfortunately many desperate persons, gamblers, blacklegs, thieves, and cut-throats; yet the place was as orderly as a New England village. There were no disturbances at night, no riots, and no lynching. It was the model town of the whole country for peacefulness and respect for law." [31]

Field's own pronouncements lead to the suspicion that he was a bit intoxicated by his rise in position from obscurity in his brother's office to czardom in a frontier town. He gloried in applying to other men principles of justice derived from his own inner consciousness, principles which had been instilled into him by the years of his early training. He seems never to have doubted his

---

[30] *Reminiscences*, pp. 29-30.

[31] *Ibid.*, p. 30. See verifying evidence of his work in Colville's *Marysville Directory*, 1855, p. v.

own wisdom in the selection and interpretation of fundamental principles. With deepest satisfaction he looked upon his work and saw that it was good. He was successful in his private affairs as well as in his public capacity. In ninety days the lots which he had signed for went up to ten times the price which he had agreed to pay for them. Gossip has it that in his efforts to sell property he appeared on the water front at San Francisco to cry the merits of Marysville real estate to new arrivals. Wherever he made the sales, he declared that he disposed of lots to the amount of over twenty-five thousand dollars. His zinc houses brought in more than a thousand dollars in rental each month. At one time he had more than fourteen thousand dollars on hand, in addition to the money received from rentals and the sale of property. A large part of this money came in fees for his services as alcalde.[32] His economic success was quite as great as that of large numbers of the men who had hurried directly to the mines. It is not surprising that he was pleased with and somewhat inclined to boast of his achievements, and that his self satisfaction gave added heat to the fury with which he met the bitter personal controversy and the changes of fortune which were soon to come.

The duties of the alcalde came to an end with the installation of local officers under the new California constitution in April or May, 1850. At that time William R. Turner, a hot-tempered, opinionated, but none too learned Texan, came to Marysville to serve as district judge. Field may have been jealous because of the loss of his own prerogatives in the town. However,

[32] *Reminiscences*, p. 30.

according to his own account, he tried to be courteous to the new judge. Having on hand a number of copies of the New York *Evening Post*, he sent them to Turner. That paper, however, was vigorously anti-slavery, while Turner was a true son of the South. He suspected that he was being insulted, or at least that Field was an Abolitionist. At any rate, he was unfriendly to Field from the beginning.[33]

On June 7 Field appeared in Turner's court as attorney in a suit against Captain John Sutter. Turner over-ruled Field on a preliminary motion, whereupon Field arose and asked to be allowed to read the relevant provision of the law. Turner replied that he knew the law and that his mind was made up, and ordered Field to sit down. Field stated that he took exception to the decision of the court and appealed from the order. "I fine you two hundred dollars," snapped Turner. "Very well," replied Field. Turner boosted the fine to three hundred dollars and eight hours' imprisonment, and, enraged that Field still insisted on having the last word, he finally ordered him fined five hundred dollars and imprisoned for forty-eight hours.[34]

Field declared that he was not disrespectful to Turner in the court room. As to that, stories differ.[35] As Field left the room a friend told him not to mind what the

[33] *Ibid.*, p. 33.

[34] *Ibid.*, pp. 34-35; *District Court Record Book*, p. 9.

[35] See the depositions in *Proceedings of the Assembly of the State of California, Second Session, 1851, on the petition of Citizens of Yuba and Nevada Counties for the Impeachment of William R. Turner* (a compilation of depositions and documents made in 1878 by Field himself or someone working under him; hereinafter cited as *Proceedings of the Assembly*). An example of contrary assertions is that of "Stranger," in the Marysville *Transcript*, June 15, 1850, reprinted in Turner, William R., *Documents in Relation to the Charges Preferred by Stephen J. Field and Others* (published in 1853; hereinafter referred to as *Charges of Judge Field*), p. 7: "After a decision had been given by Judge Turner, in which Judge Field

judge said, for Turner was an old fool. Field replied, "The judge is a d—d old jackass." Turner's landlord heard the comment, and opened the door of the court room and shouted, "Judge Turner, Judge Field says you are a d—d old jackass." [36] Turner, sputtering wrathfully, ordered Field locked in his own office—there being no jail in town.

Field went to his office, but immediately sent for Judge Haun of the County Court. After a talk with Haun he sued out a writ of habeas corpus before him, and at a public hearing that evening was discharged, on the basis of the testimony of the sheriff and four members of the bar, because no warrant had been issued for the arrest.[37] The crowd gave three cheers for Field and three for Haun, and three groans for Turner. Turner was burned in effigy in the public plaza,[38] a matter with which Field declared he had nothing to do.

On the following day, Saturday, the District Court adjourned without proceedings "on account of the ill health of the judge." [39] On Monday Turner ordered Field re-imprisoned, and fined Judge Haun fifty dollars and ordered that he likewise be imprisoned forty-eight hours for contempt of the District Court in releasing the prisoner. Field again appeared before Haun on writ of habeas corpus. While the hearing was in process the sheriff appeared and took Field away. Turner dismissed

was an attorney, Judge F. hurriedly arose, and with an air of consequence, told the Court that its decision was incorrect, and not in accordance with the law. He was ordered to take his seat—he refused, and was then fined. He still persisted in talking—said that he had a right to be heard, and still continued to talk, and did talk, until the Court imposed a fine to the extent of the law, and imprisonment of forty-eight hours."

[36] *Ibid.* (manuscript), p. 96.
[37] *Ibid.*, p. 100.
[38] *Reminiscences*, p. 38.
[39] *District Court Record Book*, p. 10.

Field from the bar for suing out the writ, and likewise disbarred two of his colleagues, Mulford and Goodwin, for "having denounced the proceedings of this Court and set at defiance its authority, and vilified the same." [40]

Evidently the rough crowds in Marysville gloried in the controversy. The fact that many of them sided with Field enraged Turner all the more. He vowed time and again that he would kill Field. Such a solution was not uncommon at the time. Field asked Judge Bennett, of the state Supreme Court, what he should do about it. Bennett advised him to get a gun and use it the first time Turner appeared. Field was by no means eager to kill his enemy, but he determined to defend himself. He bought guns and learned to shoot from his pockets. Then he sent word to Turner that he would not avoid him, and would shoot to kill if he were attacked. [41] "Go tell him," he said, "I do not want any difficulty, that I am the son of a clergyman, a Doctor of Divinity in New England, who taught me to avoid breaches of the peace and difficulties; but that old clergyman, if he thought I gave up my right to my share of the sidewalk to any man, would not let me come into his house, and by —— I would not, and if he came at me in a threatening manner I would shoot him." [42]

Field declared that thereafter, in the saloons of Marysville, he often went up to within three feet of Turner and called for a drink. He saw him many times in the streets and saloons. There was fascination in the danger. Previously he had not gone into gambling saloons. Now he went wherever there was a crowd. In passing Turner he always turned and looked straight at him. "It was nothing I suppose but pure deviltry," he said, yet he

[40] *Ibid.*, pp. 10-11.
[41] *Reminiscences*, pp. 43-45.
[42] *Ibid.* (manuscript), pp. 114-15.

realized that was really the only safe course. Any sign
of fear would have meant his death.[43] An enemy has
maliciously left another version of affairs. According to
his account Field was kept busy dodging Turner. It was
a common remark that Turner had disbarred Field in two
respects: He had stopped Field from practicing law, and
had also "stopped his grog." When Turner was in town
Field visited only those saloons which had two doors, and
when Turner entered at one Field went out at the other.[44]
The accuracy of this version is undoubtedly open to some
question.

Field appealed to the state Supreme Court in the matter of his disbarment. Gregory Yale, one of the friends
he had made on the trip from Panama to San Francisco,
aided him in the presentation of motions.[45] The Supreme
Court in its first action ordered the record of the District
Court to be brought up.[46] After going over the record
the Supreme Court reversed the order of dismissal and
ordered Turner to reinstate Field.[47] Turner's decisions in
the cases of Mulford and Goodwin were also reversed.[48]
Turner maintained that he was tricked by the three men,
saying that although he had remained in Marysville for
about a week after the close of the session of the Court,
the appeal to the Supreme Court had not been made until
he left for the mines, where he did not receive the
summons which was delivered at his office.[49] In the
meantime one hundred and forty-three people—Field

[43] *Ibid.*, pp. 117-18.
[44] Terry, D. S., in *Character and Career of Stephen J. Field as It is
Known in California* (a compilation of articles written chiefly by Terry,
and published by his friends in 1889 after his death), p. 47.
[45] *Reminiscences*, p. 41.
[46] *People* ex rel. *Stephen J. Field* v. *Turner*, 1 Cal. 152.
[47] Ex parte *Stephen J. Field*, 1 Cal. 187. See also *Reminiscences*, p. 58.
[48] *People* ex rel. *Mulford* et al. v. *Turner*, 1 Cal. 143.
[49] *Charges of Judge Field*, pp. 3-4.

says "all the prominent citizens of Marysville" [50]— believing that the Governor could suspend a judicial officer, sent a petition to Governor Burnett urging the suspension of Turner. Field's name led the list. The Governor took no action, however.

Throughout the summer, newspapers of Marysville and Sacramento carried the slanderous or all but slanderous charges of opposing parties. On July 27, shortly after they were ordered reinstated, Field, Mulford, and Goodwin published a signed article in the Placer *Times* saying that Turner was a man of "depraved tastes," "vulgar habits" and "ungovernable temper," and that he was "reckless of truth," and "grossly incompetent." [51] Turner replied in a "Letter to the Public" on July 30, in which he called Field and his associates "perjured damned villains." [52] He evidently assumed that he would have to restore the men to their positions at the bar, as ordered by the Supreme Court, but on October 28 he cited the three men to appear before him and show cause why they should not be re-expelled for their printed statements concerning him as a judge.

Though expecting to be disbarred in any case, the three men decided to appear before the judge and give as many blows as possible in the verbal battle which was likely to take place. Field was heard to say on the evening before his appearance in court that he would read at all hazards a document accusing Turner of being corrupt and unfit for office. [53] At the hearing Field, when asked to show cause why he should not be expelled from the bar, arose and began to read aloud the affidavit of a man who declared that Turner had said he would dismiss the three

[50] *Reminiscences*, p. 42; see also pp. 210-13, Exhibit F.
[51] *Charges of Judge Field*, p. 16.
[52] *Ibid.*, p. 10.
[53] Deposition of W. H. Richardson, *Proceedings of the Assembly*, p. 78.

men no matter what they did or said.[54] Turner stopped
the reading, saying that the document was not respectful.
Field then began to read his answer to the order to show
cause. According to a comment made several years
later,[55] and judging by the fact that he nowhere preserved it among the numerous documents which he had
printed for his own vindication, Field in time became
somewhat ashamed of the answer which he read in court
and of the manner in which he read it. Turner preserved
it, however. Field gave four reasons why he should
not be expelled, saying, of Turner: "*First*—That he is
grossly incompetent to discharge the duties of his office.
Second—That he is guilty of gross oppression and tyranny
in office. *Third*—That he is guilty of gross indecency in
language and conduct. *Fourth*—That he is guilty of
gross immorality." [56]

As described by a friend of Turner's, Field "went on
reading the paper until he got to a portion of it which
was derogatory to Judge Turner's character, as was supposed by Judge Turner, who immediately stopped him
from reading further, stating that it was disrespectful to
the Court. Judge Field replied in a theatrical manner—
what did you say, sir; thank you, sir—at the same time
bowing backwards and forwards, until he reached the
door, passing back and forward. He then commenced to
read again, and was stopped by the Court, at which time
he passed off with the same gestures. At this time there
was stamping of feet in the court room by his friends." [57]

Field and his friends were again expelled.[58]

Field appealed to the state Supreme Court. He tried
to get an attachment of the person of Turner for refusing

[54] *Ibid.*, pp. 22-23, Exhibit G.
[55] *Reminiscences*, pp. 107-8.
[56] *Charges of Judge Field*, p. 17.
[57] Deposition of W. H. Richardson, *Proceedings of the Assembly*, p. 78.
[58] See the order of dismissal, *Proceedings of the Assembly*, p. 25.

to obey the order of the Court to reinstate the three men. The attachment was refused, on the ground that the last dismissal was for a new offense.[59] In another action, however, the Court vacated the order expelling the offenders, and directed that they be reinstated.[60] Nevertheless the controversy between Field and Turner continued to rage,[61] and Field argued no cases before the District Court.

[59] *People* ex rel. *Field* v. *Turner*, 1 Cal. 188.

[60] *People* ex rel. *Field* v. *Turner*, 1 Cal. 190.

[61] For instance, take the following letter of Turner's of Dec. 12, 1850, in a Marysville paper: "Who then is Stephen J. Field? This man who, skulking behind the attenuated and pusillanimous form of a country editor, hurls forth his lying slang and abuse, which, forsooth, he has neither the manliness or courage to openly father! This man who has tried to make the public take sides in a purely personal quarrel, which his own Falstaff disposition forbade his alone assuming! This man whom I have published as a 'perjured damned villain,' whom I attempted to chastise with a switch, and who has no courage to resent the former, and just speed enough in his system to avoid the latter! This man of such judicial power, who, in a *personal* matter, cries, Caesar-like, to the public, '*Help me, Cassius, or I sink,*' and on my approach, 'his coward lips do from their color fly!' This man, in a word, whose life, if analyzed, would be found to be one series of little-minded meanlinesses, of braggadocio pusillanimity, and contemptible vanity, which, when known, will sink him so low in public estimation that the hand of the resurrectionist can never reach him. Such is Stephen J. Field, who, having failed to *awe* me by his great legal ability, and who vainly thought to defy my court with impunity, now behind numerous editorial squibs, seeks to inflame the public mind by making charges which are as false as the heart which conceives them is cowardly and dastardly. Whatever I have said, I reiterate *I can prove*—whatever I have done, judicially, or otherwise, I reiterate I hold myself amenable, not only to the laws which I am alleged to have violated, but also personally responsible in any and under all circumstances."—Reprinted from *Charges of Judge Field*, pp. 17-18.

Field replied to Turner's letter in the Marysville *Herald* of December 21, saying that it was a "shameless lie" that Turner had ever attempted to chastise him with a whip or that he had ever fled from Turner. He had not avoided him. In spite of Turner's printed statements he (Turner) had let it be known that if any one attempted to call him to account his oath of office would require him to obtain an indictment of such person.—*Reminiscences*, p. 60.

In the fall of 1850 an election was to be held for members of the legislature which was to meet in January, 1851. Field decided to become a candidate. Among his admitted motives was that of bringing about the reform of the judiciary and of getting rid of Turner. He failed to obtain the nomination of the Democratic party. Refusing to give up, he ran on an independent ticket. He set out to get acquainted with his constituency, traveling all over the district, making friends, and trying to get out a vote. The task was difficult because of the nature of the population. It was made up chiefly of transients, men who were there in search of gold, and who, once they had it, expected to go back home or at least to return to a more civilized section of the country in which to live. They were little concerned about the government of California, so long as they could go on mining without interruption.

He made speeches at many places. His enemies used the slavery question to make trouble for him, showing that David Dudley Field had become a prominent Abolitionist, and insisting that Stephen held the same convictions. The rivalry and bitterness between the Abolitionists and the advocates of slavery were so intense that the result of the election might turn on that matter. Field tried to destroy its effectiveness so far as he was concerned by admitting that he had one brother who was a Free Soiler, but volunteering further that he had another brother who was a slave holder.[62] As for himself, he said, he was neither the one nor the other. He thought that slavery was a matter to be decided by each state for itself.

He found the campaign an intensely interesting experience. He learned much of the country, of the mines,

[62] *Ibid.*, pp. 47-49. One brother, Matthew, was building bridges in Tennessee at the time. See Pierce, F. C., *Field Genealogy*, p. 622.

and of the ways of the rough miners with whom he came in contact. He also learned something of the judicial methods of the mining communities. On one occasion he rode into a settlement where a man was being tried by a lynch jury. He took an interest in the prisoner, went around and talked with him, and concluded that he was probably innocent. He knew, however, that such juries seldom failed to convict. At a lull in the proceedings he announced himself, told why he was there, and asked that all present stop and drink with him. While they were drinking he talked with the man who appeared to be in charge and led him to speak sentimentally of his home and his mother. Then he turned the conversation to the prisoner, and suggested that he might have a home somewhere and loved ones who needed him. He kept the crowd drinking until they were in a mellow mood, and then, by an eloquent appeal to their sympathies, he persuaded them to send the man to Marysville for trial. He was convinced that he had saved the man's life. "Of all things which I can recall of the past," he declared, "this is one of the most pleasant." [63]

He won a seat in the legislature, but, much to his disappointment, he did not carry Marysville. He attributed the loss of a majority of the local votes to his actions in connection with another criminal case. A man who was charged with murder seemed in danger of being lynched. Field helped to get him away secretly and send him to Sacramento, where he would be sure to get a fair trial, and in doing so angered many of the people in his own community. [64] The Turner faction had fought his candi-

---

[63] *Reminiscences*, pp. 51-54.

[64] *Ibid.*, pp. 50-51.   He declared, "When the civil tribunals are open and in undisturbed exercise of their jurisdiction, a resort to violence can never be approved or excused."   No consideration of votes could change his attitude.

dacy with great bitterness, however, and it seems quite possible that Field was not as popular or Turner and his friends as unpopular in Marysville as Field believed. Since he ran for the legislature as an independent, Field did not have the campaign funds of a party chest at his disposal. His friends showed no enthusiasm when it came to paying expenses. As a result he found himself in debt for a considerable sum at a time when he was badly in need of income. Examples of the bills which he had to pay were those for refreshments for voters on the day of the election. He had told saloon keepers in the vicinity of the polls to be liberally disposed toward his friends on that day. That some of them took him quite literally is indicated by an itemized bill from a saloon in Downie-ville, which called for $298.75 for four hundred and sixty drinks and two hundred and seventy-five cigars.

When the legislature met, Field gave his first efforts to striking a blow at Judge Turner. He drafted a bill for the reform of the judiciary and succeeded in having it passed. It rearranged the judicial districts and created one new district, and provided that the incumbent judges should be assigned to such of the rearranged districts as were designated by the numbers by which their former territories had been called. As a matter of fact, only one judge was required to move. Turner had been judge in the eighth district, which embraced Marysville and vicinity. Under the new arrangement the eighth district, which he was required to take if he were to remain a district judge, was in the comparative wilderness of Trinity and Klamath Counties, in the extreme northwestern part of the state.[65] Field successfully sponsored another bill which provided that attorneys and counsellors could be dismissed only by the Supreme Court, and then only after

---

[65] "An Act Concerning the Courts of Justice in this State, and Judicial Officers." *California Laws*, 1851, p. 9.

the Court had followed a prescribed procedure as to
hearings.[66] The purpose of the act was to protect attorneys against the personal prejudices of such judges as
Turner.

Not yet satisfied, Field presented petitions signed by
many of his friends and Turner's enemies asking for the
impeachment of Turner, and in various ways gave this
movement energetic support. A committee was appointed
and many depositions were taken concerning the details
of the Field-Turner controversy.[67] Field testified at
length, and submitted with his testimony many documents to verify his statements. Apparently, however, he
did not present his answer to the Court when Turner
ordered him to show cause why he should not be
re-expelled from the bar. The testimony on Turner's
side was directed chiefly toward showing that he was a
man of good character, and that the proceedings in his
court were habitually orderly, while at the same time
revealing Field as a haughty and insolent person. An
important part of Turner's political capital was a letter
from Henry Clay expressing complete confidence in him.
Clay said, "The accounts of the disturbances near you
reached me, and I take pleasure in expressing my conviction of the propriety of your official conduct, in the
trying riotous proceedings in which you had to act a
prominent part." [68] The opinion of a man like Henry
Clay was not to be wholly ignored.

The testimony was reported to the assembly on April 15.
There was still much business before the legislature, and
many members wanted to finish it as soon as possible and
go home. It was thought that an impeachment trial

---

[66] "An Act Concerning Attorneys and Counsellors at Law." *Ibid.*, p. 48.
[67] See *Proceedings of the Assembly.*
[68] Printed in the San Francisco *Picayune*, April 14, 1851, reprinted in
Charges of Judge Field, p. 29.

before the Senate would take at least a month, and there was much opposition to prolonging the session in this way. Some evidently thought that Field had already carried his vindictiveness far enough. "Judge," they said to him, "what's the use of pressing this matter? You have sent Turner where there are only grizzly bears and Indians; why not let him remain there? He can do no harm there." [69] One of Turner's friends spread the rumor that Field was willing to drop the matter. As the result a motion for indefinite postponement carried, fifteen to twelve. Actually, Field had wanted the prosecution to continue, particularly because he knew that if it did not, the outcome would be interpreted as a vindication of and a victory for Turner.

Turner went off into the fastnesses of the North, as provided by the act of the legislature, but the dregs of the controversy remained to cause unpleasantness for Field for some years, since by no means all the popular sympathy had been on his side. He was a bit too lordly and suave in his manner, and too sublimely confident of his own rectitude, to be acclaimed a hero by the rougher elements of pioneer California. A few years later one more scene occurred in the struggle between the two men. Turner ran for re-election to his office. The election was contested in the courts, and the matter was carried on appeal to the Supreme Court. Field was at that time a member of the Court. Turner made loud complaint about Field's being on the bench, thinking he had no chance to get an unbiased hearing. When the case came up Field withdrew from the bench and left the argument to be heard by his colleagues, whose decision was such as to allow Turner to retain his office. [70] Turner was amazed at Field's action. Soon afterward he sent a friend to find

[69] *Reminiscences*, pp. 62-63.
[70] *Saunders* v. *Haynes*, 13 Cal. 145 (1859).

out if Field would speak to him. The following is Field's account of his answer:

"I answered that under no circumstances would I ever consent to speak to him; that he had done me injuries which rendered any intercourse with him impossible; that the world was wide enough for us both, and he must go his own way. . . . The next morning he stationed himself at the foot of the stairway leading up to the Supreme Court rooms, which was on the outside of the building, and, as I passed up, he cried out: 'I am now at peace with all the world; if there is any man who feels that I have done him an injury, I am ready to make him amends.' I turned and looked at him for a moment, and then passed on without saying a word. On the following morning he took the same position and repeated substantially the same language. I stopped and gazed at him for a moment, and then passed on in silence. This was the last time I saw him." [71]

"In thinking over my difficulties with Turner at this distant date," he said in the summer of 1877, "there is nothing in my conduct which I in the least regret. Had I acted differently; had I yielded one inch, I should have lost my self-respect and been for life an abject slave. There was undoubtedly an unnecessary severity of language in two or three passages of my answers to his attacks; and some portion of my answer in court to his order to show cause why I should not be re-expelled from the bar might better have been omitted. I have since learned that one is never so strong as when he is calm, and never writes so forcibly as when he uses the simplest language. My justification in these particulars, if they require any, must be found in the savage ferocity with which I was assailed, the brutal language applied to my

[71] *Reminiscences*, pp. 105-6.

character and conduct, and the constant threats made of personal violence. Malignity and hate, with threats of assassination, followed me like a shadow for months. I went always armed for protection against assault. I should have been less or more than a man had I preserved at all times perfect calmness either in my language or conduct." [72]

The controversy was now closed, save as it might be used as campaign material against him later on, and except as it lived in the effects which it had left upon the mind and character of the headstrong and self-confident individual who had been involved.

[72] *Ibid.*, pp. 107-8.

CHAPTER III

PROBLEMS OF FRONTIER LIFE

The fact that a fracas such as the Field-Turner controversy could take place among judges, legislators, and prominent citizens tells much of the rough, unformed character of the state of California in the early days. In the session of the legislature which met in San José in January, 1851, rugged, sun-tanned, bewhiskered frontiersmen daily entered the legislative halls and laid their guns upon their desks or tucked them away close at hand. The day might eventually come when peace and order would be maintained by civil officers, but for the time being these men, as well as the common run of men throughout the state, were equipped to care for themselves. In the absence of a tradition which limited parliamentary combat to the use of the powers of oratory, the ever-present guns at times threatened to come into play. On one occasion, after Field had made a speech in the assembly concerning the Turner impeachment, B. F. Moore, another member, ostentatiously cocked his pistols and laid them in the open drawer before him, and in a speech made a deliberate personal attack upon Field.[1]

Field was enraged, but for the time being he kept his hot temper under control. After the vote on impeachment had been taken he set out to get satisfaction from Moore. He prepared a challenge, and sought someone who would carry it to Moore. None of his friends would serve, pleading as their reason the fact that the constitution of the state disbarred from political life all persons

[1] *Reminiscences*, p. 66.

convicted of participation in dueling. Field was quite despondent until he came upon David C. Broderick, President of the Senate, a man who had little fear in him, and who was to become one of the two prominent political bosses of the state during the decade of the fifties. Broderick offered to carry the challenge.[2] Moore refused either to fight or to apologize. Broderick thereupon sent word that on the following day Field would rise in the assembly and denounce him. He was told that Field would be shot in his seat. Broderick replied that others would be shot too. Moore's friends urged him to apologize. The next day Field, with a group of his friends seated around him, arose and addressed the chair. The speaker of the assembly, who had been forewarned, recognized Moore instead of Field. Moore read a retraction of his assertions about Field, and the trouble was over.[3]

His aid endeared Broderick to Field, and an incident which occurred later in the session deepened the friendship. Field was standing in a saloon with some of his friends, when Broderick suddenly seized him and shoved him out of the room. Unknown to Field, a brother of Judge Turner's had entered the saloon and had drawn a gun on him. In gratitude Field thereafter gave Broderick vigorous political support. He spent large sums of money for him each year, and campaigned for him. Many people were surprised, Field said, that he would associate with Broderick, "whose habits of life and general character had little to attract one like myself." [4] Broderick's help to him at San José was the cause.

Rough as they were, it is not to be inferred that Field and his colleagues spent most of their time in the legisla-

---

[2] *Ibid.*, p. 67.
[3] *Ibid.*, p. 69.
[4] *Ibid.* (manuscript), pp. 156-57.

ture gunning for one another, or even in advancing
private quarrels.   Only one other legislature had met
since the adoption of a constitution by California, and
the state had not gone through the usual territorial stage
during which political life might have been organized.
Hence a great deal of political foundation work needed to
be done, work the character of which was made all the
more complex because of the abnormal conditions produced by the gold rush.   Field and the more able of his
colleagues set out to lay the needed foundations.

Field was a member of the Judiciary Committee.
Another man was chosen as chairman, for political
reasons, but Field declared, "I was foremost in the Committee." [5]   As a member of this Committee, his greatest
contribution was in the writing of the civil and criminal
practice acts.   He took most of the work upon himself.
He disregarded the work of the preceding legislature and
took the civil and criminal codes of procedure recommended by David Dudley's committee to the New York
legislature as his guide.   He modified and added to these
codes to meet the particular needs of California.   He
said of the task: "The amount of labor bestowed on these
acts will be appreciated when I say that I recast, in the
two, over three hundred sections, and added over one
hundred new ones.   I devoted so much attention and
earnestness to the work, that in a short time the legislature placed implicit confidence in everything relating to
the judiciary which I recommended.   The criminal
practice act, for instance, remodelled as stated, con-
sisting of over six hundred sections, was never read before
the legislature at all.   The rules were suspended and the
bill read by its title and passed.   When it came before
the Governor, on the last day of the session, he said he

[5] *Ibid.,* p. 131.

could not sign it without reading it, and it was too late for him to do that. I represented to him that its passage was essential to secure the harmonious working of the laws already passed. Turning to me he said, 'you say it is all right?' I replied, 'yes'; and thereupon he signed it." [6]

The acts became the basis of similar acts in a number of other western states. Field was extremely proud of his work. Referring to it nearly ten years later, when he was Chief Justice of the state Supreme Court, he said: "It is not within the wit of man to devise more simple rules of pleading than those prescribed by the practice act of this state, and there is no excuse for any departure from them." [7] His ability to adjust the acts to the needs of California indicates that he had not been idle at the time when David Dudley was working at the task of codification a few years earlier.

Perhaps the most important contribution which he made in the civil practice act was the provision giving legal status to the rules adopted by men in the mining camps for their own government. A section dealing with justices' courts read as follows:

In actions respecting "Mining Claims" proof shall be admitted of the customs, usages, or regulations established or in force at the bar, or diggings, embracing such claim; and such customs, usages, or regulations, when not in conflict with the constitution and laws of this state, shall govern the decision of the action.[8]

While the provision seems simple enough, it became highly significant in the political life of California. Thus far the political organization of the state had made no detailed attempt to legislate concerning the multitude of

[6] *Reminiscences*, p. 65.

[7] *Coryell* v. *Cain*, 16 Cal. 567 (October term, 1860).

[8] *California Laws*, 1851, Sec. 621, p. 149.

problems which grew out of the relations of miners to one another in the ownership and working of their claims. For the sake of order the miners had adopted their own bodies of rules in particular camps, and when necessary had set up tribunals for enforcing them. The rules varied somewhat from section to section, but they bore great similarity. For the most part they were modelled after similar rules which had prevailed in mining regions in other parts of the world. "They were not the spontaneous creation of the miners of 1849-50. Historical accuracy ascribes a different origin to them. They reflect the matured wisdom of the practical miner of past ages, and have their foundation . . . in certain natural laws, easily applied to different situations, and were propagated in the California mines by those who had a practical and traditional knowledge of them in their varied form, in the countries of their origin, and were *adopted,* and no doubt gradually improved and judiciously modified by the Americans." [9]

Field and other legislators knew that the legislature had not the requisite practical knowledge for the enactment of laws necessary for the regulation of mining life and activities, and that the government would fail in the attempt to enforce laws not acceptable to the miners themselves. It was evident that the miners' own rules were fairly adequate. Hence it was that Field wrote the provision making these rules applicable in the justices' courts of the state. No such provision was adopted for the higher courts, but the pressure upon the other courts for its recognition was so great that the Supreme Court came to assume the acquiescence of the legislature in the extension of the provision, and followed it where no

[9] Yale, Gregory, *Legal Titles to Mining Claims and Water Rights in California* (1867), p. 59.

adequate rule was furnished by the common law.[10] Even the federal government was eventually compelled to place its stamp upon the regulations adopted by the miners.[11] Field also incorporated into the civil practice act provisions making liberal exemptions from forced sale of the personal property of debtors. In addition to the articles usually exempted he included farm implements, work animals, tools and implements of mechanics, and the instruments and libraries of professional men.[12] Although generous humanitarian legislation has characterized much of the frontier law-making experience, it is to be noted that at this time Field's leadership in the movement suggested a tolerance and human sympathy quite different from the rigid attitude toward debtors which had been taken by his forbears, and which seemed more nearly to characterize him in his later years. He took pride in the fact that he supported a homestead exemption bill, and that he helped successfully to resist a reduction of the exemption from five thousand to three thousand dollars.[13] For the time being he was to be reckoned among the liberals, the sponsors of so-called social legislation.

He drafted also "An Act Concerning Divorces." Other than the customary justifications for granting divorces he listed "extreme cruelty in either party; or for habitual intemperance; or for wilful and continued desertion, by either party, for the period of three years; or for wilful neglect, on the part of the husband, to provide for his wife the common necessaries of life, having the ability to provide the same, for the period of three

[10] *Ibid.*, p. 60.
[11] See Field's discussion in *Jennison* v. *Kirk*, 98 U. S. 453.
[12] *Reminiscences*, p. 75.
[13] *Ibid.*, p. 75; *California Laws* (1851), p. 296.

years." [14]   Here again was to be found a liberality of viewpoint not in harmony with the tenets of Puritanism, an attitude which showed the man in sympathetic contact with the social problems of his time and desirous of solving them, even if he had to change legal customs which had been long established.

With the responsibility of these and other acts on his hands, one of them being a charter for Marysville,[15] Field was a busy man at San José. He kept two clerks, at his own expense, to help him with the tasks which he had assumed.[16] He worked much alone in shaping the acts which he sponsored. This may have been due to the fact that there were few men in the legislature who had been intensively enough and broadly enough trained in the law to be able to work shoulder to shoulder with him. It may have been due also to the fact that in most things he was a man who was sufficient unto himself, and who did not easily adjust himself to others or work well with them. It is evident that he was eager to place his own stamp upon the institutions of the state, and that he succeeded in doing so. Whether or not such a desire always worked to the good of the state, it offers a clue to the character of Field which is not to be ignored in a study of his life.

When the legislature adjourned on the first of May Field returned to Marysville. He had no money, and was in debt to the amount of eighteen thousand dollars, which bore interest at the rate of ten per cent a month. His *Reminiscences* are vague as to just what happened to his money. Once, speaking of the period following his

---

[14] *California Laws* (1851), p. 186.

[15] *Ibid.*, p. 330.

[16] Mott, Judge Gordon N., San Francisco *Alta*, June 30, 1884.

disbarment he said: "Having nothing else to do, I went into speculations which failed, and in a short time—a much shorter time than it took to make my money—I lost nearly all I had acquired and became involved in debt." [17] Elsewhere he said, "My ventures, after my expulsion from the bar, in June, 1850, had proved so many maelstroms into which the investments were not only drawn but swallowed up." [18] At another point he declared that the expenses of his campaign for the legislature, together "with various losses and numerous adventures and speculations that I entered into swept away my fortune." [19] An enemy declared in later years that Field had been an inveterate gambler, and that his money was probably lost in gambling saloons.[20] Mining ventures of some kind seem to have been involved. In looking back upon these experiences he is reported to have said that he made a lot of money and lost a lot, and came out with what he started with—nothing.[21]

The proprietor of the United States Hotel agreed to trust him for his meals until he could improve his fortunes. He rented a small house for eighty dollars a month, put a cot in the garret and a minimum of office furniture on the ground floor, and was ready to practice law again [22]—for Judge Turner was at Marysville no longer. A Marysville newspaper of May 20 carried a card announcing "Stephen J. Field, Attorney and Counselor at Law, Office on 2d Street next door to Ford & Goodwin's old stand." [23] Here he began the task of

---

[17] *Reminiscences*, p. 46.

[18] *Ibid.*, p. 75.

[19] *Ibid.* (manuscript), p. 158.

[20] Terry, in *Character and Career of Stephen J. Field*, pp. 47-48.

[21] Statement of Irwin B. Linton, in interview with author, Feb. 22, 1928.

[22] *Reminiscences*, p. 76.

[23] Marysville *Herald*, May 20, 1851.

earning money to pay his debts. A directory of 1853 shows that he had moved to a location over the El Dorado saloon, on the west side of "D" Street between First and Second, while two years later he was in the United States buildings on the other side of "D" Street.

The ruinous rate of interest, ten per cent a month, had had much to do with his financial disasters,[24] but he now set out to pay all that he owed, including the full amount of the interest, in spite of the fact that the current rate was falling rapidly. In 1852 it declined to three per cent a month, and soon afterward to two and a half per cent, where it stood for some time.[25] Field said of his achievement: "My business soon became very large; and, as my expenses were moderate, within two years and a half I paid off all my indebtedness, amounting with the accumulations of interest to over thirty-eight thousand dollars. Part of this amount was paid by the surrender of the property mortgaged, or a sale of that previously assigned, but the greater part came from my earnings. I paid every creditor but one in full; to each I gave his pound of flesh, I mean his interest at ten per cent a month. I never asked one of them to take less than the stipulated rate. The exceptional creditor was Mr. Berry, a brother lawyer, who refused to receive more than five per cent a month on a note he held for $450." [26]

For some years the bar at Marysville had the most lucrative practice of any in the state outside of San Francisco.[27] Field shared in this prosperity. It is reported, however, that experience had not yet taught him how to keep a surplus, once he had won it. Most of the members

[24] For a statement of the mortgages against his property, the sale of it, and its value as estimated by the returns in rentals, see *Benham* v. *Rowe*, 2 Cal. 387 (1852).

[25] Bancroft, H. H., *History of California*, Vol. VII, p. 162.

[26] *Reminiscences*, p. 78.

[27] Shuck, Oscar T., *Bench and Bar in California* (1889), p. 149.

of the Field family gathered in Stockbridge in 1853 for the golden wedding of the parents. Henry has recorded that Stephen "could not be spared" [28] to attend because he was busy establishing the institutions of a frontier state. Another person has recorded, however, undoubtedly not without malice, that Field left for the East with about ten thousand dollars in his possession, got as far as San Francisco where he lost all his money in a gambling saloon, and was obliged to borrow money to take him back to Marysville.[29] In the following year he went into partnership with Samuel B. Smith. Leaving his practice in the hands of his partner he now made a belated trip to the home of his parents.[30] In 1855 he was again at work in Marysville.

He would have liked to continue his legislative experience. In the summer of 1851 he decided to run for the state Senate. He was a Democrat, and since the Democrats were well in the majority at that time a nomination was almost the equivalent of election. A majority of the delegates chosen to the county convention favored his candidacy. Some of them could not go to the convention, however, and sent him their proxies filled out in blank. He turned them over to supposed friends, to be voted for himself, giving one man ten votes, another five, and another two. When the convention met the man with ten votes sold them for the promise of the office of sheriff for his partner, an office which was supposed to be worth thirty thousand dollars a year. The man with five votes sold out for a county judgeship. Field was defeated by two votes. His reaction can be best described in his own words:

[28] Field, *Life of David Dudley Field*, p. 63.
[29] Terry, quoted in *Character and Career of Stephen J. Field*, p. 48.
[30] *Reminiscences*, p. 98.

"For the moment I was furious, and hunted up the man who had held my ten proxies, and had been seduced from my support. When I found him in the room of the convention, I seized him and attempted to throw him out of the window. I succeeded in getting half his body out, when the bystanders pulled me back and separated us. This was fortunate for both of us; for just underneath the window there was a well or shaft sunk fifty feet deep." [31]

Though he continued active in politics and made some attempt to influence legislation, this was his last attempt to secure a seat in the legislature.

As indicated by these various experiences, difficulties among frontiersmen were frequently characterized by rabid abuse, and often by physical violence. Field's troubles with district judges were not yet over. As the result of his judiciary bill the district at Marysville was vacated, and a new judge, Gordon N. Mott, was chosen by joint vote of both houses of the legislature. Afterward there was a dispute as to whether Mott's term ran until 1852, or merely until an election could be held in the fall of 1851. At an election proclaimed by the Governor in 1851 a new judge, William T. Barbour, was elected. Mott refused to give up his office, and the dispute was carried to the Supreme Court.[32] Field argued the case for Mott. Barbour won, and was offended at Field for the part he had played. When Barbour ran for re-election in 1853 Field opposed him. Harsh words passed between them, and Barbour challenged Field. He then claimed that Field had challenged him, and insisted on the right to choose the weapons and the place of combat. He chose to fight in a room twenty by twenty, the duel to be started with pistols and ended with Bowie

[31] *Ibid.*, pp. 76-77.
[32] *People* ex rel. *Barbour* v. *Mott*, 3 Cal. 502.

knives. Field, declaring that he believed Barbour to be a coward, accepted. Barbour backed down on the use of knives, then insisted on fighting in the open instead of in the room, and finally walked off without fighting at all, saying he would defend himself if attacked.[33] The next day, according to Field's account, Barbour came up behind him, put a pistol to his head, and ordered him to draw and defend himself. Field called him a cowardly assassin and told him to "shoot and be damned." Barbour turned and walked away.[34] Another version, one which is perhaps not well substantiated, is to the effect that Barbour applied not a gun but his toe, and that Field fled to his office and locked the door.[35] Barbour further antagonized Field by distributing copies of Turner's book which gave his side of the Field-Turner controversy and by writing a letter to Turner declaring that he had caught Field in the street and had given him a whipping in the presence of a large crowd.[36]

In spite of the enmity between the judge and himself, Field continued to practice before the District Court. For a time Barbour consistently ruled against him, but he usually won his cases when he appealed them to the Supreme Court. Then Barbour turned and began to rule consistently in favor of Field, embarrassing him even more than before, for as a result his opponents often won in the Supreme Court, while he gained a reputation for losing before that Court.[37] After a time Barbour tired of the controversy, and made peace overtures. In Field's

[33] *Reminiscences*, pp. 86-89. See verifying letter, Mott to Field, April 26, 1876, *ibid.*, pp. 219-23.

[34] *Ibid.*, pp. 89-90. See verifying letter, L. Martin to Field, March 21, 1854, *ibid.*, pp. 223-24.

[35] Terry, in *Character and Career of Stephen J. Field*, pp. 40-41.

[36] *Judge Turner's Defense* (1857), pp. 6-7, a second edition of *Charges of Judge Field*.

[37] *Reminiscences*, p. 91.

own words, "Judge Barbour said to me he was willing to meet me half-way and let bygones be bygones and I replied 'yes if there are no explanations, because I won't explain anything and any attempt at explanation would only revive the old difficulties.' Accordingly we met together and took a glass of wine and I said 'here is an act of oblivion to the past but no explanations.' " [38]

Field was always an enemy of trials by lynch juries, which continued to be held frequently for a number of years throughout the state, and used every effort to protect prisoners from their judgments. An exciting event occurred at Downieville on July 5, 1851. Just prior to July 4 a Democratic convention had been held there—the same convention at which Field had attempted to throw a man out of a window. The convention drew a great crowd of people, many of whom remained in town over the holiday. William Walker, a man of magnetic personality who in later years by his expeditions into Mexico and Nicaragua was to acquire the title of "the Gray-eyed Man of Destiny," had presided over the convention. With Field from Marysville were William M. Stewart, afterwards a United States senator from Nevada, Charles N. Felton, who was to be a congressman from California, and Charles S. Fairfax, who might have boasted of the fact that he was the last Lord Fairfax. All of these remained in town to enjoy the excitement of the celebration of the country's independence.

Toward the end of the day the town was giving evidence of the gallons of liquor which had passed over its many bars. In one of the saloons at a gambling table sat a beautiful young woman of twenty whose name was Juanita. Juanita was fascinating to the crowd of rough, bibulous men in the saloon, but she was not much

[38] *Ibid.* (manuscript), pp. 194-95.

respected by them, due to the fact that the man with
whom she lived was not her husband. A big Scotchman
named Jock Cannon was able to see through drunken eyes
enough of the loveliness of Juanita's bare shoulders to stir
hot desire in his giant physique. As he brought down a
heavy hand upon her shoulder she leaped to her feet with
a dagger in her hand. Jock drew back. Next morning,
still drunk, he found his way to her house, and had kicked
down the door before his friends arrived and took him
away. He went back again, and Juanita plunged a
butcher knife into his breast.

The townsmen, sullen and peevish with headaches of
the morning after their drunken celebration, raised a cry
for the death of the murderer. A lynch court was
organized in the briefest time, and Juanita and her
man were hauled before it for trial. The man was
released, but Juanita was sentenced to be hanged. Field
and his friends from Marysville were much distressed.
"Find Walker," he shouted. "If anybody can handle this
mob he can." But alas, William Walker had ridden out
of town two hours earlier.

"With this hope gone, young Steve Field tried the
persuasive power of his own tongue—and even in his
youth Field had gained fame as a pleader and knockabout
orator. See this tall, spare, black-headed youngster in his
long surtout and frilled stock mount a barrel in the heart
of the mob. He has the face of a knight, all glorified by
his high purpose.

" 'Gentlemen of Downieville, you cannot hang a
woman! Think, I beg you! Our fair California has
been one of the sisterhood of states not ten months. Her
fame is world wide. Would you have it rolled off the
whole world's tongue that California men are cowards
enough to——'

"A voice from the mob—'Aw, to hell with him!'
Steve Field is knocked off the barrel and rolled in the
dust." [39]

After an hour in which to prepare herself Juanita was
led away to her doom. Field and his comrades went
sadly back to Marysville.

Field carried a derringer pistol and a bowie knife until
the summer of 1854 when he made his first visit to the
East. "I found that a knowledge that they were worn
generally created a wholesome courtesy of manner and
language," he said. [40] Even the courts of law were not
free from threats of violence. At one time, when he was
attorney in a suit over a mining claim, he discovered that
the constable had received two hundred dollars to sum-
mon as jurors persons chosen by the other side. On the
night before the trial he overheard an offer being made
to one of the jurors. On the day of the trial he discussed
the case for three hours. Then, turning on the jury, he
astonished them by accusing them of having been corrupted. Pointing to one of the jurors he declared: "I
know that you . . . have been approached. Did you
spurn the wretch away who made a corrupt proposal to
you, or did you hold counsel, sweet counsel, with him?
I know that you [pointing to another juror] talked over
this case with one of the other side at the house on the
hill last night, for I overheard the conversation—the
promise made to you and your pledge to him." In the
otherwise deadly quiet of the room he heard the click,
click of the cocking pistols. "There is no terror in your
pistols, gentlemen," he warned; "you will not win your

[39] This account is taken from the chapter on "The Hanging of Juanita"
in Ritchie, Robert Welles, *The Hell-roarin' Forty-Niners*. Ritchie gathered
his data from an account by Charles N. Felton, one of the Marysville group,
which was recorded in an Old Timer's scrap-book found in Downieville.

[40] *Reminiscences*, p. 84.

case by shooting me; you can win it only in one way—by evidence showing title to the property; you will never win it by bribery or threats of violence." [41] Overawed by Field's exposure, the jury gave a verdict for his client. He speedily won an enviable reputation as a lawyer. Of the sixty cases in which he appeared before the Supreme Court of the state he won forty-one and lost nineteen. He took forty cases to the Supreme Court himself, and appeared for the respondent in twenty.[42] Controversies over mining claims brought the highest fees. He left to clerks such matters as the enforcement of mortgages and the collection of debts, unless contests were made on them. Of his methods of work it has been said that "he left nothing to chance. . . . He had no faith in the vulgar conception of inspiration; to him, success signified the legitimate consequence of logical thought and untiring industry. Not that he believed that thorough preparation was incompatible with such flashes of rhetoric as were evoked by the fervent heat of intellectual controversy." [43]

"He was distinguished at the bar for his fealty to his clients, for untiring industry, great care and accuracy in the preparation of his cases, uncommon legal acumen, and extraordinary solidity of judgment," said Judge Baldwin. "As an adviser, no man had more the confidence of his clients, for he trusted nothing to chance or accident when certainty could be attained, and felt his way cautiously to his conclusions, which, once reached, rested upon sure foundations, and to which he clung with remarkable pertinacity. Judges soon learned to repose confidence in his opinions, and he always gave

[41] *Ibid.*, pp. 81-83.

[42] These data were compiled from an examination of the *California Reports* during the years when Field practiced at the bar.

[43] Bancroft, H. H., *Chronicles of the Builders*, Vol. I, p. 415.

them the strongest proofs of the weight justly due to his conclusions." [44]

Along with his vocation he kept up many civic and social interests. He was a Mason. He was one of the directors of the first historical society of California.[45] He was a member of the Yuba Guards, a military, civic, and social organization of Marysville, in which he came in contact with many men whom he was to know in professional life in the years to come. For a time he was a frequent attendant at the Presbyterian church, which was organized in the latter part of 1850. In 1854, the Reverend William McKip, an Episcopal minister who came to be known as the "Missionary Bishop of California," preached in Marysville. As the result of his inspiration, Field and others organized St. John's Episcopal Church and erected a brick building at the corner of Fifth and "E" Streets. Field was "first warden" of the church until he left Marysville. It may be questioned, of course, whether his activities in this direction had any very deep religious significance. The church was a symbol of respectability and stability, qualities which apparently seemed to Field at least as important as religious devotion.

Although Field was prospering financially and was rapidly becoming a leader in the California bar, he was not satisfied with his position. It seems probable that he was more eager to create or mold institutions which would stand as monuments to his memory than to use the law as an instrument for the protection of the property of others, even with the reward of high fees for his

[44] Sacramento *Union*, May 6, 1863.
[45] *Papers of the California Historical Society*, Vol. I, Part I (1887) Introduction, p. xvii, note 1. The first society was organized on April 29, 1852.

services. He was constantly in touch with politics, and in 1857 his name was again mentioned for office. The legislature of that year had the task of electing two United States senators, one for a full term of six years and another for a short term of four years. Field's friend, David C. Broderick, at that time the strongest political leader in the state, forced his own nomination for the long term. Field was among the aspirants for the short term. He received seven votes on each of several ballots, but never more than that number. Broderick agreed to use his influence for William M. Gwin if Gwin would surrender all the California patronage to him. Gwin agreed, and Field and other aspirants withdrew in his favor.[46]

Field at no time had any real chance of election. It was said that he "was in the list mainly to prepare his way to the Supreme Court bench, a position more congenial to his nature and training, and much coveted by him. Likewise it was a place he could fairly hope to obtain; one that he could well honor." [47] He seems to have withdrawn his name from the senatorial contest with the understanding that he was to be nominated for the position of state Supreme Court judge later in the year.

He received the nomination, as was generally expected. Although it was believed that he would easily win at the polls, the election was hotly contested. The Turner affair came into the light again, to be used as a political scandal. A second edition of the papers compiled on Turner's side of the controversy was brought out as "Judge Turner's Defense," [48] and was widely circulated. Although Field was called a Broderick man, Broderick refused to support him. The break was due to the war-

---

[46] See O'Meara, James, *Broderick and Gwin* (1881). See also Lynch, Jeremiah, *A Senator of the Fifties; David C. Broderick.*

[47] O'Meara, *Broderick and Gwin*, p. 160.

[48] See advertisement, Sacramento *Democratic State Journal*, Sept. 12, 1857.

fare between Broderick and Gwin. Although Gwin had agreed to surrender all patronage to Broderick, President Buchanan had ignored Broderick's recommendations and had asked for recommendations from Gwin. Nothing averse, Gwin gave them. There was a legend that once after a futile visit to the White House Broderick, leaving, had paused on the front steps to send echoing out over Lafayette Park a denunciation of the administration that, for its vocabulary of adjectival expletives, would have been worthy of Field himself [49]—for Field had a vocabulary of high vituperative excellence. Broderick returned to California and declared war on the Gwin faction, but Field declined to have any part in it, whereupon Broderick included Field in his list of enemies.

There was also opposition to Field among certain groups, due to his supposed hostility toward the settlers, in connection with the controversies between people who had come into California and had settled on vacant land without taking the trouble to secure title to it, on the one hand, and owners who claimed large tracts as grants from the Spanish or the Mexican government, but whose evidence of title was incomplete, on the other. Field was thought to favor the paper titles as against the rights of the squatters,[50] wherever such titles were not obvious forgeries. Indeed, as will be seen later, the title even to the site of Marysville itself, for which Field had written the deed, would have been unsettled if the squatters had had their way. This fact may have helped to develop Field's convictions on the subject.

Field's opponents were Nathaniel Bennett, Republican, who had previously served a year and a half as one of the original members of the Court, and James H. Ralston, candidate of the American party and the Settlers' and

[49] Lynch, *David C. Broderick*, p. 162.
[50] Sacramento *Bee*, July 15, 28, Aug. 3, Sept. 5, 1857.

Miners' party. At the election of September 2, 1857, Field received 55,216 votes, considerably more than a majority of all the votes cast.[51] He carried all but two counties, Alameda and San Francisco, which gave majorities for Bennett.[52] These were, of course, the most populous counties in the state.

Both Republicans and Democrats rejoiced at his election. A Republican paper of Sacramento expressed pride in the New England men who had come into the state. "With their thoroughly inbred, or rather inborn, principles of freedom, how we of the North may congratulate ourselves upon every political promotion of which any one of them is the deserving object. You can no more eradicate their natural Republican sympathies and sentiments than you can take out their hearts and then converse with them as living men." [53] A Democratic paper was highly indignant at this attempt of the Republicans to claim Field as their own. He was not a Republican. He had been a Yuba County Democrat in the legislature. Were he less widely known he might be injured by these Republican statements, but as it was he would "only smile at the shallow artifice that would thus draw him to the embrace of the colored population." The Democrats had nominated him and had triumphantly elected him, and were well satisfied with their selection.[54]

"When he took his seat upon the bench," said a California lawyer, "Judge Field possessed the express confidence of not only his party, but of the opposition. His reputation as an enlightened leader of his profession had spread to all parts of the state, and the general hope

[51] Davis, W. J., *History of Political Conventions in California*, p. 84.
[52] Sacramento *Democratic State Journal*, Oct. 6, 1857.
[53] Quoted in *ibid.*, Oct. 15, 1857.
[54] *Ibid.*

and conviction were that he would be, not a partisan, but a thoroughly upright and honest judge." [55]

Peter H. Burnett, who had been the first Governor of the state, had been elected to fill a short term on the bench, to run until January 1, the time when Field was to take his seat at the beginning of his regular term. During the month of September Chief Justice Murray died. Burnett was appointed to fill the remainder of Murray's term, and the short term was offered to Field, thus making it possible for him to go on the bench immediately. He hesitated to accept because he had planned to go East before beginning his judicial tasks, but was told that he would be permitted to go anyway. [56] He had gone to Sacramento to argue cases before the Court when, on October 13, 1857, he received his appointment to the bench. [57] He surrendered his private practice and accepted. He suffered financially by the change in position. "A greater pecuniary and personal sacrifice, in our opinion, has never been made by a public officer in the state . . .," said a Democratic paper. [58] During his last year at private practice he earned forty-two thousand dollars. [59] His salary as Supreme Court justice was only six thousand.

[55] Schuck, *Bench and Bar in California*, p. 159.
[56] *Reminiscences*, p. 99.
[57] *Ibid*.
[58] Sacramento *Democratic State Journal*, Oct. 14, 1857.
[59] Society of California Pioneers, *Obituary Record*, Vol. VI, p. 170.

CHAPTER IV
FROM THE BAR TO THE BENCH

The Supreme Court of California was composed of three members, of whom the eldest in point of seniority was Chief Justice. Two judges could hear arguments in cases, and could give decisions if they agreed. Thus far since the Court was organized it had frequently happened, due to death or resignation, that there were but two judges on the bench. When they disagreed no decision could be given. Leave of absence was granted freely, and at least one of the judges was absent from the state much of the time. During the period of seven years in which the Court had been in existence, a total of eight judges had retired from the bench. Since not more than three sat at any one time, this meant a rapid turnover. It meant, further, that there were likely to be frequent reversals of decisions, and that little could be done toward working out an established system of precedents. Add the fact that some of the judges were anything but capable and that others were notoriously dishonest, and it is not surprising that much important work of a judicial nature remained to be done.

Of Field's colleagues on the bench, former Governor Peter H. Burnett was probably a fair administrator and a man of sound integrity, but he was not more than mediocre in his capacity as a judge. His lack of firmness was shown in a case having to do with the ownership of slaves, in which he gave the opinion of the Court. He declared that the law had been violated, but he disposed of that particular case by saying: "This is the first case;

and under these circumstances we are not disposed to rigidly enforce the rule for the first time. But in reference to all future cases, it is our purpose to enforce the rules laid down strictly, according to their true intent and spirit." [1] Terry agreed with the result without accepting the reasoning involved. If Field sat in the case he recorded no expression of his opinion.

David S. Terry, a man with a great deal of legal ability, had been on the bench since the latter part of 1855. He was a Southerner, with a violent temper and strong prejudices. In 1856 he had become involved in a brawl with the vigilance committee which was organized to bring about a state of order in San Francisco, which could not be secured through the corrupt city government. Terry lost his temper and stabbed a member of the committee. The man was dangerously wounded, and Terry was imprisoned by the committee. Only the recovery of his victim prevented the trial and execution of the Supreme Court judge by a popular tribunal.[2]

Terry became Chief Justice at the time of the death of Murray, in 1857. He remained on the bench for two years, when he resigned, after some trouble with David C. Broderick, to challenge Broderick to a duel. Broderick was killed in the combat. Field was absent from the state at the time of the duel. He knew the two men well, and thought that if he had been present he could have made peace between them.[3]

Joseph G. Baldwin and W. W. Cope, who succeeded Burnett and Terry, were judges of considerable ability. Baldwin, particularly, did much to give the Court standing before the public, and in the period in which he served he took second place only to Field.

---

[1] Ex parte *Archy*, 9 Cal. 147 (January term, 1858).
[2] See Wagstaff, A. E., *Life of David S. Terry*, pp. 97-136.
[3] *Reminiscences*, pp. 101-2.

The position of justice of the Supreme Court was such as to offer a challenge to the best energies of capable and energetic men. Like the legislature, the Court had to deal with new types of situations which were puzzling in their intricacy. The common law of England had been adopted,[4] to apply where it was not inconsistent with the constitutions of the United States and of California, but the problems which arose in this pioneer mining state were very different from those which had been settled by the common law of England. To be sure, there were usually principles that were in some sense applicable— principles which were not always in harmony with one another. The judges had to select from among the principles offered those which would lead to the wisest decisions in terms of the welfare of the state. Hence, their conceptions of what was going on in the practical affairs of their jurisdiction were quite as important as their abstract learning in the province of law. Their own social philosophies took on significance, as well as their mastery of the tools of logic. Of necessity, in spite of the assumptions of the doctrines of the separation of powers, the Supreme Court was in effect highly influential as a legislative as well as a judicial body.

Complexity was added to the duties of the judges by the fact that the treaty between the United States and Mexico provided that all property rights which had existed under the Mexican régime should be respected by the new sovereign. Hence it devolved upon the judges to discover and understand the laws by which these rights were defined. Judge Baldwin declared: "The bench and bar in California, generally, have not been familiar with these laws; it has been exceedingly difficult to procure copies of the Mexican statutes, and sometimes impossible

[4] *California Laws* (1850), p. 219.

to procure the works of the most distinguished commentators on the Spanish civil code. And even when procured, it was equally difficult to obtain correct translations of such laws and of the works of such law writers. Add to this the fact that nearly all the Mexican orders, laws, decrees, etc., respecting California, are still in manuscript, scattered through immense masses of unarranged archives, almost inaccessible, and known, even imperfectly, to scarcely half a dozen persons, and will it appear surprising that errors have been committed by our judiciary?" [5]

Viewed as a whole, it seems no exaggeration to say that the task of the California judges was such that they were "required to frame a state jurisprudence *de novo*—to create a system out of what was at the time a mere chaos." [6] If it meant hard work, however, it meant also an opportunity for capable men to leave their imprint upon the plastic institutions of the state. It seems evident that the desire for this kind of self-expression had much to do with Field's decision to seek the position. It was a position which could utilize his best energies. It meant not only the maintenance of order of the type for which he had been responsible as alcalde at Marysville, but also the orderly arrangement of the then confused tangle of principles, rules, and laws by which the state was to be governed. This phase of his task would call into action the results of the training in the processes of reasoning which he had received from his father and Mark Hopkins, and from the study and practice of law. For an opportunity for the fullest expression of his best powers he could scarcely have done better than accept a position on the bench of the Supreme Court of California.

[5] *Hart* v. *Burnett*, 15 Cal. 530, 611 (1860).

[6] Pomeroy, J. N., "Introductory Sketch," p. 25, *Some Account of the Work of Stephen J. Field*, edited by S. B. Smith and C. F. Black.

Significant as an exposition of Field's social and legal philosophy is a dissenting opinion which he read not long after becoming a member of the Court. It is important both in the light of his past life and of his future life in California and on the bench of the Supreme Court of the United States. It is significant in spite of and also because of the fact that it does not in all respects harmonize with trends in his thinking which had been revealed earlier, or with dominant trends which were to be seen later on. His life was not so simple as to be explained by threads of unity which ran smoothly from beginning to end. The cross threads and those which began and ended abruptly, or which seemed to do so, are to be considered as well.

The legislature of 1858 passed "An Act to Provide for the Better Observance of the Sabbath." Among other things it provided that stores should be closed on Sunday. An Israelite violated this provision of the act by doing business on Sunday. He was imprisoned for the violation, and an appeal of habeas corpus was taken to the Supreme Court.[7] Justices Terry and Burnett, constituting a majority of the Court, holding that the act deprived the accused of the right to acquire property,[8] and that it discriminated in favor of one religious profession,[9] declared it unconstitutional. Field dissented. Discussing first the point of religious discrimination, he declared that the law treated of business matters, not religious duties. In fixing a day of rest it established only a rule of civil conduct. "Religious profession springs from matters of faith, and religious worship is the adoration of the soul." The law, he declared, placed no restraint upon freedom of worship.

[7] Ex parte *Newman*, 9 Cal. 502 (April term, 1858).
[8] Constitution of 1849, Art. I, Sec. 1.
[9] *Ibid.*, Sec. 4.

The purpose of the law, as he interpreted its provisions, was to preserve health and promote good morals. It was within the province of the legislature to pass such laws. It was not, he said, the province of the judiciary to pass upon the wisdom of legislative policy. In spite of this statement, however, he continued with a justification of the act of the legislature, and in the process of doing so he gave a clear statement of many of his own social conceptions. His authorities as well as his ideas are worthy of note:

"In its enactment, the legislature has given the sanction of law to a rule of conduct, which the entire civilized world recognizes as essential to the physical and moral well-being of society. Upon no subject is there such a concurrence of opinion, among philosophers, moralists, and statesmen of all nations, as on the necessity of periodical cessation from labor. One day in seven is the rule, founded in experience and sustained by science. There is no nation, possessing any degree of civilization, where the rule is not observed, either from the sanctions of law, or the sanctions of religion. This fact has not escaped the observation of men of science, and distinguished philosophers have not hesitated to pronounce the rule founded upon a law of our race."

In a succeeding century, perhaps, science would not with exactness approve all of Field's statement. Neither would philosophers be regarded as the best of authorities. He continued, however, with an analysis of the social and economic relations of men in society which would merit anywhere the serious attention of careful students:

"It is no answer to the requirements of the statute to say that mankind will seek cessation from labor by the natural influences of self-preservation. The position assumes that all men are independent, and at liberty to work whenever they choose. Whether this be true or not in theory, it is false in fact; it is contradicted by every day's experience. The relations of superior and subordinate, master and servant, principal and clerk, always have and always will exist. Labor is in a great degree dependent upon capital, and unless the exercise of the power which capital affords is restrained, those who are obliged to labor will not possess the freedom for rest which they would otherwise exercise. The necessities for food and raiment are imperious, and the exactions of avarice are not easily satisfied. It is idle to talk of a man's freedom to rest when his wife and children are looking to his daily labor for their daily support. The law steps in to restrain the power of capital. Its object is not to protect those who can rest at their pleasure, but to afford rest to those who need it, and who, from the conditions of society, could not otherwise obtain it. Its aim is to prevent the physical and moral debility which springs from uninterrupted labor; and in this aspect it is a beneficent and a merciful law. It gives one day to the poor and dependent; from the enjoyment of which no capital or power is permitted to deprive them. It is theirs for repose, for social intercourse, for moral culture, and, if they choose, for divine worship. Authority for the enactment I find in the great object of all government, which is protection. Labor is a necessity imposed by the condition of our race, and to protect labor is the highest office of our laws."

He recognized that the legislators who passed the law might have had various motives for doing so, and that among them might have been the pressure of constituents whose desire for the law grew out of religious convictions. He thought this no valid objection. It would be fortunate for society, he said, if all wise civil rules obtained a ready obedience from citizens, "not merely from the requirements of the law, but from conscientious or religious convictions of their obligation." "It would be, indeed, singular," he declared, "if a wise and beneficent law were the subject of objection, because suggested by the principle of a pure religion. Christianity is the prevailing faith of our people; it is the basis of our civilization; and that its spirit should infuse itself into and humanize our laws, is as natural as that the national sentiment of liberty should find expression in the legislation of the country."

He emphasized the fact that judicial interference with matters of legislative discretion would be a usurpation of power which did not belong to the judiciary. "That the legislature possessed the power to legislate for the good order, the peace, welfare, and happiness of society, is not denied. The means by which these ends are to be effected are left to its discretion. The existence of discretion implies a liability to abuse, but because the discretion of the legislature may be abused, its acts are not, for that reason, void. . . . There is no single power which may not be so exercised as to become intolerable. . . . It is to be supposed that the members of the legislature will exercise some wisdom in its acts; if they do not, the remedy is with the people. Frequent elections by the people furnish the only protection, under the Constitution, against the abuse of acknowledged legislative power."

These sentences, had logical consistency been the element of major importance, could have been quoted against him with devastating effect in later years, when he denounced the doctrine which they expressed, and demanded that the judiciary keep a watchful eye and a restraining hand upon the doings of the legislature.[10]

The fact that similar Sunday laws had been passed and upheld in other states brought out a discussion of his

[10] See, for example, his dissent in *Munn* v. *Illinois*, 94 U. S. 113, discussed below, Chap. XIV.

conception of the nature of law. "The law is a science," he declared, "whose leading principles are settled. They are not to be opened for discussion upon the elevation to the bench of every new judge, however subtle his intellect, or profound his learning, or logical his reasoning. Upon their stability men rest their property, make their contracts, assert their rights, and claim protection. It is true that the law is founded upon reason, but by this is meant that it is the result of the general intelligence, learning, and experience of mankind, through a long succession of years, and not of the individual reasoning of one or of several judges. . . . It is possible that some intellects may rise to the perception of absolute truth, and be justified in questioning the general judgment of the learned of mankind. But before the legitimate and just inference arising from the general acquiescence of the learned can be avoided, the error in the principles recognized should be clearly shown. We should not blindly adhere to precedents, nor should we more blindly abandon them as guides."

This case is significant here chiefly for what it tells of the thought world of Field himself. Its value for this purpose is limited by the fact that his ideas undoubtedly changed from time to time. Another limitation is that which applies to most judicial opinions, namely, that it resembled an argument so arranged as to make possible only one conclusion, rather than an attempt at an unbiased discussion of all phases of the subject.

It should be said that three years later a similar Sunday law was declared valid by the Supreme Court·of California.[11] Justices Baldwin and Cope had supplanted Terry and Burnett. Baldwin gave the opinion of the Court, referring with approval to Field's dissenting

[11] Ex parte *Andrews,* 18 Cal. 678 (July term, 1861).

opinion in the preceding case and ignoring the opinion of the Court given by Terry.

California had been a part of the United States but a few months when it was noised abroad that fortunes in precious metals were waiting to be gathered from her mountainsides. Thousands upon thousands hurried into the erstwhile thinly settled country to participate in the gleaning. Inevitably the question arose as to who owned the minerals before they were collected by the miners. Upon the answer might hang the solution to all sorts of problems having to do with their disposal. Neither Congress nor the legislature of California settled the question. It was brought before the Supreme Court of the state, and the perplexed judges had to work out a solution.

In 1853, in *Hicks* v. *Bell*,[12] Justice Heydenfeldt, of the state Supreme Court, went back to an English case [13] of the sixteenth century to show that under the common law mines and minerals had been the property of the king, and did not pass from him even though he gave up the title to the land on which they were located. The Justice took this fact as proof that the minerals, by common law, were attributes of sovereignty, and belonged always to the sovereign. California had been ceded by Mexico to the United States, and the title to precious metals must also have passed in the deal. But, continued the Justice, "it is hardly necessary at this period of our history to make an argument to prove that the several states of the Union, in virtue of their respective sovereignties, are entitled to the *jura regalia* which pertained to the king at common law." The minerals now belonged to the State of California. Though the United

---

[12] 3 Cal. 219 (July term, 1853).

[13] *The Queen* v. *The Earl of Northumberland*, 1 Plowden 310 (1568).

States owned the public lands, it did so only as a private proprietor, and not as sovereign. The state owned the minerals on the public lands as well as on the estates of private citizens. Although thus far all who chose to do so had been tacitly permitted to work mines of gold and silver, the state had the sole power to authorize the working of the mines and to pass laws for their regulation.

In the first years of frantic activity most of the mines were located either on public lands or on private tracts which were so large that the use of the land brought no great loss upon the owners. Conditions changed, however. Settlers poured in, and land was taken up for farming purposes as well as for mining. Gold was discovered upon improved lands which had become private property. Under the decision of the Court it appeared that until the state declared otherwise, miners had the right to go on private land and carry on operations, in spite of the injury to the property. In 1855 Justice Heydenfeldt, dismayed by the use to which his previous decision was being put, said *obiter dicta,* "We did not, in that case, intend to go further than to decide the right of all citizens to dig for gold upon the public lands; for although the state is the owner of the gold and silver found in the lands of private individuals as well as the public lands, yet to authorize an invasion of private property, in order to enjoy a public franchise, would require more specific legislation than any yet resorted to." [14]

This mild statement, however, was quite ineffective in checking the inroads upon private property.

The first case of the kind upon which Field was called to pass was *Biddle Boggs* v. *Merced Mining Company.*[15]

[14] *Stoakes* v. *Barrett,* 5 Cal. 36, 39 (January term, 1855).
[15] 14 Cal. 279.

Biddle Boggs had leased from John C. Fremont [16] at a rental of a thousand dollars a month the huge Mariposa estate, the title to which Fremont had secured only after extended litigation. The estate had been originally granted to Juan B. Alvarado by the Mexican government. It contained ten square leagues of land, but its boundaries were undefined, except that it was to be located within the limits of a much larger territory. Within this territory Fremont himself marked out the boundaries of his own estate. It was surveyed in 1855 and patented in the following year, whereupon it was leased to Boggs.

In 1851 the Merced Mining Company had started mining operations within the limits of the larger territory. Fremont was reported to have assured the company that the point where it was located was not within the limits of his own estate, and to have urged the expenditure of money for the improvement of the mines. Several thousand dollars were invested. When the estate was surveyed, however, it was cut out in such a way as to bring the mining area within its borders. Boggs laid claim to the mine and brought suit for the minerals involved.

Justices Terry, Burnett, and Field constituted the personnel of the Supreme Court at the time. Heydenfeldt was now a lawyer in private practice, and as counsel for the respondent he opposed the position which he had taken with regard to the ownership of minerals in *Hicks* v. *Bell*. Burnett gave the opinion of the Court. He too went back to the sixteenth century English case as a basis for his argument. He held that the title to the minerals had passed from Mexico to the United States. They were not essential to the existence of government, however, he declared, and so could not be called attributes of

[13] For a detailed study of Fremont, see Nevins, Allan, *Fremont, The West's Greatest Adventurer.*

sovereignty. That being the case, the title to them remained in the United States, regardless of the fact that California had become a state, and the title to the land was vested in a private individual. Boggs, as the lessee of Fremont, had only the same right to dig for minerals which belonged to the United States as had any other miner, and could not claim the fruits of the labor of others nor prevent their continued operations. Although the United States had not specifically granted the right to dig for minerals on private property, the conditions in California were unusual, and the granting of the right was to be presumed.

Terry concurred in the judgment, which was announced at the January term of 1858, but Field dissented.

The value of the property immediately involved ran into many thousands of dollars, while it was evident that vast fortunes would be indirectly affected by the decision of the Court. Interested parties followed the judges with jealous watchfulness, and charges of corruption were liberally made. It would be difficult either to prove or to disprove the charges. They are significant at least in so far as they show the atmosphere amid which the judges performed their tasks. The best known accusations were published about 1860 in an anonymous pamphlet of an "Ex-Supreme Court Broker," called *The Gold Key Court or the Corruptions of a Majority of It*.[17] Shortly after Burnett gave the opinion of the Court in the Fremont case he was supplanted on the bench by Judge Baldwin, who had been an attorney for Boggs, or for the Fremont interests. According to the "Ex-Supreme Court Broker," a motion was made soon afterward to have the case re-argued, but "the argument was put off from time to

[17] A copy of this colorful but perhaps not too authetic pamphlet is to be seen in the Henry E. Huntington Library, San Marino, Calif.

time until Fremont sent Col. James, of Mariposa, to Baldwin with his, Fremont's bonds, secured on the property for $100,000. After this the opinion was written by Field before he went East [on his wedding trip, in the summer of 1859], he receiving $25,000 of Fremont's bonds for this service, and at the same time a certain attorney was employed to bribe Terry, but Terry obstinately refused to sign the opinion, and Baldwin dare not, as he had been counsel in the case, as it appeared of record. After Field returned from the East he received an additional $25,000 from Fremont by the hands of James, after which the case was re-argued and Cope [who in the meantime had supplanted Terry] signed the opinion with Field, reversing the former judgment of the Court."

Field's opinion was read at the October term of the Court, in 1859. He did not attempt to decide the question as to who owned the minerals in the soil, saying that that decision was to be postponed until it could be presented to a full bench. However, he declared that there was no federal license to work mines on the public lands except that of forbearance, and that such a license could not apply to private lands where the government was ignorant of the fact that these lands were being worked. Neither was there any valid license from the state. If the United States owned the minerals it did so only as a private proprietor, except for the matter of exemption from state taxation, and it had no right to authorize the entry upon private lands for the removal of the minerals, when private property was thereby injured or destroyed.

If we disregard stories of corruption and look to the general conceptions of welfare which were back of the decision—as, for the most part, it seems wisest to do—the following quotations are significant: "The doctrine of an unlimited general license—put forth in many instances, and advocated by the defense—is pregnant with the most pernicious consequences. If upheld, it must lead to the spoliation of landed estates, under the pretense of mining, without possibility of protection or redress on the part of the owner." "There is something shocking to all our ideas of the rights of property in the proposition that one man may invade the possessions of another, dig up his fields and gardens, cut down his timber and occupy his land, under the pretense that he has reason to believe there is gold under the surface, or if existing, that he wishes to extract and remove it."

By this decision the Fremont estate was given protection against the miners. Later, in a test case,[18] the whole question of the ownership of the minerals was again presented, this time before a full bench. Field gave the opinion of the Court. Like his predecessors in dealing with the question, he went back to the sixteenth century English case for the basis of his argument. He held that although minerals had been the property of the crown, they were not attributes of sovereignty. In the case of the public lands received from Mexico by the United States, the ownership of the minerals had also passed to the United States, but only in its capacity as private owner, and not as sovereign. Hence, the title did not pass to the state through its claim to sovereignty. When the United States, in 1851, made provision for confirming the grants of land to private individuals made by the Mexican government it had not reserved the minerals. Hence, it was to be assumed that the minerals now belonged to those who owned the land.

So it was that one of the bitterly controversial problems of California was settled. Logically the decision was determined by "attributes of sovereignty," the knowledge of which the judges acquired by digging far back into

[18] *Moore* v. *Smaw*, 17 Cal. 199 (January term, 1861).

the records of the past. Actually, if we disregard all accusations of corruption, it was determined by the ideas of the judges as to what rule would work best amid the unprecedented conditions of pioneer mining and agricultural life.

Many of the problems having to do with the validity and boundaries of grants of land that had been made by the Mexican government were handled by federal officials and federal courts, but they provided also a great many controversies for the state Supreme Court. Prior to the acquisition of California by the United States, settlers had been few and far between, and there was land enough for all. It was regarded as having little value. The wealth of the colonists consisted chiefly in cattle and horses. It was a long way to Mexico City, there were no mail service connections, and it was difficult or impossible to find competent surveyors. "This condition of things led, in some cases, without taking any steps to obtain a title, in others, after having taken only the incipient proceedings, to the practice of taking possession, or at least claiming, large tracts of land which had not been surveyed, and the boundaries of which were undefined, and even unknown." [19]

When gold was discovered throngs of Americans and foreigners crowded into the state. They, likewise without any titles, entered upon the vacant lands which they found and began agricultural developments and established towns. The land quickly took on value. Speculation began in town lots which were granted to settlers by American alcaldes. Holders of Mexican grants brought forward such evidence of title as they had, asking that

[19] Bennett, Nathaniel, in *California Reports*, Vol. I, Preface, p. vi.

they be confirmed by American courts. Along with genuine documents were presented others that were obviously forged, and still others of doubtful character. "Questions involving immense amounts of property, and of pervading interest to the public, came up for adjudication, and the courts were asked to usurp the function of the legislature, and declare papers to constitute a title, which were absolutely void." [20] In view of these facts it is not surprising that some judges were corrupted, and that false accusations were made against others. Some property interests were affected adversely whatever the decisions, and the complaints were vociferous and prolonged.

Field heard arguments in many cases based on vague and imperfect grants of land. Of these a large number had to do with the great tract of New Helvetia, which had been granted to Captain John Sutter, and which ran from below Sacramento up to and including Marysville [21]—including some land which Field had owned, and other property for which he had written deeds. He held this and many other grants to be valid even though the confirming process had never been completed by the Mexican government, though the lands in question had never been surveyed and were without defined boundaries, and though in many cases they embraced huge tracts for which the owners at the time the grants were made could have had no use. The treaty with Mexico provided that the new sovereign should give full protection to existing property rights, and Field attempted to give this protection, whatever the wisdom or the lack of it with which the Mexican government had made the

[20] Ibid.

[21] See *Ferris* v. *Coover*, 10 Cal. 589; *Cornwall* v. *Culver*, 16 Cal. 424, 429; *Moore* v. *Wilkinson*, 13 Cal. 478; *Riley* v. *Heisch*, 18 Cal. 198; *Mahoney* v. *Van Winkle*, 21 Cal. 552. These are a few of the many cases dealing with the problem. See also *United States* v. *Sutter*, 69 U. S. 562, in the decision of which Field took no part.

grants in the first place. Some grants had been made for
certain quantities of land within definite boundaries,
with the provision that any surplus found within the
boundaries was reserved to the government. Settlers
often moved onto choice bits of land within the boundaries, claiming that they were merely taking from the
surplus which belonged to the government. Field added
to his unpopularity with the settlers by holding that
where a surplus existed it could be determined and set
aside only by the government. It could not be marked
out and taken by squatters.[22]

He was interested not so much in settling individual
disputes as in working out rules which would govern the
ownership of property in the future. A striking example
of this interest is his opinion in a case which could have
been decided on a minor point, in that a wrong instruction had been given to a jury. Field said: "We do not,
however, intend to determine the appeal in this way. We
prefer to place our decision upon grounds which will
finally dispose of the controversy between the present
parties, and furnish a rule for the settlement of other
controversies of a similar character." [23]

Settlers moved onto public lands, where the title was
in the United States. Yet they carried to the courts
controversies among themselves over rights to particular
holdings. It was a general rule of law that a claimant
could win a suit only on the strength of his own title, and
not on the weakness of that of his adversary. Hence, since
in these suits neither party possessed title, it would seem
that they had no status in court. However, the rules of
law had again to be adjusted by the courts to meet the
demands of new situations. The courts took jurisdiction,
and held that as between citizens of the state, for the

[22] *Ferris* v. *Coover*, 10 Cal. 589, 621, and other cases.
[23] *Teschemacher* v. *Thompson*, 18 Cal. 11, 21-22.

purposes of the suits, the title in each case was to be treated as vested in the first possessor.[24] This solution had already been worked out with reference to mining claims and to water rights, based on the provision which Field inserted in the civil practice act when he was a member of the legislature. The miners themselves had adopted the rule that priority of occupation determined ownership. The civil practice act of the state made this rule a rule of evidence in justices' courts. The higher courts took cognizance of it for mining claims and water rights, and extended its application to public lands where it had no connection with mining or miners. It is in the opinions of Field that the steps by which the rules of law were extended and modified to meet the needs of prevailing situations are most clearly delineated.[25]

Some of the most hotly contested cases, which provoked bitter criticism of the Court, had to do with titles to property in San Francisco. One series dealt with what was commonly called the "City Slip" property. It consisted of submerged lots along the bay which by a city ordinance of 1852 had been dedicated to a public use, as a place for public docks. It was used for this purpose until December 5, 1853, when another ordinance was passed, known as Ordinance 481, which provided for the disposal of the lots at public sale. The property had become quite valuable, and it was said that the sale was planned in order to line the pockets of corrupt council-

---

[24] *Coryell* v. *Cain*, 16 Cal. 567.

[25] Charges of corruption continued to be made. It was charged in the *Gold Key Court* that Field received fifty thousand dollars in a case involving the title to Sacramento City. The charge is probably as significant of the rabid and rapacious spirit of the contestants as of anything actually done by Field.

men.[26] Certain wharf companies which stood to lose by the sale threatened to enjoin it, whereupon the council passed a second ordinance, known as Ordinance 493, which appropriated certain sums from the money about to be received from purchasers to pay damages to the wharf companies. This ordinance was passed one hour before the sale, on December 26, 1853. Lots were then sold to the amount of $1,193,550.[27] After the sale the property rapidly declined in value, and many of the purchasers were eager to withdraw from their contracts. It is said that they were shown how to do so, or how to try to do so, by their lawyer, Joseph Baldwin, who was later to be a justice of the Supreme Court.

The method used was to attack the validity of Ordinance 481, under which the sale was made. For a valid ordinance the city charter required the ratification of a majority of the persons elected to each body of the City Council. The Board of Assistant Aldermen was legally composed of eight members, but one member had resigned prior to the enactment of the ordinance. The vote on the ordinance was four to three, a majority of the seven who were then members, but not a majority of the eight legally composing the Board. On this basis it was argued that the ordinance had not been legally passed. If that was true the purchasers had received nothing from the city, and were entitled to have refunds of the money which they had paid in. In 1855 Chief Justice Murray gave the opinion of the Supreme Court declaring that the ordinance was invalid.[28] Another case giving more of the details of the situation was started, and in 1857 the

[26] Bancroft, *History of California*, Vol. VII, pp. 233-34, note 9.

[27] Soule, Frank, *Annals of San Francisco*, pp. 482-83. Accounts of many of the events are given in several of the cases, as in *McCracken* v. *San Francisco*, 16 Cal. 591.

[28] *San Francisco* v. *Hazen*, 5 Cal. 169 (April term, 1855).

Court held that Ordinance 481 had been in itself invalid, but had later been made valid through the recognition given to it by Ordinance 493. Burnett gave the opinion, Terry concurred, and Murray dissented. Baldwin, as counsel for the respondent, lost his case.[29]

The political moves which followed are not altogether clear. Apparently the legislature decided to relieve the purchasers of their bad bargains, and allowed them to make the payments on the property in scrip purchased at ten cents on the dollar.[30] The decision of the Court stood until the personnel of the bench was changed. "It would have stood forever," declared a San Francisco newspaper, "had not a combination of unscrupulous schemers been formed, who offered a logrolling firm of lawyers a contingent fee of $250,000 to overturn it. This enormous fee set influences at work to attempt to provide a court for the occasion." [31] The charge may have been without foundation. It had some apparent basis in the fact that Baldwin was elected to the Court. It may also have been known where Field stood on the question. The fact that Baldwin did not sit in the case still leaves the possibility that his influence was felt indirectly by his colleagues.

The issues were presented in a new case,[32] and Field, giving the opinion of the Court, held that Ordinance 481 had not been legally passed. Furthermore, in order to make the sale valid it would have been necessary to include a section repealing the ordinance of 1852 by which the property had been dedicated to a public use. Neither Ordinance 481 nor 493 contained such a section. The fact of the dedication of the property to a public use

[29] *Holland* v. *San Francisco,* 7 Cal. 361 (April term, 1857).

[30] San Francisco *Daily Evening Bulletin,* March 14, 1863.

[31] *Ibid.*

[32] *McCracken* v. *San Francisco,* 16 Cal. 591. See also *Grogan* v. *San Francisco,* 18 Cal. 590 (July term, 1861).

had not been presented to the Court in the earlier cases, and had not been considered by the judges. Anyway, said Field, that decision was "manifestly erroneous—setting aside fundamental principles of the law of corporations, which, however much distorted or departed from, will constantly reassert themselves." He realized that several other cases would be disposed of along with this one, and that large sums would have to be refunded by the city. "Be this, however, as it may," he declared, "it can have no weight in the determination of the case. It is our duty to pronounce the law, and with the consequences which follow we have nothing to do—whether they be to cast upon the city a liability of one dollar or of a million."

It was true that the preceding decisions had been anything but clear cut, and that they left the law of municipal corporations stated in a manner that was marked with confusion. However, it seems probable that although Field was undoubtedly interested in a clear statement of the law he was also more interested in the practical outcome of this particular controversy than his words would seem to imply. When he was preparing to leave the state bench he gave the opinion of the Court in another case which was in itself of minor importance, but which gave him the opportunity again to discuss the whole situation. He showed how the indebtedness of the city had risen with the accumulation of interest on the money which was to be refunded to the purchasers of the lots, until it now amounted to more than a million dollars, and urged that it was "desirable, therefore, not only for the claimants, but for the city, that the controversy between them should be brought to a termination."[33]

[33] *Pimental* v. *San Francisco*, 21 Cal. 352 (1863).

The San Francisco *Bulletin* was highly indignant at Field's attempt to bring about complete settlement of the controversy before he left his position of authority. "The case of the city is not hopeless yet," it declared. "Two different supreme courts have decided in two different ways on important questions in the slip suits, the city being completely victorious in the first court. Before all the new questions raised by the present efficient counsel for the city are disposed of, we shall have another entirely new supreme court." [34]

Field was accused of having speculated in the property affected by his decisions, and to have made thousands of dollars for himself out of his reversal of the earlier decision of the Court.[35] The accusation may have been, and probably was, the product of the disappointment of men whose interests were adversely affected. Nevertheless it made interesting reading for the taxpayers of San Francisco who had to bear the burden which he laid upon them. Some directed against him the milder accusation that he had been unwittingly influenced by selfish friends to believe that this particular decision was the only right one.[36] It is quite possible that in the light of calmer reflection none of these charges would have been made. Field may have been influenced solely by his desire for an

[34] San Francisco *Bulletin*, March 14, 1863. H. H. Bancroft said that the first decision against the City of San Francisco (he was under the impression that Baldwin gave it) made "the city liable to return $800,000 cash for the scrip paid in on account of the slip purchases. The city still contested the judgment, and the matter was kept in court, at enormous costs until an entirely new set of officers were on the bench, and the property had so enhanced in value that thirty-five of the purchasers of the city slips deciding to keep the lots, the city consented, and gave bonds for $1,000,000 to be paid. Six others brought suit later, and were beaten by a legal quibble as absurd as the first, which saved the city $190,000."—*History of California*, Vol. VII, pp. 233-34, note 9.

[35] *The Gold Key Court.*

[36] San Francisco *Bulletin*, Feb. 24, 1863.

orderly statement of the law, and for seeing the political life of the city managed strictly according to law. This much may be taken as true—he never doubted the rightness of his decision.

Titles to land in San Francisco gave rise to other hard fought cases in the state and federal courts. By Mexican law each pueblo, or town, was entitled at the time of its organization to a grant of four square leagues of land. Pueblo authorities granted this land to individuals, or used it as they saw fit for the benefit of the pueblo. Although it later came to be a matter of dispute, it was assumed at the time of the occupation of California by military authorities of the United States that San Francisco had had the usual type of pueblo organization, and was entitled to the usual four square leagues. The American officers in San Francisco gave away tracts for little or nothing. "It was refreshing to see with what generous liberality they disposed of lots in the city—a liberality not infrequent when exercised with reference to other people's property." [37] Squatters settled on this land, declaring that the officers had no right to dispose of it, and that as public land of the United States priority of right went with priority of possession. The disputes between the grantees and the squatters provided a great deal of work for the courts.

Further complicating the situation, the first city government of San Francisco was highly extravagant. It incurred debts for which suits were brought against the city. The creditors won the suits, execution was levied against the pueblo lands, and more territory was sold by the sheriff, at a low price, to pay the debts. Amid the tangle of alleged interests the Supreme Court decisions

[37] *Reminiscences,* p. 137.

were varied and not at all consistent. In 1855 the City Council passed the Van Ness Ordinance, which relinquished to the parties in possession on or before January 1, 1855, the property which they held, with certain exceptions. It validated certain of the alcalde sales, but ignored the supposed rights of those who had made purchases at sheriffs' sales of land which was occupied by others. Altogether the ordinance turned over to squatters property of tremendous value. It was confirmed by the legislature of 1858.

The case by which the validity of the ordinance was to be determined was before the Supreme Court for many months. Then Baldwin gave the opinion of the Court, declaring it to be valid.[38] "Attacks full of venom were made upon Judge Baldwin and myself, who had agreed to the decision," said Field. Cope had dissented. "No epithets were too vile to be applied to us; no imputations were too gross to be cast at us. The press poured out curses upon our heads. Anonymous circulars filled with falsehoods, which malignity alone could invent, were spread broadcast throughout the city, and letters threatening assassination in the streets or by-ways were sent to us through the mail."[39]

The following is probably one of the charges to which Field referred. After declaring that Baldwin had quietly bought up many of the squatter holdings before he gave the decision it continued with the statement that Field's interest had been much less, and that he had opposed the position taken by Baldwin. It continued: "About six weeks before the decision he came to San Francisco, and stopped at the St. Francis Hotel on Clay Street, where Mr. Low, of Marysville, called on Judge Field, and then and there paid to him, in coin, the sum of $10,000—(by

[38] *Hart* v. *Burnett,* 15 Cal. 530 (1860).
[39] *Reminiscences,* pp. 141-42.

the way $3,000 of this sum was soon after lost at a well-
known gambling house)—in consideration Field agreed
to sign Baldwin's opinion for that sum and $50,000 of
the Bensley Water Company's stock and also one-half
of Bensley's Settler claim on the Portrero, and Bensley
agreeing to invest $5,000 in cash in the purchase of other
claims for said Field. The stock was paid and delivered
at the same time that the money was, but there is not as
yet any record of the transfer to Field of the Settler's
claim above referred to. These facts are known to John
Parrot, Bolton & Barron, Henry S. Dexter and other
trustees of the Bensley Water Company." [40]

This case settled the matter of the ownership of land
within the city limits of San Francisco, but controversies
continued over titles to that part of the four square
leagues which lay outside the city limits. The United
States Board of Land Commissioners had in 1854 confirmed to the city the land embraced within the charter
limits of 1851, but because there was some doubt as to the
previous existence of a pueblo organization which had
been entitled to the customary grant from the Mexican
government it had refused to confirm any of the land
outside the city. An appeal was taken to the United
States District Court in the same year, but for some
reason the case was not heard—one reason apparently was
that the district judge was interested in the claims himself—and it stayed before the Court until 1864. In the
meantime Field was made a justice of the Supreme Court
of the United States, and was assigned to the tenth circuit,
which included California. He knew that the property
involved in the controversy had increased in value many
times over in the ten years during which it had been
before the District Court. He determined to have the

[40] *The Gold Key Court.*

matter settled. He drafted a bill which provided that when a district judge was interested in land claims pending before him the District Court should order the case transferred to the Circuit Court.[41] Senator Conness from California sponsored the bill. It was passed by Congress, and the case was transferred to the United States Circuit Court.

The case, which was argued before Field alone, was submitted October 4, 1864, and decided October 31.[42] As the result of his decision a decree was entered confirming the claim of the city of San Francisco to the four square leagues, with the exception of certain specified tracts which were defined in the bill passed by Congress. The federal government was allowed an appeal to the Supreme Court.

During this period, prior to the appointment of full-time circuit judges, the United States district judges often conducted the business of the circuit courts while the Supreme Court justices were in session in Washington. No sooner had Field left California for Washington than John B. Williams, styling himself special counsel for the United States, gave notice that he would, on November 21, move the Court to vacate the decree and grant a rehearing. His ground was that the decision had been rendered under a misapprehension of facts, due to the fact that his brief had been suppressed by the clerk of the Court. The district attorney declared that Williams was employed by claimants of the "outside lands," and did not represent the United States at all, and refused to have anything to do with the motion until ordered by the Attorney-General to join in it. Whether or not the district judge would have heard and decided the case, and

---

[41] See *Reminiscences*, Exhibit J, pp. 224-25. For Field's account of what happened see *ibid.*, pp. 142-51.

[42] *San Francisco* v. *United States*, 4 Sawyer 553.

so performed what Field called an "act of judicial discourtesy," remains a matter for speculation, for the
Attorney-General learned more about the nature of the
controversy, and ordered the postponement of the motion
until Field returned. When Field again took his place
on the bench of the Circuit Court, in May, 1865, he
denied the motion and scolded Williams roundly for his
conduct.[43]

The original decree was vacated, however, and another
was entered which made some further deductions from
the four square leagues. Then both the United States
and the city sought writs of appeal to the Supreme Court.
Field denied the writs, holding that the act by which the
Circuit Court was created made no provision for appeals,
and that appellate jurisdiction existed only where expressly
granted. The Attorney-General made application to the
Supreme Court for a hearing of the appeal. The Supreme
Court granted the hearing,[44] following which Justice
Nelson read the opinion. Field dissented, and Justices
Grier and Miller concurred with him. This decision was
given January 29, 1866. Field immediately drew a bill
to quiet the title of the land to San Francisco, and had it
introduced in the Senate by Senator Conness, and in the
House by Representative McRuer. It became a law on
March 8, 1866, before the case could be argued on its
merits before the Supreme Court. The appeals had to be
dropped,[45] and Field was victorious in getting his own
solution of the problem accepted.

Hubert Howe Bancroft, an admirer of Field who frequently found it necessary to moralize in his writing of
history, said of the way in which the controversy was

---

[43] The account of the happenings in the Circuit Court is included with
the case in 4 Sawyer 553.

[44] *United States* v. *Circuit Judges*, 70 U. S. 673.

[45] *Townsend* v. *Greeley*, 72 U. S. 326.

handled: "It might reasonably be questioned whether a judge should be allowed so far to interfere with matters originating in another court as to procure an act of Congress transferring it to his own court; but most men are reconciled to irregular proceedings instituted to result in better order. So nature travails, while a mountain or a mouse is born, and thenceforth throughout the ages mountains and mice abound, the former regulating the winds that cool, and the waters that fertilize the earth, the latter adding their quota to the sum of vermin without which the universe would remain unfinished. Thus society, oppressed for long years with unbearable wrongs, is suddenly aroused in all its majesty, and, ignoring the law and the machinery of justice, exacts and obtains a justice higher than the law." [46]

Whether or not we approve of Field's methods, it will not be denied that he brought order out of an extremely chaotic situation.

These groups of opinions, most of which were delivered from the bench of the Supreme Court of California, reflect the outstanding characteristics of Field's judicial work during his early years as a judge. He achieved order in the constitutional law of the state, in place of the vacillating and conflicting precedents established by former justices of the Court. His cases dealing with municipal corporations and with mortgages won him nation-wide recognition among lawyers and judges. His decisions with regard to essentially new problems of titles to property in California won and maintained for him the profound respect of his successors at the bench and bar of his adopted state for decades to come. He combined a knowledge of the law probably surpassing that of

[46] Bancroft, *History of California*, Vol. VII, p. 231.

any other man in the state with a capacity for supplanting outworn or inapplicable legal dogmas with practical doctrines which were better adapted to the existing conditions in the life around him. He revealed a great capacity for thinking in terms of so-called fundamental principles. "This quality gives a most marked unity, consistency, and universality to his decisions, not only to those connected with some single branch of the law, but to those belonging to any and all departments. His adjudications generally will thus be found related to each other, harmonious, corresponding parts of one completed system." [47]

Although it was recognized that Baldwin and Cope were learned judges and had a share in the achievements of the Court, it is said to have been "admitted by all who were personally acquainted, as contemporaries and participants, with the judicial history of the state, and it is a truth patent to all who have obtained their only knowledge from the reports of decisions during his term of office, that he assumed and maintained the position of leadership. In the fundamental principles adopted by the Court, in the doctrines which it announced, in the whole system which it constructed for the adjustment of the great questions hereinbefore described, his controlling influence was apparent; his creative force impressed itself upon his associates, guided their decisions, shaped and determined their work." [48]

It has been assumed that the philosophy of extreme individualism espoused by Field during his later years was the product of his Puritan training in New England, his study of the common law, and the practice of his profession on the frontier "at a time and in a place where the individual counted for more and the law for less than

[47] Pomeroy in *Some Account of the Work of Stephen J. Field*, pp. 30-31.
[48] *Ibid.*, pp. 27-28.

has been usual even on the frontier." [49] It is true that Field showed respect and enthusiasm for men who were able to take care of themselves in difficult situations, as he himself had done, and that as a judge he tried to avoid putting legal barriers in the way of those who played prominent parts in the life of the state. Yet it will be recalled that in the legislature he gave his best efforts to alleviating the misfortunes of debtors, and that in the Sunday law case [50] he showed a real understanding and a disposition to promote the solution of the problems of labor. The expression, "to protect labor is the highest office of our laws," does not savor of those traits of extreme individualism which in another century have been widely condemned. The statement that "frequent elections by the people furnish the only protection, under the constitution, against the abuse of acknowledged legislative power," sounds but little like the voice of Field in later years when he vigorously opposed state regulation of private enterprise. Although there is a limit to the value of quotations which are taken out of their context and applied to new situations in other decades, it seems evident that while Field's boyhood and frontier experiences may have planted in him the seeds of individualism, that individualism was for many years tempered by a calm, social point of view. Its extreme development was the product of experiences which were yet to come.

Field never attempted to disprove the charges of corruption which were made against him. They may have been so numerous as to make this impossible. Furthermore, the charges in some cases were no doubt made chiefly for the purpose of heckling the judges. Taking notice of them would have indicated that the heckling

[49] Pound, Roscoe, *Spirit of the Common Law*, p. 49.
[50] Ex parte *Newman*, 9 Cal. 502.

was a success. Field's attitude throughout was that of a man who was doing his duty as he saw it, and who was wholly unconcerned about what was said of him. In time people came for the most part to doubt that he had ever been corrupt. A grudging recognition of his probable integrity, however, did not make him popular with those whose interests had suffered at his hands.

CHAPTER V

JUDICIAL ENVIRONMENTS

When Field became a member of the Supreme Court of California he moved away from Marysville, never to return save for a few brief visits. The town had been the scene of adventures which provided material for anecdotes for his conversation through the remaining years of his life, but henceforth his adventures were to take place amid other scenes. For a time he resided at the Dawson House, in Sacramento, while he attended the sessions of the Court in the Janson Building at Fourth and "J" Streets. Between sessions he spent some time in San Francisco, which was quite a metropolis as contrasted with the country town which was the capital of the state.

Frontier life continued to provide rough and sometimes sinister drama for the Californians, even for the judges who sat on the bench of the highest court. A few months before Terry resigned his position as Chief Justice to take part in the ill-fated duel with Broderick, Field found himself in an embarrassing predicament. The situation had many angles, but it had in part grown out of the determination of the judges to keep the judiciary strictly independent of the control of the legislature. Various proposals for the coercion of the judges were suggested from time to time, and some of them were carried into effect. For example, an attempt was made to enforce the amendment to the practice act which provided that opinions of the Court should be written and filed. Most opinions had been written, but some, for one reason or another, were merely announced orally and only the decisions were recorded. Field gave the opinion of the Court on a petition filed to the Court asking that an opinion be filed in a certain case which had been decided without a statement of the reasons. The provision of the statute had not been overlooked, he declared. It was "but one of many provisions embodied in different statutes by which control over the judiciary department of the government has been attempted by legislation." To comply with the provision would be to sanction a palpable encroachment upon the independence of the department. "The legislature can no more require this Court to state the reasons of its decisions, than this Court can require, for the validity of the statutes, that the legislature shall accompany them with the reasons for their enactment." [1]

A part of the bitter feeling toward the legislature was due to the fact that an act had been passed giving the Governor the power to appoint a court reporter, instead of leaving the matter with the judges. Without consulting the Court the Governor appointed to the office a lawyer whose name was Harvey Lee. Lee was unpopular with the judges, due partly to the manner of his selection and partly to his personal traits. Two or three years earlier he had borrowed a number of law books from Chief Justice Murray. Needing money rather badly he mortgaged the books, and, when he was unable to pay his debt, they were sold and were lost to Judge Murray. As a result Lee was heartily despised by many of those who knew of the incident. There was friction among the newspapers of Sacramento over the matter of publishing opinions as they were handed down by the Court. The judges insisted on holding the opinions in their possession until they were thoroughly revised and

[1] *Houston* v. *Williams,* 13 Cal. 24, 25 (April term, 1859).

corrected, while Lee apparently shared the eagerness of certain publishers for getting the opinions before the public. In the case having to do with whether the judges could be compelled to provide written opinions at all, Field took occasion also to express himself on this matter: "The power over our opinions and the records of our Court we shall exercise at all times while we have the honor to sit on the bench, against all encroachments from any source, but in a manner, we trust, befitting the highest tribunal in the state. We cannot possibly have any interest in the opinions except that they shall embody the results of our most mature deliberation, and be presented to the public in an authentic form, after they have been subjected to the most careful revision." [2]

The clerk of the Court was Field's old Marysville friend, Charles S. Fairfax, heir to the title of Lord Fairfax. His popularity with the Court was as great as the unpopularity of Lee. Friction between the two men resulted finally in violence, and Lee stabbed Fairfax, wounding him dangerously. It was said that soon afterward Field was in the street declaring to the people that "Lee is a thief. . . . I know him to be a thief. . . . The reason the Supreme Court judges did not want him, or would not allow him, to be reporter, was, that he was a thief." He explained wherein Lee was a thief by saying that he had stolen Judge Murray's books and pawned them.[3]

Lee was at this time in the custody of an officer. Some of his friends, however, paid a visit to Field, and apparently intimated that he must either withdraw the charge which he had made or else accept a challenge from Lee. Field was willing to retract privately, but did not wish to do so publicly or by a written statement. It was

[2] *Houston* v. *Williams*, 13 Cal. 24, 28.
[3] Sacramento *Bee*, April 3, 1859.

insisted, however, that he make a public retraction.[4] Two days later a Sacramento paper published, at Lee's request, the following statement by Field:

> Shortly after the encounter between Mr. Fairfax and yourself, in the excitement of the moment, I applied to you an opprobrious epithet. This was done in the presence of several persons. The epithet was used on the authority of a statement of a gentleman now deceased. Maj. Graham, Mr. Mizner and Mr. Whitman called upon me this morning, as mutual friends, and have given me such assurance, and stated such facts in connection with the transaction to which the original charge related, as to convince me that I did you injustice in the matter. I am convinced that this charge is not properly made against you, and had its origin in misconception on the part of the gentleman from whom it first proceeded. If I had known the facts now before me, I should not have used this language, and, in justice to you, as well as to me, I avail myself of the first opportunity since being put in possession of the facts, to withdraw the charge made and the epithet used, with liberty to you to use this statement as you may think fit. I do this, of course, voluntarily, and without application or suggestion from you, and have to express my regret that I was unconsciously the means of doing you injustice—a thing I would not do willingly to any one, whatever our general relations.
>
> Hoping this explanation may be satisfactory to you, as I consider it due from me,
>
>   I am, respectfully yours, etc.,
>   STEPHEN J. FIELD.
> Sacramento, April 29, 1859.[5]

Field's enemies, including the Sacramento *Bee*, were beside themselves with glee over Field's statement. They declared it to be a matter of common knowledge that Lee

[4] Sacramento *Union*, April 4, 1859.
[5] *Ibid.*

was prepared to challenge Field if he did not retract his charge. Graham, one of the three men who had called on Field, published a statement that no threats had been made,[6] but the situation was humiliating for Field, nevertheless.

Judge Terry had been absent from Sacramento for some time. When he returned he read Field's statement, and asked him scornfully if it was true that he had made it. At that Field is said to have turned, in shame and anger, upon Judge Baldwin: "See what you have made me do, Baldwin; see what you have made me do. If Terry had been here he would not have let me . . . be disgraced. It was all your fault, Baldwin. You said worse things about Lee than I did." Baldwin had advised Field to retract his statement, saying that otherwise Lee would assault and perhaps kill him.[7]

Field touched but lightly upon this affair in his *Reminiscences*. Indeed, full records of incidents that were humiliating to him are rarely to be discovered in his own accounts. This fact is the principal limitation of his dramatic *Personal Reminiscences of Early Days in California*.

Although he was nearly forty-one years of age when he came to the bench, Field was still a bachelor. His life thus far had been rather too much disturbed by the activities around him to suggest establishing a home, although gossip has it that he was an unsuccessful suitor for the hand of at least one lady while he lived in Marysville. Undoubtedly there were but few marriageable women in California at that time in whom he would have been interested. In San Francisco, however, at 120 Bush Street, lived Mrs. Isabel Swearingen, a widow with several attractive daughters. Mrs. Swearingen boarded a

---

[6] See Graham's statement in the San Francisco *Herald*, April 9, 1859.
[7] Wagstaff, *Life of David S. Terry*, pp. 331-33.

few professional and business men, and Field when in San Francisco was occasionally among them. The eldest of the daughters, Sue Virginia, although twenty years younger than he, won the heart of the judge, and consented to be his wife. They were married on June 2, 1859, at the Grace Episcopal Church at Sacramento, in the presence of a large group. The bride and her sister Belle, who was her only bridesmaid, were very simply dressed in white muslin. The only record of the groom on that occasion is to the effect that his "boots creaked loudly as he walked up the aisle." [8] After the wedding the couple left for the East, where they visited Field's aged parents at their home in Stockbridge, and were royally welcomed at a gathering of the numerous members of the family.

Late in the same year the couple returned to California. Thereafter while in Sacramento they lived at the St. George Hotel. Much of their time, however, seems to have been spent in the home of Mrs. Field's mother, in San Francisco. Field became much attached to his wife's family, and soon stood in somewhat the position of head of the clan. His marriage lent a stability to his life which it had not possessed before. Henceforth, although the events of his life were thickly interspersed with dramatic activities, the tendency was toward order and respectability. The very nature of his task as a judge undoubtedly had much to do with the change, but to the influence of his home life may also be ascribed a share of the responsibility.

As the great national issue, the slavery question, grew more and more acute, Field aligned himself on the side of the North. He is said to have written to one of his brothers that when the infamous Dred Scott decision was set aside the nation would be free.[9] Little record has been

[8] San Francisco *Examiner*, Sept. 30, 1888.

[9] Marysville *Daily Appeal*, April 8, 1863.

preserved concerning his activities during the Civil War. It seemed for a time that there might be a severe struggle in California over whether the state should remain with the Union, secede with the South, or declare its independence and set up a separate government. Field gave his energies to the cause of the Union. He is said to have been the fifth member enrolled in a secret league which was organized to keep California loyal. Arms were purchased by the league, and companies were organized.[10] Just what part Field played remains somewhat vague.

A great many factors in connection with the war converged to direct the trend of Field's own life. The federal government sought to preserve the loyalty of California not only by providing for a transcontinental railroad, but also by strengthening the political connections between the state and the national capital. California was served by a federal circuit court, but the circuit at that time had no representative on the bench of the Supreme Court of the United States. The complicated land cases which were constantly going to that Court from California showed the need of a man on the supreme bench who knew the intricacies of the land problems, and after the beginning of the war there was much talk of reorganizing the Court in such a way as to meet the needs of California.

In addition the struggle between the North and the South, quite apart from its relation to California, provided arguments for the reorganization of the Supreme Court. That august body had made itself anathema in the North by its pro-slavery decisions in the Dred Scott case [11] and in the Booth cases,[12] incurring criticism such as had rarely been showered upon it during the period of its existence. Republicans, at the national election in the

---

[10] San Francisco *Chronicle*, April 10, 1899.
[11] *Dred Scott* v. *Sanford*, 60 U. S. 393 (March 6, 1857).
[12] *Ableman* v. *Booth*, 62 U. S. 506 (March 7, 1859).

fall of 1860, defeated the long entrenched Democrats, with a middle-western plebeian, Abraham Lincoln, as their standard-bearer, and war came to appear more and more inevitable. The Court, caught in the sectional cross-fire of rabid criticism, was in a most depressed condition. In the term beginning in December, 1860, counsel made frequent references to the situation. Caleb Cushing declared dramatically that the Court would not be in existence the following summer.[13] A number of misfortunes occurred: One justice had died the preceding May, and President Buchanan failed to appoint a successor whom the Senate would confirm; another was ill at the close of the term the following March, and died in April of the same year; still another resigned in April, 1861, to follow his state, Alabama, out of the Union. It looked almost as if Cushing's prophecy might come true.

Chief Justice Taney was already thoroughly unpopular in the North. In May, 1861, while sitting in the Circuit Court at Baltimore, he added to his unpopularity by clashing with President Lincoln. Merryman, a Southern agitator in Maryland, had been arrested by military authorities and imprisoned in Fort McHenry, on the ground that his utterances were a hindrance to the Northern cause. He petitioned Taney for a writ of habeas corpus. The writ was issued to the military commander of the fort.[14] The commander refused to obey the writ, whereupon Taney issued a writ of contempt against him, and sent a United States marshal to serve it. The marshal was excluded from the fort. Taney wrote out a full account of the affair and sent it to President Lincoln, and reminded him that it now remained for the President to fulfill his oath of office by executing the judgment of

[13] Johnson, A. E. H., "Reminiscences of Honorable Edwin M. Stanton," *Records of the Columbia Historical Society*, Vol. XIII, p. 69.
[14] See Ex parte *Merryman*, 17 Federal Cases 144, No. 9487.

the Court and releasing the prisoner. The President made no reply, and Merryman remained in prison. Sectional feeling was now too strong for the giving of much attention to the application of the technical rules of legal justice. Attempts to apply these rules amid the stress of the swelling conflict only served to make Taney the object of the attention of abusive partisans, and to create a demand for courts which would render decisions which were in harmony with the issues with which the people sympathized.

Although there were three vacancies in the Supreme Court President Lincoln hesitated to fill them. Two of the outgoing justices had resided in seceding states, and their successors, if appointed from the same localities, could not serve upon their circuits. Anyway, it was doubtful whether competent men could now be secured in those localities. He hesitated to throw all the appointments to the North, thereby making it difficult to do justice to the South on the return of peace.[15] In view of the fact that the work of the Court was being retarded by the depleted membership and by the illness of two of the remaining justices, he, in January, 1862, appointed Noah H. Swayne, of Ohio, to fill one of the vacancies. Slowly it became apparent that the South would not soon return to the Union, whereupon Congress set about to reorganize the circuits in the loyal states. In July, 1862, Samuel Freeman Miller, of Iowa, was added to the Court, and in December came President Lincoln's personal friend, David Davis, from Illinois.

For almost two years after the beginning of the war none of the decisions of the Court were particularly influential in connection with the struggle. Then arose a question concerning the legal status of the war which

[15] Message to Congress, Dec. 3, 1861. In Richardson, Jas. D., *Messages and Papers of the Presidents*, Vol. VI, p. 49.

made it seem imperative that a majority of the members of the Court should be unquestionably loyal. Thus far the United States had, in its discussions with foreign governments, declared that the revolt of the South was only an insurrection against the federal government, and that the Confederacy had no belligerent rights which could be recognized by foreign powers. Admission that the Confederacy was a belligerent power with which the United States was at war would have implied that foreign powers might recognize belligerent rights. This the United States was most eager to prevent.

On the other hand, however, in the conduct of military operations, the Confederacy was treated as a hostile government whose forces were to be met under the laws of war. Foreign vessels were excluded from Southern ports by a blockade, though Secretary Seward confused the situation by insisting in the declaration that the conflict was not a war at all. Thus, from the point of view of the United States, the question of whether or not the conflict was a war was one to be answered in terms of what use she wished to make of the laws of war. The situation was further complicated by the legal question as to whether there could be a war in the absence of a declaration by Congress, for Congress had not directly declared war on the South.

The issue was raised in the Supreme Court when former owners of ships captured under the laws of war challenged the legality of the capture, declaring that no war existed, and that the laws of war, which provided for the taking of prize, could not apply. The test case,[16] brought before the Court in February, 1863, was argued for twelve days. "Contemplate, my dear sir," wrote Charles Henry Dana, one of the counsel for the United States, to

[16] The *Prize Cases*, 67 U. S. 635.

Charles Francis Adams, "the possibility of a Supreme Court deciding that this blockade is illegal! What a position it would put us in before the world whose commerce we have been illegally prohibiting, whom we have unlawfully subjected to a cotton famine and domestic dangers and distress for two years! It would end the war, and where it would leave us with neutral powers it is fearful to contemplate! Yet such an event is legally possible,—I do not think it probable, hardly possible, in fact. But last year I think there was danger of such a result, when the blockade was new, and before the three new judges were appointed. The bare contemplation of such a possibility makes us pause in our boastful assertion that our written constitution is clearly the best adapted to all exigencies, the last, best gift to man." [17]

The five to four decision of the Court, which was handed down March 10, 1863, came as a great relief to the friends of the Union. Justice Grier, reading the majority opinion, held that the conflict was indeed a war, and that the blockade was legal. At the same time, however, he endeavored to establish the fact that the Confederacy was not a separate and independent power, entitled to be recognized as such by foreign governments. Chief Justice Taney and Justices Catron and Clifford concurred with Justice Nelson in his dissenting opinion, arguing that the status of war had never been conferred upon the struggle.

The closeness of the vote in the Supreme Court showed the danger to be very real that the conduct of the war might be at least inadvertently sabotaged by judges who were more deeply devoted either to the South or to their conceptions of the law than to the immediate needs of the government. This type of situation, together with the apprehension that others similar to it might arise,

[17] Adams, Charles Francis, *Richard Henry Dana*, Vol. II, p. 267.

made all the more insistent the demand that the personnel of the Court be so changed that the country would be in no further danger from that quarter.

It is not surprising, therefore, that Congress, on March 3, 1863, passed an act reorganizing the judicial circuit on the Pacific Coast and providing for its assignment to a tenth justice of the Supreme Court. It was probably rather generally believed, at the time the office was created, that Field would be chosen to fill it. Earlier in the same year a vacancy had occurred in the local circuit. The California senators in Washington had urged his name for the position, but he declared that he preferred to remain on the state bench. However, he volunteered the information that he would be willing to go to the United States Supreme Court if he were appointed. The entire Pacific Coast delegation worked to secure his appointment.[18] Leland Stanford, later to be prominent in the railroad history of the state, who at the time President Lincoln took office had been Governor of California, also supported him.[19]

Influence likewise came from another source. David Dudley Field, in addition to his private practice and his work for the codification of law, had also had time for politics. He had been a bitter opponent of slavery, and had played no small part in the organization of the Republican party and in the nomination of Lincoln as its standard-bearer. Consequently, as told by Henry M. Field, "While the nomination was pending, Mr. John A. C. Gray, a well-known citizen of New York, and an old friend of Mr. Lincoln, went to speak to him about it. He found the President agreed entirely on the fitness of Judge Field, and had but one question to ask: 'Does David want his brother to have it?' 'Yes,' said Mr. Gray. 'Then

[18] *Reminiscences,* pp. 115-16.
[19] Myers, Gustavus, *History of the Supreme Court,* p. 502.

he shall have it,' was the instant reply, and the nomination was sent in that afternoon, and confirmed by the Senate unanimously." [20]

Thus there were many reasons back of the appointment. Field himself stressed the need of someone on the Supreme Court who knew the peculiar conditions of California. "To bring order out of this confusion Congress passed an act providing for another seat on this bench, with the intention that it should be filled by someone familiar with these conflicting titles and with the mining laws of the Coast, and as it so happened that I had framed the principal of these laws and was, moreover, Chief Justice of California,[21] it was the wish of the senators and representatives of that state, as well as those from Oregon, that I should succeed to the new position." [22]

Senator Garrett Davis, of Kentucky, placed emphasis upon another factor. "Congress," he declared, had been "pre-eminently radical, and determined, if possible, to make the Supreme Court radical also. A tenth judge was added to the bench, and it was the purpose of the leaders that the place should be filled with a radical, and they so hoped even after his appointment." [23]

The newspapers of the East were for the most part filled with news of more dramatic interest, and had little to say about the appointment. In California, as might be expected, sentiment was divided. "The appointment of such a man to the highest judicial tribunal of the nation," said one paper, "is fortunate for the country, and will be universally regarded on this coast as a wise exercise of the appointing power." [24] "As a judicial officer," said

---

[20] Field, *Life of David Dudley Field*, note, p. 196.

[21] By seniority he became Chief Justice in 1859, when Terry resigned.

[22] Letter to his colleagues, *U. S. Reports*, Vol. 168, Appendix.

[23] *Congressional Globe*, 40 Cong. 2d Sess., p. 498.

[24] Marysville *Daily Appeal*, March 10, 1863.

another, "the appointee has not now, nor ever has had, his superior on the bench, and his selection for this responsible position will give unalloyed satisfaction to citizens generally throughout the state." [25]

The following may be taken as indicative of another point of view. A San Francisco paper thought that Field was by no means impartial in his decisions, and that he was too much subject to the influence of his friends. However, "It is admitted that he has a logical mind, accompanied with motive industry. His work never gets behind hand. Then again he has already passed upon many of the great legal questions of the country, and it is believed that he will adhere to the doctrine of *stare decisis* so far as his own decisions are concerned. The state has cause to dread new judges. People are tired of having all the decisions affecting property overturned every time a new man goes on the bench. Nearly every man of substance had been at some time victimized in the course of the legal revolutions which the almost annual crop of judges has given us. These considerations will make many cheerfully acknowledge the new judge, who would have opposed him were his antecedents only those of lawyer Field." [26]

The appointment was confirmed on March 10, 1863. At that time many state decisions were pending in cases which Field had heard with only one associate. In order that these should not have to be argued again he continued his duties for a time. On May 20 he was sworn in by his colleague, Justice Cope, as an associate justice of the Supreme Court of the United States. He chose that date because it was his father's eighty-second birthday. [27] Before he left he was serenaded by his many friends in

[25] San Francisco *Alta*, Feb. 25, 1863.
[26] San Francisco *Evening Bulletin*, Feb. 24, 1863.
[27] *Reminiscences*, pp. 116-17.

Sacramento. From Sacramento he went to San Francisco to take up his work in the new United States Circuit Court.[28]

Although he was thereafter to spend much of his time in the East he always looked upon San Francisco as his home. He lived for a time in the home of his wife's family. Then, when he built a house at 20 Ellis Street, the family moved in with him. When the mother died one of his wife's sisters, Mrs. George E. Whitney, and her family, continued to live in the home. Close as was his relationship with the Fields, it was hardly closer than that with his wife's people. When he and Mrs. Field embarked for the East, by way of Panama, one of the sisters left with them, and lived with them for many years in Washington. She took almost the place of a daughter to Field, for he had no children of his own.

California was to continue to provide him with dramatic experiences. Life in Washington was interesting, especially for the society-loving Mrs. Field, who, as the youngest and most attractive of the wives of the justices, found herself the object of much attention. But the excitement imparted by the sting of danger was still to come from California. One day in January, 1866, he received a package from San Francisco. On looking it over he was unable to determine what it was, but he concluded, in view of the time when it was mailed, that it might be a Christmas present for his wife. He started to open it, when he was struck by the black appearance

[28] It should be remembered that at this time each of the justices of the Supreme Court of the United States spent a part of every year in a federal circuit court, to which he was assigned. The United States Supreme Court was not then in session, and no order had been issued assigning Field to the tenth circuit. The Circuit Court was therefore opened by Judge Hoffman of the District Court.—Marysville *Daily Appeal*, June 2, 1863. The order of allotment was made out by President Lincoln on June 22, 1863. See 67 U. S. 7-8.

of the inside. He showed it to Delos Lake, a California lawyer who was with him. Lake cried out that it was a torpedo, and with one of the deputies of the Supreme Court he took it and dipped it in water for several minutes. Then they "took it into the carriage-way under the steps leading to the Senate chamber, and shielding themselves behind one of the columns, threw the box against the wall. The blow broke the hinge of the lid and exposed the contents. A murderous contrivance it was;—a veritable infernal machine! Twelve cartridges such as are used in a common pistol, about an inch in length, lay imbedded in a paste of some kind, covered with fulminating powder, and so connected with a bunch of friction matches, a strip of sand paper, and a piece of linen attached to the lid, that on opening the box the matches would be ignited and the whole exploded." [29]

Inside the lid of the package was pasted a clipping from a San Francisco newspaper of October 31, 1864, telling of Field's decision on the previous day in the Circuit Court, in the matter of the ownership of the four square leagues of pueblo land in and around San Francisco. The sender of the package evidently wanted it believed that he was one of the persons who lost property through that decision. His identity was never discovered.

"It has often been a matter of wonder to me," said Field, "how it was that some good angel whispered to me not to open the box. My impetuous temperament would naturally have led me to tear it open without delay. Probably such hesitation in opening a package directed to me never before occurred, and probably never will again. Who knows but that a mother's prayer for the protection of her son, breathed years before, was answered then? Who can say that her spirit was not then hovering over him and whispering caution in his ear? That I

[29] *Reminiscences*, pp. 147-48.

should on that occasion have departed from my usual
mode of action is strange—passing strange." [30]

Field lived at least a part of each of his last thirty-
five years in Washington. Until 1870 he had no fixed
residence in the capital city, but rented rooms each
fall when he returned from the long trip to the Pacific
Coast, where he spent some months holding circuit court.
In 1870, however, or very early in the following year,
he established a home in one of the historic buildings of
the city, at First and "A" Streets Northeast. The building had for many years been known as the "Old Capitol,"
and then later as the "Old Capitol Prison." It had been
fitted out for the use of Congress when the Capitol was
burned by the British in the War of 1812, and Congress
had met there from 1815 to 1819. After that it had been
used as one of the better class of boarding-houses. John
C. Calhoun had died there in 1850. During the Civil
War it was converted into a military prison, and many
grim stories have been told of life within its walls. Some
years later Field invited a group of former prisoners to
dinner at his home. He liked to tell, thereafter, how
much better they seemed to enjoy their second visit than
their first.

Until the close of the war the house was a large, gray,
barn-like structure, not in any sense attractive. When
it was no longer needed as a prison it was purchased by
George T. Brown, sergeant-at-arms of the Senate, who
put on a mansard roof, tore out and reconstructed the
inside, and built in partitions to divide the house into
three separate residences. He went into bankruptcy, and
the property was sold. There is confusing evidence as to
who owned the different residences at different times,

[30] *Ibid.*, p. 150.

but Field's brother, Cyrus, owned a part or all of the property in 1870, and Justice Field was established in the south residence not later than February, 1871. He was the equitable owner at that time, the title being in David Dudley Field. The title passed to him in 1880, by a deed which showed a consideration of twenty-five thousand dollars.[31]

Conflicting rumors said that the property was presented to Justice Field by Cyrus, by David Dudley, and, again, by Cyrus, David Dudley, and Henry. He seems at least to have been able to take his time in making the payment. In spite of the extravagant stories of wealth accumulated by speculating on the decisions rendered by the California Supreme Court, he had no large amount of money when he moved to Washington. At first his salary was six thousand dollars a year, with an additional sum for traveling expenses. Although the salary was increased to eight thousand dollars, without the expense allotment, and then to ten thousand, the office never paid well enough to provide for expensive purchases. The question of how he acquired the property is important chiefly as it has to do with whether or not he received money from his brothers. Two of them were prominent in economic and legal controversies of major importance, and some of the transactions of at least one of them were anything but creditable. The charge that Field had received money from these men, even though they were his brothers, provided a talking point for critics of the Supreme Court. As a matter of fact, if they had influence over him it was of a much more subtle nature than any that came from the transfer of property. The brothers were fond of one another. Each was interested in the achievements of the others, and it is highly probable that they were all profoundly influenced in their outlook upon

[31] *Land Records*, District of Columbia, *Liber 975*, pp. 174-75.

life by their close association. At any rate the place became Field's home, and remained so until the time of his death. For many years the four brothers met there on the thirteenth day of each February, to celebrate David Dudley's birthday.

It was a pleasant home, looking across the park to the east entrance of the Capitol, and on across the western part of the city to Georgetown. Off toward the southwest the crooked windings of the Potomac were in sight. The residence, as he bought it, was hardly large enough to provide room for his office or library. To secure the needed space he built a two-story addition at the south, over the spot where, a few years before, blind-folded prisoners had faced the firing squad. In the added room on the first floor, which was to be a reception room, he put a large mirror over the mantle piece, at the top of which was the Field coat of arms. The second story was arranged for his library. In number of volumes it was large for a private library at that time, running to about three thousand. It was predominantly legal in character, but contained many volumes on wide varieties of subjects. It was here, surrounded by his books, that he put in his long hours of hard work.

While on the state supreme bench he had been known as a hard worker. In his new position he continued to labor strenuously at his tasks, not stopping for rest even on the long voyages to and from the distant West. He was methodical and purposeful in all that he did, and little time and effort were wasted. He rigidly demanded the same efficiency of others. It was a sorry day for secretaries when they got behind with their work, and for copyists who failed to transcribe his illegibly scrawled writing into readable opinions by the time he wanted them. At times when a timid clerk approached him to have a word identified he would burst out with "How in hell do I know?" and allow the clerk to continue to do the worrying.

His working habits were disturbed by the social demands made on him in Washington. The justices of the Supreme Court and their families were prominent in society, and few evenings passed which were free from distracting entertainments. He had been used to working in the evenings. Now he found himself embarrassed by not being able to keep up with his colleagues in his preparation on cases before the Court—or perhaps, really, his embarrassment grew out of not being able to keep as far ahead of his colleagues as he desired. At any rate, he adjusted to the situation by arising early and beginning his work at seven o'clock. From that time until eleven thirty he was not to be disturbed. The afternoon, until four o'clock, was spent in the court room, after which he took some time for outdoor recreation. The new arrangement left his evenings free for social engagements.

He mixed well with the types of persons with whom he came in contact. He had a suave and courtly manner which made him the object of admiration on the part of his political associates. His rich and varied experience had provided him with innumerable stories and anecdotes, and he possessed the art of making the most of them. He was warmly devoted to his friends, yet there was enough of reserve and dignity about him that he never quite became a hail-fellow-well-met in any society. There was, and had always been, a touch of aristocracy about him.

From time to time he met people with all sorts of political connections—presidents, ambassadors, senators, representatives, and lobbyists. He came to know the prominent men at the bar throughout the country both professionally and socially, when they appeared in Washington to argue cases before the Supreme Court. Through his associations he came to know the points of view and the political, economic, and social philosophies of the representatives of prominent political groups and economic interests. If he came to know these types, however, he was virtually cut off from farmers, laborers, and small, independent property owners, who made up a large part of the population. He saw them around him but he did not meet them socially, he did not come into intellectual and emotional contact with them. These limitations may have laid the basis for the bias in outlook of which he was accused in the years to come.

Association with his colleagues was no unimportant factor in his environment. There were always from six to nine of them, with changes taking place from time to time. They were men of varied and contrasting types, most of them well beyond middle age, and usually rather firmly set in their ways of thinking and acting. Chief Justice Chase, for instance, who succeeded the allegedly pro-Southern Chief Justice Taney, had as Secretary of the Treasury risen to prominence in the Republican party, and was vigorously anti-slavery in his attitudes. He was a perennial aspirant for the presidential chair, and apparently would have been willing to accept the nomination from any party that offered it. His successor, however, Chief Justice Waite, apparently had no political aspirations, and when it was suggested that he become a presidential candidate he replied that the Supreme Court should not be used as a stepping stone to political office. Some men came to the bench with obvious eagerness, and most of them held on to their positions as long as possible, although one, Justice Davis, resigned from the bench to become a United States senator.

Justice Miller, who was a colleague of Justice Field's for more than a quarter of a century, may be taken as sharply in contrast with him in appearance, disposition, and habit. He was a great, stocky man, heavy of build and heavy of tread. He was square faced and smooth shaven. People sought his company because he rarely failed to have a good time, and in enjoying himself he radiated mirth and happiness to others. It was said that there was only one thing which he did according to a fixed schedule—go to his dinner. He worked hard, but only as he felt like it. He was accustomed to rest himself in the midst of his professional tasks by stretching out on a couch and reading paper-backed novels. His desk was always a model of confusion. He and Field were close friends, but, in view of their differences, it is not surprising that they clashed hotly at times when it was apparent that the welfare of the country would be profoundly affected by particular decisions.

The association of men of diverse characters and training sometimes brought about vigorous inter-stimulation and mutual development. Sometimes it provoked antagonisms that brought no light to the eyes of the goddess of justice. The history of the Supreme Court is in no small part a history of the way in which men of highly diverse traits, characteristics, conceptions, and ideas, have worked together or against one another in the process of guiding the orderly development and application of constitutional law.

The setting and atmosphere in which the Court did its work were not without significance. It met in what had been the old Senate chamber. As described by a contemporary observer, "The hall is small but one of the handsomest in the Capitol. It is semicircular in form, is seventy-five feet long, forty-five feet high, and forty-five feet wide in the centre, which is the widest part. A row of handsome green pillars of Potomac marble extends across the eastern, or rear side of the hall, and the wall which sweeps around the western side, is ornamented with pilasters of the same material. The ceiling is in the form of a dome, is very beautiful, and is ornamented with square caissons of stucco. A large skylight in the centre of the room lights the chamber.

"A handsome white marble clock is placed over the main door which is on the western side. Opposite, from the eastern wall, a large gilded eagle spreads his wings above a raised platform, railed in, and tastefully draped, along which are arranged the comfortable armchairs of the Chief Justice and his associates, the former being in the centre. Above them is still the old 'eastern gallery of the Senate,' so famous in the history of the country. The desks and seats of the lawyers are ranged in front of the Court, and enclosed by a tasteful railing. The floor is covered with soft, heavy carpets; cushioned benches for spectators are placed along the semicircular wall, and busts of John Jay, John Rutledge, Oliver Ellsworth and John Marshall, former Chief Justices, adorn the hall." [32] "Coming from either the House or the Senate, you seem to have entered another world. Everything is so calm and peaceful, so thoroughly removed from the noise and confusion of political strife going on in the other parts of the Capitol, that the change is indeed delightful." [33]

Too much emphasis should not be placed on the peacefulness of the court room, however, for, to use the words of Justice Oliver Wendell Holmes, "we are very quiet there, but it is the quiet of a storm centre as we all know." [34]

[32] Ellis, J. B., *Sights and Secrets of the National Capital* (1869), pp. 253-54.

[33] *Ibid.*, p. 257.

[34] Holmes, O. W., *Collected Legal Papers* (1921), p. 292.

The justices began their work in the court room each day with an impressive ritual. "At eleven o'clock in the morning, the door just back of the judges' platform is thrown open, and the marshal of the Court enters, walking backward, with his gaze fastened upon the door. Upon reaching the centre of the chamber, he pauses, and cries in a loud voice:

" 'The Honorable, the Judges of the Supreme Court of the United States.'

"All present in the chamber immediately rise to their feet, and remain standing respectfully. Then, through the open door, headed by the Chief Justice, enter the members of the Court, one by one, in their large, flowing robes of black silk. There is something very attractive about these old men, nearly all of whom have passed into the closing years of life. They ascend their platform, range themselves in front of their seats, and the Chief Justice makes a sign to the 'Crier,' who immediately makes the following proclamation:

" 'Oyez! Oyez! Oyez! [35] All persons having business before the Honorable, the Judges of the Supreme Court of the United States, are admonished to draw near and give their attendance, for the Court is now in session. God save the United States, and this Honorable Court.'

"The Judges and other persons take their seats, and the business of the day begins." [36]

It was in this setting, with all these varied influences playing upon his life, that Field took up his work in the Supreme Court. Beginning at a time when the issues of the Civil War were still undecided, he was to continue

---

[35] This is the usual form of the word. The writer from whom this quotation was taken, however, used the two words, "Oh yea," evidently trying to reproduce the word as it sounded when spoken by the crier.

[36] Ellis, *Sights and Secrets of the National Capital*, p. 258.

for more than a third of a century through a period of rapid industrial and social change, when knowledge, wisdom, and foresight on the part of the judges who interpreted and applied the country's laws were at a premium. The way in which he performed his judicial tasks becomes hereafter the outstanding feature in the story of his life.

CHAPTER VI

THE SUPREME COURT AND SECTIONALISM

During his first term in the Circuit Court of the tenth district, in the summer and fall of 1863, before he went East to take his seat with his brethren of the Supreme Court, Field spent most of his time in San Francisco, hearing cases which were chiefly of local and transient importance. One case, however, which was a trial of certain men for treason against the United States for their attempts to give aid to the South in carrying on the war, achieved both local and national prominence. The prisoners were men who had fitted out a ship in the harbor of San Francisco, and, equipped with letters of marque and reprisal from Jefferson Davis, President of the Confederacy, had been about to set out to prey upon Union vessels in the Pacific. They were caught just as they were about to leave the harbor and were brought to trial on a charge of treason. The people of California, most of whom were loyal to the Union or at least were not actively disloyal, were tremendously excited at the threat to their shipping which had been disclosed and were keenly interested in the trial.

Because of the unsettled status of the war there had been much argument as to whether or not participation in it against the Union were treason. Treason, as commonly conceived in the United States, was an ugly charge, and usually carried with it the punishment of death. Loyal citizens were willing to take up arms against the seceding states, but sentencing participants in the rebellion to death for their attempt to break away from the Union was another matter. It seemed likely that, even in the face of the clearest evidence, there would be difficulty in finding juries who would vote for conviction. Congress met the situation by limiting the penalty. By an act of July 17, 1862, it restricted the punishment of treason, when it consisted of giving aid to or engaging in a rebellion or insurrection against the United States, to ten years' imprisonment or a fine of ten thousand dollars, together with the liberation of any slaves owned, or to both penalties at the discretion of the court.

Field listened to lengthy arguments on both sides of the case before him, which was being tried by jury. It was evident, from popular reactions, that treason was still an ominous word with the masses, and that the limitation of punishment recently prescribed by Congress was little understood. Though the evidence was quite clear it was still a matter of doubt whether the jury would be unanimous for conviction. When the arguments had been completed Field delivered a comprehensive charge to the jury. He reminded them, first of all, that they were to determine the facts only. The interpretation of the law was the function of the judge. He proceeded to declare the law, interpreting it in such a way as very clearly to bring the facts which had been sworn to in the testimony within the definition of treason. Then, with equal clearness he showed how the penalty had been modified and minimized to apply to just this type of offense. The punishment was not death, but imprisonment, fine, and the liberation of slaves. When he had concluded the jury had only to declare whether it believed the facts alleged concerning the prisoners to be true. The jury so declared, and the men were adjudged guilty. Field sentenced them to the limit of the penalty.[1]

[1] *United States* v. *Greathouse*, 4 Sawyer 457 (Oct. 17, 1863).

The text of his charge to the jury has been widely praised for its clear and just interpretation of the law. It was significant in Field's life in that it indicated that in his new office he would continue to be a forceful agent in determining the course of the law and the manner of its application. It is hard to read the charge without a conviction that Field put back of it all the force of his personality, eloquence, and logic, with the determination that the jury, unless corrupt or a marvel of obtuseness, would declare the prisoners guilty. There is little doubt that he was right, but the point to be noted is that he was a dominating influence in the solution of the problem. This fact was significant not only in terms of his life in the past, but in terms of his future experiences as well.

For some time after he began his work in Washington in December, 1863, the Supreme Court functioned quietly, apparently undisturbed by the turbulence of life in its vicinity. Although a new loyal justice was now present he was not needed immediately in connection with any cases in which loyalty was likely to play an important part. Most of the opinions which he wrote dealt with land cases from California, with which he was supposed to be more familiar than his associates. Other prize cases came up, but they dealt only with the application in particular instances of laws which were fundamentally unquestioned. The right of blockade and capture did not again become a matter of controversy.

Further changes took place in the personnel of the Court. Chief Justice Taney, who had been too ill to sit during the preceding term of the Court, died in October, 1864. Since he was generally believed to be a Southern sympathizer many were glad that he was gone from the bench. The President, at the beginning of the ensuing

term, appointed Salmon Portland Chase to fill the
vacancy. Chase, as Secretary of the Treasury, had been
unable to get along with the President and other members
of the Cabinet, and had resigned. The President appointed
him in spite of the friction that had existed and in spite
of his belief that Chase would continue to be an aspirant
for the presidency, though he was reported as saying that
he would rather have swallowed his buckhorn chair than
make the nomination.[2] President Lincoln had now
appointed five of the ten judges on the bench. Justice
Catron died the following spring, and the Lincoln
appointees became the majority of the Court. The
vacancy left by the death of Catron was not filled, and
the Court thereafter never had more than nine judges.

Soon after the end of military hostilities, cases which
involved issues of the sectional struggle—most of them,
directly or indirectly, the product of the bitterness which
remained—began to come before the Court. The problem
of readjustment to a state of peace and order did not
promise to be easily solved. The South had been con-
quered by force of arms, the Confederacy had been
broken up, much Southern territory had been devastated,
and the slaves had been set free. The impoverished
citizens had to find some way of carrying on their occupations with free labor, and at the same time to readjust
themselves to life in a society where ignorant freedmen
made up a large percentage of the population. Though
they had been defeated in war the Southerners were by
no means ready to meet their former slaves as equals, and
to permit them to take part in the organization and
control of society. The bitterness of defeat was frequently
expressed in vindictive treatment of the negroes, and in
resistance to the machinations of the carpet-bag officials
from the North.

[2] *Diary of Gideon Welles*, Vol. II, p. 196.

In the North the zeal for conquest and domination did not abate immediately upon the cessation of military hostilities. Fanatical Abolitionists, with victory in sight, clamored for suffrage for the negroes, for recognition of their equality in all respects with the white population, and for suppression of the efforts of the whites to control the local governments. Confiscation of property was demanded, either for paying the war debts of the North or for providing the negroes with "forty acres and a mule." The demand for vengeance was intensified by the assassination of President Lincoln and the discovery that similar plans had been made for the assassination of the Vice-President and members of the Cabinet. "Hang Jeff Davis on a sour apple tree," lustily sang excited crowds throughout the North, and for a time it looked as if the former President of the ill-fated Confederacy might indeed be tried and executed. It was in this atmosphere of resentment and excited hostility on both sides that plans for reconstruction had to be worked out, and that the voice of the judicial department of the government had to make itself heard.

During the period of the war many people of Southern sympathies lived in the North and carried on various activities for giving aid to the Southern cause. The civil courts were at times sympathetic with these efforts, and were anything but vigorous in the prosecution of offenders. Federal officials, who amid the stress of war had brought about a predominant centralization of the government in Washington, determined that disloyal activities in the North should be stopped. To take care of such cases military tribunals were set up by authority of the President, with power to give summary trials without the aid of juries, and to execute sentences. Early in 1864 an attempt was made to have the Supreme Court review on *certiorari* the proceedings of one of these commissions, but the Court declared that it had no power to do so.[3]

In 1866, however, when the war was well over, it did take jurisdiction in a case where the constitutionality of these tribunals was brought into question.[4] Lamdin P. Milligan, a citizen and resident of Indiana, was arrested in October, 1864 at his home, by order of a military commander, and was confined in prison. He had been a member of a secret society known as the Order of American Knights or Sons of Liberty, the purpose and efforts of which were to give all possible aid to the Southern cause. The civil courts of Indiana were open and undisturbed in their proceedings, but Milligan was brought to trial before a military commission. He was found guilty and sentenced to death. He appealed by writ of habeas corpus to the United States Circuit Court in Indiana. That Court, being divided on certain questions, certified them to the Supreme Court.

The case was argued March 5 to 13, 1866. The principles involved were regarded as of very great importance, and able counsel were employed on both sides. David Dudley Field was one of the counsel for Milligan, presenting his first case before the Supreme Court since his younger brother had become a member of that tribunal. He had been an Abolitionist and a loyal advocate of the war and had many times given advice as to government policies to the President and members of the Cabinet. Now, however, he appeared on behalf of the individual and against the far-reaching extension of the powers of the federal government. His statement of his client's cause was as follows:

"It is a question of the rights of the citizen in time of war.

[3] Ex parte *Vallandigham*, 68 U. S. 243.
[4] Ex parte *Milligan*, 71 U. S. 2.

"Is it true, that the moment a declaration of war is made, the executive department of this government, without an act of Congress, becomes absolute master of our liberties and our lives? Are we, then, subject to martial rule, administered by the President upon his own sense of the exigency, with nobody to control him, and with every magistrate and every authority in the land subject to his will alone? These are the considerations which give to the case it greatest significance." [5]

The decision of the Court was announced on April 3, 1866, but the reading of opinions was postponed until December 17, to give time for their careful preparation. The Court placed the stamp of its disapproval upon the military tribunals by deciding unanimously that they had acted without jurisdiction. Justice Davis, a Lincoln appointee and personal friend of the President, speaking for himself and for Justices Nelson, Grier, Clifford, and Field, went further and declared that neither the President nor Congress had the power to institute such military commissions except in the actual theater of war, where the civil courts were not open. On this point Chief Justice Chase dissented, speaking for himself and for Justices Wayne, Swayne, and Miller.

Field later commented on the case, saying: "The decision of the Court was in favor of the liberty of the citizen. Its opinion was announced by Mr. Justice Davis, and it will stand as a perpetual monument to his honor. It laid down in clear and unmistakable terms the doctrine that military commissions organized during the war, in a state not invaded nor engaged in rebellion, in which the federal courts were open and in undisturbed exercise of their judicial functions, had no jurisdiction to try a citizen who was not a resident of a state in rebellion, nor a prisoner of war, nor a person in the military or naval

[5] Ex parte *Milligan*, 71 U. S. 22.

service; and that Congress could not invest them with any such power; that in states where the courts were thus open and undisturbed the guaranty of trial by jury contained in the Constitution was intended for a state of war as well as a state of peace, and is equally binding upon rulers and people at all times and under all circumstances." [6]

The decision brought a recurrence of popular criticism of the Court similar to that which had been showered upon it prior to and at the beginning of the war. The war-time zeal was such that there was no patience with any criticism of the measures taken to advance the cause of the Union. Questioning the acts of the martyred President, even in connection with their constitutionality, was regarded as sacrilegious and almost as a gesture of hostility to the Union. Yet the Supreme Court, having a majority of Lincoln appointees, found it necessary to determine questions of constitutionality even in the face of this opposition.

Field said of the situation: "The Court and all its members appreciated the great difficulties and responsibilities of the government, both in the conduct of the war, and in effecting an early restoration of the states afterwards, and no disposition was manifested at any time to place unnecessary obstacles in the way. But when its measures and legislation were brought to the test of judicial judgment there was but one course to pursue, and that was to apply the law and the Constitution as strictly as though no war had ever existed. The Constitution was not one thing in war and another in peace." [7]

---

[6] *Reminiscences*, pp. 160-61. (References thus noted in this and succeeding chapters, although dealing with a later period than that of Field's California experiences, are to materials which are compiled and paged with his *Personal Reminiscences of Early Days in California*.)

[7] *Reminiscences*, pp. 158-59.

In spite of their devotion to principles of constitutional law, however, Field and his colleagues, like other men, were deeply affected by their desires as to the outcome of the war. It is greatly to be doubted whether, had the Milligan case been argued before the war was near its end, the Court would have undermined the prestige of the administration by going as far as it did in the statement of its opinion. This probability is suggested by the fact that the Court refused even to take jurisdiction in a case which would have raised this issue, at a time when the war was still being carried on.[8] Though it was true that the written Constitution did not change between peace- and war-time, there were many matters upon which the Constitution expressed itself but vaguely, while the interpretation and application of its meaning was left to men, and among these men, to the justices of the Supreme Court. They, in spite of their protestations of consistency, and Field no less than his colleagues, were at times influenced in their judgments by their beliefs as to the results which would flow from them.

The Milligan case was but the beginning of many controversies which were a part of the aftermath of the war, and in which the Court had to pass upon issues which were highly charged with emotion. The two which succeeded it, and which were presented to the Court immediately following the date on which it was argued, Ex parte *Garland*[9] and *Cummings* v. *Missouri*,[10] were important not only in themselves but also in the story of Field's judicial life. The Garland case had to do with the constitutionality of the federal test oath act which was

---

[8] Ex parte *Vallandigham*, 68 U. S. 243.
[9] 71 U. S. 333.
[10] 71 U. S. 277.

passed by Congress in 1862. The act prescribed an oath which was to be taken by all federal officials who should take office subsequent to that time. Each official was required to swear that he had never voluntarily borne arms against the United States since becoming a citizen; that he had not voluntarily given aid, counsel, or encouragement to persons engaged in armed hostility thereto; that he had not sought, accepted, nor attempted to exercise the functions of any office under any authority in hostility to the United States; and that he had not yielded a voluntarily support to any such authority.

In January, 1865 the oath was extended to attorneys and counsellors of the courts of the United States. The person swearing falsely was to be adjudged guilty of perjury, and was to suffer additional penalties in that he could never thereafter hold any office under the United States. The purpose of the first act had been to eliminate from the government disloyal persons who might, from their point of vantage, give aid to its enemies. That of the second appeared rather obviously to be merely the setting aside of the privileges of a particular vocation for those who had been loyal to the government. It was the "spoils system" applied to the post-war situation.

A. H. Garland had been admitted to practice before the Supreme Court in December, 1860. He later took part in the rebellion by serving as a member of Congress in the Confederate government. In July, 1865 he received a full pardon for his offense. Thereupon he petitioned the Court for permission to resume practice before it without taking the oath prescribed by Congress. He rested his claim chiefly on the grounds that, first, the act was unconstitutional in so far as it affected his status, and second, that he was released from compliance with its provisions by the pardon of the President. Garland filed a brief in the case, and Reverdy Johnson and

M. H. Carpenter, prominent lawyers of the time, appeared for him.

Cummings v. *Missouri,* commonly spoken of as the Missouri case or cases, also dealt with the constitutionality of a test oath. This one was not prescribed by a federal act, but by a provision of the Missouri constitution. The provision had been adopted as a result of the war situation. At the beginning of the war the government of that state was in sympathy with the South, and favored secession from the Union. A bitter struggle took place in which loyal citizens took up arms and overthrew the government, and in this way maintained allegiance to the United States. Many men from the state went into the armies of opposing forces, and at home local groups sought to give aid to the causes with which they sympathized. There was intense local bitterness, and toward the close of the war the members of the winning groups sought to entrench themselves firmly in control of the political organization of the state, and in important positions in professional life as well. Delegates were elected to a constitutional convention in November, 1864. They met in January, 1865, and the following April adopted a constitution which was ratified by the people in June.

This constitution provided that all men must take an "oath of loyalty" before they could perform any of a great number of acts, of which the following is a partial list: Vote at any state or municipal election; hold any office under the authority of the state or in any corporation, public or private, established by the authority of the state; act as professor or teacher in any educational institution; hold any property in trust for any church, religious society, or congregation; practice as attorney or counsellor at law; teach, preach, solemnize marriages or perform any other duties of a bishop, priest, deacon, minister, elder, or clergyman of any religious persuasion, sect or denomination. Thus the individual could do very little indeed that was socially influential or economically important without having first taken the oath.

The following are some of the things which the individual had to declare by the oath that he had not done: Served in armed hostility against the United States or the state of Missouri; by act or word manifested adherence to the enemies of the United States or desire for their triumph, or sympathy for those engaged in exciting or carrying on the rebellion; been a member of any organization or society inimical to the government of the United States or of the state; engaged in guerrilla warfare against loyal inhabitants, or in "bushwhacking"; knowingly and willingly harbored, aided, or countenanced any person so engaged; come into or left the state for the purpose of avoiding the draft; enrolled as a Southern sympathizer to avoid military service for the Union; nor in any other manner indicated disaffection to the United States or sympathy with those engaged in rebellion. No person was to be allowed to assume any of the activities named without first taking the oath, and persons already engaged in them were to take the oath within sixty days or discontinue their activities. The result of the oath was to give to loyal citizens of Missouri almost a monopoly of the remunerative and influential positions in the state, while excluding from these positions persons who had been to the least conceivable minimum disloyal, and who were probably almost as numerous as those by whom they were being excluded.

The argument in the Missouri case was closed on March 20, 1866. When the cases were brought up for consideration in the consultation room of the Supreme Court it was decided, for some reason, that the Garland case should be argued again. Field wanted the Missouri case decided immediately, but a majority of the justices voted to hold up its decision until a vote could be taken in the Garland case. That meant postponement until the following term. Reverdy Johnson, one of the counsel, told some Missouri politicians the following summer that he had it from one of the judges that the test oath would be held unconstitutional. The information was freely used in the political struggle then going on in the state. Since Reverdy Johnson and David Dudley Field were together as counsel for Cummings, and since David Dudley Field was a brother of one of the judges, and since Justice Field was known or at least believed by some to consider the requirement of the oath to be an exercise of an unconstitutional power, there were strong suspicions that the information had come through the Field family. Justice Miller, who was then holding court in Iowa, heard of Johnson's statement, and wrote the following letter to Chief Justice Chase, which reveals something of how individual judges regarded the case:

"I call your attention to the statement of Mr. Johnson in the enclosed slip. Whatever may be our guesses at the individual conclusions of the members of the Court, it is certainly false that the Court ever decided the case, or ever took a vote upon it. Not only so but there are several members of the Court, who have never so far as I know *expressed* any opinion on the subject.

"A very animated political contest is now going on in the state of Missouri, between the radicals and their opponents; the latter including every returned rebel in the state. This contest is looked upon by both parties as settling the future of the state for years to come, not only in its political relations, but as affecting the personal safety of the respective parties.

"In this contest the stringent character of the oath prescribed by the Missouri constitution, which was before us in the case referred to by Mr. Johnson, is made a strong point in the attack upon the radicals; and the assertion that the Supreme Court of the United States has decided it to be in conflict with the Constitution of the United States is telling with fatal effect on the radicals.

"Undoubtedly this was the purpose aimed at by the motion of Judge Field, that we should decide this case, and postpone the Congressional Oath case. This move you will remember was defeated by my appeal to the Court not to decide this case if they passed the other, which succeeded by the good feeling and sense of justice of our brother Grier.

"Now shall this falsehood be permitted to work successfully its injurious effects or shall it be contradicted? The Honorable Mr. Hogan is asserting the same thing everywhere in public speeches, and so is Gen'l Blair. It was certainly a violation of judicial propriety for any judge to state what Mr. Johnson says he knows, and I do not believe any judge has said it, because it is false.

"But it seems to me that while we may well feel restrained from stating what *did* take place, there is nothing wrong, but a manifest propriety in contradicting the assertion that the Court has decided an important case, or an important principle when it has done no such thing. I think if any of the radicals of reputable standing should ask me, I should feel bound to contradict the statement, but I believe they are afraid to do so, lest the story of Johnson and Hogan might be confirmed.

"I write this in private confidence, to learn your views of the matter, and also to suggest that such a confidential communication between yourself and Senator Henderson, or Brown, or Gen'l Loan,[11] as would at least enable them to claim as boldly as Hogan and Johnson assert, might do a great deal of good without committing any impropriety; if you concur with me in this matter."

[11] Justice Miller may have intended to write "Logan" instead of "Loan."

The letter closed with a postscript suggesting that the Chief Justice say a word to some member of the group for the judiciary oath, probably referring to the issue in the Garland case.[12]

Miller's letter was dated June 5, 1866. About two weeks later J. F. Asper, a lawyer, politician, and editor of a radical newspaper in Chillicothe, Missouri, wrote as follows to Chase:

"Gen'l Blair and Hogan assert that the test oath of Missouri has been decided unconstitutional and is null and void, and the people are not bound to respect or observe it; they both assert that one of the judges told them so; that the conclusion of the Court has been arrived at, and would have been declared but for the fact that one of the judges desired that the cases be laid over for political effect.

"What I desire to know is whether any decision has been made in the cases or not, or whether any consultation has ever been held upon the case if that is proper. Of course I do not ask what the decision is, but if proper I would like to know whether any decision has been arrived at, and if proper I would like permission to use the information in such a way as would be of service in our fight here. I trust you will not consider me impertinent, or trespassing on the just reserve of the judiciary." [13]

If the Chief Justice replied to Asper's request his reply has not been filed with the letters which have been accumulated for public inspection.

Either from Chase or from some other source Field, now holding court in San Francisco, received a copy of Johnson's statement. On June 30 he wired Chase:

---

[12] Miller to Chase, June 5, 1866, with the Chase papers, filed in the Manuscript Division of the Library of Congress, Washington, D. C.

[13] J. F. Asper to Chase, June 18, 1866. Chase papers.

"Have read with amazement Reverdy Johnson's letter to Hogan on the Missouri case. Does it require any notice from judge? Please answer." [14]

On the same day he followed the telegram with a long letter in which he discussed the statement:

"I received a day or two since the correspondence between Mr. Hogan of the House of Representatives, and Reverdy Johnson in relation to the the supposed action of the Supreme Court in the Missouri test oath cases. I read the letter of Mr. Johnson with amazement, both as to the strange character of his statements, and the singular indelicacy of giving them publicity, even if they were in fact true. As we are aware no decision was reached in the cases—the only vote taken being on the question of the postponement of their consideration until the next term. As announced by you on the last day of the session they were held over under advisement. Mr. Johnson has evidently confounded the action of the Court in the military commission cases with the supposed views of some of the judges in the Missouri cases. The conduct of Johnson is indefensible—more, it merits some rebuke. How foolish he would appear if the decision of the Court should be different from what he supposes it will be, or if a re-argument should be ordered. I suppose he got what he knows on the subject from Judge Nelson with whom he was very intimate—mingled up known with other matters. I do not regret that I was never intimate with him.

"The proposed amendments to the Constitution, prepared by the committee on reconstruction, and passed by Congress appear to me to be just what we need. I think all members of the Union party can unite cordially in their support. If the President withholds his approval he will sever all connection with the Union party. Two

[14] Chase papers.

things are certain—the American people do not intend
to give up all that they have gained by the war—and
they do intend that loyal men shall govern the country." [15]
The Supreme Court reassembled the first Monday in
December, and on the fifteenth of that month the Garland case was re-argued. When the Garland and Missouri
cases came to a vote the justices divided five to four, the
majority holding the test oath provisions as they applied
to these cases to be unconstitutional. The four judges
whose appointments ante-dated the war, Wayne, Grier,
Nelson, and Clifford, joined Field in opposition to the
other Lincoln appointees, Chase, Miller, Swayne, and
Davis. Field wrote the majority opinions, while Miller
spoke for the minority.

In his analysis of the Missouri case Field stated the
offense of which Cummings was accused, summarized the
relevant provisions of the Missouri constitution, and
pointed out that offenders were to be punished by fine
and imprisonment, and that false swearing or affirmation
was punishable by imprisonment in the penitentiary.
The oath was, he declared, "for its severity, without any

[15] Field to Chase, June 30, 1866. Chase papers. The letter continued:
"I see that [Jefferson] Davis has been indicted for treason alleged to
have been committed in 1864; and I take the liberty of enclosing to you a
charge of mine in a case of treason tried in this city in 1863. I would call
your attention to some observations upon the act of July 17, 1862, which
you will find on pages four and five.

"I owe you many thanks for your letter of April 30th received in New
York a few days before I left for California, and for the many kind and
friendly expressions it contains. I remember well the conversation I had
with you in 1864 on the subject of your appointment to the place you now
occupy. But I have never told you of my interviews on the subject with
President Lincoln—nor of the telegrams and letters sent to Washington
from California urging your appointment immediately after the death of
Chief Justice Taney. I will some day speak to you of them. I did indeed
feel very solicitous for your appointment, and I always rejoiced, and do
now rejoice that you were appointed. I know of few persons who could
have filled the position so well—of none who could have filled it better."

precedent that we can discover." It was retrospective, embracing all the past from the date when the oath was taken. It was directed not merely against overt and visible acts of hostility against the government, but was intended to reach words, desires, and sympathies also. It allowed no distinction between acts springing from malignant enmity and acts which might have been prompted by charity, or affection, or relationship.

He recognized that among the rights reserved to the states was the right of each state to determine qualifications for office, and the conditions upon which citizens might exercise their callings and pursuits within its jurisdiction. However, he said, "it by no means follows that, under the form of creating a qualification or attaching a condition, the states can in effect inflict a punishment for a past act which was not punishable at the time it was committed. The question is not as to the existence of the power of the state over matters of internal police, but whether that power has been made in the present case an instrument for the infliction of punishment against the inhibition of the Constitution."

There could be no connection, he declared, between the fact that Cummings avoided the draft in Missouri and his fitness to teach the doctrines or administer the sacraments of the church. The oath "was exacted not from any notion that the several acts designated indicated unfitness for the callings, but because it was thought that the several acts deserved punishment, and that for many of them there was no way to inflict punishment except by depriving the parties, who had committed them, of some of the rights and privileges of the citizen."

In order to carry his argument Field had to prove that before the law the disabilities created by the Missouri constitution were to be regarded as penalties, as constituting punishment. He could find no such proof in any relevant law. Neither could he find it in the federal Constitution itself. Instead he had to go back to the "theory upon which our political institutions rest." The discovery of any one consistent and all-embracing theory lying back of our political institutions has long been an object of desire on the part of theorists. Few careful students will say that such a discovery has been or can be made. Yet Field believed, at least for the purpose of argument, that there was such a body of theory. In this case and in many others it provided the basis for the logical superstructures by means of which he justified his decisions.

"The theory upon which our political institutions rest is," he declared, "that all men have certain inalienable rights—that among these are life, liberty, and the pursuit of happiness; and that in the pursuit of happiness all avocations, all honors, all positions, are alike open to everyone, and that in the protection of these rights all are equal before the law." From this alleged fact he reasoned that "any deprivation or suspension of any of these rights for past conduct is punishment, and can be in no otherwise defined."

He declared that the provisions of the Missouri constitution were legislative acts which in effect inflicted punishment on a class of persons for past acts without a judicial trial. Such acts were bills of attainder, which the states were forbidden to pass. The clauses presumed the guilt of priests and clergymen and deprived them of their rights unless the presumption was removed by an expurgatory oath. They were doing indirectly that which could not be done directly. But, he said, "the Constitution deals with substance, not shadows. Its inhibition was leveled at the thing, not the name. It intended that the rights of the citizen should be secure against deprivation for past conduct by legislative enactment, under any form, however disguised. If the inhibition can be evaded by the form of the enactment, its insertion in the fundamental law was a vain and futile proceeding."

The clauses also came under the head of *ex post facto* laws, he declared, which the states were forbidden to pass. An *ex post facto* law was defined as "one which imposes a punishment for an act which was not punishable at the time it was committed; or imposes additional punishments to that then prescribed; or changes the rules of evidence by which less or different testimony is sufficient to convict than was then required." Some of the offenses, such as leaving the state to avoid the military draft, had not been violations of any law when committed. For other acts which had been recognized as crimes additional penalties were in effect imposed. Further than that, the "clauses in question subvert the presumptions of innocence, and alter the rules of evidence, which heretofore, under the universally recognized principles of the common law, have been supposed to be fundamental and unchangeable. They assume that the parties are guilty; they call upon the parties to establish their innocence; and they declare that such innocence can be shown only in one way—by an inquisition, in the form of an expurgatory oath, into the consciences of the parties."

In view of all the facts discussed, he said, the Court could only declare the clauses in question to be unconstitutional, and order a reversal of the judgment.

Completing his discussion of the Missouri case, Field then took up the Garland case in much the same way, though more briefly. He found exclusion from practice before the federal courts by requirement of an oath, which persons who had performed certain acts could not take without perjuring themselves, to be punishment for the performance of those acts. As such it came under the heads of bills of attainder and *ex post facto* laws. Attorneys and counsellors were not officers of the United States, but of the Court, admitted as such by its order, upon evidence of sufficient legal learning and fair private character. They held their office during good behavior, and could be deprived of it only for misconduct ascertained and declared by judgment of the Court after an opportunity to be heard had been afforded.

It is a matter of interest that Field's statement in this case, and other statements in similar cases where the rights of attorneys were involved, seemed charged with some of the same emotional intensity with which he had fought against his own predicament years before when Judge Turner of Marysville had disbarred him from practice.

The right of practice, he declared, once it was conferred, was not revocable at the pleasure of the Court nor at the command of the legislature. Congress might undoubtedly prescribe qualifications for the office, but it could not exercise the power in such a way as to inflict punishment against the prohibition of the Constitution. This view was strengthened in Garland's case by the fact that he had a pardon from the President relieving him from all disabilities arising from his conduct during the war.

Justice Miller, who, as was indicated by his letter to Chief Justice Chase, had felt very strongly concerning the cases from the beginning, wrote a dissenting opinion which, though it in part applied to both cases, was devoted chiefly to a discussion of the Garland case. He stressed the fact that the right to practice law in the courts as a profession was a privilege granted by law, and not an absolute right. Congress had the power to prescribe qualifications, and there was no more important qualication than loyalty to the government. While in a sense the oath looked backward it also looked to the future, in that its purpose was to bring about the establishment of a bar of unquestioned loyalty. Miller analyzed at length the nature of bills of attainder and *ex post facto* laws, and endeavored to show that the federal judiciary oath and the specified clauses of the Missouri constitution did not come within those categories. His opinion reflected throughout his sense of urgency that the control of society should be kept in the hands of men who were in sympathy with the existing political organization, although, apart from the expression of this attitude, he did not reveal himself as inept in the process of legal reasoning.

Field's almost passionate belief in the existence of inalienable rights of individuals to work out their living in their own way, as long as they interfered with no similar right of others, did not mark him as different from most of his contemporaries, save perhaps in matter of degree. The belief was, of course, emphatically in harmony with the philosophies which had prevailed both in Puritan New England and on the California frontier. It probably had much to do with the original decisions at which Field arrived in these cases as well as with the superstructure by means of which he justified them. Its use merely as a tool, however, is not to be overlooked in the chronicle of his later experience.

It would be a matter of deep interest to know the influence which David Dudley Field may have had on the decisions. He appeared as counsel in only one of the cases, but in that case he presented most of the ideas which Justice Field used in the preparation of his opinions. If the mind of Justice Field were not already made up, it seems probable that the older brother, from whom he had received much of his early legal training, would have been able to bring a tremendous influence to bear upon his judgment in connection with the cases at hand.[16]

It is to be remarked that both majority and minority opinions, though couched in terms of legal categories, fundamental principles, and inalienable rights, reveal keen insight into the nature of the political, economic, and social situations amid which the controversies arose.

Concerning the reception of the decisions Field said: "It is difficult to appreciate at this day [in 1877] the fierceness with which the majority of the Court was assailed. . . . I was particularly taken to task, however, as it was supposed—at least I can only so infer from the tone of the press—that because I had been appointed by Mr. Lincoln, I was under some sort of moral obligation to support all the measures taken by the states or by Congress during the war."[17] He characterized the following article as moderate in tone among those that appeared:

"Dred Scott Number Three has just been enacted in the Supreme Court of the United States, Justice Field, of California, taking the leading part as the representative of the majority decision against the constitutionality of the iron-clad test oath to prevent traitors from practicing before that high tribunal. . . . The country has been repeatedly admonished that such a decision would be made about this time; nevertheless a very considerable sensation was created when it was officially enunciated. All these movements are but preparations for a counter-revolution in the interest of slavery and treason. . . . Several months ago the fact that this decision was coming was communicated by someone connected with the Supreme

---

[16] The custom of more recent years which requires that a justice shall withdraw from the bench when a close relative appears as counsel seems not to have been generally followed at that time. Field had ample precedent for retaining his seat while his brother argued a case.

[17] *Reminiscences*, p. 167.

Court of the United States to a celebrated Copperhead politician in Missouri, who used it to stimulate the traitors and discourage the patriots in that state. . . . Can it be expected that a tribunal committed to a policy so cruel and disastrous can retain, or deserve to retain, the confidence of a free people? I learn that the opinion of Justice Field against the test oath, like that against military trials in time of war, goes outside of the immediate case in issue and indulges in a fierce onslaught on test oaths in general. If so, it will only add another reason for such a reorganization as will prevent the judges in the last resort from becoming the mere agents of party, or the mere defenders of rebellion. The adage, constantly quoted, that 'whom the gods wish to destroy they first make mad,' is having a pointed illustration in these successive judicial assaults upon the rights of the people. Although the supreme judges hold for life, there is at once precedent, necessity, and law for such a change in the present system as will in a short time make it a fearless interpreter of republican institutions, instead of the defender and apologist of treason." [18]

A California newspaper, discussing the cases in a similar vein, remarked that the radical judge who used to sing of John Brown's body with so much zeal and talk like Garrison in the atmosphere of California had suddenly become very high-toned and somewhat dizzy on the supreme bench.[19] Leland Stanford said that McRuer, representative from California who had voted against George S. Boutwell's new test oath bill, had "fallen immensely in popular favor in consequence of his vote on Boutwell's test oath bill. Field is repudiated. The fact is in these times a man's political character is as sensitive and needs to be as carefully guarded to avoid

[18] "Occasional," *The Press*, Philadelphia, Jan. 15, 1867.
[19] Sacramento *Union*, Jan. 16, 1867.

taint as a woman's character for chastity. A suspicion of weakness is accepted as sufficient for condemnation." [20] It was true that the emotions of the people were keyed to a high pitch, and that conflict even with mere popular whims often brought a politician into general condemnation. But although Field lost prestige with the Republicans and with the Union party of California he won applause in other quarters. He was thereafter looked upon by Democrats in the South as the guardian of their liberties in the Supreme Court, and he was talked of as a potential candidate for the presidency. Anyway, whatever his popularity or lack of it, the opinions succeeded in making him a nationally known figure.[21]

In the meantime the legislative and executive branches of the government were at odds over plans for reconstruction in the South. Congress was dominated by such extreme Abolitionists as Charles Sumner in the Senate and Thaddeus Stevens in the House of Representatives. These men were eager to rule the Southern whites with an iron hand, while giving protection and political privileges to the negroes. President Johnson favored the speedy restoration of the Southern states to their former

[20] Letter to Cornelius Cole, in *Memoirs of Cornelius Cole*, p. 260.

[21] A few other test oath cases were argued before the Court. In *Blair* v. *Thompson & Ridgely*, announced in 1870 but not published in the official reports, the Court divided four to four on the question of whether the Missouri oath was valid when resorted to as a test for voting. Justice Wayne, who had voted with the majority in *Cummings* v. *Missouri*, had died in the summer of 1867, and his place had not yet been filled. The other members voted as in the preceding case. See the New York *Tribune*, Feb. 1, 1870. In the term of 1872-73 Justice Field spoke for the Court in *Pierce* v. *Carskadon*, 83 U. S. 234, holding that a West Virginia law granting the right to a rehearing only on the basis of a war-time test oath was unconstitutional, as determined by *Cummings* v. *Missouri* and Ex parte *Garland*.

places in the Union, upon their ratification of the Thirteenth Amendment to the Constitution, by which the slaves were set free.

"It would have been most fortunate for the country had this condition been deemed sufficient and been accepted as such," said Justice Field. "But the North was in no mood for a course so simple and just. Its leaders clamored for more stringent measures, on the ground that they were needed for the protection of the freedmen, and the defeat of possible schemes for a new insurrection. It was not long, therefore, before a system of measures was adopted, which resulted in the establishment at the South of temporary governments, subject to military control, the offices of which were filled chiefly by men alien to the states and indifferent to their interests." [22]

Friction existed between the President and Congress almost from the beginning. The friction grew worse with time, until the President narrowly escaped removal from his office as the result of a trial for impeachment. His opposition to the rigorous measures of Congress were without avail. In order to prevent his appointing Supreme Court justices who held ideas similar to his own Congress in the summer of 1866 passed a bill providing that no vacancy in the Court should be filled until the membership stood at a chief justice and six associate justices.[23]

After its decisions in the Milligan case and in the test oath cases the Court was watched with hostile suspicion. It was looked upon as in league with a disloyal President against the patriotic measures of Congress. As further

[22] *Reminiscences*, p. 156. See also acts of Congress March 2, 1867, March 23, 1867, July 19, 1867, March 11, 1868, and June 25, 1868.

[23] *Cong. Globe*, 39 Cong., 1 Sess., pp. 3699, 3922.

war and post-war legislation came before it, said Justice Field, "its action thereon was watched by members of the Republican party with manifest uneasiness and distrust." Many suspected that "the sympathies of the majority of the Court were with the Confederates. Intimations to that effect were thrown out in some of the journals of the day, at first in guarded language, and afterwards more directly, until finally it came to be generally believed that it was the purpose of the Court, if an opportunity offered, to declare invalid most of the legislation relating to the Southern states which had been enacted during the war and immediately afterwards. Nothing could have been more unjust and unfounded." Many things had been done, however, he said, which could not be sanctioned under the Constitution.[24]

The reconstruction acts which were passed in March, 1867, providing for military governments throughout the South, seemed to many people to be nearly duplicating the military tribunal proceedings which had been declared unconstitutional in the Milligan case. No sooner had the acts been passed than efforts were made to prevent their being carried out. In *Mississippi* v. *Johnson*[25] a suit was brought in the Supreme Court to prevent the President from carrying the acts into effect in the State of Mississippi. The case was argued on April 12, 1867. It occasioned a great deal of discussion and considerable uneasiness as to the outcome. On April 14 Francis Lieber wrote to Charles Sumner saying: "I imagine that at no time in our history have there been so many ears pricked up, in all portions of our country, for a coming decision of a tribunal, as at present for the decision of the Supreme Court. . . . As it appears to me, the Court has only to decide between two laws presumed to conflict,—a neces-

[24] *Reminiscences*, p. 157.
[25] 71 U. S. 475.

sary consequence of an enacted (or written) constitution.
It leads to many inconveniences; but where parties
contend, justice has to be done. If we could obtain some
archangels to sit after each Congress, to decide on the
laws of Congress, then we might make the *constitutionality* a general question; but with all respect for our
Supreme Court,—or for many of the judges at least,—
I have never seen the angelic wings penetrating the
gown. . . ." [26]

The Court, on April 15, unanimously refused to take
jurisdiction in the case and pass upon the constitutionality
of the reconstruction acts. It could not enjoin the
President in the performance of his official duties, said
Chief Justice Chase. He showed how largely this was a
matter of expediency by saying:

"Suppose the bill filed and the injunction prayed for
allowed. If the President refuses obedience, it is need-
less to observe that the Court is without power to enforce
its process. If, on the other hand, the President complies
with the order of the Court and refuses to execute the
acts of Congress, is it not clear that a collision may occur
between the executive and legislative departments of the
government? May not the House of Representatives
impeach the President for such refusal? And in that
case could this Court interfere, in behalf of the President, thus endangered by compliance with its mandate,
and restrain by injunction the Senate of the United States
from sitting as a Court of impeachment? Would the
strange spectacle be offered to the public world of an
attempt by this Court to arrest proceedings in that
Court?

"These questions answer themselves."

On the same day on which this decision was given an
attempt was made to get at the reconstruction acts in

[26] *Life and Letters of Francis Lieber,* edited by Thos. S. Perry, pp. 371-72.

another way. A bill was filed to prevent officers of the executive department from enforcing the acts. The case, *Georgia* v. *Stanton*,[27] was argued about two weeks later and the decision was announced May 13, 1867, although the opinion was not read until February 10, 1868, partly, perhaps, because of the intensity of popular feeling at the time. Again the Court refused to take jurisdiction, holding that the enforcement of the acts came under the head of political measures, which the Court had no power to enjoin.

There is room for much difference of opinion both as to the wisdom and the motives of the Court. James Ford Rhodes, historian, has this to say: "The Supreme Court had acted with great prudence. Had the cases of Mississippi and Georgia been considered on their merits little doubt can exist, to argue from the decision of the Court in the Milligan case the preceding December, that a majority of the judges would have pronounced the reconstruction acts unconstitutional. Current gossip had it that such was the belief of five of the nine judges and, had such a decision been rendered, the Constitution already strained would have been put to a severer tension. One thing is sure: The Republican majority in Congress and among the Northern people was determined to have its way and would no more be stopped by legal principles and technicalities than it had been by the President's vetoes."[28]

In 1868 the validity of the reconstruction acts was questioned in another type of case. In 1867 the appellate jurisdiction of the Supreme Court had been extended to cover habeas corpus cases appealed from the circuit

[27] 73 U. S. 50.
[28] Rhodes, J. F., *History of the United States*, Vol. VI, p. 74.

courts. The purpose of the act had been to give protection to persons who might not be able to get it in the circuit courts of the South, where local feelings and prejudices were dominant. The act was turned to a use quite other than that which was intended. An editor, McCardle, wrote articles criticizing the policies of the United States government. He was imprisoned by military authorities, and was to be tried by a military tribunal which was set up by the reconstruction acts. When the Circuit Court denied him a writ of habeas corpus he appealed to the Supreme Court. The Court decided that it had jurisdiction.[29] The case was then argued on its merits March 2, 3, 4, and 9, 1868. David Dudley Field, Jeremiah S. Black, and William L. Sharkey appeared for McCardle, and Matthew Hale Carpenter, Lyman Trumbull, and James Hughes for the government.

The court room was tense with repressed excitement. Carpenter wrote to his wife on March 3, "I spoke two and a half hours today, and did as well as I expected or hoped to do. I am praised nearly to death. I had half of the Senate for an audience. Miller's face was as the face of an angel radiant with the light of joy; Davis and Field looked troubled; Nelson, Clifford and Grier dead against me. But I shook them up and rattled their dry bones."[30] After the argument Secretary of War Stanton exclaimed fervently, with tears in his eyes, "Carpenter, you have saved us."[31] The remainder of the argument was postponed until March 9, because of the fact that Chief Justice Chase was called from the bench to preside over the Senate while it sat as a court of impeachment for the trial of the President.

[29] Ex parte McCardle, 73 U. S. 318.
[30] Ashley, H. D., "Matthew Hale Carpenter as a Lawyer," *Green Bag* (1894), Vol. VI, pp. 442-43.
[31] Ibid., p. 444.

Field said of the presentation and disposal of the case: "Seldom has it been my fortune during my judicial life, now (1877) of nearly twenty years, to listen to arguments equal in learning, ability, and eloquence. The whole subject was exhausted. As the arguments were widely published in the public journals, and read throughout the country, they produced a profound effect. The impression was general that the reconstruction acts could not be sustained; that they were revolutionary and destructive of a republican form of government in the states, which the Constitution required the federal government to guarantee. I speak now merely of the general impression. I say nothing of the fact, as the Court never expressed its opinion in judgment. The argument was had on the 2d, 3d, 4th, and 9th of March, 1868, and it ought to have been decided in regular course of proceedings when it was reached on the second subsequent consultation day, the 21st. The judges had all formed their conclusions, and no excuse was urged that more time was wanted for examination. In the meantime an act was quietly introduced into the House, and passed, repealing so much of the law of February 5th, 1867, as authorized an appeal to the Supreme Court from the judgment of the Circuit Court on writs of habeas corpus, or the exercise of jurisdiction on appeals already taken. The President vetoed the bill, but Congress passed it over his veto, and it became a law on the 27th of the month. Whilst it was pending in Congress the attention of the judges was called to it, and in consultation on the 21st they postponed the decision of the case until it should be disposed of. It was then that Mr. Justice Grier wrote the following protest, which he afterwards read in Court:

In Re McArdle   Protest of Mr. Justice Grier

The case was fully argued in the beginning of this month. It is a case that involves the liberty and rights not only of the appellant, but of millions of our fellow-citizens. The country and the parties had a right to expect that it would receive the immediate and solemn attention of this Court. By the postponement of the case we shall subject ourselves, whether justly or unjustly, to the imputation that we have evaded the performance of a duty imposed on us by the Constitution, and waited for legislation to interpose and supersede our action and relieve us from our responsibility. I am not willing to be a partaker either of the eulogy or opprobrium that may follow; and can only say:

> Pudet haec opprobria nobis,
> Et dici potuisse; et non potuisse repelli.[32]

R. C. GRIER.

I am of the same opinion as my brother Grier, and unite in his protest.

FIELD, J.

After the passage of the repealing act the case was continued; and at the ensuing term the appeal was dismissed for want of jurisdiction. . . ." [33]

The diary of Gideon Wells for March 23, 1868 contains the following entry: "The judges of the Supreme Court have caved in, fallen through, failed, in the McCardle case. Only Grier and Field have held out like men, patriots, judges of nerve and honest independence.

"These things look ominous and sadden me. I fear for my country when I see such abasement. Fear of the usurping radicals in Congress has intimidated some of these judges, or, like reckless Democratic leaders, they are willing their party should triumph through radical folly and wickedness.

"These are indeed evil times! Seward has on more than one occasion declared that he controlled Judge

---

[32] Field's translation: "It fills us with shame that these reproaches can be uttered, and cannot be repelled." From Ovid *Metamorphoses*. Book I, lines 758-59.

[33] *Reminiscences*, pp. 172-73. The case was Ex parte *McCardle*, 74 U. S. 506.

Nelson. Whether he is, or has been, intriguing in this matter, or taken any part, is a problem." [34]

As an indication of the way in which the judges were watched prior to and at the time of the McCardle case Field told the following story of his own experience. He was invited by Samuel Ward, a prominent lobbyist, to a five o'clock dinner which was being given in honor of the Secretary of the Treasury, McCulloch. "Some of the brightest spirits of Congress were present. As we took our seats at the table I noticed on the menu a choice collection of wines, Johannisberg among others. The dinner was sumptuously and admirably served. Our host saw that the appropriate wine accompanied the successive courses. As the dinner progressed, and the wine circulated, the wit of the guests sparkled. Story and anecdote, laughter and mirth abounded, and each guest seemed joyous and happy. At about eight songs had been added to other manifestations of pleasure. I then concluded that I had better retire so I said to my host, that if he would excuse me, I would seek the open air."

Field had no more than left when Rodman M. Price, former Governor of New Jersey, arrived, having been under the impression that the banquet began at eight o'clock. He was told to take Field's place at the table. He had been traveling in the South, and proceeded to tell of some of his experiences. He closed by expressing the opinion that "the whole reconstruction measures would soon be 'smashed up' and sent to 'kingdom come' by the Supreme Court." A reporter from the *Evening Express* came in at that moment, heard what Price said, and asked a waiter who he was. The waiter picked up the card at Price's elbow and saw that it bore Field's name. The reporter, elated by his scoop, hurried away to write it up.

[34] *Diary of Gideon Welles*, Vol. III, p. 320.

The *Express* carried the story the next day, without mentioning any names, and the following day a Baltimore paper disclosed the fact that Field was the judge who had attended the banquet. On January 30, 1868 Mr. Scofield, a representative from Pennsylvania, introduced in the House of Representatives a resolution directing the committee on judiciary to inquire into the facts, and report if they would justify action by impeachment. After some debate the resolution was passed, ninety-seven to fifty-four, thirty-four not voting.[35] Field said of it: "The resolution was evidently intended to intimidate me, and to act as a warning to all the judges as to what they might expect if they presumed to question the wisdom or the validity of the reconstruction measures of Congress. What little effect it had on me my subsequent course in the McCardle case probably showed to the House. I had only one feeling for the movement—that of profound contempt; and I believe that a similar feeling was entertained by every right-thinking person having any knowledge of the proceeding." [36]

The facts of the situation soon became known, and caused much merriment. On June 18, 1868, the resolution of the House of Representatives was laid on the table.

After the disposal of the McCardle case other attempts were made to secure a decision of the Supreme Court as to the constitutionality of the reconstruction acts, but all of them failed. When the Southern states in time found their way back to their former status in the Union they did it without help from the Court. The Court however

[35] See 40 Cong., 2d Sess., pp. 863-65. Johnson, representative from California, said: "If the gentlemen on the other side desire to impeach that judge because he is as spotless in character as the robes of the goddess of justice, let them give us a fair proceeding." *Ibid.*, p. 863.

[36] For the story in full as told by Field see his *Reminiscences*, pp. 174-79.

did pass many times upon questions which had to do with property rights in the South. Most of the cases grew out of the seizure of the property of Southerners under an act of Congress of July 17, 1862, entitled "An Act to Suppress Insurrection, to Punish Treason and Rebellion, to Seize and Confiscate the Property of Rebels, and for Other Purposes." The act, like many others of the period, indicated confusion as to the status of the war. In part it seemed to be based upon the municipal powers of government, and in part upon war powers. In the first prominent case arising under the act [37] the majority of the Court held that though in part it was a municipal act applying to rebellious citizens certain provisions were based upon the laws of war, and in terms of these laws the confiscation of enemy property was legitimate.

Field dissented. He declared that while Congress had at hand war powers which it might have used, it could not in the same act confuse these powers with the power of legislating for the purpose of punishing offending citizens. This act, he said, was directed "against persons who have committed certain overt acts of treason." It was a municipal act. As such it was subject to the limitations of the Constitution affecting the taking of property—that it should be done by orderly judicial process. "There is no difference in the relation between the owner and his property and the government, when the owner is guilty of treason and when he is guilty of any other public offense. The same reason which would sustain the authority of the government to confiscate the property of a traitor would justify the confiscation of his property when guilty of any other offense."

In most, although not all, of the confiscation cases which came before it the Court upheld the actions of the

[37] *Miller* v. *United States*, 78 U. S. 268 (1870).

government. In most, although not all, of the same cases, Field dissented, usually standing alone. He gave different reasons for dissenting in different cases, and from a standpoint of law these opinions are no doubt worthy of study. In the biography of the man, however, they are less important than the fact that he usually found one legal reason or another for arguing and voting in favor of the rights of the original owners of the properties. His attitude throughout seemed to be that the conflict between the North and the South should be brought to a close as soon as possible. Recriminatory acts against the South—such as limiting their vocational, economic, and political rights, governing them by arbitrary military tribunals, confiscating their property, compelling them to receive negroes on a basis of social equality with themselves,[38] and requiring them to give places to negroes or juries [39]—were to be deplored and to be checked wherever possible.

The various Supreme Court cases arising out of the issues of sectionalism had numerous prominent elements of significance in Field's life. Suffice it to say that two very different elements which are worthy of note and recollection were his use of the doctrine of inalienable rights, and his establishment of himself as the judicial spokesman of the rights of the defeated citizens of the South. The former gives a clue to his judicial methods, and the latter to certain political aspirations which were to appear later on.

[38] Voting with the majority in the *Civil Rights Cases*, 109 U. S. 3 (1883).
[39] Dissent in Ex parte *Virginia*, 100 U. S. 339 (1880).

CHAPTER VII
GREENBACKS IN THE SCALES OF JUSTICE

The controversies which came before the Supreme Court were of many kinds and of varied importance. Those which provided the great amount of routine work for the judges called for no great extension of legal principles which were already established. They were of interest chiefly to the contending parties alone, and were quickly forgotten by others, even by the judges themselves. There were other types of cases, however, which, though fewer in number, caused the judges more work and more worry, and demanded more of them in the way of creative effort. While logically these cases were subject to the application of established legal principles, these principles often clashed irreconcilably with each other, or, while stamping a given course of action as legally just, worked obvious injustice from a common sense point of view, or failed to get at the heart of the situation at all. When the Constitution, the enacted laws, and the common law were all silent with regard to the basic problems before the Court, or were in conflict, or spoke in uncertain generalities, the judges had to forsake their traditional passivity and become, in effect, legislators. They had to evaluate the existing situations in terms of their own knowledge and experience, and then find legal principles which they could develop far enough to justify their decisions.

The knowledge, experience, social philosophies, courage, and inventive genius of the judges varied with each individual. Hence it was that these decisions, which

were often fraught with tremendous importance in the
developing life of the country, were the objects of violent
controversies among the judges, and were arrived at only
after compromise or were pronounced by bare majorities of the Court, with the minority judges protesting
vociferously. Field participated in many decisions of
this kind. Among them, obviously were certain of the
cases having to do with the issues of sectionalism. Other
cases of special interest to him were those dealing with
currency problems growing out of the Civil War, with
the immigration of Chinese into California, and with the
varied attempts at state control of private enterprise. At
times he was the outstanding figure in the judicial efforts
to solve these problems, while at other times, in so far as
records remain, he was much in the background. Yet the
judges were so intimately associated that the position of
every member of the Court was a matter of importance,
whether he was in the foreground or not.

It has been conventional to assume that if judges were
deeply learned in the law little attention needed to be
given to their learning or their lack of it in the fields of
economics, sociology, and psychology. To some extent
the assumption has been only conventional. Furthermore, it has rarely been possible to attain outstanding
proficiency in law without at the same time acquiring
considerable knowledge of allied fields. Emphasis in the
appraisal of judges, however, has been upon their capacity
to render decisions clearly in harmony with pre-existing
laws. In the great policy-making cases, however, their
economic and social ideas have often seemed far more
important than their stock of legal lore. Such would
seem to have been true of Field and his colleagues in the
numerous cases which had to do with the critical currency problems of the country immediately after the war.

For a time, although his vote was of great importance and his advice may have played a part in determining the policy of the Court, Field was not one of the prominent judges in the judicial controversy. Chase, in the early years, was undoubtedly the star in the performance, with Miller, and, a little later, Strong and Bradley, playing prominent rôles. Then, with the prophetic voice of a great dissenter, Field came to the front, and remained there until he alone of the dissenting group was left to proclaim the coming of tragedy unless the country returned to the wise policy of the fathers.

The trouble began when the representatives of the recently established Republican party found themselves, or thought themselves, unable, either by taxation or by the conventional means of borrowing, to raise money fast enough to carry on the war against the Confederacy. The currency system of the country then consisted of gold and silver, which were used in all monetary transactions by the national government, and of paper money issued by state banks under state laws requiring its redemption in coin on demand. Soon after the war began the state banks found themselves unable to meet the unusual strain, and suspended specie payment. The federal government then had likewise to suspend, in order to protect its supply of gold and silver. For currency it had thereafter to choose between using the notes of state banks in its transactions, and issuing notes of its own.

Chase, then Secretary of the Treasury, was opposed to using the state bank notes. These notes, over-issued and insufficiently protected, had played a part in many financial disasters hitherto, and he favored forcing their withdrawal rather than the extension of their use. He planned to get rid of them by placing on them a gradually increasing federal tax, while their place would be taken by the notes of a newly established national banking system. This program was eventually adopted, though much of the legislation was not passed until after he had left the Treasury and gone to the Supreme Court. While he was Secretary the government, in order to relieve the pressing need for currency, issued so-called irredeemable notes to a final total of $450,000,000, of which $50,000,000 was to be held in reserve. Chase was reluctant to sponsor the issue, but finally concluded that it was necessary to do so.

To secure their acceptance as money the notes, or "greenbacks," as they soon came to be called, were made receivable "in payment of all taxes, internal duties, excises, debts, and demands of every kind due to the United States, except duties on imports, and of all claims and demands against the United States of every kind whatsoever, except for interest upon bonds and notes, which shall be paid in coin; and shall also be lawful money and a legal tender in the payment of all debts, public and private, within the United States, except duties on imports and interest as aforesaid."

The notes circulated in most places without difficulty, but such gold and silver as were still current immediately disappeared. Hopes of preventing depreciation were not realized. Gold sold on the market at a premium the amount of which varied with the successes and failures of the Union armies. Prices leaped to higher levels. People who had contracted debts before the legal tender acts were passed canceled them by paying in depreciated paper money. As had been usual in times of inflation, debtors prospered, while creditors and persons receiving traditionally fixed wages and salaries found themselves losers.

The constitutionality of the legal tender acts was soon questioned in cases arising in a number of state courts. In the first test case, which was tried in New York in

1863, Chase sent David Dudley Field and S. A. Foote to appear before the court for the United States Treasury. George Ticknor Curtis wrote to Chase remonstrating against this attempt to influence a decision of a state court. The New York judges, and Pennsylvania judges before whom a similar case was tried, demonstrated their loyalty by sending word to Chase that they had held the acts valid.[1]

In California the notes were not well received. There the state constitution had forbidden the use of any instrument of credit as money, while a plentiful supply of a substantial circulating medium was furnished by the mines. A sack of gold dust was better than a roll of bills. Many believed that much of the prosperity of the state was due to the fact that the use of paper money was prohibited.[2] Hence, although some greenbacks found their way into the state, they were accepted with great unwillingness. Business men in San Francisco agreed to blacklist and refuse further credit to debtors who insisted on paying their debts in anything but gold and silver. The legislature passed an act to establish the validity of contracts which provided that payments should be made only in coin, and by means of these contracts most business was transacted on a gold basis.

Field was on the state bench at that time, but he carefully avoided expressing any opinion as to the constitutionality of the acts. The subject was mentioned in a case which was argued before him in 1862.[3] A taxpayer had insisted on paying his taxes in greenbacks, and when the collector refused to accept them the taxpayer applied for a mandamus to compel him to do so. Field, speaking

---

[1] Hart, A. B., *Salmon Portland Chase*, p. 389.

[2] See Moses, Bernard, "Legal Tender Notes in California," *Quarterly Journal of Economics*, Vol. VII, pp. 1 ff.

[3] *Perry* v. *Washburn*, 20 Cal. 318.

for the Court, held that taxes were not debts within the meaning of the legal tender acts, and therefore the state could not be compelled to accept paper money in payment of its taxes. He declared that for the purpose of that decision it was not necessary to meet the arguments which had been raised concerning the power of Congress to make government notes a legal tender. "The question is one of great magnitude and importance," he said, "upon which the first legal minds of the country differ; and until it is legitimately and directly before us, we have no disposition—nor indeed would it be proper—to express or even intimate an opinion upon it."

The statement suggests that at this time he at least had considerable doubt as to the constitutionality of the acts. In view of his enthusiasm for the prosecution of the war it seems probable that if he had been whole-heartedly in favor of the acts he would have taken the occasion to place the stamp of his judicial approval upon them—in spite of the apparent intermittent appearance of some squeamishness as to the use of *obiter dicta*.

When the notes were issued few people looked upon them as anything more than a temporary instrument for carrying on the war, and it was expected that they would be redeemed when the emergency was over. This was the firm belief of Chase. "My whole plan," he declared, "has been that of a bullionist and not that of a mere paper money man. I have been obliged by necessity to substitute paper for specie for a time, but I have never lost sight of the necessity of resumption. . . ." [4] When the war closed, in 1865, Chase was on the bench of the Supreme Court, and Hugh McCulloch was Secretary of the Treasury. McCulloch was just as eager as Chase to return to specie payments and get rid of the irredeemable

[4] Letter to S. De Witt Bloodgood, New York, May 9, 1864, in Schuckers, J. W., *Life of Salmon Portland Chase*, p. 402.

paper money. With the consent of Congress he entered upon a policy of gradual withdrawal of the greenbacks. The policy of contraction soon met with strong opposition, however. In the excitement of the era of plentiful money people had recognized new necessities, acquired new luxuries, and learned to live with an extravagance which they had not known before. In the West a great deal of money had been spent for farm equipment of various kinds. All this involved the incurring of new debts. A contraction of the currency would mean that debts would be harder to pay, and strict economy would have to be substituted for the recently acquired habits of spending. Hence, contraction was opposed, and the opposition was justified in terms of any economic theory that seemed to lend plausibility to the contention.[5] Members of Congress, reflecting the sentiment of their constituents, put a stop to the cancelation of the greenbacks.

The sentiment for a plentiful paper currency was not unanimous, however. The various groups of creditors were eager to return to a specie basis as soon as possible, and others who had no immediate interests involved were convinced that the welfare of the country depended upon a contraction of the currency. Feverish speculation, which had been stimulated by the war and by money inflation, still continued. The wealth of the country was being manipulated by a rising group of promoters and speculators, who were undeterred in their get-rich schemes by even minimum standards of business ethics. It was hard to tell what might be the final results in terms of national economic welfare.

An example of the evils which the currency situation made possible was the gold conspiracy in Wall Street,

[5] For a study of this situation see Wildman, M. S., *Money Inflation in the United States.*

in September, 1869, in which Jay Gould and James Fiske, Jr., of the Erie Railroad, cornered the gold market and brought on the panic of "Black Friday." When attempts were made to prosecute them David Dudley Field and his partner manipulated certain corrupt judges with such skill that the Erie men went unpunished. Henry Adams said of David Dudley Field in this instance that "his power over certain judges became so absolute as to impress the popular imagination; and the gossip of Wall Street insisted that he had a silken halter round the neck of Judge Barnard and a hempen one round that of Cardozo." [6]   With the wide-spread corruption of the business world, of the bar, and of the judiciary, of which this example was but one of many, it is not surprising that persons who placed a part or all of the blame upon the inflated currency should urge vigorously the return to a specie basis.

Congress, it would appear, was the body which should have taken action to solve the currency problems. Nevertheless, it failed to act.   In the first place, the problems were too intricate for the understanding of the members. This is not surprising in view of the fact that most of these men were predominantly politicians, while even trained economists were in violent disagreement as to the operation of so-called laws of currency. A second reason for the inactivity of Congress was the fear of loss of prestige with the country. The prospect of the next election was ever in the minds of the legislators. The obsession was deadly to the possibility of vigorous and unbiased activity. The result was that the attempt at a solution was left to the Supreme Court, which was assumed to be purely a judicial body, the members of

[6] Adams, Henry, "The New York Gold Conspiracy," *Historical Essays,* p. 331; reprinted from the *Westminster Review,* October, 1870.

which necessarily had superior training only in the field of law.

Many cases having to do with the financial system of the country came before the Court. The first to challenge the constitutionality of the legal tender acts was *Hepburn* v. *Griswold*,[7] an appeal from a Kentucky court, which was argued in the term of 1867-68 and re-argued December 10, 1868 in order that the government might be represented by counsel in a case of such importance to it. The Court now had only eight members, owing to the death of Justice Wayne the preceding summer. Either no agreement could be reached by the justices or else it was thought unwise to announce any decision at the time. At any rate, the case remained undecided for more than a year after the date of the argument.

During that year, however, the Court disposed of certain other cases dealing with related phases of the problem. In one of these Chief Justice Chase, speaking for a unanimous Court, held that the United States notes were exempt from state taxation, because of the fact that they were obligations of the national government. The quality of these notes as legal tender belonged to another discussion, he said.[8] In another case he held, again speaking for a unanimous Court, that the clause making the notes a legal tender for debts had no reference to taxes levied by the states.[9] In still another he held that a contract made prior to the passage of the legal tender acts calling for payment in "gold and silver coin, lawful money of the United States," could not be fulfilled by the payment of United States notes.[10] Justice Miller

[7] 75 U. S. 603.
[8] *Bank* v. *Supervisors*, 74 U. S. 26.
[9] *Lane County* v. *Oregon*, 74 U. S. 71.
[10] *Bronson* v. *Rodes*, 74 U. S. 229. In *Butler* v. *Horwitz*, 74 U. S. 258, Chase and Miller took the same relative positions as in *Bronson* v. *Rodes*.

dissented, and Justices Swayne and Davis made it clear that while they concurred in the judgment they were not to be bound by any implications that might be drawn from the text of the opinion. This reservation indicated that somewhere in connection with the currency problems there were important points upon which the justices were not agreed. Finally, in *Veazie Bank* v. *Fenno*,[11] Chase upheld the constitutionality of a prohibitive tax upon the note issues of state banks, Justices Nelson and Davis dissenting.

The trend of these decisions was, without passing directly on the legal tender question, to limit the meaning of the acts, and to protect the national banking system which Chase had sponsored. It is significant that Chase chose to write all the opinions himself.

The Hepburn case finally came to a vote. On November 27, 1869, after a discussion in the conference room lasting three or four hours, the justices divided four to four. This meant that the legal tender acts would stand. It had been thought that Justice Grier would vote against the constitutionality of the acts. Had he done so the majority would have been five to three against them. The venerable Justice had grown quite feeble in recent years, and his mind was not as clear as it had been in former times. Some of his colleagues believed that he was voting against his real desires and tried to persuade him to change his vote. He refused to do so, the case was passed over, and another was taken up. It likewise depended on the question of the constitutionality of the legal tender acts.[12] Justice Grier here so voted as to hold the acts unconstitutional. His colleagues tried to show him his inconsistency, and in the end he was persuaded to change his vote in the Hepburn case. The result was to

[11] 75 U. S. 533.
[12] *Broderick's Executor* v. *Magraw*, 75 U. S. 639.

declare the legal tender acts unconstitutional in so far as they applied to contracts made prior to the passage of the acts. A week later the Court, because of Justice Grier's mental condition, delegated a committee, of which Field was one,[13] to urge him to resign from the bench. Said Justice Miller, writing for himself and the other dissenting justices, Swayne and Davis, "these are the facts. We make no comment. We do not say that he did not agree to the opinion. We only ask, of what value was his concurrence, and of what value is the judgment under such circumstances?" [14]

Justice Grier took the advice of his colleagues and resigned. His resignation stated that he was to leave the bench February 1, 1870. The majority opinion on the Hepburn case was written by Chief Justice Chase, and was read and agreed to in conference January 29. It would have been delivered two days later as a five to three decision of the Court had it not been delayed a week to give time for the preparation of the dissenting opinion.[15] It was delivered on February 4. Since Grier had now departed it stood technically as a four to three decision.

Chase pointed out in his opinion that the federal government was one of delegated powers, and that the Constitution contained no specific grant of power to make notes or bills of credit a legal tender for debts which had already been contracted. He argued further that such a measure was not a means appropriate, plainly adapted, or really calculated to carry into effect any express power vested in Congress, and that it was incon-

---

[13] Hughes, Charles E., *The Supreme Court of the United States*, p. 76.

[14] Except for the clause above noted the facts of this paragraph are taken from the *Miscellaneous Writings of the Late Hon. Joseph P. Bradley*, edited by Charles Bradley, pp. 73-74.

[15] Chase's statement in *Knox* v. *Lee*, 79 U. S. 457, 572.

sistent with the spirit of the Constitution and was prohibited by it. It had been strenuously argued that the legal tender acts had been a part of the exercising of the war powers of the government. Chase attempted to refute this argument by declaring at length that the notes would have circulated as money if they had not been made legal tender, and hence that the legal tender provision was not essential. Notes that were not made legal tender circulated along with the greenbacks during the war, he said, and did not depreciate below them.

It is a significant commentary on the issues of the case that Chase, unable to support his statements either by exact provisions of law or an unquestionable array of facts, was compelled to rely on such arguments as begin with "All modern history testifies. . . ," and "It is denied by eminent writers. . . ." His decision in very large part rested upon neither law nor provable facts, but upon the economic theories which he held.

To some extent it must have been embarrassing to him to have to attack the position which he had defended when he was Secretary of the Treasury. He attempted to explain his change of views in the following statement—"felicitous language," [16] Field called it:

"It is not surprising that amid the tumult of the late Civil War, and under the influence of apprehensions for the safety of the Republic almost universal, different views, never before entertained by American statesmen or jurists, were adopted by many. The time was not favorable to considerate reflection upon the constitutional limits of legislative or executive authority. If power was assumed from patriotic motives, the assumption found ready justification in patriotic hearts. Many who doubted yielded their doubts; many who did not doubt were silent. Some who were strongly averse to making gov-

[16] *Reminiscences*, p. 157.

ernment notes a legal tender felt themselves constrained to acquiesce in the views of the advocates of the measure. Not a few who then insisted upon its necessity, or acquiesced in that view, have, since the return of peace, and under the influence of calmer time, reconsidered their conclusions, and now concur in those which we have just announced. These conclusions seems to us to be fully sanctioned by the letter and spirit of the Constitution."

Justices Nelson, Clifford, and Field concurred with Chase. Miller dissented, speaking for himself and for Swayne and Davis. He attempted to prove that the legal tender acts were necessary incidents to the war powers which were specifically granted to Congress. After describing the general situation at the beginning of the war he said: "A general collapse of credit, of payment, and of business seemed inevitable, in which faith in the ability of the government would have been destroyed, the rebellion would have triumphed, the states would have been left divided, and the people impoverished. The national government would have perished, and with it, the Constitution which we are now called upon to construe with such nice and critical accuracy.

"That the legal tender acts prevented these disastrous results, and that the tender clause was necessary to prevent them, I entertain no doubt." [17]

Government paper money which was not made a legal tender would not have met the needs of the situation, he argued. "What was needed was something more than the credit of the government. That had been stretched to its utmost tension, and was clearly no longer sufficient in the simple form of borrowing money." His argument on this point, like that of Chase, was weakened by the necessity of resorting to such generalities as begin with "All experience proves. . . ." The fact that the

[17] 75 U. S. 633.

government notes had retained some value instead of depreciating to nothing was due, he said, to the fact that "when by law they were made to discharge the function of paying debts, they had a perpetual credit or value, equal to the amount of all the debts, public and private, in the country. If they were never redeemed, as they never have been, they still paid debts at their par value, and for this purpose were then, and always have been, eagerly sought by the people."

The real division in the Court was upon the merits of conflicting financial policies. Justice Miller, along with the masses of the people in the section of the country from which he came, looked upon the greenbacks as a great economic panacea. Chief Justice Chase, feeling responsibility for their having been issued, saw the evils which he had hoped to prevent had come to pass, and that there was no probability that Congress would take action to check them. He concluded that any measure having the results which seemed to have come from the legal tender acts could not be necessary to the execution of any of the powers conferred by the Constitution— that the acts could not be constitutional. One of his biographers says dogmatically: "The real difficulty with the decision was that it was an attempt to make up for the failure of Congress to bring the country back to a specie basis; in view of the probable shock of an immediate change it seems very unlikely that the decision would ever have been pronounced, had McCulloch been allowed to continue his contraction policy so that the defects of the system might gradually have righted themselves." [18] Full and complete proof of this statement could not easily be gathered, but there was a great deal of circumstantial evidence in its support.

[18] Hart, *Salmon Portland Chase*, p. 398.

Sentiment was sharply divided over the legal tender question.[19] A year earlier it had been said that "nearly everybody who has opened his mouth on the legal tender question for three or four years back has been suspected of prejudice or passion or selfishness in all he said about it."[20] This was no less true now. Chase was bitterly criticized in official circles for his change of front and his condemnation of "irredeemable paper currency."[21] Although the decision applied only to contracts made prior to the date of the legal tender acts much of the reasoning was also applicable to contracts made afterwards, and it was suggested that the Supreme Court was watching the effects of the decision before taking the final plunge and declaring the acts unconstitutional for all contracts. "Should this occur," said a prominent newspaper, "the theory and effects of contraction will receive an illustration of a crucial character. But we wish to raise our voice in emphatic protest against the country's being mangled and slaughtered, while the Supreme Court is making experiment upon the laws of currency."[22] On February 9 Senator Wilson introduced a bill to increase the membership of the Court to ten,[23] hoping presumably to bring about a reversal of the decision.

The personnel of the Court was to be changed without further action from Congress. Shortly after the beginning of President Grant's term an act had been passed to raise the membership of the Court to nine

[19] See comments in Warren, Charles, *The Supreme Court in United States History*, Vol. III, Chap. XXXI.

[20] The *Nation*, Feb. 25, 1869.

[21] See the Boston *Daily Advertiser*, Feb. 9, 1870.

[22] *Ibid*.

[23] *Cong. Globe*, 41st Cong., 2d Sess., p. 1128.

justices. The President had appointed his Attorney-General, Ebenezer Rockwood Hoar, to the vacant seat left by Justice Wayne, but the appointment was rejected by the Senate. In December, after Justice Grier had resigned but before he had left the bench, the President had appointed Edwin M. Stanton to take his place. Stanton died, however, four days after his appointment was confirmed, and Grier, after attending the funeral of his intended successor, returned to his place on the bench. The President made no further appointments until Grier had withdrawn.

On February 7, the date on which the legal tender case was decided, President Grant sent to the Senate the names of two appointees to the existing vacancies. They were William Strong of Pennsylvania, and Joseph P. Bradley of New Jersey. Strong had been a judge of the Supreme Court of Pennsylvania for eleven years and had written an opinion upholding the constitutionality of the legal tender acts. Bradley was a prominent and able lawyer, who had included the Camden and Amboy Railroad among his clients. He was thought to believe the legal tender acts to be constitutional. It was freely asserted at that time that railroad interests wanted the legal tender decision reversed, so that the corporations would be able to pay in greenbacks the debts which they owed in bonds issued prior to the date of the legal tender acts.[24]

It was widely and vigorously asserted for many years that President Grant appointed the two men for the purpose of changing the position of the Court on the legal tender acts. Many pages have been written to prove that the President did not know and could not have known what the decision of the Court was at the time

[24] Schuckers, *Life of Salmon Portland Chase*, p. 260.

he sent in the appointments.[25] However, one of the members of the Cabinet knew in advance what the decision would be, and there is no proof that he kept the knowledge to himself. Two weeks before the decision was given Chase called on George S. Boutwell, Secretary of the Treasury, and told him what the decision would be. He said his reason for sharing the secret with Boutwell was that he anticipated serious financial disturbances when the decision was given, and he wished the Secretary to be prepared in advance.[26]

Whether or not the appointments were made with the legal tender acts in mind, it is now generally recognized that there were relatively few able lawyers and judges to select from who did not accept the acts as constitutional.

Strong became a member of the Court on March 14, 1870, and Bradley took his seat March 24. At that time there were on the docket two cases, *Latham* v. *United States*[27] and *Deming* v. *United States*,[27] the decisions in which depended in part upon the status of the legal tender acts. At an earlier date the Chief Justice had been about to assign a date for hearing the arguments in the Latham case when Justice Miller requested that the matter be postponed until it could be taken up in conference. In the conference room he pointed out that the legal tender question was involved, and expressed the hope that the cases would not be taken up until the two vacancies on the bench were filled. Chase said he thought the legal tender question was settled, but his colleagues did not commit themselves. On March 25, the day after Bradley took his seat, Attorney-General Hoar moved

[25] See, for example, Hoar, George F., *The Charge Against President Grant and Attorney General Hoar.*

[26] Boutwell, G. S., *Reminiscences of Sixty Years in Public Affairs,* Vol. II, p. 209.

[27] 76 U. S. 145.

that the Latham and Deming cases be set down for
argument, and suggested a reconsideration of the legal
tender question. In conference on the following day it
was decided by a vote of five to four to grant the reconsideration of the question, the two new justices voting
with the three who had dissented in the Hepburn case.

The argument was scheduled for April 4. Prior to the
session on the following Monday, when the order for
the argument would have been announced, Chase showed
to the other justices a letter which he had received from
James M. Carlisle, one of the counsel, claiming that the
legal tender phase of the cases had been settled by the
Hepburn case. On the following Thursday the Court
heard the Attorney-General and Carlisle on this point.
On Friday an order was issued providing that the arguments in the cases should be heard on April 11, Chase
announcing that he, Nelson, Clifford, and Field dissented
from the order. He based the dissent in part upon the
allegation that the action was a violation of a rule of the
Court which provided that a question which had been
settled by the Court should not be reopened unless justices
who had voted for the decision favored a rehearing.[28]

The events of April 11 were in sharp contrast with the
usual dull routine of court-room procedure. As described
by a newspaper reporter who was present, "There was a
very lively scene at the Supreme Court this morning, the
oldest lawyers practicing there having witnessed nothing
like it in their day. It arose in connection with the legal
tender case which it was expected would be again argued
on its merits. At the proper hour Mr. Potter of New
York, who is counsel in one of the cases on which the
Court had consented to hear further argument, in effect

[28] The facts of this and the preceding paragraph are gathered from
Schuckers, *Life of Salmon Portland Chase*, Chap. XXVIII, and from pages
63 to 70 of the Bradley *Miscellaneous Writings*.

asked for a postponement for the reason that the senior counsel was engaged elsewhere and another was absent on account of illness. The Attorney-General responded against postponement and in the course of his remarks spoke of the necessity for an early hearing and decision, because the country is disturbed and will continue to be disturbed until the whole question at issue is settled. He also alluded to the fact that these two cases involve points somewhat like those in the case recently decided, and in reply to Mr. Potter denied that any order had been made which precluded a rehearing on the point then decided.

"The Chief Justice here interrupted to say that according to his recollection, such an order had been made.

"This was said with evident feeling, and Justice Miller remarked with equal feeling, that he knew of no such order.

"Justice Nelson came to the rescue of the Chief Justice, and Justice Davis spoke up, saying he concurred with Justice Miller. The Chief Justice repeated his statement with emphasis and hardly-suppressed passion, and then upon the suggestion of Judge Davis, who remarked that it was not worth while to bandy words, it was decided that the case might go over to next Monday.

"The Attorney-General in the meantime bowed to the recollection of the Chief Justice, and merely expressed his regret that in a matter of this importance there was no record.

"The point on which this dispute, so astonishing in the Supreme Court, turns, seems to be, whether there was or was not such an order made when Mr. Evarts was Attorney-General, as prevents a further hearing on the question whether the legal tender act applies to debts contracted before its passage." [29]

[29] Boston *Daily Advertiser*, April 12, 1870.

A week later a crowd gathered in the court room to
hear the argument of the cases, the controversy between
the judges having achieved great notoriety. Another
case was being argued, however, and the Latham and
Deming cases were not reached. The talk about the
Court was that the justices had settled their differences.[30]
When the cases came up two days later counsel for the
appellants requested that they be dismissed. Justices
Miller and Bradley expressed doubt that the appellants
had a right to withdraw at this time, whereupon the
Court, evidently determined to have no more public
scenes, left the room for a conference. There only
Justice Bradley strongly urged refusal to grant the
request.[31] The Court returned and announced that it
was unanimously decided that the appellants might
withdraw, and the cases were therefore dismissed.[32]

Although these cases were removed from the docket
the proceedings had been effective notice to the country
that the legal tender decision would be reversed at the first
opportunity. Chase believed that the opposing justices
had intended to bring about this result. He was unwilling that his version of all that had happened should
remain untold, so he prepared a statement for himself
and for Nelson, Clifford, and Field, in which he gave an
account of the events of the recent months and intimated
strongly that the Supreme Court had been packed for the
purpose of reversing the legal tender decision. He filed
this statement with the records of the Court. Thereupon
Miller prepared, for signature by Swayne, Davis, Bradley,
Strong, and himself, a statement in which he attempted
to refute the charges, and showed the efforts of the Chief

[30] *Ibid.*, April 19, 1870.
[31] Shuckers, *Life of Salmon Portland Chase*, p. 264.
[32] 76 U. S. 145.

Justice to prevent a reconsideration of the legal tender question. When he heard that the other statement was being prepared Chase withdrew his own, so that neither remained with the Court. Most of his own statement was published four years later as a chapter in his biography,[33] while the other appeared more than thirty years later in the published papers of Justice Bradley. The bitter feeling among the justices which prevailed at that time and which is evidenced by these papers has probably never been surpassed in the history of the Court.

The annual term of the Court came to a close without further significant efforts toward the solution of the legal tender problem. There was relief in Washington that the matter was dropped for the time. Newspaper and magazine articles indicate that there was widespread feeling that the Court was going outside its province in meddling with the problem at all. Some held that "it is a great error to suppose that we can with safety rely upon a court to employ a legislative function and restore the country to specie payments."[34] Others agreed with Henry Adams that "no one who holds strong convictions against legal tender as a measure of finance is likely to trouble his mind with the question whether such a power has or has not been conferred by the Constitution upon Congress. Though it were conferred in the most specific terms language is capable of supplying, there could be no excuse on that account for changing an opinion as to its financial merits; and its financial merits are not a subject for lawyers, or even for judges, as such, to decide. These happily rest on principles deeper than statute or than constitutional law. They appeal to no written code; and whenever the public attempts to over-

[33] Schuckers, *Life of Salmon Portland Chase*, Chap. XXVIII.
[34] *Harper's Weekly*, April 16, 1870.

rule them, the public does so at its own peril." [35]   Still others felt that, whatever the intrinsic merits of the controversy, it would be exceedingly bad form for the Court to reopen the question and possibly flatly reverse the position which it has taken. Such action would lower the prestige of the Court. It would violate popular conceptions of the consistency of its decisions by showing the influence of particular individuals on the bench, as contrasted with the influence of abiding principles of law.[36]

At the next term of the Court the legal tender question came up again, in two cases, *Parker* v. *Davis* [37] and *Knox* v. *Lee,*[37] usually referred to as the legal tender cases, which had been held over from the previous year. It was known by all the justices that the question was almost sure to be reopened, but some apparently sought to delay the cases while others wanted to get at them as soon as possible. The justices who had formerly been in the minority resented the attempts which were made to postpone the arguments. When on April 12, 1871, they

[35] Adams, Henry, "The Legal-Tender Act," *Historical Essays*, p. 315; reprinted from the *North American Review*, April, 1870.

Adams got a great many of his ideas directly from Chase, with whom he became intimate, and for whom he had a high personal regard. He said of the Chief Justice: ˙ "Like all strong-willed and self asserting men, Mr. Chase had the faults of his qualities. He was never easy to drive in harness, or light in hand. He saw vividly what was wrong, and did not always allow for what was relatively right. He loved power as though he were still a senator. . . . Legal tender caused no great pleasure or pain in the sum of life to a newspaper correspondent, but it served as a subject for letters, and the Chief Justice was very willing to win an ally in the press who would tell his story as he wished it to be read."—*The Education of Henry Adams*, p. 250.

[36] See a collection of such comments in Warren, *The Supreme Court in United States History*, Vol. III, Chap. XXXI.

[37] 79 U. S. 457.

were put off because of the illness of Justice Nelson,
Justice Swayne filed a statement telling of the many
delays that had already taken place and saying, "It is due
to this Court and to the public, that both of these cases
shall be decided, and the important question which they
present be put at rest as speedily as can be done with
propriety. It is to be hoped that the early restoration of
the health of Mr. Justice Nelson will enable us to hear the
further argument and announce our conclusion within
the residue of the term." [38]

On the question as to whether the legal tender issue
should be raised in these cases the Court again divided
five to four, with the same alignment of particular individuals. The arguments were finally heard, and on May
1, 1872, still another time with the same five to four
alignment, it was decided that the legal tender acts were
constitutional as to contracts made both before and after
the acts were passed. In order to give full time for the
preparation of the opinions they were not read until
January 15, 1873.

Justice Strong gave the opinion of the Court. He held
that the existence of a power might be inferred not only
because it was appropriate to the exercise of some other
power which was specifically granted—such as that of
carrying on war, or borrowing or coining money—but
also from a grouping of powers already conferred. Since
the legal tender acts played a part in providing money for
carrying on the war he declared that they were constitutional unless they were forbidden by the Constitution.
To show the part which the acts had played in the
conduct of the war he traced briefly the financial history
of the war period and then said in summary:

"Something revived the drooping faith of the people;
something brought immediately to the government's aid

[38] *United States Reports*, 20 Law. Ed., pp. 290-91.

the resources of the nation, and something enabled the successful prosecution of the war, and the preservation of the national life. What was it, if not the legal tender enactments?"

He agreed that previous decisions of the Court should not be indiscriminately over-ruled, but pointed out that the reversal of decisions was not unknown, either in this country or in England. The decision in the Hepburn case had been rendered by a less number of judges than the law provided, while the case at hand had been heard and decided by a full Court. In view of the far-reaching consequences of the decision the Court felt obliged to speak in justification of the legal status of the acts.

Justice Bradley wrote a concurring opinion, agreeing with Justice Strong and holding in addition that since the United States government was a national government it possessed as an attribute of sovereignty the power to issue paper money and to make it a legal tender. Chief Justice Chase and Justices Nelson, Clifford, and Field stood together, as they had done from the beginning. All but Nelson wrote long dissenting opinions. Something of the nature of the arguments and of the panorama of logical display can be learned by an examination of the forty-seven page opinion written by Field. He had voted consistently with Chase throughout the controversy, but, hot-tempered and opinionated as he was inclined to be at times, he had thus far said little on the subject in public. In this opinion he expressed himself with force and eloquence. The opening paragraphs stated his position:

"Nothing has been heard from counsel in these cases, and nothing from the present majority of the Court, which has created a doubt in my mind of the correctness of the judgment rendered in the case of *Hepburn* v. *Griswold*, or of the conclusions expressed in the opinion of the majority of the Court as then constituted. That judgment was reached only after repeated arguments were heard from able and eminent counsel, and after every point raised on either side had been the subject of extended deliberation.

"The questions presented in that case were also involved in several other cases, and had been elaborately argued in them. It is not extravagant to say that no case has ever been decided by this Court since its organization, in which the questions presented were more fully argued or more maturely considered. It was hoped that a judgment thus reached would not lightly be disturbed. It was hoped that it had settled forever that under a constitution ordained, among other things, 'to establish justice,' legislation giving to one person the right to discharge his obligations to another by nominal instead of actual fulfilment, could never be justified.

"I shall not comment upon the causes which have led to a reversal of that judgment. They are patent to every one. I will simply say that the Chief Justice and the associate justices, who constituted the majority of the Court when that judgment was rendered, still adhere to their former convictions. To them the reasons for the original decision are as cogent and convincing now as they were when that decision was pronounced; and to them its justice, as applied to past contracts, is as clear today as it was then."

He argued at great length, as Chase had done in the Hepburn case, to show that the legal tender quality of the greenbacks had contributed nothing to the assistance of the government. "Without the legal tender provision the notes would have circulated equally well and answered all the purposes of the government—the only direct benefit resulting from that provision arising . . . from the ability it conferred upon unscrupulous debtors to discharge with them previous obligations." Since the

power to make the notes a legal tender gave no assistance
in the exercising of the powers specifically granted by the
Constitution it did not belong to the national government—which was a government of delegated powers.
He referred rather scornfully to the "general and loose
statements" of his opponents, and promised to confine
himself to a discussion of the powers conferred by the
Constitution. In a short time, however, he found himself
discussing, not law, but the confused economic facts and
theories involved in the operation of the legal tender acts.
He called himself back by saying, "It is foreign, however,
to my argument to discuss the utility of the legal tender
clause. The utility of a measure is not the subject of
judicial cognizance, nor, as already intimated, the test of
its constitutionality." Continually, however, he found
himself carried away again into the field of economics,
where he discussed not constitutional law but what he
called a "universal law of currency."

He stressed heavily the subject of the impairment of
the obligation of contracts. The Constitution did not
specifically deny to the federal government the power of
such impairment, but he was sure that it was denied by
implication. He thought that the payment of money
owed by the government in a medium cheaper than that
used at the time the obligation was incurred was a form
of repudiation. "Repudiation in any form, or to any
extent, would be dishonor, and for the commission of this
public crime no warrant, in my judgment, can ever be
found in that instrument [the Constitution]." Though
he did not use the terms it is evident that his conceptions
of natural rights were again playing their part in his
judicial work.

He had less to say about the constitutionality of the
legal tender acts as they affected contracts made after
their enactment, but he thought them bad even here.

The greenbacks were widely in use, but not to the same extent everywhere, as for example in the "Pacific States, where the constitutional currency has always continued in use." It was the duty of Congress to provide a uniform standard of value. He did not see how this could be maintained with the fluctuating notes. They were merely promises to pay, and their value depended upon the confidence entertained by the public in their ultimate payment. Their value could never be uniform throughout the Union, but would be different in different portions of the country; "one value in New York, another at New Orleans, and still a different one at San Francisco."

His final paragraph contained an eloquent peroration: "I do not yield to anyone in honoring and reverencing the noble and patriotic men who were in the councils of the nation during the terrible struggle with the rebellion. To them belong the greatest of all glories in our history,— that of having saved the Union, and that of having emancipated a race. For these results they will be remembered and honored so long as the English language is spoken or read among men. But I do not admit that a blind approval of every measure which they may have thought essential to put down the rebellion is any evidence of loyalty to the country. The only loyalty which I can admit consists in obedience to the Constitution and the laws made in pursuance of it. It is only by obedience that affection and reverence can be shown to a superior having a right to command. So thought our great Master when he said to his disciples: 'If ye love me, keep my commandments.'"

Had Field been free frankly to ground his arguments on facts and theories of finance, from which it is quite apparent that they were derived, rather than upon doctrines of constitutional law, they would have stood out

with greater clearness. In spite of his superior qualities
as a logician he was unable gracefully to perform the feat
in logical gymnastics which he had set for himself, and
his opinion as written is by no means free from confusion.
It can only be said that his colleagues were no more successful. The justices, specialists in the interpretation of
law, were performing a legislative function in the field
of finance, but were compelled by tradition to conceal
the fact behind an embankment of legal terminology.

The fact that Field, in his last paragraph, by implication tried to ground his discussion in the appeals of
religion, leads back to the subject of how much he
resembled the old minister at Stockbridge. Such appeals
would have some effect upon countless people who would
never follow or would be untouched by legal and economic reasoning. For this reason his Yankee shrewdness
may have led him to use them. But his resemblance to
his father goes deeper than that. He was arguing about
matters concerning which he had deep convictions, and
in terms of principles which he deemed fundamental and
abiding. His task was not unlike that of the minister in
the pulpit, and psychologically it is not surprising that
when he sought to express his deep convictions he turned
to the ideology in which in the days of his boyhood such
convictions had been customarily phrased. It may be
said, of course, that if the paragraph reveals economic
arguments taking shelter behind the rhetorical trappings
of both law and religion it is not the first time that such
a technique has been used. Nevertheless there remains
the suggestion that as the minister saw in religion a set
of principles and a body of doctrine which, interpreted
with due care, would serve as an unerring guide to the
solution of almost any problem, so Justice Field saw
similar possibilities in the law. He never doubted the

correctness of his own interpretation. Here, perhaps, is the source of the ringing finality of many of his dissenting opinions.

The reversal of the decision of the Court produced elation in some quarters and bitter disappointment in others. Apart from the particular issue involved the reversal impaired the prestige of the Supreme Court, an institution that, in spite of the criticism that was poured out upon it from time to time, was still guarded by a halo of sanctity. When dissentions arose within the Court, tending to dispel the halo, cries of resentment and protest went up from the devotees. The atmosphere of sanctity around the Court, which had been created by a variety of influences over a long period of years, was presumably an asset in that it gave weight to the decisions of the Court. At times, however, it was a liability, in that it tended to prevent the Court from being seen and understood as a very human institution, made up of men who, save for a presumably superior training in law, were little different from thousands of their fellows. It was also a liability in that it played a part in compelling the justices to couch in terms of constitutional law and judicial precedents arguments which had their basis in the field of economics, and which were good or bad depending not upon any erudite knowledge of law, but rather upon the interpretation of economic conditions.

Although each of the justices retained the conviction that he had been "right" in his respective position and his opponents had been wrong, the worst of the friction among them gradually disappeared. Chase, however, felt very deeply on the subject of his defeat. He asked Boutwell, Secretary of the Treasury, why he had permitted the appointment of judges to over-rule him. He expressed great dissatisfaction with his life and labors on the bench, and said that if it were possible he should be glad to exchange positions with Boutwell.[39]

The legal tender decision which was of major importance to the country had now been made. Other cases growing out of the legal tender acts were, however, to come before the Court. Field read a majority opinion holding that a contract which called for payment "in specie" meant payment in gold or silver, rather than in United States notes, and could be enforced.[40] Miller and Bradley dissented. In another case Miller gave the opinion of the Court, upholding the legal tender decision.[41] Field, of course, dissented. "We have recently had occasion to express on this subject our views at large," he said, "and to them we adhere. We have considered with great deliberation the views of the majority, who differ from us, and we are unable to yield our assent to them. With all proper deference and respect for our brethren, we are constrained to say that, in our judgment, the doctrines advanced in their opinions on this subject are not only in conflict with the teachings of all the statesmen and jurists of the country up to a recent period, and at variance with the uniform practice of the government for nearly three-quarters of a century, but that they tend to break down the barriers which separate a government of limited powers from a government resting in the unrestrained will of Congress."

Chase and Clifford concurred in this unyielding affirmation of the position which they had taken in the Hepburn case, and had held ever since. If Nelson voted in the case he went over to the majority.

---

[39] Boutwell, *Reminiscences of Sixty Years in Public Affairs*, Vol. II, p. 210.

[40] *Trebilcock* v. *Wilson*, 79 U. S. 687.

[41] *Dooley* v. *Smith*, 80 U. S. 604.

Shortly afterward the Court heard arguments in another case which showed in striking fashion the evils of a fluctuating currency.[42] Damages had been awarded in a lower court for property destroyed by a collision of two canal boats. The value of the property was estimated in gold, but the Court did not specify that the damages were to be paid in gold. Greenbacks, then much depreciated, were offered but were not accepted, and the matter was carried to the United States Circuit Court. That Court issued an order that the damages be paid in greenbacks, and fixed the amount at a total of greenbacks which at that time was equal to the assessment in gold. An appeal was taken to the Supreme Court, which ordered the payment of the greenbacks at the figure set by the Circuit Court, although by this time paper money had so appreciated as greatly to increase the indemnity.

Field and Clifford joined with Chase in a dissenting opinion in which he pointed out what seemed to him the obvious injustice of rendering judgments payable in legal tender currency. Hardly anything fluctuated more than such judgments, he said. Every day witnessed a change. The judgment debtor gained by depreciation and lost by appreciation. There was no reason why such judgments should not be entered originally for payment in coin, in which case justice would be done to all parties. Chase's opinion, indeed, might almost be interpreted as a message to the lower courts telling them how they might avert some of the evils which flowed from the legal tender acts.

In the following year the Court decided another legal tender case on the basis of previous decisions, and again the three minority justices held to their dissent.[43] Chase

---

[42] *The Vaughan and Telegraph,* 81 U. S. 258.
[43] *Railroad Co.* v. *Johnson,* 82 U. S. 195.

died before the next case was decided, but Field and Clifford held staunchly to their positions.[44]

In the meantime the money policy of the government remained a live subject of controversy throughout the country. Arguments ranged all the way from those which demanded an immediate return to a hard money basis and the retirement of the greenbacks, to those which called for further liberal issues of paper money. When the slump in business occurred in the fall of 1873, following the panic which began with the collapse of Jay Cooke's banking house, a return to a specie basis became increasingly difficult. The next session of Congress was given over almost wholly to a discussion of the currency problem. The debates, not wholly unlike the opinions of the justices of the Supreme Court, were excellent examples of the rationalizing ingenuity of men in finding economic doctrines to support the legislation which they desired. The widespread demand for more paper money, coming chiefly from the South and West, finally secured the enactment of a bill which provided that enough additional notes should be issued to bring the total in circulation up to $400,000,000. Creditor groups organized in vigorous opposition to the bill. They were greatly relieved when it was vetoed by President Grant. It was not passed over the veto. Its enactment had marked the high tide of the struggle for an enlarged circulation of paper money. Agitation for more greenbacks did not cease, but the disposal of those already in circulation provided the highly controversial currency problem of the years immediately following.

The population of the country continued to grow, and in spite of the pinch of hard times during the decade

[44] *Maryland* v. *Railroad Co.*, 89 U. S. 105.

of the seventies industrial and agricultural activities continued to expand, bringing the need for a larger supply of a circulating medium of exchange. No more paper money was issued, and confidence in the credit and good faith of the government became more firmly established. Hence the greenbacks slowly appreciated in value, and the problem of returning to specie payments became less and less difficult. On January 14, 1875, a bill was passed providing that beginning January 1, 1879, greenbacks should be redeemed in coin upon presentation.[45] It was not stated whether the notes, once they had been redeemed, could be reissued. An act of May 31, 1878, provided that when the notes were returned to the Treasury they might be reissued from time to time, as the exigencies of the public interest might require.[46] While popular agitation for a plentiful money supply was finding futile expression in the greenback party movement, which gradually merged into the free silver controversy, this act of 1878 provided one more important legal tender case for the Supreme Court. The case, *Juilliard* v. *Greenman*,[47] was decided in March, 1884.

By this time only Field remained to represent the minority justices, and only Miller and Bradley remained from the majority which had reversed the Hepburn case decision. The legal tender issue was not as fresh as it had once been. It had been in existence for a number of years, and nothing startling seemed to have happened as a result of it. Whether or not the existing currency arrangement was in harmony with the logic of the Constitution and with judicial utterances in the past, it was a practical working arrangement, and although it was

---

[45] 18 Stat. 296.
[46] 20 Stat. 87.
[47] 110 U. S. 421.

not without opposition it was generally accepted
throughout the country. Hence it is not greatly surprising that if one group of justices had strained a bit
their power of constitutional interpretation to uphold
the legal tender acts as they applied to a war-time emergency, another group now stretched their power a bit
further, and upheld the right of the government to issue
legal tender notes in time of peace.

Justice Gray, successor to Justice Clifford, gave the
opinion of the Court. He held that the government had
the power of issuing legal tender notes not only as a
resulting power from the powers specifically granted,
but also as an attribute of sovereignty. The states had
no power of coining and issuing money; therefore it must
be inferred that the power resided in the federal
government.

This time there was no wrangling in the Court. Nine
members were present, and all who had come to the
bench since the decision in the legal tender cases voted
with the majority. Field, the one minority justice, read
a dissenting opinion in which no former colleague
remained to concur. There was no note of surrender in
what he had to say. In so far as he argued the case in
detail his reasoning was similar to that which he had
used twelve years earlier, but the tone of his opinion was
not quite the same. It was not written with the restraint
of its predecessor. His earnestness and intensity of
expression were redoubled, and it is hard to believe that
exasperation and anger were not rumbling in undertone
to the ringing prophecy that change in the position of
the Court would yet come, or else evil for the country
would befall. He began:

"From the judgment of the Court in this case, and
from all the positions advanced in its support, I dissent.
The question of the power of Congress to impart the

quality of legal tender to the notes of the United States, and thus make them money and a standard of value, is not new here. Unfortunately it has been too frequently before the Court, and its latest decision, previous to this one, has never been entirely accepted and approved by the country. Nor should this excite surprise; for whenever it is declared that this government, ordained to establish justice, has the power to alter the condition of contracts between private parties, and authorize their payment or discharge in something different from that which the parties stipulated, thus disturbing the relations of commerce and the business of the community generally, the doctrine will not and ought not to be readily accepted. There will be many who will adhere to the teachings and abide by the faith of their fathers. So the question has come again, and will continue to come until it is settled so as to uphold and not impair the contracts of parties, to promote and not defeat justice."

He declared that if there was anything in the history of the Constitution which could be established with moral certainty it was that the framers of that instrument intended to prohibit the issue of legal tender notes both by the general government and by the states. He discussed the financial history of the country to show the working of the "universal law of currency," using Justice Story, Chief Justice Marshall, George Bancroft, Daniel Webster, and Chief Justice Chase as his authorities. He declared that the legal tender measure was passed as one of over-ruling necessity in a perilous crisis of the country. Now it was advocated as one that might be adopted at any time. "Never before was it contended by any jurist or commentator on the Constitution that the government, in full receipt of ample income, with a treasury overflowing, with more money on hand than it knows what to do with, could issue paper money as a

legal tender. What in 1862 was called the 'medicine of
the Constitution' has now become its daily bread. So it
always happens that whenever a wrong principle of conduct, political or personal, is adopted on a plea of
necessity, it will be afterwards followed on a plea of
convenience."

He denounced the argument that the power of issuing
the notes belonged to the government as an incident of
sovereignty. There was no such thing as a power of
inherent sovereignty in the government of the United
States. It was a government exclusively of delegated
powers. Sovereignty resided in the people, and Congress could exercise no power which the people had not,
through the Constitution, entrusted to it. Anyway, he
doubted whether the power of issuing the legal tender
notes was necessarily an attribute of sovereignty. "The
power to commit violence, perpetrate injustice, take
private property by force without compensation to the
owner, and compel the receipt of promises to pay in place
of money, may be exercised, as it often has been, by irresponsible authority, but it cannot be considered as
belonging to a government founded upon law."

Again and again throughout the opinion he alluded to
the fact that the government was founded to "establish
justice," while now justice was being violated by acts
which permitted the impairment of contracts between
private parties. It seemed so obvious to him that the
strict observance of the provisions of contracts was a
fundamental principle of justice that the fact needed
no proof at all. "Mr. Madison," he said, "in one of the
articles in the *Federalist,* declared that laws impairing
the obligation of contracts were contrary to the first
principles of the social compact, and to every principle
of sound legislation. Yet this Court holds that a measure
directly operating upon and necessarily impairing private

contracts, may be adopted in the execution of powers specifically granted for other purposes, because it is not in terms prohibited, and that it is consistent with the letter and spirit of the Constitution."

With no abatement of earnestness he brought his argument to a close: "From the decision of the Court I see only evil likely to follow. There have been times within the memory of all of us when the legal tender notes of the United States were not exchangeable for more than one-half of their nominal value. The possibility of such depreciation will always attend paper money. This inborn infirmity no mere legislative declaration can cure. If Congress has the power to make the notes a legal tender and to pass as money or its equivalent, why should not a sufficient amount be issued to pay the bonds of the United States as they mature? Why pay interest on the millions of dollars of bonds now due, when Congress can in one day make the money to pay the principal? And why should there be any restraint upon unlimited appropriations by the government for all imaginary schemes of public improvement, if the printing press can furnish the money that is needed for them?"

Here, as in many of Field's other opinions, a conception of relativity seemed to have no place. Either a certain thing must happen or an alternative of a particular kind, usually one very much to be dreaded, must follow. The possibility of a great many other types of adjustment than those which he detailed seemed never to have occurred to him. It did not necessarily follow, as subsequent history has shown, that if a certain amount in legal tender notes was issued the amount would be increased and its value would depreciate indefinitely. Logically that might have happened, but more than the logic of a few chosen principles must be taken into account in predicting the future. The Supreme Court did not set the limit to the issue of notes, but, some time later, Congress did set such a limit. Field took no account of this possibility in his predictions. He might well have achieved greater accuracy had he remembered that the Supreme Court was only one of a great many instruments of control which would play a part in determining the financial policies of the country. This is not to suggest that he was in any sense naïve, but only to indicate that in the tireless pursuit of the solutions of problems through the application of legal principles by the courts he tended to over-emphasize the importance of selected principles, and to disregard too much the determining influence of the whole welter of human experience.

Time has proved that in this case, as in many others, Field was wrong in his predictions as to the evil days which were to come. In view of the evidence of the past he seems to have had quite as good a basis for his position as his colleagues had for theirs. He might quite easily and logically have been right—had not other things happened in the meantime to change results. Though the worst never came to pass, however, in spite of the fact that the Supreme Court never accepted his point of view and his conclusions, his prophecies are not necessarily to be regarded as being without value. They may have played some part in shaping the body of opinion back of the legislation which determined the outlines of the currency system of the country. That is to say, the effectiveness of his warnings may have been such as to keep his prophecies from coming true. Such a conclusion may seem to label the Supreme Court as a propagandist institution which popularizes the ideas and conceptions of its members. If so, it is not for us to argue that the label is altogether a misnomer, but rather to suggest that if Field differed from his colleagues in his resemblance to the prophets of religion the difference was one only of degree.

It may be that it was his own love of power which in large part supported his desire to have the financial system of the country determined by the Supreme Court rather than by Congress—for if Henry Adams was right in saying that Chase loved power as though he were a senator [48] he might with equal truth have said the same of Field. Opinions will differ, however, as to whether such legislative power should be exercised by men who are in office for life, and who only in a very limited sense are responsible to the people for what they do—this especially in view of the fact that the reasons for decisions must be couched not directly in terms of the social, economic, and political issues involved, but in the phraseology of legal doctrine which may have had little or nothing to do with the making of the decisions. Field, however, and for all we know his colleagues as well, had no fear of the responsibility of decisions of major importance, and he had more faith in his own judgment than in that of the chosen representatives of the people. He was quite as eager to shape the course of national policies as he had been, when a state judge, to play a dominating rôle in California.

[48] *The Education of Henry Adams*, p. 250.

CHAPTER VIII
CHINESE IMMIGRATION

It seems a long way from a subject of great national economic importance, such as the legal tender value of United States notes, to the problem of restricting the immigration of Chinese into a few states along the Pacific Coast, and chiefly into California. Yet it is a commonplace in the experience of judges that they must be constantly dealing with situations and problems as diverse as these. Furthermore, if the race problem in California was not as important to the country as a whole as were many others with which Field had to deal it was still not without significance, and it played no small part in the course of his judicial life.

The story began back at the time when Field himself first journeyed to California. Along with the motley hordes that poured into that region after the discovery of gold came hundreds of pig-tailed Orientals from the Celestial Empire. These representatives of an ancient civilization were made welcome, for a very short time, and then race prejudice began to appear. This prejudice, whatever its justification, has been the source of friction throughout the subsequent history of the state. For many years it expressed itself either in direct maltreatment of the Chinese by people of the white race, or in legislation prejudicial to their interests. From time to time the legislation came before the courts, and judges had either to apply it or declare it invalid. In this work Field played a prominent part. He was constantly aware of the problem, for it was a critical element in the life of his state. As a judge, however, he could deal with it only intermittently and to a limited extent, when particular controversies were presented in court. He was limited by the extent of the controversies which were brought before him, and by the nature and extent of the laws and ordinances involved. Due to this fact as well as to other reasons his decisions often, though not always, gave the impression that he was trying to sabotage the efforts of the people to get rid of the unwelcome visitors. When this happened the hardy and opinionated pioneers let no reverence for Justice Field as the spokesman or mouthpiece of the law hinder them from venting their disapproval.

Self-confident as Field was, it probably bothered him little that other men disagreed with him, but when the disagreement interfered with his political aspirations it caused trouble. Furthermore, the rankling bitterness over the problem caused measures to be taken in various parts of the state which he regarded as shameful and "unworthy of a brave and manly people." [1] He had an intense pride in California, and was proportionately shocked and humiliated when anything was done which, in his estimation, brought disgrace upon the state.[2] Rights which he considered "inalienable" for all men were freely violated in laws and ordinances which were aimed at the Chinese. These violations drew fire in his decisions, while he at the same time was earnestly trying to find a way to solve the whole problem created by the presence of the despised aliens. Few problems provided greater difficulties for him than these.

It was about the middle of the decade of the fifties that anti-Chinese legislation began to appear. Before

---

[1] *Ho Ah Kow* v. *Nunan,* 5 Sawyer 552, 564.

[2] Statement of Emelia Field Ashburner in interview with author in San Francisco, Calif., June 18, 1929.

Field took his seat on the state supreme bench the Court declared unconstitutional an act assessing on the masters of ships a tax of fifty dollars for each Chinaman whom they brought into the country, holding that such a tax was an interference with foreign commerce.[3] An act of 1858 to "prevent the further immigration of Chinese or Mongolians to this state" was quietly declared unconstitutional without any opinions being written and filed.[4] In 1862 the legislature passed what in the title was declared to be "An Act to Protect Free White Labor against Competition with Chinese Coolie Labor, and Discourage the Immigration of Chinese into the State of California." The validity of the law was contested before the state Supreme Court in the same year,[5] and as Chief Justice of that Court Field made his first public utterances on the Chinese immigration problem.

The title of the act declared the purpose to be to discourage immigration. This, in terms of previous decisions, would appear to be unconstitutional, and the Court so declared, Justice Cope reading the opinion and Justice Norton concurring with him. The body of the act was so worded, however, that it did not necessarily imply all that was included in the title. The principal section stated:

There is hereby levied on each person, male and female, of the Mongolian race, of the age of eighteen years and upwards, residing in this state, except such as shall, under laws now existing, or which may be hereafter enacted, take out licenses to work in the mines, or prosecute some kind of business, a monthly capitation tax of two dollars and fifty cents; which

[3] *People* v. *Downer,* 7 Cal. 169, on basis of the *Passenger Cases,* 7 Howard, 283.

[4] Stated in argument for appellant, *Lin Sing* v. *Washburn,* 20 Cal. 534, 538.

[5] *Lin Sing* v. *Washburn,* 20 Cal. 534.

tax shall be known as the Chinese Police Tax; provided, that all Mongolians exclusively engaged in the production and manufacture of the following articles shall be exempt from the provisions of this Act, viz.:   Sugar, rice, coffee, tea.

Field dissented from the decision of the Court, declaring that he was unable to perceive in what way the act interfered with the power of Congress to regulate commerce.   It was his opinion that the act "does not interfere with the landing of Mongolians within the state; it does not impose any tax upon them as emigrants; nor is it directed to their exclusion from the state.   The title of the act, it is true, is open to criticism, but the title is never held to control the legislative intent."   Such intent, he argued, was to be sought in the body of the act.   The act "imposes no tax as a condition of the landing of Mongolians; nor does it require their removal from the state in case of their refusal to pay the tax levied."   The penalty for refusal to pay was merely the seizure of property.

He may have been right in declaring that the act embodied no intent to interfere with foreign commerce. The available evidence, however, indicates that it was another attempt to make life unpleasant or unprofitable for Chinese in California, and to reduce the number of them who were to become permanent residents.   If this was true Field could hardly have been unaware of it, but he may have thought the evidence too tenuous for use in invalidating an act of the legislature.

This case by itself is not particularly important in the story of his attempts to deal with the Chinese problem. It is important, however, if the reader keeps in mind the range of things Field takes "judicial notice" of in different cases.   The tax in this particular act, quite evidently, as counsel declared, was not large enough to have much effect on Chinese immigration, but, it was argued, if this tax were upheld much larger ones could subsequently be passed. This act was but the entering wedge. Field replied: "The objection that if there is the right to levy the tax in question there is no limit to the power of the state, and the tax may be made so great and oppressive as to drive all Mongolians from the state, does not alter the question. All power, wherever lodged, is subject to abuse." The reply was characteristic of him in his early years as a judge. In later years he came to feel more keenly a need for perpetual watchfulness in protecting society from legislative abuse.

It was some years before another Chinese case was tried before Field. In the meantime many things had happened. China, reluctant to open her doors to the commerce of other nations, was gradually being persuaded to do so, and the port of San Francisco was sharing in the profits of the trade. In 1868 Anson Burlingame, who had won the confidence of the Chinese government, helped to arrange between China and the United States a treaty by which the citizens of each country were given the rights of the "most favored nations" in the other. The treaty was hailed in the United States as a great achievement, because of the commercial possibilities involved. With the increase of commercial privileges, however, came a like increase of Chinese immigration, chiefly of laborers, into the western states. These laborers competed actively and successfully with white laborers, and did, for instance, a substantial part of the work in the construction of the Central Pacific Railroad. Many of them hired out to work on farms. They served as cooks and helpers in many households. They took over a large part of the laundry business in the cities, and made themselves generally useful wherever unskilled labor was needed. They lived on next to nothing, and worked for wages which

white men would not accept. Add to these facts their
peculiar mannerisms of speech, of dress, and of general
living, and it is not surprising that the Chinese were
highly unpopular with a large percentage of the Californians, particularly of the workers, and that they
became increasingly unpopular with the increase in the
number of yellow immigrants arriving in the country.
By treaty they were guaranteed equal protection with
the citizens and subjects of other nations, but illegal persecutions continued, and persistent efforts were made to
render California an undesirable domicile for the
Oriental laborers.

Field was of course aware of what was going on. He
had been promoted to the bench of the Supreme Court
of the United States in 1863, but he returned to the
Pacific Coast each spring to hold Circuit Court. In performing their Circuit Court duties many of the
Supreme Court judges were in the habit of delivering
lengthy charges to grand juries on various aspects of
the duties of citizens. Field was no exception. In his
lecture to a grand jury in San Francisco in the summer
of 1872, although no Chinese cases were pending before
the Court, he discoursed at length upon the way in
which the obnoxious aliens were being treated. He
remarked that "although there may be reasonable differences of opinion with respect to the wisdom and
policy of encouraging the immigration to this country
of persons, between whom and our people there is such
marked dissimilarity in constitution, habits and manners; yet so long as our country seeks to enlarge her
commerce by treaties with Asiatic countries, and to
secure protection to her own citizens in those countries
by pledging protection to their citizens in this country,
it is the duty of the government to exert its power, its

entire power if necessary, to enforce its obligations in this respect." [6]

Furthermore, independent of such considerations of duty or interest, he said, it was base and cowardly to maltreat these people while they were within the jurisdiction of the United States. "If public policy requires that they should be excluded from our shores," he continued, "let the general government so provide and declare, but until it does so provide and declare, they have a perfect right to immigrate to this country; and whilst here they are entitled, equally with all others, to the full protection of our laws. It is unchristian and inhuman to maltreat them, as has been sometimes done by disorderly persons, we are sorry to say, in this district." [7]

Most of the Chinese immigrants were men, but some of the enterprising males brought over women of their race and set them up as prostitutes. They did a thriving business. The state legislature tried to stop the importation and might have been successful to some degree had it not allowed the desire to exclude as many Chinese as possible to govern its choice of words. It passed an act providing that persons of a wide variety of classifications, ranging from those merely lacking in funds to those steeped in debauchery, should not be allowed to land in the state unless the master, owner, or consignee of the ship on which they came would put up for each person a bond of five hundred dollars, to guarantee that he would not become a charge of the state. Pursuant to the law, certain Chinese women were held at the port of San Francisco as "lewd and debauched," for whom no bond was put up. The women, or their representatives, appealed to the state courts, but no relief was granted. Thereupon an appeal was taken to the United

[6] 2 Sawyer 667, 680-81.
[7] Ibid.

States Circuit Court, on the ground that the statute was in conflict with the treaty with China, and with the Constitution of the United States. The case was tried before Field, who declared the statute unconstitutional.[8]

"A statute thus sweeping in its terms, confounding by general designation persons widely variant in character, is not entitled to any very high commendation," he remarked. A state had the power to exclude foreigners only as it was necessary to do so for self-defense. Further than that the control of immigration was exclusively in the hands of the general government. The wide range of persons prescribed in the statute showed that its purpose was not that of defense.

Continuing his opinion he endeavored to instruct his fellow Californians as to what ought and what ought not to be done in dealing with the Chinese, in a manner not unlike that hitherto used by his father in giving much-needed advice to his parishioners: "Where the evil apprehended from the ingress of foreigners is that such foreigners will disregard the laws of the state, and thus be injurious to its peace, the remedy lies in the more vigorous enforcement of the laws, not in the exclusion of the parties. . . . So if lewd women, or lewd men, even if the latter be of that baser sort, who, when Paul preached at Thessalonica, set all the city in an uproar (Acts xvii, verse 5), land on our shores, the remedy against any subsequent lewd conduct on their part must be found in good laws or good municipal regulations and a vigorous police."

As for the feeling against the Chinese which was ascribed to the belief that the dissimilarity in physical characteristics and in language, manners, religion, and habits would always prevent any possible assimilation of

[8] In re *Ah Fong*, 3 Sawyer 144 (Sept. 21, 1874).

them, it might be justified, but the state could not "exclude them arbitrarily, nor accomplish the same end by attributing to them a possible violation of its municipal laws." With clear insight into the actual situation he continued:

"It is certainly desirable that all lewdness, especially when it takes the form of prostitution, should be suppressed, and that the most stringent measures to accomplish that end should be adopted. But I have little respect for that discriminating virtue which is shocked when a frail child of China is landed on our shores, and yet allows the bedizened and painted harlot of other countries to parade our streets and open her hells in broad day, without molestation and without censure."

The California pioneers did not meekly respond to wise exhortation when their prejudices and economic interests were involved. They repeatedly found ways of reminding the incoming Orientals of their unpopularity. The coming of hard times made matters worse. In 1877 came the break in the San Francisco stock market, the failure of crops on the farms, the slump in business, and widespread unemployment. The Chinese became to some extent the scapegoat of the ills of the laborers, and race riots took place in many parts of the state. The laborers of San Francisco found leadership in Dennis Kearney, a demagogic Irishman. In the meetings held on the sand lots of Market Street they gathered around him by the thousands, and shouted loud applause as he declaimed against all capitalists and as he closed every fiery speech with the battle cry, "The Chinese must go!" In the spring of 1878 delegates were chosen to a state constitutional convention, and one third of them bore the stamp of Kearney's newly organized workingmen's party.

A large percentage of the members of the constitutional convention were eager to see an end to Chinese
immigration into the state, or found it expedient to
appear to be so. The difficulty lay in the barriers set up
by the federal Constitution and repeatedly observed by
the courts. The problem was debated at length and
with all the powers of oratory possessed by the members.[9]
All sorts of notions were expressed concerning it, ranging
from those of persons who thought the Chinese ought to
be forcibly removed from the state, to those of others who
declared that there were no constitutional measures which
could be taken. Samuel M. Wilson and others of the able
corporation lawyers in the convention, many of them
close friends of Justice Field, urged that immigration
could be legally stopped only by the federal government,
and that those who wanted it stopped should work for
federal action. Others argued, however, that settled law
did not always remain settled when courts became convinced of the urgent necessity for change. As an example one lawyer mentioned the Granger cases,[10] which had
been decided the previous year, and the decision of which
had come as a rude shock to conservative lawyers. "The
decision of the Court . . . was a surprise to the legal fra-
ternity, and contrary to the law ideas of the bar, not only
in San Francisco, but all over the state, and all over the
United States. Notwithstanding that, the decisions
were made in obedience to the necessities of the case,
in obedience to the demand of the great body of the
people of the United States. And whenever law is so
exclusive that it ceases to supply the wants of the people,

---

[9] For a discussion of the controversy in the constitutional convention see
Swisher, C. B., *Motivation and Political Technique in the California Constitutional Convention of 1878-79.*

[10] 94 U. S. 113 ff. For Field's dissent in these cases and a discussion of
his attitude see Chap. XIV.

that it ceases to protect the people, . . . it ceases to become good law for the people. And I say now that if we pass these provisions and bring this matter before the Supreme Court of the United States, presenting it as it can be presented, I believe they will find a way to relieve us from our burdens, as they did the farmers of Illinois." [11]

Judging by his dissenting opinions in the Granger cases Field, however, would not have been stirred to action by such an appeal.

Another member of the convention, a prominent lawyer from San Francisco, offered the suggestion that "now, it is possible, barely possible, that as the science of jurisprudence grows, it has taken, and will take, steps in advance as to what are understood to be popular rights. I do not suppose there is a distinguished lawyer on this floor . . . who would undertake to say that in five years, or ten years, the higher courts may not have taken advanced doctrines as to what are considered popular rights. Such advances are necessary in order to keep pace with the changed conditions of things. The bearing of circumstances may change and alter the condition of things, and the law, being a progressive science, will move along and keep pace with this change; and if we put a clause in the constitution that will permit this question to be reopened and re-examined, no man need be afraid of this being in the nature of a defiance of the Constitution of the United States. It is the only way to test it." [12]

The believers in jurisprudence as a progressive science were not numerous enough or well enough organized to

[11] Wyatt, N. G., in *Debates and Proceedings of the Constitutional Convention of the State of California*, edited by E. B. Willis and P. K. Stockton, p. 681.

[12] Barnes, W. H. L., in *Debates and Proceedings of the Constitutional Convention*, p. 690.

secure the adoption of a well-constructed article on the subject of the Chinese. A wordy article was adopted incorporating some provisions that were later to be held unconstitutional, but a clear and direct attack upon the problem was not made. The conservatives, who were in agreement with Field and who probably discussed the matter with him, for the most part had their way. It was evident that unless the federal government could be persuaded to act, Chinese would continue to come in, and their persecution would go on.

It was shortly after the new constitution was adopted, in the summer of 1879, that Field gave his next decision in a Chinese case.[13] The Chinese were notoriously penurious. If they were convicted of crime and fined by a court they refused to pay the fine, preferring to go to prison instead, where the government had to support them. The Board of Supervisors of San Francisco found a way to make the prospect of imprisonment a terror to Orientals, however, by the simple measure of prescribing that all male prisoners should have their hair cut to a maximum length of one inch. The Chinese at that time wore their hair braided in long queues. The loss of his queue subjected a man to disgrace among his people, and was presumed likewise to bring heavy penalties in the life to come.

Soon after the ordinance was passed a Chinaman was sentenced to pay a fine of ten dollars, or spend five days in the county jail. He refused to pay the fine and was taken to jail, and, in spite of his protests, his queue was cut off. He brought suit against the sheriff for thus maiming him, and the matter was carried to the Circuit Court of the United States. The complaint averred, as

[13] *Ho Ah Kow* v. *Nunan*, 5 Sawyer 552 (July 7, 1879).

stated by Field in his opinion, "that the defendant knew of this custom and religious faith of the Chinese, and knew also that the plaintiff venerated the custom and held the faith; yet, in disregard of his rights, inflicted the injury complained of; and that the plaintiff has in consequence of it, suffered great mental anguish, been disgraced in the eyes of his friends and relatives, and ostracized from association with his countrymen; and that hence he has been damaged to the amount of ten thousand dollars."

The ordinance was attacked on the grounds that it exceeded the authority of the supervisors, and that it was special legislation against a class of persons entitled to equal treatment with all others under the jurisdiction of the United States. Field agreed with these contentions. The cutting of the hair of every male person to within an inch of the scalp could not be maintained as a measure of discipline or as a sanitary regulation, he declared. "A treatment to which disgrace is attached, and which is not adopted as a means of security against the escape of the prisoner, but merely to aggravate the severity of his confinement, can only be regarded as a punishment additional to that fixed by the sentence. If adopted in consequence of the sentence it is punishment in addition to that imposed by the Court; if adopted without regard to the sentence it is wanton cruelty." In either case it was beyond the powers of the Board of Supervisors as conferred by the state legislature.

The ordinance was special legislation against a class, he maintained, being intended only for the Chinese of San Francisco. It "is known in the community as the 'Queue Ordinance,' being so designated from its purpose to reach the queues of the Chinese, and it is not enforced against any other persons. The reason advanced for its adoption, and now urged for its continuance, is, that only the dread of the loss of his queue will induce a Chinaman to pay his fine." This, Field said, was super-adding torture to imprisonment.

The ordinance was general in its terms, and on its face applied to all men under the same circumstances. That was not proof against discrimination, however, he declared. "The statements of supervisors in debate on the passage of the ordinance cannot, it is true, be resorted to for the purpose of explaining the meaning of the terms used; but they can be resorted to for the purpose of ascertaining the general object of the legislation proposed, and the mischiefs sought to be remedied. Besides, we cannot shut our eyes to matters of public notoriety and general cognizance. When we take our seats on the bench we are not struck with blindness, and forbidden to know as judges what we see as men; and where an ordinance, though general in its terms, only operates upon a special race, sect or class, . . . we may justly conclude that it was the intention of the body adopting it that it should only have such operation, and treat it accordingly." However general the terms of the act, he continued, it subjected the Chinese to cruel and unusual punishment, just as, for instance, a similarly general act would impose such punishment upon Jews by compelling all persons to eat pork.

Field may have been profoundly just in looking to matters of general knowledge to determine the meaning, or purpose, of the act. His position, however, seems a far cry from that which he had taken in his first Chinese case, when he had refused to look even as far as the title of the act.

Having disposed of the ordinance he turned again to instruction and exhortation on the race problem in California: "We are aware of the general feeling— amounting to positive hostility—prevailing in California against the Chinese, which would prevent their further immigration hither and expel from the state those already here. Their dissimilarity in physical characteristics, in language, manners and religion would seem, from past experience, to prevent the possibility of their assimilation with our people. And thoughtful persons, looking at the millions which crowd the opposite shores of the Pacific, and the possibility at no distant day of their pouring over in vast hordes among us, giving rise to fierce antagonisms of race, hope that some way may be devised to prevent their further immigration. We feel the force and importance of these considerations; but the remedy for the apprehended evil is to be sought from the general government, where, except in certain special cases, all power over the subject lies."

It was not believed that the appeal to the general government would ultimately be disregarded, he said, but, "be that as it may, nothing can be accomplished in that direction by hostile and spiteful legislation on the part of the state, or of its municipal bodies, like the ordinance in question—legislation which is unworthy of a brave and manly people. Against such legislation it will always be the duty of the judiciary to declare and enforce the paramount law of the nation."

One group of people—the Chinese themselves—greeted the decision with joy and gratitude. A memorial, beautifully lettered in gold, was sent to Field. Thereafter, when he stayed at the Palace Hotel in San Francisco, on his annual trips to California, he was fairly swamped with attentions from pig-tailed Mongolians, who with pathetic eagerness sought to perform services for him.[14] The case received much attention from the bar throughout the country, and the decision was gen-

[14] Statement of Charlotte Anita Whitney in interview with author, June 14, 1929.

erally received with favor. The popular reception in California, however, was anything but favorable. The comment of the San Francisco *Argonaut* may be taken as very mild and sane, as compared with many others. If even this comment is unfair it is nevertheless not without significance:

"We are not in sympathy with sentimental judges, and while we regard that character of legislation and judicial decision that appeals to the prejudice and passion of the ignoble mob as greatly to be condemned, we believe that less hurt comes from it than that sickly sentimentality so apparent in the decisions of courts, and so especially notable in this opinion of Messrs. Field and Sawyer against the cutting off of Chinamen's queues. It is bad law—unquestionably bad law. The power exists to cut off a man's ears or his head for crime. To invoke the Fourteenth Amendment as authority for the protection of vermin in a pagan's hair, and to reason that the soul of a soulless heathen is to be endangered, the sensibilities of a fatalist wounded, or the social status of an Asiatic coolie injured, by cutting his hair in prison, is a little too absurd for us to seriously consider. Looked at through the blue spectacles of a New England Sunday-School teacher it may go down; but to those who stand on this verge of the continent, confronting the incoming hosts of barbarians who threaten our civilization and our government, it is altogether ridiculous." [15]

The situation was complicated for Field by the fact that he was beginning to be looked upon as a possible Democratic candidate for the presidency. If he was to enter politics it was most unfortunate that he had to stir up the wrath of his fellow Californians against himself.

[15] July 26, 1879.

He realized as much, and tried to allay the ill will through a public statement of his views on the Chinese question, which he gave in an interview with Frank M. Pixley of the San Francisco *Argonaut* and Whitelaw Reid of the New York *Tribune*. "Independent of the legal questions involved," he said, "I am of the opinion that no good can come from resort to small vexations against the Chinese. To deny to them the privilege of sending to China their dead, to cut off their queues, to subject them to inconveniences and petty annoyances, is unworthy of a generous people, and will result in no practical benefit."

He continued his statement by urging the modification of the treaty with China in such a way as to limit immigration to this country. "We are alarmed upon this coast at the incursion of Chinese. It is not avarice, greed, or cowardice that prompts us, and all classes of our society, to say to the law-makers and opinion-makers of the East that we have a serious apprehension of the consequences of Chinese immigration. In the language of Senator Booth, we declare that it is our conviction 'that the practical issue is, whether the civilization of this coast, its society, morals, and industry, shall be of American or Asiatic type.' It is to us a question of property, civilization, and existence. We are in earnest, we are compelled to be, and what we now demand is that the American people shall consider this question." [16]

In March of the following year Field again stated his position for the public, reiterating what he had said many times before concerning the futility and unworthiness of petty persecutions of the Chinese, and the necessity of a modification of the treaty between the United States and China so that the immigration of laborers might be restricted. This statement was in the

[16] *Argonaut*, Aug. 9, 1879.

form of a letter to John F. Miller, who in the constitutional convention had been chairman of the committee on Chinese, and who was soon to be chosen United States senator from California.[17] Miller replied by saying that Field had discovered "the only practical, statesmanlike plan for the settlement of the burning question of the present age."[18] Miller began a campaign for the modification of the treaty with China, a task which was probably made easier by the support of Field. No treaty could be framed prior to the date of the nominating convention of 1880, however, and in spite of the fact that he is said to have written the plank adopted by the Democratic National Convention urging upon Congress the suppression of coolie immigration, Field continued to be regarded as the enemy of the people because of his Chinese decisions.

Before the year was ended commissioners were sent to China to secure a new treaty. They returned with an agreement that whenever it appeared to the United States that Chinese immigration was injurious to its interests Congress might regulate, limit, or suspend it. Early in 1881, according to custom, copies of the treaty were secretly printed for each United States senator. In some way the document was immediately made public, and was reprinted widely throughout the country. Its provisions were bitterly attacked in California, partly because it was looked upon as a Republican measure, and partly because it contained the usual "most favored nation" clause, which, many people insisted, would confer the right of naturalization upon the Chinese. Suspicious newspapers and politicians railed against the proposed menace, and the treaty was bitterly attacked in the state legislature. News of the California opposition

[17] The letter was published in the San Francisco *Call*, Mar. 21, 1880.
[18] Quoted by Francis G. Newlands in the *Argonaut*, June 28, 1884.

reached Washington, and the California senators and representatives began to show uneasiness about the meaning of the treaty and about the risk of supporting it. It would have meant political extinction for any Californian who voted for a treaty which conferred the right of naturalization upon Chinese.

John F. Swift, one of the commissioners who had helped to draft the treaty, a Californian and a friend of Field's, saw that something must be done quickly or the treaty would be lost. He hurried to Field's home, on Capitol Hill, in Washington, and was received in Field's study. He explained the nature of the treaty, the attacks that were being made upon it, and its probable fate unless the senators could be convinced that it did not naturalize Chinamen. "I fully examined that question before signing, and it does not naturalize Chinamen," Swift declared. "It could not do so if it tried, and it does not try. I want you, Judge Field, to help us. Your opinion will settle it with the senators. Will you examine the subject and express an opinion?"

"Very good, Mr. Swift," said Field, after reflecting a moment, "I will hear you on that question. I am in the habit of listening to argument, and my mind is trained by that habit to reflect and deliberate while it is going on before me. I think best and quickest while so engaged. Imagine yourself addressing the Court on the point made against your treaty, and argue it to me. Go on."

Swift proceeded to argue the matter, showing, among other things, that the United States did not confer the right of naturalization to any nation by treaty, and that it naturalized not on the basis of nationalities, but of races. After perhaps ten minutes Field interrupted him: "That is enough. You are right; you need go no further. Take your decree. The Court stands adjourned." He touched a bell upon the table. A servant appeared. "Send around my carriage at once; I am going out. I will do my best, Mr. Swift, to put this matter in the proper light with the senators from the Pacific Coast, and all whom I can see and talk with. The treaty must not be lost." In a few minutes he was driving at full speed through the streets of Washington looking up senators, and for days he made it a point to be always on hand to explain away doubts and settle questions of international law. The treaty was confirmed.[19]

It was not until 1882 that Congress passed an act, pursuant to the treaty, suspending the immigration of Chinese laborers for ten years. In the meantime the yellow Orientals continued to monopolize the laundry business in San Francisco, and to carry it on in foul-smelling wooden shacks in various parts of the city. Both the Chinese and their laundries were highly unpopular wherever white people lived. In June, 1882, an ordinance was passed providing that in order to establish, maintain, or carry on a laundry in certain sections of the city the consent of the Board of Supervisors was to be secured, and that consent should not be given until the applicant secured the recommendation of not less than twelve citizens and taxpayers in the same block. A certain Chinaman who had been in business for eight years could not obtain the necessary recommendations to enable him to continue it legally, and immediately fell afoul of the law. The controversy came before Field in the Circuit Court.[20]

[19] This is the story as told by John F. Swift and published in the *Argonaut*, July 11, 1885.

[20] In re *Quong Woo*, 13 Fed. 229 (Aug. 7, 1882).

Field decided against the ordinance. He saw it as a pernicious arrangement, since if the right to conduct a business could be made to depend on twelve persons it might as easily be made to depend upon the unanimous consent of all the people living in the block. Or, instead of citizens and taxpayers a certain number of Irishmen, for instance, might be made the arbiters of the right to do business. Indeed, the matter might be carried to almost any extreme. Field did not mention here, as in his first Chinese case, that the fact that a power might be abused was no proof against its existence.

He considered the ordinance objectionable because it was directed against the laundry business as such. The business was not against good morals or contrary to public order or decency, he declared. If it was conducted in an offensive or dangerous manner or if the particular buildings used were such as to endanger public safety, the Board of Supervisors might take action on these matters, but the ordinance at hand was directed against the business as such, and could not be sustained.

All this may have been good sense and sound logic, although there were points to be made on the other side, but to the people of California it was just another decision in favor of the Chinese. Two and a half years later Stephen Mallory White, a political enemy of Field's who was later to be a United States senator from California, tried to make capital of this decision in a long letter to President Cleveland. He argued that the presence of laundries hurt the value of adjacent property, and that it was only rational that those whose interests were affected should be consulted. He implied that Field had said there was nothing offensive about a Chinese laundry, and then declared in rebuttal that "if you have never had the pleasure of passing by a Celestial washhouse you cannot arrive at any sort of a correct

conclusion as to the structure of Field's judicial nose
and if you ever visit San Francisco or even this town
(Los Angeles) and approach such an institution you will
wonder *what does offend* Field's senses. . . ." [21]

Field gave other important opinions in Chinese cases
during that same year, but for the moment it is interesting to look ahead to January, 1885, when he spoke for
the Supreme Court of the United States in another San
Francisco laundry case.[22] This case also had to do with
the validity of a San Francisco ordinance. The section
in question provided that no person in a public laundry
within a certain area of the city should wash or iron
clothes between the hours of ten in the evening and six
in the morning. Work on Sunday was prohibited by
the same section, but the Court refused to discuss that
provision, since the plaintiff had only been convicted for
working at night. Since the date of his first laundry case,
Field's attitude toward anti-Chinese legislation seemed to
have changed considerably. The change may have been
due to the fact that the exclusion of Chinese under the
provisions of the new treaty was not proving as effective
as he had expected. At any rate, his decisions were now
much more frequently against the Chinese. In this case
he claimed to see no discrimination which gave cause for
legal complaint, and handed down an opinion which is
noted for its clarity of expression on the subject of classification for the purpose of legislation. He had labeled
the ordinance before the Court in the previous case as
an attempt to restrain the Chinaman's liberty to follow
his occupation on the grounds of the "miserable pretense that the business of a laundry . . . is against good

[21] In manuscript letters of Stephen Mallory White, in the library of
Stanford University.
[22] *Barbier* v. *Connolly*, 113 U. S. 27 (Jan. 5, 1885).

morals, or dangerous to the public safety." In the second ordinance, however, he could see no discrimination against the Chinese. Neither of the ordinances mentioned the Chinese, but both were framed to deal with Chinese laundries in the same part of the city. Nevertheless the facts of which he took judicial notice in the two cases were very different. In his opinion in the case now before the Court the heart of his position was that "the provision is purely a police regulation within the competency of any municipality possessed of the ordinary powers belonging to such bodies. And it would be an extraordinary usurpation of the authority of a municipality, if a federal tribunal should undertake to supervise such regulations."

Another case depending upon the same section in a similar ordinance was before the Supreme Court at that time, and Field gave the opinion of the Court about two months later.[23] Counsel attacking the ordinance had pressed him much harder than in the previous case. They quoted him extensively in the "Queue Ordinance" case, where he had eloquently proclaimed that legislation hostile to a class was forbidden by the Fourteenth Amendment, and that "against such legislation it will always be the duty of the judiciary to declare and enforce the paramount law of the nation." They quoted him in the same case where he declared the seriousness of the race situation in California. They quoted him again in the same case where he held that "we cannot shut our eyes to matters of public notoriety and general cognizance. When we take our seats on the bench we are not struck with blindness, and forbidden to know as judges what we see as men; and when an ordinance, though general in its terms, only operates upon a special race, sect or class, we may justly conclude that it was the intention of

[23] *Soon Hing* v. *Crowley*, 113 U. S. 703 (March 16, 1885).

the body adopting it that it should only have such operation, and treat it accordingly."

Counsel declared earnestly that the situations were strikingly similar, and that the ordinance now before the Court, like that in the "Queue Case," was hostile and discriminating legislation against a class. "If the 'Queue Ordinance' contained inherent evidence of its unconstitutionality, and special class legislation, which is prohibited by the Fourteenth Amendment, we insist the context of the laundry ordinance under consideration presents the same palpable vices; and that if it was proper, as it was certainly just, from the circumstances shown, to award relief to the party injured in the former case, it would certainly be equally proper and just that the petitioner should be awarded a like opportunity to be heard, and if wrongfully imprisoned, restored to liberty. In the former case evidence *aliunde* was permitted to be given to show the 'Queue Ordinance' was the result of unwarrantable class legislation, and if the same vice is not apparent on the face of the ordinance set up in the petition of the petitioner in this proceeding, he is prepared to establish *aliunde* that it is of the same pernicious character." [24]

In giving the unanimous opinion of the Supreme Court, however, Field referred to none of his earlier opinions except to that in the other laundry case recently decided by the Supreme Court. In so far as he answered the arguments of counsel he did it in the following paragraph:

"The principal objection . . . of the petitioner to the ordinance in question is founded upon the supposed hostile motives of the supervisors in passing it. The petition alleges that it was adopted owing to a feeling of antipathy and hatred prevailing in the city and county

[24] Brief of counsel for plaintiff, p. 24.

of San Francisco against the subjects of the Emperor of China residing therein, and for the purpose of compelling those engaged in the laundry business to abandon their lawful vocation, and residence there, and not for any sanitary, police, or other legitimate purpose. There is nothing, however, in the language of the ordinance, or in the record of its enactment, which in any respect tends to sustain this allegation. And the rule is general with reference to the enactments of all legislative bodies that courts cannot inquire into the motives of the legislators in passing them, except as they may be disclosed on the face of the acts, or inferrible from their operation, considered with reference to the condition of the country and existing legislation. The motives of the legislators, considered as the purposes they had in view, will always be presumed to be to accomplish that which follows as the natural and reasonable effect of their enactments. Their motives, considered as the moral inducements for their votes, will vary with the different members of the legislative body. The diverse character of such motives, and the impossibility of penetrating into the hearts of men and ascertaining the truth, precludes all such inquiries as impracticable and futile. And in the present case, even if the motives of the supervisors were as alleged, the ordinance would not be thereby changed from a legitimate police regulation, unless in its enforcement it is made to operate only against the class mentioned; and of this there is no pretense."

Field's cleverness in phrasing his argument will hardly be denied. It is left for the reader to decide whether he maintained consistency with his earlier declarations.

In order not to lose the thread of the story it is necessary now to return to the events of 1882. Much litigation grew out of the application of the Chinese immigration restriction act which was passed in that year. By the act the masters of ships were forbidden, under penalty, to bring in Chinese laborers "from any port or place." After the act was passed a Chinaman who had been in the United States for six years left San Francisco as a waiter on a ship. During the voyage he was at no time off the ship, but when the return trip to San Francisco was made the captain refused to permit him to land, pleading fear of the penalties of the restriction act. The controversy reached Field in the Circuit Court.[25] He declared that the waiter had a perfect right to land, saying that the ship was itself territory of the United States, while the act applied only to Chinese brought from some "foreign port or place."

Another case had to do with certain laborers who had been on the same ship and whose situation was the same except that they had had a few hours of shore leave in foreign ports. Field held that they, likewise, were not the persons whom the act was intended to keep out.[26] They had been in the United States when the act was passed, and in spite of their shore leave in foreign ports had not really been beyond its jurisdiction. The act should be construed in such a way as to protect them. "All laws should be so construed, if possible, as to avoid an unjust or absurd conclusion. . . . And in illustration of this doctrine the construction given to the Bolognian law against drawing blood in the street is often cited. That law enacted that whoever thus drew blood should be punished with the utmost severity, but the courts held that it did not extend to the surgeon who opened the vein of a person falling down in the street in a fit. The application sought to be made of that law

[25] In re *Ah Sing*, 13 Fed. 286 (Aug. 27, 1882).
[26] In re *Ah Tie*, 13 Fed. 291 (Aug. 29, 1882).

to the surgeon was hardly less absurd than some of the applications which, without much reflection, are sought to be made of the act of Congress."

The treatment given to a certain Chinese merchant likewise stirred him to scorn.[27] The restriction act provided that Chinese persons who were not laborers and who sought admission to the country should bring with them certificates from the government of China telling their occupations and present places of residence in China. A merchant who had been in Panama for a number of years came to the port at San Francisco, but, although he was able to prove his occupation by parol evidence, he had no certificate from the government of China. Since he had not lived in China for many years he quite obviously could not provide a certificate which would meet all the terms of the act. Field ruled that he should be admitted without a certificate. The purpose of the act, he declared, "will be held to be, what the treaty authorized, to put a restriction upon the emigration of laborers, including the skilled in any trade or art, and not to interfere, by excluding Chinese merchants, or putting unnecessary and embarrassing restrictions upon their coming, with the commercial relations between China and this country. Commerce with China is of the greatest value, and is constantly increasing.[28] And it should require something stronger than vague inferences to justify a construction which would not be in harmony with that treaty, and which would tend to lessen that commerce. It would seem, however, from reports of the action of certain officers of the government—possessed of more zeal than knowledge—that it is

[27] In re *Low Yam Chow*, 13 Fed. 605 (Sept. 5, 1882).

[28] Here in a footnote he gave figures to show the amount of exports to and imports from China in recent years.

their purpose to bring this about, and thus make the act as odious as possible."

The operation of the restriction act soon revealed signs of many leaks by which persistent Chinese laborers continued to slip into the country. Field stopped one of the leaks by holding that a laborer of the Chinese race was excluded even though he was a citizen of a country other than China.[29] He stopped another when he refused to allow a Chinaman, who was temporarily absent from the country, to bring a wife with him on his own re-entry certificate.[30] The legal fiction that two people became one when the marriage ceremony was performed did not apply under the restriction act, he declared. "We are not insensible to the earnest remarks of counsel as to the hardship of separating man and wife. With our notions of the sacredness of that relation, they appeal with striking force. But here the relation was voluntarily assumed in the face of the law forbidding her coming to the United States without the required certificate. He can return with and protect his child-wife in the Celestial Empire."

Chinese laborers who by the Treaty of 1880 had a right to continue to live in the United States, and who desired to leave the country temporarily and then return, were given certificates to show their identity and status. The certificates caused an enormous amount of trouble. They were lost, or misused in various ways, and oftentimes it was not clear to what extent they had to be employed as evidence. Chinamen appeared at the port at San Francisco and claimed the right to land, but for one reason or another could not produce certificates.

[29] In re *Ah Lung,* 18 Fed. 28 (Sept. 24, 1883).
[30] In re *Ah Moy,* 21 Fed. 785 (Sept. 22, 1884).

The courts for a time admitted parol evidence that the applicants had been in the United States before and had the right to return, and it was soon evident that a mass of litigation would arise out of the subject. The Chinese committed perjury with great facility and perfect equanimity. Those who were now seeing the shores of the Occident for the first time made oath that they were just returning to California after a visit to the homeland, and their racial brethren corroborated with similar testimony. To the Americans all Chinese looked pretty much alike, so that identification was well nigh impossible. Hence the excluded persons were coming in, after all, by the simple expedient of making oath to statements which were false but which could not easily be disproved. Congress, to check the abuse, redrafted the restriction act in 1884, and provided that immigration officers should accept no evidence of a right to enter except the authorized certificates. It now appeared that none of the unwelcome immigrants would get into the United States except such as were smuggled in. Field did his part in keeping them out by ruling against them in doubtful cases.[31] Then arose another case which provided violent controversy in the Court. The Treaty of 1880 gave the right of continued residence in the United State to Chinese laborers who were here at the time when the treaty was made. Subsequently it was recognized by the courts that these laborers had a right to return to this country after a temporary absence if they could submit the required evidence of their identity. A certain laborer who was in the United States in 1880 left for Hawaii in 1881, and returned after the second restriction act was

[31] See In re *Ah Kee*, 21 Fed. 701 (Sept. 22, 1884), and In re *Kew Ock*, 21 Fed. 789 (Sept. 22, 1884). However, he ruled against requiring a certificate from a Chinaman who had been born in the United States.—In re *Look Tin Sing*, 21 Fed. 905 (Sept. 29, 1884).

passed, in 1884. This restriction act declared that the only acceptable evidence of a right to enter the country was the certificate which was to be issued to the laborer when he left. This Chinaman had left before the date of the first restriction act, however, when no certificates were issued or required. Obviously therefore he was not able to submit a certificate, yet he demanded admission to the country on the basis of the provisions of the treaty.

The case was argued in the Circuit Court before Justice Field, Circuit Judge Sawyer, and District Judges Hoffman and Sabin.[32] The judges clashed vigorously in their attempts to arrive at a decision. Field held that the laborer could not be allowed to enter the country, while the other judges were in favor of admitting him. A certificate of division of opinion was entered, and the case was carried to the Supreme Court of the United States.[33]

Counsel here used the same methods that were to be used in the last of the laundry cases, as described above,[34] in that they went back to Field's earlier opinions in which he had insisted on merciful and generous treatment for the Chinese, and quoted from them frequently and at length. Field had once scoffed at the attempt to exclude a Chinese merchant through the application of an act which had neglected to take into account men in his position, and the words that expressed Field's scorn were read before him and his brethren of the Supreme Court. He had scolded officials for interpreting an act of Congress in such a way as to violate the declared intent of a treaty when it could be interpreted otherwise, and his words were read before him. Again and again selected passages from his opinions were chosen and read before

[32] In re Cheen Heong, 21 Fed. 791 (Sept. 29, 1884).

[33] Chew Heong v. United States, 112 U. S. 536 (argued Oct. 30, 1884, decided Dec. 8, 1884).

[34] Soon Hing v. Crowley, 113 U. S. 703 (March 16, 1885).

the Court.[35] Counsel applied all of these to the case at hand. It was that of a man who without doubt had had a right to remain in the United States, for he had been here when the treaty was made. Congress now required a certificate of re-entry for laborers returning from abroad, but this man could not possibly have one, for the government had not begun to issue certificates when he left. Congress had merely forgotten to provide for men in his position, as they had for those in the position of the Chinese merchant who lived in a foreign country.

Seven members of the Supreme Court, speaking through Justice Harlan, refused to apply the act of Congress in such a way as to exclude the Chinaman at the bar. Field, as might be expected from his earlier position in the same case, dissented, and Justice Bradley voted with him. In his dissenting opinion Field gave one of the clearest expositions of the development of the Chinese problem in California that is anywhere to be found. He followed the history of the situation down to the time when, in order to prevent the restriction act from being rendered impotent through the notorious capability of the lower classes of Chinese for perjury, Congress had modified the act to make a certificate the only acceptable evidence of a right to enter the country. Upon this act he based his decision. "If the construction I give works hardship to any persons," he said, "it is for Congress, not this Court, to afford the remedy. This Court has no dispensing power over the provisions of an act of Congress."

As he was to do in the laundry case, he for the most part ignored the heckling of counsel as they quoted embarrassingly from his earlier opinions, though he did go so far as to say, when speaking of the extent to which anti-Chinese legislation could have been passed without

[35] See briefs for appellant, on file at the Library of Congress.

violation of the Treaty of 1868, that "subsequent reflection has convinced me that my views on this subject require modification." He closed his opinion with words which show quite clearly his reasons for wanting his views accepted by the majority of the Court:

By the act of 1884, he said, "the door is effectually closed, or would be closed but for the decision of the Court in this case, to all parol evidence and the perjuries which have heretofore characterized its reception. But for this decision, nothing could take the place of the certificate or dispense with it; and I see only trouble resulting from the opposite conclusion. All the bitterness which has heretofore existed . . . on the subject of the immigration of Chinese laborers will be renewed and intensified, and our courts there will be crowded with applicants to land, who never before saw our shores, and yet will produce a multitude of witnesses to establish their former residence, whose testimony cannot be refuted and yet cannot be rejected. I can only express the hope, in view of the difficulty, if not impossibility, of enforcing the exclusion of Chinese laborers intended by the act, if parol testimony from them is receivable, that Congress will, at an early day, speak on the subject in terms which will admit of no doubt as to their meaning."

Some of his fellow Californians were much pleased by Field's dissent,[36] but he was by this time so widely disliked and distrusted in California that the trend of a few opinions on the Chinese problem was of no avail in bringing him popularity.[37]

Federal machinery for keeping Chinese laborers out of the United States continued to operate and to be made

[36] *Argonaut,* Jan. 10, 1885.

[37] For further causes of his unpopularity see succeeding chapters.

more effective. There were abuses such as Field had predicted, but Congress forestalled them in 1888 by going even further than his expressed hopes and passing an act which excluded the laborers even if certificates had been issued to them. In an opinion that was to become well known in constitutional law Field upheld the right of the national government to exclude foreigners, even if it was done clearly in violation of a treaty, as in this case.[38] Treaties were of no greater legal obligation than acts of Congress, he declared, and the last expression of the sovereign will must prevail. As for the justice of what had been done, he declared that the Court was not called upon to censor the morals and motives of Congress. "Whether a proper consideration by our government of its previous laws, or a proper respect for the nation whose subjects are affected by its action, ought to have qualified its inhibition and made it applicable only to persons departing from the country after the passage of the act, are not questions for judicial determination." Counsel had urged that even where treaties were abrogated property rights were customarily still recognized, and that the absentee Chinese had property rights in the privilege of returning which had been guaranteed to them under the treaty. Field was rarely slow in raising his voice on behalf of the rights of property, but he saw no such rights involved here. "Between property rights not affected by the termination or abrogation of a treaty, and expectations of benefits from the continuance of existing legislation, there is as wide a difference as between realization and hopes."

The Supreme Court continued to support the government in its efforts to exclude the Chinese. Even Chinese who were citizens of the United States had difficulties. Field gave the opinion of the Court in a case which

[38] *Chae Chan Ping* v. *United States,* 130 U. S. 581 (May 13, 1889).

denied the right of re-entry to a Chinaman who claimed to be a citizen, but who could find no white person who could testify to the fact.[39] He claimed that Chinese testimony was too apt to be perjured to be of value, and that if this man was admitted on Chinese testimony others would enter in the same way, who had never before been in the United States. This was carrying suspicion a bit too far for Justice Brewer, Field's nephew, who now sat on the supreme bench, and he dissented from his uncle's opinion.

Matters went still further. Chinese in the country were required to obtain certificates of residence to show that they were not persons who had been smuggled into the country. If they failed to obtain the certificates, and were unable to obtain identification by "at least one creditable white witness," they might be taken before a judge and ordered deported. The Supreme Court upheld the measure.[40] It was too much for Field, however, and he dissented, with the vigor characteristic of his opinions. In the year before he left the bench he concurred in a decision that was intended to check the extreme to which national anti-Chinese legislation was now going.[41] The Court here invalidated an act which provided punishment of both imprisonment at hard labor and deportation for Chinese found unlawfully in the United States. Field had participated in decisions affecting the Chinese problem during almost his entire judicial life. Something of the feebleness that had reached him at last was in evidence here as he declared pleadingly that "It is to be hoped that the poor Chinamen, now before us seeking relief from cruel oppression, will not find their appeal

[39] *Quong Ting* v. *United States*, 140 U. S. 417 (May 11, 1891).
[40] *Fong Yue Ting* v. *United States*, 149 U. S. 698 (May 15, 1893).
[41] *Wong Wing* v. *United States*, 163 U. S. 228 (May 18, 1896).

to our republican institutions and laws a vain and idle proceeding."

The line of Field's Chinese decisions, running over a period of nearly thirty-five years, followed a jagged seam. It is not surprising that this is so, in view of the network of interlocked and conflicting principles that was involved. He was a statesman—his enemies would have said a politician—as well as a judge. He gave weight to principles that were political, or economic, or moral, or religious, or all of these, as well as those that were legal. In his use of legal principles he chose one type on one occasion, and another on another occasion. At one time he ranged widely for his evidence, and at another he narrowed his vision to the obvious meaning of legal phrases. Back of it all was the man who used principles and rules of evidence for the achievement of the ends which he thought most worth while.

CHAPTER IX
THE OCTOPUS

When Field was elected as a member of the Supreme Court of California in 1857 the thinly settled pioneer state had no lines of railroads within its borders. When he resigned from the Supreme Court of the United States forty years later California was connected with the East by three transcontinental lines, and hundreds of miles of railroad track provided a network which gave one or more transportation outlets to every important section of the state. The railroads made it possible for the state to become the thrifty commonwealth into which it developed during the latter half of the nineteenth century. On the other hand, most of the lines within the state were knitted together into one great corporate organization, with tentacles stretched out to every locality which had goods to buy or sell, with rates of transportation set arbitrarily at "all the traffic will bear." Consequently, they were looked upon rather generally not as beneficent feeders of an infant commonwealth, but as a gigantic octopus, sucking at the life-blood of the state.[1] The clash of viewpoint and of economic interest forced the courts to become arbiters in controversies many of the aspects of which were new to the judges. In the absence of legal precedents and legislative enactments it was inevitable that the judges' personal conceptions of the economic and social values in the clashes between the railroads and the people should play a very large part in guiding their decisions.

[1] See, for example, Norris, Frank, *The Octopus*, a novel which was built around the story of the Southern Pacific Railroad.

In California, as in other parts of the country, many short lines were built by small companies. These, however, soon fell into the hands of the builders of the Central Pacific Railroad, and were amalgamated into their system. Four men provided most of the energy and ingenuity which carried forward the Central Pacific project. They were Leland Stanford, Collis P. Huntington, Charles Crocker, and Mark Hopkins. In the beginning of their California history they were shrewd small-scale business men, with eager eyes upon the flood of gold that was pouring out of the mines. At the early beginning of the railroad era in the state they conceived of a project for building a line eastward from Sacramento to the Territory of Nevada. They may have planned to operate the road themselves, but they probably intended to unload their interests for as much cash as possible when the project was completed.[2] At any rate, they organized the Central Pacific Railroad Company, under a charter from the state, and began work.

A transcontinental railroad had long been considered in the East, and numerous surveys for proposed roads had been made. The coming of the Civil War made it imperative that something be done to tie up California with the Union, for there was a real possibility that the state might give aid to the cause of the South, or, what was perhaps even more probable, might take this opportunity to declare its independence and set up a Pacific republic. Congress made provision for the donation of land and the lending of funds to build a railroad. The Union Pacific Railroad was chartered to run westward from the Missouri River. To the Central Pacific Railroad, already chartered by California, similar grants and loans were made, and the privilege was given it to build

[2] For the railroad history of this period see Daggett, Stuart, *Chapters on the History of the Southern Pacific.*

eastward from the California line until it met the Union Pacific coming from the East. The grimly energetic builders, employing the hated Chinese as laborers, and struggling against tremendous odds of every kind, completed their task in 1869. They made the construction of the road quite profitable to themselves by forming construction companies of which they were the principal stockholders, and then, as directors of the railroads, awarding to themselves exorbitant sums for their work. However, the road was built, it seemed likely to become prosperous, and the builders, instead of selling out, retained their holdings. They began to build branch roads in the state, and they forced other roads to sell out to them. In a short time they had close to monopoly interest in the California transportation facilities.

Perhaps only men with a ruthless sort of energy could have built the Central Pacific Railroad, in the face of the business and engineering difficulties which they met. However, the builders carried the same ruthlessness into their subsequent operations, where it had striking disadvantages. During the sixties Californians were enthusiastic almost to the point of hysteria about the building of new railroads, and lavishly voted subsidies for them. Some of them were constructed, but oftentimes the funds were squandered by pirates, leaving the people heavily in debt for the subsidies voted, and with little or nothing to show for them. The Stanford group acquired such roads as were built, and set rates to suit themselves. When localities acquired their hostility, rates were boosted. When the people, in self-defense, sought to build new lines, the Stanford group either beat them to it or constructed rival lines and competed them out of existence. Expenses were paid by boosting rates in localities where there was no competition. If in the building of new lines by the Stanford group certain towns failed to make the desired concessions and contributions, the roads were apt to be built two or three miles away, leaving the offending places stranded, as far as railroad transportation was concerned. All this stirred the people to rage, and enthusiasm quickly turned to hate. The much wanted railroads were soon symbolized as a menace to civilization.

Discrimination of one kind or another resulted in threats of regulatory legislation. Stanford either attended the sessions of the state legislature himself or kept agents there, openly or secretly, when legislation affecting railroad interests was being considered.[3] In 1877-78 Stanford and a corps of lieutenants succeeded in wrecking a recently established board of railroad commissioners whose investigations and activities were proving embarrassing to the railroads.[4] The political life of the state was rapidly being honeycombed by railroad influence, while in the East Collis P. Huntington was doing his part by lobbying in Congress.

Stanford participated in state politics before he began building railroads, and was Governor during the term of 1862-63, after having been defeated for the same office for the preceding term. He established himself with the local politicians, and his political activities in favor of his railroad probably began at this time. He was in contact with Justice Field, who was then Chief Justice of the state Supreme Court. He had personal acquaintance with Abraham Lincoln, and recommended Field to him for a position in the federal Supreme Court.[5] The two men, Stanford and Field, were in frequent contact from that time on.

[3] See Stanford testimony before the Pacific Railway Commission, quoted, In re Pacific Railway Commission, 32 Fed. 241, 246 (1887).

[4] Swisher, Motivation and Political Technique in the California Constitutional Convention of 1878-79, pp. 53-54.

[5] Myers, Gustavus, History of the Supreme Court, p. 502.

Certain provokingly intangible facts need to be taken into account if we are to gain a more than superficial understanding of the relation of the railroads to the political life of the state, and to the courts. Railroad agents may, at times, have bought votes in the legislature, and decisions in the courts. It seems evident that there was trading of this kind, though probably there was less of it than was at the time supposed. In addition there were various means of putting pressure on legislators and judges, such as are common to similar political situations. In a study of Field and his colleagues, however, these methods are probably not important. Another type of fact is more significant. For instance, when Leland Stanford gave a banquet at his palatial home in San Francisco Field, if in California at the time, was apt to be there. If he were not there some of his colleagues on the district or circuit benches were likely to be present. It was well nigh assured that some of the best lawyers in the state, such as Creed Haymond, or S. M. Wilson, who were in the employ of the Central Pacific, would be in attendance. It would be a gathering of men who were at the top of the business and political life of the state. The same men came together on many other occasions. Upon the death of a person of prominence it was the fashion to call on other notables to serve as pall-bearers, and it was not uncommon that a federal judge and a prominent railroad official strode side by side. They had bonds of personal acquaintance and friendship, and, undoubtedly, a common sense of superiority to the masses of the people. In their continued association they developed to some extent common ways of thinking about the social and economic problems with which they were in more or less constant contact.

When Stanford, out of the fortune which he had accumulated in his railroad enterprises, founded a uni-

versity in memory of his son, Field, along with many
other prominent men of the state, was made a trustee.
The appointment may have been made more to do honor
to the new university than to Field, but to that extent, at
least, the fact is significant. Mrs. Field and Mrs. Stanford
were close friends, and were much together. When after
Stanford's death the federal government tried to collect
more than fifteen million dollars from his estate to apply
on the debt owed by the California railroads to the government, Field, although he wrote none of the court
opinions, gave every possible assistance to Mrs. Stanford
in protecting her interests.[6] The government failed to
collect.[7] "Always your faithful friend," Mrs. Stanford
signed herself in a letter to him shortly after the case was
won, "and my prayers for years of usefulness here in
this life."[8]

Such was the nature of some of the personal and social
bonds between Field and the railroad builders. Other
bonds, while their existence can not be conclusively
proved, may well have existed. For instance, the dominating energy and the unyielding perseverance with
which the builders fought for what they wanted was also
strikingly characteristic of certain members of the Field
family—Cyrus, struggling against heavy odds to lay the
Atlantic cable; David Dudley, striving to create and
secure the adoption of his codes of law; and the Justice,
fighting for his interpretation of state and federal laws.

[6] Statement of Irwin B. Linton in interview with author, Feb. 22, 1928;
also of Charlotte Anita Whitney in interview with author, June 14, 1929.
[7] See *United States* v. *Stanford*, 69 Fed. 25; 70 Fed. 346; 161 U. S. 412.
[8] Clipped from the foot of one page of a letter of November 3, 1896.
The clipping is filed with the volume of manuscript letters to Stephen J.
Field which is in the library of the University of California. It is a matter
for regret that when these letters were filed those written by the railroad
builders were not submitted, except in one notable instance. That there
were such letters is proved by the fact that signatures of Huntington and
Stanford were clipped from them and filed.

The Stanford motto, *"Labor omnia vincit,"* [9] might well have been the Field motto, too. As long as their interests did not conflict this common apostleship of the strenuous life may have been a dominating force for unity of thought and action. Furthermore, Justice Field, even without any personal sympathy with the builders, would almost undoubtedly, with his paternal interest in California, have agreed with Stanford that every consideration of basic railroad problems only brought into stronger relief the interdependence of transportation with every other material interest of the state. "It is so interwoven with every element of progress and prosperity that to inflict upon it an injury is to strike a blow equally at every other material and commercial interest." [10] It is not surprising that he was impatient with the resentment stirred by what he regarded as minor and temporary ills.

With the immense amount of corruption in railroad affairs that appeared in the years following the Civil War people grew uneasy about the possibility of collecting the millions of dollars loaned to the Pacific railroads on second-mortgage bonds. An attempt was made to collect the interest before the principal fell due, but the Supreme Court declared that it could not be done. [11] Congress then went to work on a bill which was to provide that twenty-five per cent of the net earnings of the debtor corporations should be set aside, to become a sinking fund for the payment of the debts when due. Huntington did his best to protect the interests of his company, but was unable to prevent a bill from being passed. The builders were much worried at this depletion of their

[9] See the San Francisco *Call,* Oct. 14, 1882.

[10] *Ibid.,* Aug. 27, 1882.

[11] *United States* v. *Union Pacific,* 91 U. S. 72.

available funds, and David D. Colton, who was now in a position of prominence among them, "declaimed bitterly against the communistic tendencies of the times." [12] "When men like Thurman and Edmunds advocate the passage of such a bill, what protection is there for property in this country?" he asked in a letter to Huntington.[13] He continued significantly, "I have had several long talks with Judge Field and the hope of the country is in the Supreme Court if the nation is to be saved from disgrace. I know you are having a fearful time there and I had hoped they would adjourn today but no such good news."

The bill was no more than passed when the builders were planning a suit which would bring the act before the Supreme Court. Albert Gallatin, the owner of five shares of stock in the Central Pacific Railroad, brought suit in the United States Circuit Court against the company in such a way as to involve the constitutionality of the act, doing it presumably at the instance of the directors. "Judge Field will not sit in the Gallatin case," Colton wrote to Huntington, "but will reserve himself for his best effort (I have no doubt) on the final termination of the case at Washington before a full bench. I think that is wise, as then Judge Sawyer will hear the case here, and if Judge Field should take our view of the case on final argument before the Supreme Court, it would have more weight with that Court than if he had rendered a decision before in our favor in California." [14]

[12] *Colton* v. *Stanford*, 82 Cal. 351.

[13] Aug. 9, 1878; in the San Francisco *Chronicle*, April 18, 1885.

[14] Letter of September 20, 1878; in the San Francisco *Chronicle*, April 18, 1885. It was one of the defects of the Circuit Court system then in use that the Supreme Court justices, after having given decisions in cases in the circuit courts, often sat in the Supreme Court to hear appeals from decisions which they had given in the lower courts.

Huntington replied, "I think you are right about Field not sitting in the Gallatin case." [15]

In the Circuit Court a demurrer was interposed by the defendants, Judge Sawyer ruled *pro forma,* and the case was carried up to the Supreme Court. Evidence was forwarded to the Attorney-General of the United States by interested citizens of California to show that the railroads were really both plaintiff and defendant in the same case, and he interposed on the part of the government to save the sinking fund act, or the Thurman Act, as it was called, from being thrown out by the Court because of ineffective argument for its constitutionality. The case was well argued on both sides, and when a decision was reached Chief Justice Waite gave the opinion of the Court, holding the act to be constitutional.[16] Field dissented, as did also Justices Strong and Bradley.

"The decision will, in my opinion, tend to create insecurity in the title to corporate property in the country," he declared. He saw the relation of the federal government to the railroad companies as twofold—that

---

[15] Letter of September 30, 1878; *ibid.* These letters came to light after the death of Colton, when his wife was engaged in a controversy with the other builders over his share of the property. See *Colton* v. *Stanford,* 82 Cal. 351. Much embarrassing information was disclosed through the letters which were read in evidence, and the originals seem to have disappeared when the controversy was ended. Some of them, but not all, were printed in the volumes of testimony that were taken. The Huntington letter which, as published by the San Francisco *Chronicle,* contained the above-quoted reference to Field, was included in the printed testimony, but this quotation was omitted. The two Colton letters, along with many others, were not printed. There is apparently no way of proving that the *Chronicle,* which was hostile to the railroads and to Field, did not invent the sentences referring to him. On the other hand, it would be equally difficult to prove that his friends did not suppress the embarrassing sentences. They attracted a great deal of attention, and were evidently never satisfactorily explained.

[16] *Sinking Fund Cases,* 99 U. S. 700 (May 5, 1879).

of sovereign, and that of contractor. As a lender of
money the government was merely in the position of
any other creditor, and could not of itself modify the
contracts which it had made. The Central Pacific Railroad Company was created by charter of the State of
California, he said, and its charter was not subject to
modification by the federal government. His emphatic
delineation here of state and federal powers carried some
suggestion of a political platform upon which he might
become the standard-bearer of the Democratic party. In
view of his subsequent reversal of his ideas about the
Central Pacific charter, in a case where taxes were being
levied not by the federal government but by the state,[17]
it is evident that the observer should not take his legal
arguments too seriously. The heart of his attitude was
in his fear of creating "insecurity in the title to corporate
property in the country," or, we may suspect, in making
insecure the titles of Stanford, Huntington, Crocker,
Hopkins, Colton, and others, to the winnings of the
Central Pacific.

While there was little danger to be feared from discriminating legislation by the federal government, the
property rights of wealthy railroad men were not as
safe in California as they might have been. Their
unpopularity had been constantly increasing, and the
hard times of the latter part of the decade of the seventies
made matters still worse. The organized workingmen
who roared applause to the slogan, "The Chinese must
go," fixed their attention not merely upon the Orientals,
but upon their employers as well, and Stanford and his
brethren came in for their share of threats and denunciation. The impoverished farmers sputtered with impotent

[17] *Central Pacific* v. *California*, 162 U. S. 91 (March 16, 1896).

rage over the exorbitant and discriminatory charges of the railroads. When delegates went to the Constitutional Convention of 1878-79 representatives of almost all groups, except from the railroads themselves and their attorneys, went with the determination to place the obstreperous corporations under an unbreakable system of control.

Field had no patience with the disturbances created by the followers of Kearney—"those damned Kearneyites," he called them explosively.[18] He told Frank Pixley, of the *Argonaut,* who was another of those who were accustomed to gather in Stanford's banquet hall, that there were boundless opportunities for remunerative labor up in Oregon and Washington Territory, where he traveled on his circuit. There was no lounging, no tramps, no grumbling, and no poverty. "This," said Pixley, "justifies us in withholding our sympathy from the broad-shouldered, full-necked, brawny idlers that throng our sand lots, blaspheming God and cursing free institutions, because they can not, by simply lifting their grimy hands in applause of ranting demagogy, earn their beer and bread." [19]   Pixley published Justice Field's dissent in the sinking fund cases under the title of "Law, Morals, and Common Sense." He gave unqualified approval.[20]

Although the railroads had some of their most capable politicians in the Constitutional Convention they were unable to withstand the onslaught of popular indignation which was pouring out against them.[21]   A railroad commission was provided for in the constitution, where a lobbyist-ridden legislature could not get at it. Some

[18] Statement of Irwin B. Linton in interview with author, Feb. 22, 1928.
[19] *Argonaut,* Oct. 5, 1878.
[20] *Ibid.,* Nov. 15, 1879.
[21] For the story of the Constitutional Convention see Swisher, *Motivation and Political Technique in the California Constitutional Convention of 1878-79.*

delegates foresaw the possibility that the railroads would attempt to control the commission instead of getting rid of it, but the simple faith of most of the delegates that phrases in a constitution possessed a magic potency all their own, prevented their reasoning very far into the intricate possibilities of the future. The railroad commission was to have extensive powers of investigation and regulation of railroad activities and charges, and the state Board of Equalization was to levy taxes on the railroads, in such manner and extent that they should in the future bear their full share of the burden of state taxation.

Persons who owned mortgaged property had complained bitterly because they had to pay taxes on the entire value of their property, while the holders of the mortgages paid no taxes at all. The new constitution provided that debtors should pay only on the value of the property less the amount of the mortgages, while the mortgaged value was to be assessed to creditors. The principal railroads, however, were mortgaged for at least all they were worth. If mortgage credits were deducted from their taxable value they would pay no taxes at all. Some of the bonds were held by the federal government and some by owners who were widely scattered over the country. It was feared that if the railroads themselves escaped taxation the tax would be lost entirely, because of the inability to collect it from creditors. Anyway, few people wanted to see the railroads themselves escape. Accordingly it was provided that railroads should not have the right of deducting the amount of their mortgage debts from the value of their taxable property. Some of the advocates of rigid control of the railroads were suspicious of the plan for denying them this privilege, particularly as some men known to be railroad agents spoke plausibly in its favor. They feared that the shrewd attorneys were laying a trap by means of which their clients could escape all taxation.

The new constitution was adopted in spite of the bitter opposition of the railroad and banking interests of the state. Taxes were levied under the new scheme. The railroads protested that the method was unconstitutional, and refused to pay. When their property was put up for sale Huntington found friendly judges to issue injunctions, which were dismissed after the date set for the sale.[22] The railroads failed to bring the state Supreme Court to their way of thinking,[23] and thereupon they transferred their efforts to the federal Circuit Court, where Justice Field lent a sympathetic ear to their pleas.[24] The first Circuit Court case was merely a preliminary movement, to determine whether that Court could take jurisdiction. Highly skilled lawyers, including such friends of Field's as Delos Lake and Creed Haymond, appeared for the railroads.

Field declared that according to his way of thinking the jurisdiction act for the Circuit Court should be so interpreted as to require an action of this kind to be settled in the state courts. However, the federal Supreme Court had decided otherwise,[25] and the Circuit Court must take the case. Nothing more than this need now be decided, he said. Another suit involving the merits of the controversy would have to be brought. It was not necessary to determine at this moment whether the Fourteenth Amendment applied to corporations as well as to natural persons. However, it might not "be out of place to make some suggestions as to the force of the

[22] Fankhauser, W. C., *Financial History of California,* p. 301.

[23] *S. F. & N. P. Railroad* v. *Board of Equalization,* 60 Cal. 12 (January term, 1882).

[24] *San Mateo* v. *Southern Pacific R. R. Co.,* 13 Fed. 145 (July 31, 1882).

[25] *Railroad* v. *Mississippi,* 102 U. S. 135.

Fourteenth Amendment, in order to draw the attention of counsel to the difficulties in its application to the present case, which they must be prepared to meet on trial." Although the amendment was passed to validate the civil rights act for the protection of negroes, the generality of its language made it applicable to all persons, he said. Equality of protection was made the constitutional right of every person. This implied that he should be subjected to no greater burdens nor charges than such as were equally imposed on all others under like circumstances. No one could be arbitrarily taxed on his property at a different rate from that imposed upon similar property of others, similarly situated. Property might be classified and taxed at different rates, but "arbitrary distinctions not arising from real differences in the character or situation of the property, or which do not operate alike upon all property of the same kind similarly situated, are forbidden by the amendment." Without directly saying so he implied that corporations were entitled to the same protection as natural persons.

He closed his discussion of the controversy which was soon to be brought before him by saying that "As thus seen, the question which will be presented for our determination on the trial of this case is one of the greatest importance. We express no opinion upon it, but invite for it the most thoughtful consideration of counsel. And in their discussions the control of a state over corporations of its own creation, where a reserved power of amendment is embodied in their charters or imposed by the Constitution, should be considered. The general tendency of modern decisions is to treat corporations with this reserved power as subject at all times to the will of the state as to their rights, powers, and liabilities. Such unlimited control, asserted in some cases, would, indeed, leave them not only out of the protection of the Fourteenth Amendment, but also out of nearly all protection, except such as the legislative pleasure of the hour may permit."

This opinion was read on July 31. From August 21 to 29 the case was argued in full before Field and Circuit Judge Sawyer.[26] There were able attorneys on both sides, but the railroads were quite obviously in the most capable hands. Delos Lake had died, in the interval between the two cases, and his place had been taken by J. Norton Pomeroy, of the Hastings Law School. In the words of Pomeroy's son, his father's acquaintance with Field had "ripened into a warm and devoted friendship. Between them there was an intellectual sympathy at almost every point; and on Judge Field's part the help-fulness and solicitude, one may almost say, of an elder brother." [27] Pomeroy's argument was delivered in the driest possible fashion, wearying exceedingly the crowd in the court room,[28] but the opinions of the judges, when they were read September 25, followed closely the lines which he had drawn.

The railroads claimed that in the assessment of their property the Fourteenth Amendment was twice violated. They were denied the equal protection of the laws when they were not allowed to deduct the amount of their mortgages from the assessable value of their property, and they were denied due process of law when no right had been granted to be heard concerning the value of the property and for the correction of errors after the assessment had been made. The attorneys for the county and state claimed that the state had unlimited power to tax, that classification for the purpose of taxation was

[26] *San Mateo* v. *Southern Pacific*, 13 Fed. 722 (Sept. 25, 1882).

[27] Pomeroy, J. N., Jr., "John Norton Pomeroy," *Great American Lawyers*, Vol. VIII, p. 123.

[28] Statement of Frank Monckton in interview with author, June 28, 1929.

legitimate, that the Fourteenth Amendment was adopted for the protection of the negroes and should be restricted to that end, that corporations were not persons, that the statute requiring railroads to submit to the Board of Equalization statements of the amount and value of their property provided for all the hearing that was necessary, and that the tax provisions were to be treated as conditions upon which the railroad corporations were allowed to continue their existence.

Field accepted the arguments of the railroads, and overthrew those of the state. As he saw it the Fourteenth Amendment gave the same protection to persons organized in corporations as to those doing business as individuals. Citing an extended list of services which were being performed by corporations he declared that "it would be a most singular result if a constitutional provision intended for the protection of every person against partial and discriminating legislation by the states, should cease to exert such protection the moment the person becomes a member of a corporation." He declared equality and uniformity of taxation—terms which had been deliberately left out of the new constitution because of the fear of what judges might do with them—to be measures of the equal protection guaranteed by the federal Constitution. The right to a hearing after the assessment had been levied was likewise a fundamental element in "due process of law." The power to amend charters did not give the power to confiscate property already acquired. The state could not withdraw the corporations "from the guaranties of the federal Constitution."

Hence it was that two years of railroad tax assessments were thrown out by the Court as invalid. The questions presented had been examined with a painful anxiety to reach a right conclusion, declared Field, "aware as the

Court is of the opinion prevailing throughout the community that the railroad corporations of the state, by means of their great wealth and the numbers in their employ, have become so powerful as to be disturbing influences in the administration of the laws; an opinion which will be materially strengthened by a decision temporarily relieving any one of them from its just proportion of the public burdens." That consideration, however, could not be allowed to affect the judgment of the Court. "Whatever acts may be imputed justly or unjustly to the corporations, they are entitled when they enter the tribunals of the nation to have the same justice meted out to them which is meted out to the humblest citizen. There cannot be one law for them and another law for others."

The San Francisco *Chronicle* predicted that a few more such decisions would stir up a feeling in most of the states against the federal judiciary which would call for some power greater than a court to quell.[29] "While the hireling sheets of monopoly are exulting over the decision, another class is mourning the fact that the circuit in which California is unfortunately included is presided over by Justice Field. These sorrowful ones do not assert that the eminent Justice is not conversant with the law; their only complaint is that whenever he has a case before him in which the community and the corporations are arrayed against each other, his lights always lead him to discover points against the people."[30] The *Argonaut*, however, was delighted, declaring that "the spirit of communism that took its rise at the sand lot; that was fanned into a flame of passionate resentment against railroad corporations by party demagogues; that forced its way into the new constitution, through the efforts of

[29] Sept. 27, 1882.
[30] San Francisco *Chronicle*, Sept. 28, 1882.

malignant journalists and the cowardice of political
leaders, and that now dominates both political parties,
has met its check and rebuke from the Circuit Court of
the United States." [31]

This case, commonly called the San Mateo case, was
hurried on to the Supreme Court of the United States,
where it was argued December 19 of the same year, with
such men as Roscoe Conkling, George F. Edmunds, and
S. W. Sanderson appearing for the railroads. It was at
this time that Conkling made the assertion that one reason for the framing of the Fourteenth Amendment was
the pleas of men of big business for protection from
oppressive state legislation.[32] Californians watched eagerly
for the decision, but the matter dragged on for a year
without an expression from the Court. Shortly after the
argument an incident happened which put Field further
in bad odor. Stanford gave a dinner at Chamberlin's
restaurant, in Washington, to Conkling, Sanderson, and
other railroad attorneys. A little earlier in the day Field
drove out to the Arlington Hotel, in search of Sanderson.
Finding that he had gone to the Stanford dinner Field
followed him, and remained for the repast. Much surprise was expressed that he would attend a banquet of
this kind while the railroad case was still pending before
the Supreme Court. Said the correspondent of the
Chronicle, "The unanimous verdict of lawyers and others
is that Justice Field did a very indelicate thing, to say the
least, in view of the fact that he tried the case in California originally. No other member of the United States
Supreme Court participated in the banquet. Indeed, it
is safe to say that no other of the justices were invited for
the reason that it was known they would not attend." [33]

[31] Oct. 7, 1882.
[32] See Chap. XVI.
[33] San Francisco *Chronicle*, Dec. 27, 1882.

It had been agreed on both sides that the San Mateo case should be used to test the validity of the California taxing system, and when it was appealed to the Supreme Court, stays were issued in other cases then pending before the Circuit Court. When the Supreme Court failed to give an immediate decision other cases were initiated in California, however, in which counsel on both sides advanced new arguments in addition to those already brought forth. On September 17, 1883 Field gave the Circuit Court decision in the Santa Clara case,[34] deciding six similar cases which were before the Court at the same time. His opinion was much the same as that given in the San Mateo case. He ignored many of the new arguments advanced by the railroads, saying that it was unnecessary to pass upon them, since the decision was determined by the application of the Fourteenth Amendment. One plea he did notice, however. It had been argued that since the Central Pacific and Southern Pacific had been made instruments of the federal government in the performance of its functions, their franchises could not be taxed by the state. He replied that where the companies were originally chartered by the state, even though the general government for its own convenience conferred additional privileges, they were not exempt from the taxing power of the state unless Congress declared them to be so. Congress had not so declared.

Deciding this point against the railroads, however, did not prevent the final decision of the cases from being in their favor.

At the end of his opinion he added two long paragraphs of advice to the state on the subject of taxing railroads. "I am profoundly sensible," he said, "of the irritation which a supposed desire to escape from the just burdens of government naturally creates. The more powerful,

[34] *Santa Clara* v. *Southern Pacific Railroad*, 18 Fed. 385 (Sept. 17, 1883).

the more wealthy, the party, the more intense the feeling, and it finds expression in words of bitter complaint, not merely against the party, but sometimes, also, against any administration of justice which tolerates such supposed evasion. It is sometimes forgotten that the courts cannot supply the defects of the law, not always correct the mistakes of public officers, nor the errors even of learned counsel. Certainly no member of this Court would countenance the escape of anybody from his just obligations, but it cannot, with any seeming justice, declare that one party shall discharge an obligation which the law, properly administered, would impose upon another." He declared that the Court's duty was to administer the law as it found it, not to make it, never forgetting the great principles for the protection of private rights which were embodied in the national Constitution.

The railroads should be taxed, he said, but no unjust discrimination should be made against them. His solution was that the railroads should be assessed at their true value, but that since they were mortgaged for their full value or more, the railroads should be allowed to pass the indebtedness on to the creditors. It was true that many of the bonds were held outside the state, but the property in the hands of the corporations stood as security for the bonds. The railroads would pay the taxes to the state, but they would deduct the amount of the taxes from the amount of the mortgages against them.

However wise this plan may have been, its application would have seemed to free the hated corporations from paying any taxes out of their own coffers. The state was determined to compel them to disgorge.

The Santa Clara case was carried to the Supreme Court. In the meantime things were happening in connection with the San Mateo case. It had been agreed upon as a test case, but technically it involved assessments on only a few miles of railroads in San Mateo County, amounting to only a few thousand dollars. The records are not perfectly clear as to just what happened, but apparently the railroads decided that the Santa Clara would be a better test case than the earlier one from San Mateo. In collusion with certain San Mateo County officers they paid, or pretended to pay, the taxes due to that county, and received a receipt for them, and the county officers set out to get the case dismissed—in spite of the fact that the real backing of the argument against the railroads was provided by the state, and not by the county. Attorneys for the state did their best to prevent the case from being dismissed, but without success.[35] Chief Justice Waite gave the opinion of the Court dismissing the case, replying to the argument that this was a test case by saying that the Santa Clara case (which had not yet been argued before the Supreme Court) contained all the issues presented in that from San Mateo.[36]

The Santa Clara case was argued before the Supreme Court January 26-29, 1886, and the decision was given on May 10, 1886.[37] Chief Justice Waite, reading the opinion of the Court, held that it was not necessary for the Court to pass upon the question of discrimination against the railroads in the constitution of California, since the assessments involved had to be declared invalid on a minor ground. The Board of Equalization had included in its assessment of the railroad property the fences along the line, whereas the constitution of the state permitted that Board to assess only the specified property such as the franchise, roadway, roadbed and rolling stock, which did not include the fences. This had been one of

---

[35] See the briefs submitted on the motion to dismiss; see also Fankhauser, *Financial History of California*, pp. 302-4.

[36] *San Mateo* v. *Southern Pacific*, 116 U. S. 138 (Dec. 21, 1885).

[37] *Santa Clara* v. *Southern Pacific*, 118 U. S. 394 (May 10, 1886).

the points stressed before the Circuit Court, but Field
had not taken it into account in his opinion. Thus, once
more, the courts failed to solve the problem of the constitutionality of the California railroad assesment scheme.
Popular pressure was so great that the officials of the roads
voluntarily paid considerable sums to the state, but they
themselves virtually dictated the amount.

Field, in his concurring opinion, regretted that the
Court had not decided the important question of whether
there was unlawful and unjust discrimination against the
defendant in the scheme of assessment used, from which
the Fourteenth Amendment afforded relief. Again, as
he had repeatedly done in earlier cases, he stressed the
number of business and industrial activities that were
being carried on by corporations. It was a matter of the
greatest interest to them that their property should be
assessed only in like manner as that of natural persons.
The question was whether the state might "prescribe rules
for the valuation of property for taxation which will vary
according as it is held by individuals or by corporations.
The question is of transcendent importance, and it will
come here and continue to come until it is authoritatively
decided in harmony with the great constitutional amendment which insures to every person, whatever his position
or association, the equal protection of the laws; and that
necessarily implies freedom from the imposition of
unequal burdens under the same conditions."

Other tax cases were started in the state courts of
California, carried to the United States Circuit Court by
the railroads, and appealed to the Supreme Court by the
state. They were argued January 11-13, 1888, and
decided on April 30, 1888.[38] The Court decided against
the state on two grounds, first, that the Board of Equalization included in the assessment the value of the railroad

[38] *California* v. *Central Pacific*, 127 U. S. 1 (April 30, 1888).

steamships which completed the railroad journey across the San Francisco Bay, and which the state Supreme Court had decided that the Board had not the power to tax; second, that the assessments included the value of franchises which were conferred by the federal government, which franchises the state had no power to tax. Justice Bradley spoke for the entire Court in giving the opinion.

California was eventually driven to re-assess the railroads, with an eye to what they would probably consent to pay. The courts, whatever their motives, had been little more than obstructions to the state in its attempts to collect the taxes which it had levied. Whatever the truth may have been, the appearance was that the judges, in their attempts to apply old principles of law to new situations, had been used as tools by the shrewd agents of the railroad corporations.

The California railroads made one more attempt to secure the protection of the Supreme Court of the United States against state taxation before Field left the bench. Their franchises had been assessed by the state, and they apparently sought to make use of this fact to invalidate the whole assessment, claiming that federal franchises were involved which the state had no right to tax. This time they failed. Chief Justice Fuller accepted the finding of a lower state court that federal franchises were not involved.[39] Justice Field gave a dissent that was not untouched with exasperation, emphasizing the privileges that had been conferred upon the railroads in question by the federal government, and protesting against state interference with these privileges. This dissent is of

[39] *Central Pacific* v. *California*, 162 U. S. 91; *Southern Pacific* v. *California*, 162 U. S. 167 (March 16, 1896).

interest in contrast with his earlier one in the sinking
fund cases. There, when the federal government had
sought to direct the use of a portion of the funds of the
railroads, Field had stressed the rights of the corporations
under California laws, holding that the relation of the
federal government was only that of any creditor under
similar circumstances. Here, basing his arguments on the
same federal and state statutes which he stressed in the
sinking fund cases, but quoting certain phrases which he
had seen fit to ignore in the earlier cases, he emphasized
the powers of the federal government over the railroads
and declaimed against the encroachments of the state
upon the federal province. The statutes were the same;
the arguments conflicted; but, in both cases, *the interests
to which he sought to give protection were the same.*
When the Santa Clara case was before the Circuit Court
he had rejected a railroad argument by saying that even
if federal franchises were involved they might be taxed
by the state unless Congress had forbidden such taxation,
and Congress had not so spoken. On other grounds,
however, he had decided that case in favor of the railroads. Indeed, in studying Field's record in connection
with the California railroads we find no record of an
opinion which would work injury to the corporations.

Officers of the federal government were uneasy about
the possibility of recovering the funds loaned by the
government to the railroads. In 1887 Congress provided
for the appointment of a commission which was to
inquire into the affairs of the debtors. If witnesses refused
to provide the information or papers asked for the commission was empowered to call on the federal courts to
enforce obedience. Stanford was called before the
commission, and was quizzed mercilessly about his lobbying activities and the details of railroad expenditures which
he had made. He admitted that he and his agents spent

much time with the legislature when their interests
needed protection, but denied that he knew of any
expenditures to corrupt legislators. When pressed to
explain the use of money which was accounted for only
by certain vouchers he declared, time and again, that he
had no recollection of the details of the expenditures.
The commission was not convinced, and appealed to the
Circuit Court to compel him to be more talkative and
to provide further material evidence.

Field heard the plea of the commission. In his opinion
he denied that the commission was a judicial body, and
declared that the Court could not compel the production
of evidence except by regular judicial proceedings.[40] He
denounced the inquisition which the commission was
making, and declared: "Of all the rights of the citizen,
few are of greater importance or more essential to his
peace and happiness than the right of personal security,
and that involves, not merely protection of his person
from assault, but exemption of his private affairs, books,
and papers from the inspection and scrutiny of others.
Without the enjoyment of this right, all other rights
would lose half their value. The law provides for the
compulsory production, in the progress of judicial proceedings, or by direct suit for that purpose, of such
documents as affect the interests of others, and also, in
certain cases, for the seizure of criminating papers
necessary for the prosecution of offenders against public
justice, and only in one of these ways can they be
obtained, and their contents made known, against the
will of the owners."

The declaration in behalf of the rights of personal
liberty is impressive. To some it may seem antiquated, in
view of the interlocking dependency of individuals and
interests upon each other. Others would be more

[40] In re *Pacific Railway Commission*, 32 Fed. 241 (Aug. 29, 1887).

impressed if they did not suspect that the concept of liberty was here chiefly a tool to prevent Stanford from being required to give information that would be embarrassing to him and to the railroad corporations.

If the evidence shows on the part of Justice Field a bias, conscious or unconscious, in favor of the railroads and their builders, there were limits beyond which he would not go. Although letters showing his close personal relationship with Stanford, Huntington, and others, have been carefully destroyed, other letters, providing evidence of his independence from their control, have been preserved. Congress had made a grant of land to the Oregon and California Railroad, including in the grant the provision that the road should be completed by a certain time. The road was not completed at the date specified, and a controversy arose with private individuals as to the ownership of the land. A case involving the question was argued before the Supreme Court on March 31, 1891. Field was ill at the time, and was unable to be present. After the argument the railroad men were decidedly worried as to how the case might turn out. On April 3 I. E. Gates, Huntington's agent in New York, wrote to Field telling him that Huntington was sorry that on account of his illness he had been unable to sit in the case.

After indicating the nature of the case Gates continued: "In case the Court should find any difficulty in its determination of the case, Mr. Huntington would be very much obliged if, before any decision should be rendered against the Oregon & California Railroad Company, you would ask the Court to order a re-argument of that question at a time when you could sit and participate in the hearing. Mr. Huntington would have written to you directly himself, but he is now on the way to California to attend the April meetings."

Field lost no time in replying: "Your letter of yesterday has been received. I am very much surprised at its contents. I would not have believed that any person would have presumed to write to me as to proceedings in the Court of which I am a member and to ask me to take certain action in those proceedings should they result in a particular way. With your long experience you must have known the impropriety of such a communication to a judicial officer. You have written I am sure without due consideration, and, as I fear, been prompted by your counsel who is certainly aware of the impropriety of such a letter.

"You state that Mr. Huntington would have written himself had he not already left for California. Had he done so, and his letter been of the tenor of yours, I should have replied to him in stronger terms than I do now. If either he, or the railroad company which he represents, or yourself, desire any action taken by the Court of which I am a member, there is only one course to pursue, and that is to apply for such action in open court by proper proceedings, upon notice to the adverse party."

After an interval of a few days Gates replied to Field's "favor of the 4th inst.," in a stammering letter in which he expressed his sorrow that he should have written anything "which was in any wise indecorous or improper." [41]

During the following summer it was generally understood that relations between Field and the railroad

---

[41] These letters are in the volume of manuscript letters to Field which is on file in the library of the University of California. The Gates letters are originals, written on Huntington stationery. Field's reply is a copy, on Supreme Court stationery, evidently made at the time the letter was written.

company were pretty severely strained.[42] Stanford and Huntington were not as friendly at this time as in the earlier years of their association. It is a matter of conjecture whether if the appeal had come from Stanford instead of Huntington Field's answer would have been just the same. Anyway, the appeal was unnecessary. The Court gave a unanimous decision in favor of the railroad.[43]

[42] The *Wave*, July 11, 1891.

[43] *Bybee* v. *Oregon and California R. R. Co.*, 139 U. S. 663 (April 20, 1891).

CHAPTER X

THE GAME OF POLITICS

Prior to the time when the slavery question became a sharp political issue all the members of the Field family had claimed membership in the Democratic party. In the early fifties, and perhaps even before that time, David Dudley Field began to align himself with the so-called Free Soil groups, and when the Republican party was organized he was for a time prominent among the leaders. Justice Field never really left the ranks of the Democratic party. At the outbreak of the war the old party lines in California were for a time obliterated, and loyal citizens came together in a Union party for the purpose of aiding in the conduct of the war. Some who shared in the work of the new organization undoubtedly remained to hold strategic positions in the Republican party after the war had come to an end, but Field maintained his allegiance as a Democrat, in spite of the fact that he had been appointed to the supreme bench by a Republican President. Although his alignment may have been due in part to his devotion to party principles it seems evident that he was driven back into the Democratic camp by the hostility which he encountered as the result of his decisions in the test oath cases and in other cases in which he tried to protect the interests of the defeated Southerners.[1] The California Democrats gave him recognition in the Democratic National Convention in 1868 by offering him, rather late in the proceedings, as their candidate for the presidency. He was nominated

[1] See Chap. VI.

as the man who had been the guardian of the Constitution against the assaults of the radicals. He received little support at the time, however. There was a maximum number of but fifteen votes cast for him on any ballot.[2]

It was conventional to assume that when men were appointed to judicial office they left party politics behind. Most men who have taken seats on the bench of the Supreme Court have justified the assumption by withdrawing from their partisan activities, although Chief Justice Chase and others in the history of the Court have remained ardent aspirants for political office. The prestige of the Court has been greatly enhanced and its decisions have been given added weight because of the belief that the justices, unlike other government officials, are not affected by political motives. In their positions of retirement behind the scenes of active political life Field and his colleagues had not the same temptation to partisanship as other public servants, but occasionally some unusual controversy drew them toward the edges of the fray. The struggle of their respective parties to seat Rutherford B. Hayes and Samuel J. Tilden in the presidential chair in 1877 engulfed certain members of the Court in what might be called a tidal wave of party politics, and of these members Field, at least, was never quite the same after the experience. He revealed thereafter an interest in participation in party politics which was hardly compatible with traditional conceptions as to the non-partisanship of judges.

Since the close of the term of James Buchanan in 1861 the presidency had been regularly awarded each four years to the candidate of the Republican party. The Democratic organization had been shattered on the reefs of slavery and secession. Attempts to rebuild it to the point where it could wage a successful battle in a national

[2] New York *Evening Post*, July 9, 1868.

conflict with the Republicans had failed again and again. The party was still divided, and the taint of disloyalty to the Union was still upon it. However, at the time of the election in the fall of 1876 people were growing weary of the corruption of government in the Grant régime, and were losing interest in the zeal of the radicals for ruling the South with a heavy hand. It looked as if Governor Tilden of New York, the Democratic standard-bearer, might have some chance of success.

The total popular vote showed a majority for Tilden, and it seemed at first that a majority of the electoral votes also was his. The election was close in certain states where majorities had been declared for Tilden, however, and the Republicans, refusing to accept defeat, laid claim to them. Politicians rushed to Louisiana and Florida to engage in the scramble for votes. Both parties claimed these states, and there were violent disagreements over elections in South Carolina and Oregon. There seems to have been ample evidence of intimidation and fraud on the part of both parties. Rival sets of returns were sent to Washington, whereupon there was violent disagreement as to who had the power to determine which returns should be counted. If the power was exercised by the President of the Senate, a Republican, he would doubtless count the electoral votes for Hayes, while if disagreement threw the election into the House of Representatives, which was Democratic, Tilden would be elected.

Partisan feeling ran high, and press and platform carried the rumblings of another civil war. Politicians used all their wits to win the contest for their respective candidates, and to do it in such a way as to make the results acceptable to the people. Both the Senate and the House of Representatives appointed committees to work out solutions. The committees met many times, both separately and together. One was predominantly

Democratic and the other predominantly Republican. Each sought a way to win the presidency for its own party, and to make its method seem orderly and just. Plans were discussed for a commission which would sit in judgment over the sets of conflicting returns. Members of neither party would trust the action of a committee the majority of which was made up of their opponents, and from the beginning there was some talk of using the justices of the Supreme Court. They affected to believe that the justices would not be swayed by partisanship, but each party fought for the selection of justices who had been affiliated with it.[3]

Justices Clifford and Field were the only pronounced Democrats on the bench. Justice Davis had vacillated so much in his affiliations that nobody knew just where he stood. All the others were Republicans. Many possible arrangements of the commission were discussed, and the politics of Davis came in for much speculation. The final arrangement was that Clifford, Field, Miller, and Strong were to be members of the commission, and were to choose another member from among the other associate justices. It was presumed that the choice would fall upon Davis, who would "maintain the tribunal's equipoise." [4] Clifford, now the senior member on the bench of the Supreme Court, was to be chairman of the committee. In addition to the justices on the committee there were to be five members from the Senate, of whom three would be Republicans and two would be Democrats, and five members from the House, of whom two would be Republicans and three would be Democrats, or a total of fifteen. Thus, of the total there would be seven Republicans and

[3] Northrup, Milton Harlow, "A Grave Crisis in American History," *Century*, October, 1901, pp. 923-34. Northrup was secretary of the special committee of the House of Representatives.

[4] *Ibid.*, p. 926.

seven Democrats, with Justice Davis classified as an independent. "In the ponderous Illinois jurist was centered the hopes of Democracy, the apprehensions of Republicanism." [5] Then, to the dismay of the Democrats, Davis was elected to the United States Senate by the legislature of Illinois. He accepted the position and resigned from the bench, to give up his seat on March 4, 1877.

The four justices spent many hours discussing the question as to who should be the fifth justice on the commission. Although it was generally believed that Davis was now disqualified, or at least would not serve on the committee, since he was soon to become a member of the Senate instead of the Supreme Court, three of the four justices still preferred him if he would serve. Miller, believing that Davis had disqualified himself, favored Bradley or Hunt. They finally offered the position to Davis, but he declined to serve. [6] Bradley was then chosen. He was a Republican, but he had never been notably active in politics except to run for Congress in 1862, when he was soundly beaten. Field is said to have had hopes that he could draw Bradley to the support of the Democrats, and bring about the election of Tilden. [7] Some of the justices had expressed themselves as reluctant or unwilling to serve on the commission. Field was quite willing to serve, though he claimed that the commission was unnecessary. His idea of the correct procedure was that the electoral votes should be opened before a joint convention of the two houses, and if there was inability to agree on the votes the House of Representatives should then elect the President, and the Senate should elect the

[5] Ibid., p. 933.

[6] New York Sun, Jan. 31, and Feb. 1, 1877.

[7] Statement of Irwin B. Linton in interview with author, Feb. 22, 1928. Linton was Field's secretary for many years.

Vice-President.[8]   This method, of course, would have resulted in the election of Tilden.

The commission met for organization January 31. The clerk of the Supreme Court administered the oath to Justice Clifford, who administered it to the other fourteen members.   All bound themselves impartially to examine and consider all questions submitted to the commission and to give a true judgment thereon.[9]   The bench, at which nine men were accustomed to sit, had to be extended to hold fifteen.   Clifford, a ponderous and testy Democrat who had been appointed during the presidency of James Buchanan, took the seat usually occupied by Chief Justice Waite, and his four brethren ranged themselves two on either side, "looking somewhat bare in their accustomed places without their accustomed robes." [10] There was perhaps a suggestion that they had been divested of their supposed judicial impartiality as well as of their robes.   The five senators sat to the right of the justices, and the five congressmen on the left.

On the following day the two houses of Congress met in joint session to count the electoral votes.   Field and Miller, representing the electoral commission, had seats at a bench directly in front of the clerk's desk.[11]   The galleries were filled with politicians and celebrities who were there to witness the beginning of the struggle for the presidential prize.   The count was begun by states, and proceeded as far as Florida when objections were made to the returns which were offered.   The dispute was referred to the electoral commission in the Supreme Court room.   Prominent lawyers in Congress assembled

[8] Doyle, John T., "The Electoral Commission of 1877," *Some Account of the Work of Stephen J. Field*, edited by Smith and Black, note, p. 415.

[9] See Sec. 2 of act of Congress providing for the commission in *Proceedings of the Electoral Commission*, p. 1.

[10] New York *World*, Feb. 2, 1877.

[11] *Ibid.*

in the court room to act as "objectors" for their respective parties. Among them were Charles O'Conor, Jeremiah S. Black, John A. Kasson, William M. Evarts, Stanley Matthews, and David Dudley Field. This older brother of Justice Field claimed that he had voted for Hayes, but had been shocked by Republican efforts to steal the election from Tilden. He came to the House of Representatives late in 1876, to fill a vacancy, presumably at the instance of Tilden.[12] The first meeting of the electoral commission found him on guard as a Democratic watchman. This was the first time he had served in any elective political office. He was widely known, however, not more for his efforts to bring about the codification of law than for his malodorous influential connections with the schemings of Jay Gould and other ruthless capitalists of New York, and for his service as counsel for the notorious Tweed. His principles stood in low repute, but his opponents feared him for his driving energy and his matchless ingenuity in the defense of his clients. He, a physical giant, arose as spokesman for the Democrats, while Evarts, small and withered, opened for the Republicans, "making in mere matter of bulk a tolerably sharp contrast."[13]

The work of the commission was now under way. The "objectors" were allowed limited periods in which to present their arguments, and testimony was presented to the commission. The situation seemed not greatly different from the trial of a case before the Supreme Court. "For all the new interest which hangs around the old chamber," said an observer, "it has not lost its air of strict seclusion. The curving and cushioned seats of spectators were full, but they were not crowded. There was room and more for counsel, and as the commission retains the

[12] Field, *Life of David Dudley Field*, p. 270.
[13] New York *World*, Feb. 2, 1877.

doorkeepers and attendants of the Supreme Court the
doors are kept and errands decorously done by a set of
gray-haired men who could not be more irreproachable
in plush and powder. The sole, solitary spot of life and
confusion in this venerable body, something less than a
week old, is a forgotten, shelf-like mantelpiece of a
gallery where the press stands, with an officer in at odd
moments to see that the press doesn't smoke." [14] It was
"an uncommonly dry, cool and judicial atmosphere,"
and was said to place a vigorous constraint upon the jury-
lawyer mannerisms of David Dudley Field.[15] Evarts
spoke with a vigorous intensity, the impulse driving him
"past the normal and proper close of every sentence." [16]
He looked "as if he had dried away from his clothes, which
hung and swung at every turn." [17] Charles O'Conor, on
the other hand, a head taller than Evarts, and large, stood
calmly with his coat tightly buttoned and spoke quietly
and earnestly, "deliberate to the last degree." [18]

When the arguments were heard the doors were closed,
and the commission deliberated in secret. It had first to
decide whether it would make use of any evidence other
than that contained in the papers which had been sent to
the President of the Senate. If not, its task would be
hardly more than declaring whether these papers had
been presented in the proper form, and it seemed quite
probable that the Republican votes might have to be
validated. On the other hand, if the commission could
make use of the ample evidence of intimidation and fraud
at and after the date of the local elections its task would
be greater, and it was apparent that some of the votes
might go to the Democrats. The loss of any votes at all

[14] *Ibid.*, Feb. 3, 1877.
[15] *Ibid.*
[16] *Ibid.*, Feb. 6, 1877.
[17] *Ibid.*
[18] *Ibid.*

would mean the defeat of the Republicans. The commission divided, eight to seven. Eight Republicans voted against going behind the returns, and seven Democrats voted in favor of doing so. Commissioners on each side offered profound reasons for their decisions, but no one paid much attention to the arguments. All attention was upon the fact that the alignment was political. On minor points Bradley and others at times seemed to side with opponents, but when it came to serious decisions such as this they remained loyal to their party interests. It is said that Bradley was pale and trembling when he gave his opinion, impressed with the overwhelming responsibility resting upon him,[19] but he voted with the Republicans.

Field, arguing at his best, supported the cause of the Democrats. In closing his long, persuasive speech he said: "Mr. President, I desire that this commission should succeed and give by its judgment peace to the country. But such a result can only be attained by disposing of the questions submitted to us on their merits. It cannot be attained by a resort to technical subtleties and ingenious devices to avoid looking at the evidence. It is our duty to ascertain if possible the truth, and decide who were in fact duly appointed electors in Florida, not merely who had received certificates of such appointment. That state has spoken to us through her courts, through her legislature, through her executive, and has told us in no ambiguous terms what was her will and whom she had appointed to express it. If we shut our ears to her utterances, and closing our eyes to the evidence decide this case upon the mere inspection of the certificates of the governor and canvassing board, we shall abdicate our powers, defeat the demands of justice, and

---

[19] Cox, S. S., *Three Decades of Federal Legislation* (1886), p. 653.

disappoint the just expectations of the people. The country may submit to the result, but it will never cease to regard our action as unjust in itself, and as calculated to sap the foundations of public morality." [20]

Thus the main issue with regard to the Florida votes was decided, eight to seven, in favor of the Republicans. If there had been any hopes that the justices on the commission would vote without regard to party affiliations they were now dispelled.

The electoral vote of Louisiana was next submitted to the commission. There was much evidence of corruption in connection with it. In a committee of the House of Representatives David Dudley Field, here unhampered by any atmosphere of judicial calm, subjected J. Madison Wells, Republican, to a merciless cross-examination. To the delight of the Democrats and the wrath of Republicans he uncovered shocking evidence of the devious doings of certain Republican agents in connection with the Louisiana ballots. The electoral commission decided, however, by the familiar party vote of eight to seven, that it could not go behind the returns in search of evidence. In many ways the credentials of the electors were challenged, but, eight to seven, the commission voted that it had no power to make inquiry.

In this way the struggle continued without change throughout the month of February. The final outcome of the eight to seven alignment was that Hayes was declared elected, with one hundred and eighty-five votes, against one hundred and eighty-four for Tilden. Hayes had received all the challenged votes, and the Republicans remained in power by a majority of one.

The Republicans were of course elated. They turned to the scramble for political patronage which characterized

[20] *Proceedings of the Electoral Commission*, p. 249.

the beginning of each administration, and showed no further interest in the Supreme Court. The Democrats, enraged that they had been duped into accepting the device of an electoral commission, made venomous attacks upon the Republican justices, particularly upon Bradley. So great had been the pressure upon him from both sides during the month of February that he cut himself off from callers, refused to read the papers, and finally stopped opening his personal mail.[21] Because he had been the fifth justice on the commission the public seemed to place upon him the burden of the political misdeeds of all. It is only fair to say that he seemed to have given all his energies to an attempt to arrive at an unbiased opinion, but with the Democratic public this fact did not matter. His son declared that he was unjustly made the final arbiter: "I say unjustly because he was by belief, by association, by past history, as staunch a Republican as any of those members of the commission who were deliberately selected by reason of their known political predilections."[22]

In Monticello, New York, Miller, Strong, and Bradley were hanged in effigy. Bradley, hanging between his two colleagues, bore the inscription, "I am crucified between two thieves."[23]

Field was no less enraged than his fellow Democrats, and seems not to have kept his opinions entirely to himself. He was accredited with starting the report that Bradley had read to Clifford and himself an opinion favoring Tilden in the Florida case, and then, after a night session with influential Republicans and certain western railroad men, had made use of most of the same

---

[21] Bradley, *Miscellaneous Writings*, p. 9.

[22] *Ibid.*

[23] New York *World*, March 9, 1877.

opinion but so changed it as to give his decision for Hayes.[24] Bradley, hearing of the charge while Field was in California, wrote to Field demanding that he prove the charge or else retract it. Field replied that what he had said had been misinterpreted and exaggerated, and that he had said nothing derogatory to Bradley's honor or integrity.[25]

In September of the same year Bradley wrote a letter to the Newark *Advertiser* concerning the charges which were still being made about him. He told how, at the time, he had pondered over the alternatives in the Florida situation, being now on one side and now on the other. At last he had discarded all that he had written and prepared a short opinion which he delivered to the commission, and which he still believed to be right.[26] Field remarked, in sending a copy of this letter to Tilden, "The language of the letter justifies some of the comments of the press upon the change of views which the judge experienced shortly before the vote was taken in the Florida case." [27]

Some of the Democrats on the electoral commission had wanted to issue a minority report. A proposed report was prepared by Congressman Josiah G. Abbott, and offered to his colleagues for consideration. It discussed in detail the controversies over the electoral votes in the four disputed states, attempting, of course, to justify the claims of the Democrats. It attempted to express the feelings of the minority members in the following closing paragraphs:

[24] See Poore, Ben. Perley, *Perley's Reminiscences*, pp. 331-32.

[25] Bradley, *Miscellaneous Writings*, p. 10.

[26] Bigelow, John, *Letters and Literary Memorials of Samuel J. Tilden*, pp. 568-69.

[27] Field to Tilden, *ibid.*, pp. 567-68.

The undersigned believe the action of the majority of the commission to be wrong, dangerous, nay, ruinous in its consequences and effects.

It tends to destroy the rights and liberties of the states and of the United States and the people thereof; because by it states may be robbed of their votes for President with impunity, and the people of the United States have foisted upon them a chief magistrate, not by their own free choice expressed, but by practices too foul to be tolerated in a gambling hell.

By the action of the commission the American people are commanded to submit to one as their chief magistrate who was never elected by their votes, whose only title depends on fraud, corruption, and conspiracy.

A person so holding that great office is a *usurper,* and should be and will be so held by the people.

As much a usurper as if he had signed and held it by military force; in either case, he equally holds against the consent of the people.

Let the people rebuke and over-rule the action of the commission. The only hope of the country rests on this being done, and done speedily and effectually, so that it may never become a precedent to sustain wrong and fraud in the future.

It is the first and highest duty of all good citizens who love their country to right this foul wrong, as soon as it may be done under the Constitution and laws.

Let it be done so thoroughly, so signally, so effectually, that no encouragement shall be given to put a second time so foul a blot on our national escutcheon.[28]

The report did not say how "this foul wrong" could be righted. It is hard to see what the people could have done, short of rebellion against the rule of the newly elected President, and it is equally hard to see how that could have been justified "under the Constitution and laws." Indeed, certain parts of the report read as if they were intended covertly to urge the people on to the new

[28] Bigelow, John, *Life of Samuel J. Tilden,* Vol. II, Appendix A, p. 403.

civil war which at times during the controversy had
been freely predicted. It is hardly surprising that some
of the Democratic members of the commission thought
it best not to aggravate further the disturbed condition
of the country by signing and publishing the document.
Field was not one of these, however. He saw the report
and approved it. "I know that it was a disappointment
to me," he said many years later, "that the address, either
as prepared, or as it might be amended by suggestions of
members of the Democratic minority, was not published." [29] Upon reflection Abbott himself came to see
so much political dynamite in the report that he filed it
away with the request that it be not published until after
his death." [30]

Hayes took the oath of office privately on Saturday,
March 3, 1877, and the formal inauguration was held on
the following Monday. It was reported that at the
inauguration the master of ceremonies "bowed in six
large, bald-headed men in gowns, the Supreme Court of
the United States, and with them one man of girth
without a gown, David Davis, the newly elected senator,
sitting with his brethren of the bench for the last time." [31]
Field and Clifford were conspicuously absent. A dis-
gruntled Democratic newspaper declared that they had
manifested a sense of propriety by staying away, and
that if they had stayed away from the electoral commission it would have been still better.[32] A Republican
paper, however, declared that in remaining away from
the inauguration "Justices Clifford and Field were guilty
of an act of discourtesy as discreditable and unworthy as

[29] Field to John Bigelow, Feb. 2, 1894, in Bigelow, *Letters and Memorials
of Samuel J. Tilden*, pp. 538-39.

[30] John Bigelow to Field, Jan. 31, 1894, *ibid.*, p. 537.

[31] New York *World*, March 6, 1877.

[32] New York *Sun*, March 6, 1877.

it was uncalled for and undignified. The only explanation of their conduct . . . is that, not being able to forget that they were Democrats, they were unable to remember that they were justices." [33]

It is quite possible that if these two Democratic justices had refused to serve on the electoral commission there would have been no commission at all. In that case it is impossible to tell how the crisis would have been resolved. The two men may or may not have blamed themselves for taking the positions. Clifford remained on the bench as long as possible, in spite of poor health and a failing mind, in the vain hope of seeing his successor appointed by a Democratic President.[34] Field, having entered the lists for his party, was loath to withdraw. The sting of defeat, which usually stimulated him to redoubled efforts, may have had something to do with it, while a fondness for the exercise of power undoubtedly played a part. At any rate, he not only maintained his interest in seeing the Democrats oust their opponents from control of the federal government, but began to look upon himself as a potential candidate for leading his party on to victory.

[33] Chicago *Tribune*, March 6, 1877.
[34] The *Nation*, July 28, 1881.

CHAPTER XI
GROOMED FOR THE PRESIDENCY

With the Republican President in office as a result of the decisions of the electoral commission the Democratic politicians had to endure four more years without political power or patronage. The Hayes administration gave rise to fewer grievances than had the two preceding administrations under President Grant, but the Democrats already had grievances enough and to spare, and they husbanded their righteous indignation for another battle. There were no outstanding leaders. Tilden was still a potential leader, but he had by no means a universal following among the discordant factions of the party in different sections of the country. There was a gambler's chance that any one of a dozen or more men might lead the party in the next campaign, and might even succeed in getting to the White House.

It seems evident that other members of the Field family had a great deal to do with stimulating Justice Field's interest in the presidency and with launching his name as a candidate. Each of the brothers was ambitious for himself and for the others. David Dudley and Cyrus had achieved both fortunes and reputations. David Dudley, in his unceasing busyness, was engaged in activities that were more reputable than his connections with Wall Street. For many years he had labored to bring about the codification of law, a cause in which he believed with all the zeal of a religious devotee. The results of his work were spreading not only throughout the United States but also throughout the world. He met with tremendous opposition of various sorts, and he reacted to the opposition with all the indominable force of his nature. This struggle tied in with the political situation. After he had espoused the cause of Tilden in the Hayes-Tilden controversy Tilden had the fortune or the misfortune to oppose part of Field's code in the New York legislature, whereupon the Democratic leader at once became anathema to the father of the codes.[1]

Tilden also made an enemy of Cyrus Field prior to the election of 1880. Through his pioneering success in laying the Atlantic cable Cyrus as well as his brother had become an internationally known figure. Though he was not trained in law he had many characteristics in common with his brothers. In the days when the locomotive symbolized the acme of force and energy he was characterized as a "locomotive in trousers." [2] After laying the cable he invested heavily in elevated railways in New York City. In 1879 when Field was in London pushing the stock Tilden suddenly unloaded heavily on the New York market, and the reaction put Field in a sorry financial plight.[3] Tilden now had two enemies among the Fields, and the Fields were not noted for forgiving their enemies. They had wealth, they had a learned brother of whom they were proud, and they loved distinction. It is not surprising that they were accused of setting out to chastise Tilden and capture the presidency for the family.

Neither Justice Field nor his brothers, however, made a direct appeal for political support. When in 1876, shortly after the nomination of Tilden, a San Francisco reporter had asked Justice Field what he thought of the candidates he had replied grandiloquently, "My present

---

[1] "Gath," in the Cincinnati *Enquirer*, June 19, 1880.
[2] See Clews, Henry, *Twenty-eight Years in Wall Street* (1887), p. 659.
[3] See account in the San Francisco *Chronicle*, June 21, 1880.

office is foreign to politics, and forbids my canvassing the merits or demerits of the gentlemen who are now striving for the chief magistracy." [4] His public attitude continued to be that of a man who was restrained by the duties of his office from taking any part in politics, and who with great reluctance allowed his name to be used by his friends. A number of things which were done quietly, however, now stand out as preliminary steps in his campaign. In the summer of 1877 he dictated to a stenographer his *Personal Reminiscences of Early Days in California*, parts of which had excellent possibilities as a campaign biography. In the following year he compiled and edited the proceedings of the California assembly with regard to the impeachment of Judge Turner,[5] evidently hoping to be prepared in advance for any use which his opponents might attempt to make of the Turner controversy in the presidential campaign.

In addition to the preparation of these documents he took occasion in a number of his Supreme Court opinions to state firmly and clearly a doctrine dear to the heart of most Democrats, that of states' rights.[6] In his test oath decisions shortly after the close of the Civil War he had made himself popular in the South by his defense of the rights of the former rebels. Now, although only in a dissenting opinion, he boosted his reputation tremendously in Virginia by declaring that states could not be compelled to accept negroes as jurors.[7] His fellow Democrat, Justice Clifford, concurred in his opinion.

The nominal management of his campaign was in the hands of men who were relatively inconspicuous in public

---

[4] Quoted in the San Francisco *Call*, June 22, 1880.

[5] *Proceedings of the Assembly.*

[6] Ex parte *Virginia*, 100 U. S. 339 (March 1, 1880); *Virginia* v. *Rives*, 100 U. S. 313 (March 1, 1880); *Sinking Fund Cases*, 99 U. S. 700 (May 5, 1879).

[7] Ex parte *Virginia*, 100 U. S. 339 (March 1, 1880).

life, such as Samuel B. Smith of New York, who in the early days had been Field's partner in Marysville, and L. Q. Washington of Virginia. In spite of the fact that Field was a relatively poor man his managers showed evidence of having plenty of money to spend. A large volume containing well written encomiums on Field and detailed approving analyses of his judicial work was provided for.[8] On April 25, 1880, the New York *Sun* published his *Reminiscences* in a full page of fine print. It was also issued in pamphlet edition.[9] The story was told in the third person instead of the first, and some points were omitted, such as the manner in which he had suggested himself as candidate for the position of first alcalde of Marysville, his failure to get Judge Turner impeached, and his refusal to accept an apology from Turner. The document was prefaced by a brief account of his family connections. On June 17, 1880, his friends were said to be scattering over Cincinnati, where the Democratic National Convention was to meet, thousands of pamphlets containing a portrait and this sketch of his life.[10] The Cincinnati *Commercial* of June 19 gave all of its first page and a part of the second page to the same story.

The talking points which were enumerated in Field's favor as a presidential candidate were as follows:

1. His pluck shown in various contests.
2. His comparative youth and personal vigor.
3. His record as a war Democrat.
4. His states' rights record.
5. His hard money record.

[8] *Some Account of the Work of Stephen J. Field*, edited by Smith and Black. Although the book was not published until 1881 it bears evidence of having been planned for use in the campaign had Field been nominated. A second edition was published in 1895.

[9] *Opinions and Papers of Stephen J. Field* (two-volume edition), No. 44.

[10] New York *Tribune*, June 18, 1880.

6. His strict construction of the Constitution.
7. His antagonism to presidential election frauds.
8. His freedom from entangling party complications.
9. His never having voted a Republican ticket.[11]

A great deal was said about his decisions in the test oath cases and about his opposition to the radical persecution of the Southerners after the war. It was believed that his decisions would win him the support of the Southern states. The West was claimed for him because of the fact that he was a Californian. It was hoped that on the first ballots in the Convention the votes would be scattered among so many candidates that Tilden would be unable to get the majority required for the nomination, and that he would withdraw in favor of Field, out of gratitude for the support which Field had given to him when on the electoral commission.

The nature of the personal influence of Field's brothers was a matter of great uncertainty. Former Senator Gwin of California, who was working for Field, had an interview with Tilden. It was reported that Tilden told Gwin that his relations with the other Fields would not influence him, and that as far as he was concerned Justice Field had no brothers.[12] Tilden's brother declared the report untrue, saying that Justice Field's name had not been mentioned during the interview.[13] Some admirers of Cyrus and David Dudley Field thought that their prestige would be of great help. Other persons thought Justice Field terribly handicapped as a candidate, saying that if one brother did not kill him the other would. "Judge Field . . . has worse relatives than Grant," said

[11] New York *Sun*, quoted in *Opinions and Papers*, No. 41.

[12] New York *Herald*, June 16, 1880; San Francisco *Call*, June 17, 1880.

[13] New York *Herald*, June 18, 1880; Cincinnati *Commercial*, June 19, 1880.

a Washington magazine.[14] David Dudley was shrewd enough to refrain from open campaigning, and claimed that he had nothing more than a brotherly interest in the contest.[15] Either he or Cyrus chartered a car in which a crowd of Field advocates went from New York to the Convention.[16] In another car rode a part of the Tammany Hall delegation, whose allegiance had been temporarily captured by the Fields. Arriving in Cincinnati the members of this delegation began with enthusiasm to circulate the New York *Star*, the organ of Kelly, their leader, which was loaded with Field literature.[17]

If Field's test oath and negro juror cases had made him popular in the South his Chinese and railroad decisions had already made him thoroughly distasteful to large numbers of Californians. It was said that in the state Democratic convention not more than twenty-five delegates favored him, and these refused to demonstrate their weakness by coming out in his behalf. All but two of them—and these two cast their votes by proxy—came out in favor of other men, though it was noticeable that none voted for Tilden.[18] Allen G. Thurman received the largest number of votes in the state convention, while Tilden and Seymour received considerable numbers.[19] It was declared that resolutions would have been passed opposing Field's candidacy had not his friends agreed not to work for him.[20] Samuel M. Wilson, a leading attorney for the Central Pacific Railroad, failed to secure election as a delegate to the National Convention, but he went

---

[14] The *Republic*, April 11, 1880.

[15] Cincinnati *Enquirer*, June 19, 1880.

[16] Sacramento *Record-Union*, June 19, 1880.

[17] Cincinnati *Commercial*, June 20, 1880.

[18] Richmond *Dispatch*, June 15, 1880.

[19] Davis, *Political Conventions in California*, p. 422.

[20] Richmond *Dispatch*, June 15, 1880.

anyway, to do what he could for Field.[21] So also did Lloyd Tevis, president of the Wells and Fargo Express Company.[22]

The publicity work of the Field managers spread to the Pacific Coast. A number of the Democratic clubs in California, alarmed by it, met to denounce the men in the East who were campaigning for Field.[23] Field entertained some of the California delegation at his home in Washington prior to the date of the Convention,[24] but failed to win all of them over, and it was evident at Cincinnati that the delegation was divided. Members of other delegations sought to solidify the Californians for their local candidate,[25] but without avail. The division was highly disturbing to the morale of the Field crowd.

It was common gossip in Cincinnati that Field was a representative of capital. He was said to be the favorite of the Central Pacific Railroad, and it was believed that through Cyrus Field he was connected with capitalist interests in the East. The purse of Cyrus himself was said to be well lined, and to promise to be a fruitful source of Democratic sustenance in case his brother was nominated. The Field managers declared that Tilden would not be nominated, and therefore would not contribute heavily to the campaign. They hinted that the Field contributions would be wholly adequate as a substitute.[26]

Field's managers were the first to get under way in Cincinnati. The campaign was, to quote a newspaper correspondent, "brought here in sections from Washing-

<hr />

[21.] San Francisco *Chronicle*, June 23, 1880.

[22] Richmond *Dispatch*, June 15, 1880; Chicago *Tribune*, June 18, 1880.

[23] San Francisco *Call*, June 18 and 22, 1880; New York *Herald*, June 18, 21, 1880.

[24] San Francisco *Chronicle*, June 16, 1880.

[25] *Ibid.*, June 23, 1880.

[26] New York *Tribune*, June 22, 1880.

ton and set up on arrival." [27]   Headquarters were "in a
great spreading room at the Gibson for the better
convenience of Southerners. . . . Further up town is
the business of Field's boom, Beverly Tucker in command,
a Virginian of thirty years' training in politics, apt to
over-manipulate, but in this matter successful. Col.
Washington is another Virginian in the same work." [28]
Said a local paper, "Justice Field had a boom yesterday
in the shape of a band wagon drawn through the streets
by six white horses, and ornamented with Joe Seiter as
pilot on the driver's seat." [29]   A New York correspondent
in Cincinnati wrote a vivid, though unsympathetic,
description of the Field campaign:

"The movement in support of his nomination is the
only one which has been forwarded in this city by a
liberal use of money and by spectacular effects. It is
well known that, for some time past, the Judge has been
appealing to the country through a literary bureau,
modeled after the one in which Tilden employed his
nincompoops in 1876. Several journalists have been
retained in his service and have acted as his agents in the
manipulation of Southern delegates. While the politicians
of the party were quietly consulting in the city, in the
hope of harmonizing the factions, the Field movements
burst upon them in all the glory of banners, band wagons
and biographies. They have inspected with curiosity,
and have returned to their work. This manifestation of
what money will do deserves especial consideration,
because it is, up to this time, the sole exhibition of its
kind in Cincinnati. No other candidate has even his
name displayed on a poster, either in the street or any of
the hotels.

[27] New York *World*, June 22, 1880.
[28] *Ibid.*
[29] Cincinnati *Commercial*, June 20, 1880.

"There are not even placards to guide the stranger to the headquarters of the delegations. No candidate except Field has chosen to advance his fortunes by displaying anything which could appeal to the eye or the intellect, and the method pursued by him has impressed the kind of delegate known as 'Moss-back' with astonishment. The first and second pages of the Cincinnati *Commercial,* which are ordinarily reserved for the most important news of the day, were covered this morning with an elaborate biography of Judge Field. This advertisement must cost a handsome amount. A large wagon, draped in national colors and containing a brass band, dispensed music from one end of the city to the other this afternoon, and upon banners which hung from the sides of the wagon were the words: 'Stephen J. Field. We must have the Pacific states.'

"A delegate, who was unacquainted with the majesty of the Field family, impatiently declared such displays were all nonsense. He added that the party didn't care a copper for the Pacific states, and couldn't get them if it did.

" 'What we do want and must have,' said he, 'is New York and Indiana, and the returning boards.' Having said that he was a delegate from one of the states which Judge Field claims to be able to carry, he was asked if all this enthusiasm was spontaneous production of the Pacific Slope. 'No,' he replied, 'this cry comes out of the mouths of Cyrus W. Field and David Dudley Field in New York. They are the persons who want the Pacific states, and they are paying for these biographical advertisements and band wagons, but it wont work.' Indeed, the average Democrat delegate seems to believe that money spent for banners, music, and long advertisements of a candidate's remarkable history is not placed where it will do the most good. It seems to him an indefensible waste of something which ought to have gone into his own pocket. This delegate's eyes brightened for a moment as the Field missionary band began to play 'Dixie,' a melody which the leader had probably chosen as appropriate for a Democratic convention, but he soon turned away with a look of disgust on his face and sought comfort at the bar." [30]

In spite of the sounds and signs of triumph which the Field managers were displaying they were having troubles. The Pacific Coast delegations were not falling into line. California remained recalcitrant. It was a discouraging task to play up the qualifications of a man whose own state was against him. The opposition was not confined merely to the delegates. Telegrams kept pouring in from Democrats back home urging the withdrawal of Field's name,[31] and letters were received by newspapers in the East reiterating and explaining the causes of the local hostility.[32] For a time during the days prior to the opening of the Convention reports declared that Field seemed to be making fully as much progress as any other candidate, but the reporters may have been deceived by the display, rather than influenced by any accurate knowledge of what politicians were thinking. By the time the Convention was about to open the Field boom seemed to be in eclipse. Few people were to be found at the Gibson House, and little attention was paid to the band wagon. Field was not attacked, except by the barbed pens of a few nervously energetic newspaper men. He was merely ignored.

Such expressions of opinion as there were indicated that the party had no expectation of carrying the Pacific states, while the Southern states, where Field was said to

[30] New York *Times*, June 20, 1880.
[31] San Francisco *Alta*, June 22, 1880.
[32] See for example the Richmond *Dispatch*, June 15, 1880.

be strong, would vote for any Democratic candidate who was nominated. The appeal had to be made to the doubtful states, such as New York and Indiana. Some of his economic principles were against him, notably those having to do with paper currency. His nomination would inject a strange issue, one delegate declared, while the need of the party was for a strong ticket and a light platform. "There is no talking over the money question; it has dropped out of sight. The swift march of events, resumption and prosperity, has solved the question for the time and silenced the war of the 'hards' and 'softs' in the Democratic party." [33] Hence it was that while one newspaper declared on June 22 that Field was probably accumulating votes as fast as any other candidate,[34] another congratulated the civilized world that his invaluable services on the supreme bench were likely to be secured for four years longer.[35]

Tilden lent interest to the general situation by a letter in which he declined to be a candidate. Seymour had also declined. There were many other candidates, but none were particularly prominent. Bickering, trading, posing, boasting, and prophesying went on through the days in which politicians were pouring into Cincinnati from all parts of the country. Finally, on June 23, came the first show of hands.

It was a sultry, hot day. In spite of rules as to admission visitors jammed into the hall in droves, struggled for seats, and, exhausted, packed themselves in like sardines. Men pulled themselves out of their coats and fanned their streaming faces and soggy bosoms with their hats. "Heat, flies and discomfort," scrawled a reporter, in his efforts to

---

[33] New York *Herald*, June 22, 1880.

[34] Washington *Post*, June 22, 1880.

[35] New York *Sun*, quoted in the Sacramento *Record-Union*, June 23, 1880.

picture the occasion.[36] The chairman rapped for order
and announced that the Reverend Doctor Taylor would
lead the assembly in prayer. That gentleman arose, a
clergyman "with a bald head, a bombazine jacket, and a
profound sense of the importance of his duty." [37] Some
of the delegates arose, and "the ludicrous and incongruous
scene was presented of a few hundred men standing in
prayer while as many thousands, mistaking the purpose,
shouted vociferously, 'Sit down!' 'Down in front!' and
'Oh do sit down!' Meantime Dr. Taylor communicated
a great deal of information concerning the fundamental
principles of the great Democratic party and everybody
in the great hall yawned, whispered, chatted and suggested to a thoughtful mind whether the Almighty was
being particularly honored by the marked inattention
of the assemblage." [38]

The matter of credentials was taken up, and, in
harmony with the report of the committee on credentials,
the Tammany delegation was ruled out. Two rival delegations had come from New York, one representing the
Tilden group and the other under the leadership of Kelly
of Tammany Hall. Kelly had declared that he was ready
to support any candidate who might be nominated except
Tilden,[39] and although the Field managers declared that
they had made no advances to the Tammany Democrats [40]
many of them had been quite friendly, and many potential
votes were lost with the action of the Convention.
Efforts were made to over-rule the action of the committee but they failed, and the Tammany delegation sat
outside the rails. During the hours through which the

[36] New York *Herald*, June 24, 1880.
[37] *Ibid.*
[38] *Ibid.*
[39] Chicago *Tribune*, June 19, 1880.
[40] New York *Tribune*, June 22, 1880.

controversy went on the temperature rose higher and higher, and the audience in the great hall grew more and more restless.

At length the Convention was ready for the nomination of candidates for the position of leadership in the next battle with the Republicans. The names of the states were called alphabetically, and in that order the nominations of favorite sons were made. Alabama and Arkansas had no candidates to present. When California was called J. E. McElrath, of Oakland, a squarely built, business type of man, arose, mounted the platform, and delivered a speech in nomination of Justice Field. The speech was a matter-of-fact statement of Field's claims to qualification for the presidency, told at rather too great length. McElrath was not an orator. As he faced the sweltering audience he read his speech in a deliberate manner, with the thumb of his left hand in the arm hole of his vest, while he gesticulated with his right hand.[41] One observer thought the gesticulation funny, rather than impressive, since, "as his arms went up, his eyes went down to the manuscript which lay on the desk before him." [42] "Neither the people nor the delegates cared to tax their minds in an attempt to analyze the greatness of Field's legal triumphs, which were not described in a popular or entertaining way." [43] As an oratorical effort the speech "was a decided failure. Unrelieved by eloquence, wit or humor, it wearied the Convention, and evoked cries of 'time, time; cut it off,' &c., from the impatient delegates." [44] The confusion in the hall was so great that few could hear what the speaker was saying,

[41] *Ibid.*, June 24, 1880.
[42] Chicago *Tribune*, June 24, 1880.
[43] New York *Times*, June 24, 1880.
[44] Cincinnati *Enquirer*, June 24, 1880.

and when he sat down he was greeted with sighs of relief and weak applause.

After an interval the nomination was seconded by a man named Brown, from Colorado, "who looked like the 'lime kiln man,' and so waved his arms and flourished his head as to excite pity in some breasts and such indignation in others that he was compelled to yield by a storm of catcalls and hisses, after which he hid his face in his hands and buried his confusion near the skirts of the president." [45] The restless mob, adversely impressed by Field's spokesmen, had turned "thumbs down."

The names of other states were called and other men were placed in nomination, in speeches that were better adapted to the audience. Before the Convention adjourned for the day the first ballot was taken. Field was fifth from the highest in number of votes, with Hancock, Bayard, Payne, and Thurman ahead of him. He received sixty-five votes out of a total of seven hundred and twenty-eight. Only six of the twelve votes from California were cast for him, and only one of the six from Colorado. He received only two votes from Massachusetts, none from Connecticut, and none from New York. He showed no strength at all in the large, central states of the country. His friends were mortified and chagrined at his beggarly array of votes,[46] while the spectators, who had condemned him the instant he was nominated, regarded giving him any votes at all as superfluous folly.[47] His managers had declared that his strength would develop after the first ballot, when the usual votes for favorite sons had been cast, but his showing at the beginning was so poor that expectation of anything better appeared fantastic indeed.

[45] New York *Herald*, June 24, 1880.

[46] New York *Tribune*, June 25, 1880.

[47] Cincinnati *Enquirer*, June 25, 1880.

The second ballot was taken on the following day, and sixty-five and one-half votes were counted for Field. Then it was discovered that Hancock's strength had grown tremendously. Delegations began to change their votes in his favor, and the Field votes went with the landslide. Hancock, a general during the Civil War, not more than average in intelligence and not more than mediocre as a politician, was declared the Democratic candidate for the presidency of the United States. He and his colleague, English, were to make a poor showing against the Republican opponents, Garfield and Arthur.

Field had been assured that early in the proceedings he would receive at least two hundred and fifty votes,[48] and he had evidently been more easily convinced as to the nature of his support than a seasoned politician would have been. Many persons, however, had apparently believed up to the time of the Convention that he would make a fair showing. The intolerant reaction of the Convention to his nominating speeches doubtless counted heavily against him. He had little hold on the loyalty of the politicians who were present as delegates. That, however, was true of all the candidates. They were pretty much pawns in the hands of the schemers who traded and bargained over them.[49] "There was no personal enthusiasm on the part of the mass of any candidate's supporters, not even those of General Hancock himself. Most of the men who were supporting Payne, Bayard, Field, Thurman, and Randall, really cared very little personally for their candidates. They saw the one withdrawn without regret; and when they felt like it abandoned the other with the greatest alacrity." [50]

[48] Field, *Record of the Family*, p. 107.

[49] New York *Times*, June 24, 1880.

[50] New York *Tribune*, June 25, 1880.

Although Field's friends had not hesitated to use for him all the propaganda methods characteristic of political campaigns he himself had sat in the background, and had at no time taken an open and active part in the movement. A newspaper, in presenting brief biographies of many candidates, had closed its paragraph on Field by saying that he "will serve—if nominated and elected! !" [51] He was not among the defeated aspirants who sent telegrams of congratulation to General Hancock—he was a judicial officer who could take no part in the game of politics! When interviewed concerning the late experience he declared that it was but an episode in his life, and would soon be forgotten. He would have nothing more to do with politics. He liked his position, and was devoted to the philosophy and practice of law. He considered that his defeat was due to the lack of support in his own state. When asked if he would go into politics again he vigorously answered, "Never!" [52]

In spite of the claims that he was an unwilling candidate, both friends and enemies who knew him well have given assurance that he wanted very much the distinction of being President. They have likewise expressed the assurance that he would not have filled the office well. He was typically a man with the proverbial "legal mind," and belonged on the bench rather than in an executive position. Field was not a "man of the people." He did not adjust himself readily in relationships with the masses, and he was proud of his difference from others, of his superiority. However laudable this may have been it did not help him as a politician, and it would not have helped him in the handling of the innumerable human problems which face every President. In harmonizing different factions of his party, in distributing the patron-

[51] New York *Herald*, June 22, 1880.
[52] "Celebrities at Home," The *Republic*, July 4, 1880, p. 310.

age, in recommending adjustments of the intricate problems connected with the tariff, in dealing with the currency problems of the country, he would undoubtedly have exercised an intolerant dogmatism that would not have promised well for his administration. Indeed, the lamentable failure of his campaign for the nomination may have augured well for what his administration would have been. He knew the "game of politics" from the outside, but he knew it as a student and not as a successful practitioner.

With the pride and confidence which he had in himself he evidently felt that there was no office too great for him to fill in an able and distinguished fashion. He was evidently unaware of the extent to which, during the years which he spent on the bench, his subtle enslavement to particular dogmas and principles had gone on while his capacity for adapting easily and rapidly to new circumstances had at least not developed. Instead of fitting in well with all phases of the life around him he had the habit of insisting that circumstances be adapted meticulously to suit his own ideas, or else he must register a protest or withdraw himself entirely. While on the bench he was noted for the number of occasions on which he felt it necessary to register dissent in forceful opinions rather than acquiesce when the majority was against him. Such a tendency might be laudable in that it showed him to be tenaciously loyal to his principles, but it did not mark him as a man adapted to the give and take of political life.

CHAPTER XII

MORE POLITICS

With the lamentable failure of their campaign in 1880 Field's brothers evidently surrendered the hope of making him President. In spite of their wealth they had not been able to master the technique of politics. Most of his eastern friends, and even Field himself, accepted his defeat as final. Somewhat surprisingly, however, his name continued to be mentioned in California for the position of Democratic standard-bearer. He himself may have had nothing directly to do with this fact. The suggestions seem to have come from a small group of conservative leaders in the state. They were evidently received warmly by lawyers long established in their profession, particularly those who were employed by corporations, and were supposed to have the backing of the principal railroad men in the state. His railroad and Chinese decisions from 1880 until after the date of the Democratic National Convention in 1884 were of such effect as to make him the object of the envenomed bitterness of the masses of the people in California, while the railroad decisions strengthened him with the railroad leaders and with other conservative minorities. While he was being attacked by such newspapers as the San Francisco *Chronicle,* he received periodic encomiums from the *Argonaut.* In 1882 the San Francisco *Evening Post* gave him publicity by publishing a condensed version of his *Personal Reminiscences of Early Days in California.*[1]

In February, 1884, public attention was turned to him by an anonymous letter of inquiry, copies of which were

[1] San Francisco *Evening Post,* April 15, 22, 1882.

addressed to many "representative Democrats" throughout the state, requesting opinions as to the most available
man for the Democratic nomination, and closing with
the query, "What do you think of the availability of
Justice Stephen J. Field as a presidential candidate?" [2]
The letter was effective in giving new life to political
gossip. From that time on throughout the spring there
were rumors that a vigorous campaign for Field was
being organized. The state convention was to be held in
June. "I beg to call attention," wrote one of his political
enemies to another, "to the fact that an effort is being
made for the election of a Field delegation, and that your
county is reckoned by his friends, as one in which to
operate successfully. Being forwarned is to be forearmed.
So saith the *Scripture.*" [3] Politicians in many other
counties seem to have received similar warnings, for
twenty-two county conventions instructed against supporting Field in the state convention. [4]

Early in March James A. Johnson, editor of the San
Francisco *Alta*, a well-written, pro-railroad newspaper,
wrote to Field offering to aid in the promotion of his
candidacy. Field replied that he had not the political
aspirations which were attributed to him. It was only
out of deference to the wishes of his friends that he had
not long since declared in print that his name could not
be used in any political contest. "I have looked over the
whole matter, and months ago, as I told you last summer,
I came to the conclusion that it will serve no useful
purpose to bring me out as a candidate for the presidential nomination." He would be proud to have the support

[2] San Francisco *Call*, Feb. 10, 1884.

[3] Williams, of 320 Sansome Street, San Francisco, to S. M. White of Los
Angeles. Among the letters to White on file in library of Stanford
University.

[4] Terry, in *Character and Career of Stephen J. Field*, p. 23.

of California, he said, but "there is no use in disguising the fact that owing to prejudices in certain quarters it will be difficult to obtain it. I shall certainly not deny my record to secure any one's support."

He continued with a discussion of his record: "My judicial opinions on subjects of interest in California —the position of the Chinese in the state, the taxation of property of railways, and the Mexican land grants—have, I am aware, given offense to a large number of people who would have had me disregard the law, the treaties with China and Mexico, and the Constitution, to carry out their views and schemes. I could not thus do violence to my convictions of duty—the thing was impossible. Indeed, I would not have changed a line of what I wrote, had I known beforehand that for it I should lose the support of California, nor would I now change a line to secure the vote of every man in the state.

"One of these days our good people will see their error, and then they will do me full justice. I am content to wait for their ultimate judgment of approval, which, sooner or later, will certainly come. They will then admit that a just judge could not ignore the law or treaties, or the Constitution, however offensive and detested the persons protected by them may have been. And as to railway taxation, all will then acknowledge that, under any just administration of the government, associated capital can not be assessed on different principles and taxed at different rates from individual capital. And as to the Mexican grants, it will not then be questioned that the grantees had a right to stand upon the plighted faith of the government, under the treaty which gave us the magnificent domain of California, that they should be protected in all their rights of property. But enough of this. Sufficient it is to say that my strong inclination has long been, and still is, against being in the political contest of this year. I am content to remain where I am. There I may do some good, and, after all, position is only desirable as a means of doing good." [5]

Some weeks later, when a delegation from Missouri went to Washington to urge him to permit his name to be used, he replied with much the same statement. When asked if he would accept the nomination if it were offered him he replied: "Such a contingency is scarcely possible. I have made no effort to secure the nomination, and have discouraged all efforts on the part of my friends to that end. But there is no instance in the history of the country where the nomination of a national convention actually tendered has been refused, and I have no idea that I should prove an exception." [6]

The leadership of the Democratic party in California was dominated by men of the type which fought the railroad interests in the constitutional convention. Throughout the spring of 1884 a special session of the legislature had been in session for the purpose of aiding the state in collecting railroad taxes and in keeping the corporations in hand. Pro-railroad men had successfully blocked all such efforts. When the Democratic state convention met at Stockton on June 10 it of course condemned the Republican party for the failure of the legislation. By going farther than this, however, it showed that it was more than a Democratic convention. It took account of the fact that certain Democrats then in office had been faithless to the people. The fifth resolution of the platform said, in part:

That while no amount of care can at all times prevent the intrusion into parties of faithless men, who enter with a false pledge upon their lips merely to ruin and betray—yet the

[5] Quoted in Gorham, G. C., *Biographical Notice of Stephen J. Field*, pp. 79-80.
[6] Quoted, *ibid.*, p. 81.

party becomes responsible for the conduct of such recreant members only when, having discovered them, it fails to condemn their course; that it is the duty of a party, if it is true to itself and to the people, to expel from its ranks and denounce as unworthy of public trust and lost to all sense of honor, traitors and pledge-breakers. Therefore we do now denounce railroad commissioners Carpenter and Humphreys, who have broken their pledges with reference to freight and fare reductions; Lieutenant-Governor John Daggett, whose casting vote was ever thrown into the scale to turn the balance against the people; Attorney-General Marshall, who violated his solemn pledge, taken at San José, that in the collection of revenues from railroads there should be no compromises; and those Democratic senators and assemblymen who at the late session of the legislature proved faithless to their pledges and betrayed the cause of the people—men whose recreant conduct has since met with such emphatic denunciation and rebuke at the hands of their own local constituencies.[7]

The platform declared that the administration of the state government had been greatly embarrassed by the interference of the federal judiciary with the collection of state taxes on the property of railroad corporations, and invoked remedial legislation from Congress. It recognized the importance of railroads to the state but declared that "we view with alarm the power of the railroad monopoly as manifested in its pernicious and corrupting interference in politics and in its control of officials elected by the people."

Samuel J. Tilden and Thomas A. Hendricks were declared to be the choice of the Democracy of California for President and Vice-President, with Allen G. Thurman as second choice for President if Tilden failed to accept the nomination. The twenty-third and final resolution of the platform read as follows:

[7] See platform in Davis, *Political Conventions in California,* pp. 456-60.

That the Democracy of California unanimously repudiates the presidential aspirations of Stephen J. Field, and that we hereby pledge ourselves to vote for no man as delegate to the national convention of July 8, 1884, who will not before this convention pledge himself to use his earnest endeavors to defeat these aspirations.

When the platform was presented to the convention a delegate moved that the twenty-third section be stricken out. Francis G. Newlands, corporation lawyer from San Francisco, seconded the motion and, in spite of hisses, groans, cat calls, and cries of "Time, time!" made a powerful speech in defense of Justice Field. He told of Field's decisions which gave protection to personal liberty, he analyzed the Chinese situation, and showed that although Field had struck down obnoxious local legislation he had done more than any other person to secure restrictive legislation by the federal government. In his railroad decisions he had been subject only to the dictates of the law. He had merely insisted on equal rights for all. The Governor, in calling the recent special session of the legislature, had proposed that the railroads be permitted to pass on a proportionate share of their tax indebtedness to their bondholders, a plan which Field had suggested in the Santa Clara case.[8] A bill embodying the plan was said by the anti-monopolists to have been defeated by the railroads. That did not indicate that Field was a railroad agent. "Had he been ambitious for office, had he been a demagogue, had he been desirous of prostituting his high functions to the desire of elevation to the presidency, he would have decided the queue cases against the Chinese, and the railroad cases in favor of the people. And had he done so, he would have violated his conscience and stained his brilliant record. . . . I think

[8] See Chap. XI.

the decisions of Mr. Justice Field were right; but is this convention to be a court of appeals in which everything decided in courts of justice must come?"

"The fact is, gentlemen," Newlands continued, "Mr. Justice Field, in his official capacity, is the friend of no one, the enemy of no one; but the upright, impartial judge—a judge who braves the present and looks to the future for vindication. It causes me no little mortification that the career of so distinguished a man should need vindication at my hands. I appeal to no man to support Mr. Justice Field simply because his decision in this or that case was right. His claims to the presidency do not rest upon his decisions in individual cases. They rest upon his distinguished career as a legislator, jurist, constitutional expounder, and statesman, and upon his brilliant public services. But when it is sought to assail him with reproach and calumny because of decisions which have run counter to popular feeling, it is the right and privilege of every friend not only to vindicate the decisions called in question, but to recall to minds clouded with prejudice his entire judicial history, replete with splendid efforts and crowned with successful struggles in behalf of constitutional law and individual rights. . . . I am admonished that my time has expired. I will only add that this resolution repudiating the honorable aspirations of a great and eminent man is a gratuitous insult, and as such I denounce it." [9]

When Newlands took his seat D. M. Delmas, who had opposed the railroads in the Santa Clara case, obtained the floor. "I admired the gallant manner in which the gentleman who has just addressed you has defended his friend, Mr. Justice Field," he said, "and therefore I desired, for one, that he should have all the time he

[9] As quoted in the *Argonaut*, June 28, 1884, which had reprinted from the San Francisco *Alta*.

wanted to vindicate his friend. And now, gentlemen, what is your verdict?" A voice shouted "Guilty!" and the hall resounded with applause.

Delmas continued with an attack on Field's Chinese and railroad records. He concluded: "When the people of this state undertook to collect from corporations their share of the revenue under the constitution, who was it that brought the state to the pitiful pass that it must beg such beggarly pittances as they were minded to pay? Stephen J. Field. We have been told that, in all these decisions, the learned justice followed the dictates of his own conscience. If the conscience of Stephen J. Field is so constituted that he believes that the people have no rights, and can form no laws that are binding on the railroads, is that a reason why the people should select him as their standard-bearer? When the Democratic party still holds to the doctrine that it is the people, and not the railroads, that own this state, will it accept that as a reason for accepting Stephen J. Field as its standard-bearer? I have seen this commonwealth, in her legislative halls being overwhelmed by corruption; but may I never see her in the attitude that some Democrats would have placed her in, licking the hand that smites her and accepting from the railroad corporation their chosen candidate, Stephen J. Field." [10]

The resolution was retained by a vote of 453 to 19.

Newspapers such as the *Alta* could find no words too harsh for their descriptions of the action of the convention. Pixley, of the *Argonaut*, week after week gave free play to his excellent capacity for vituperative expression. "The most contemptible thing of all," he said, "was the abject cowardice of the minority of Democratic gentlemen who allowed the vile mob to run over and frighten them from standing boldly up to the vindication

[10] San Francisco *Examiner*, June 12, 1884.

of Stephen J. Field. A Democratic state convention, 453 to 19, attempted, with deliberate insolence, to insult the only candidate that the California Democracy ever had for the presidency, and the only one it ever ought to have until the communists and sand-lotters have ceased to intimidate gentlemen, and ceased to have influence in the Democratic party." [11]

M. D. Boruck, a prominent Californian who was notoriously pro-railroad, declared that D. M. Delmas should be punished for his speech before the convention. "The Supreme Court of the United States will not be setting a good example if they allow D. M. Delmas, an officer of the Court, to practice before it again until he makes reparation for his contempt of that body, in impugning the motives, and charging dishonesty upon one of its most honored members. They owe it to their colleague, that D. M. Delmas should purge himself of this contempt." [12]

Field was quoted as saying of the situation: "There is a radical element in California politics that alarms the conservative element in that state, without regard to party organization, as dangerous to the rights of property. I have never swerved from my duty not to pander to that element, which is therefore hostile to me. But politicians have done so, and this is the secret of the resolution which has been aimed at me. This element does not constitute a majority in the Democratic party of California, but it is large enough to intimidate its organization. This element resented certain judicial decisions of mine, not one of which would I retract to receive the nomination. Therefore the action of the convention is no surprise or disappointment to me. Most assuredly I have not desired any support which was not the result

[11] *Argonaut,* June 28, 1884.
[12] San Francisco *California Spirit of the Times,* June 21, 1884.

of an open and frank appeal to public opinion, and as you know, I said months ago that I did not expect to receive this support, and it was so stated in public print. I have not sought a nomination, and if I have allowed my name to be used, it was in deference to the opinions of friends in different parts of the country, who acted without reference to California sentiment. The matter is with them and not with me. I don't suppose they will modify their action because they fail to receive support in a quarter where they never expected it." [13]

A friendly biographer said that in referring to the action of the convention Field simply remarked that better and wiser men than he had been reviled, persecuted, and driven from their country for causes which were afterwards repeated to their honor, and for which monuments were erected to their memory, and that he was content to abide his time.[14] There is reason to suspect, however, that in his more private utterances there was somewhat more of vigor and less of piety.

His friends in California continued to agitate for him. The *Alta* suggested Roswell P. Flower, of New York, as a running mate. "Field and Flower" would be a good campaign slogan, it thought.[15] Judge Gordon N. Mott, Field's old friend in Marysville, now a feeble old man, declared, "If I can live to see Stephen J. Field President of the United States, I will die contented." [16] The most eager of friends, however, had soon to admit that their hopes were of no avail. They were able to build up no strength for their candidate, and at the national convention they found sentiment for Grover Cleveland so

[13] San Francisco *Alta*, June 18, 1884.
[14] Gorham, *Biographical Notice*, p. 81.
[15] San Francisco *Alta*, June 30, 1884.
[16] *Ibid.*

strong that Justice Field's backers "abandoned all hope
and would not put his name forward to be slaughtered." [17]

In November, 1884, Grover Cleveland was elected
President in the race against James G. Blaine, Republican
candidate. In 1882 a Democratic Governor had been
elected in California by a majority of more than twenty-
three thousand over his Republican opponent. In this
election, however, Blaine received some thirteen thousand
more California votes for the presidency than Cleveland.
Conservative Democrats and Republicans were secretly or
openly gleeful at the Republican landslide, looking at
the result as flowing from the action of the Stockton
convention. "Hon. Stephen J. Field of the United States
Supreme Court may well feel proud of the indorsement
given him by the people of California," wrote M. D.
Boruck. "It is true that the state went largely Republican, but in that very result the honor came to Judge
Field, in the fact that the people overwhelmingly defeated
the scoundrelism of the Stockton convention, which
distinguished itself in its low, degrading, infamous insults
offered Judge Field. The people of California have
avenged him, and in scoring a great triumph for themselves, secured a still greater one for him in the fact that
those who stood by him were not of his own political
faith. His enemies, so far as he was concerned, 'builded
better than they knew.' " [18]
The defeat of the California Democrats was realized
by the leaders with humiliation, and a further blow was
added the following January when Leland Stanford,
president of the Southern Pacific Railroad Company,
was elected to the United States Senate by the state

[17] *Ibid.*, July 12, 1884.
[18] San Francisco *California Spirit of the Times*, Nov. 22, 1884.

legislature. At the time of the first Democratic presidential victory in a quarter of a century the California Democratic leaders appeared to be impotent. This was exasperating, particularly since there would be patronage to be distributed. Said the *Argonaut:* "Boruck, in his *Spirit of the Times,* with inexcusable malice and altogether indefensible vindictiveness, reprints the roll call of the Stockton convention on striking out the resolution censuring Mr. Justice Field. . . . We are informed that Judge Field carries this printed list in his hat, and that whenever any of these names are presented for office he will see to it that they are not appointed if he can help it. The election of Governor Stanford will aid to hold up the Judge's hands. Not only are they very good friends, but these same men who are, and have been, so vindictive against Judge Field, are conspicuous enemies of the railroad, and are most of them defamers and opponents of Governor Stanford and his associates. This will be a difficult political combination for a set of politicians whose inexcusable conduct led the Democratic party from twenty-seven thousand majority to thirteen thousand minority." [19]

The executive committee of the Democratic party met in San Francisco January 15 to decide on a course of action. They asked Stephen M. White,[20] of Los Angeles, who had been president of the Stockton convention, to meet with them. At the meeting they determined to put up a bold front, stand by the action of the Stockton convention, and fight and belittle the Field faction of the party. Barclay Henley, a California representative in Congress, cheered them on, telling them that they were just right, and that no backward step should be

[19] *Argonaut,* Jan. 31, 1885.
[20] For a biography of White see Dobie, Edith, *The Political Career of Stephen Mallory White.*

taken. It was a strange spectacle in Washington, he said, to see a small junta, most of them in the pay of the railroad, undertaking to control the party, "and through Field here declaring that no member of, or sympathizer with, the Stockton convention should be recognized by the administration." "That," he continued, "is what Field told me, and right there the fight commenced. Field is simply a d—d fool and can't begin to win this fight." [21]

W. D. English, chairman of the executive committee, wanted the position of collector of the port at San Francisco. The committee was backing him. The conservative, or Field faction, was pressing Jesse D. Carr for the position. Carr was a heavy stockholder in the *Alta,* which had backed Field. Each group determined to show President Cleveland that it represented the Democratic party of California, and was entitled to the patronage. The entrenched leaders arranged to have a large delegation in Washington at the time of the inauguration, and the conservatives did the same. The former wrote numerous and lengthy letters to prove their status, and Field and others made personal calls to achieve the same ends. The liberals called county meetings to endorse the work of the Stockton convention, and the conservatives very quietly circulated an endorsement of Field, to prove that he was the true Democratic leader. White wrote to Henley to get a copy of the paper so that he might publish the names of those who had signed it. He implied that the political future of such persons would be very dark indeed.[22]

It looked bad for the liberals when Field, the only Democrat on the bench of the Supreme Court, administered the oath of office to Cleveland's cabinet officers. He

[21] Henley to White, Jan. 27, 1885. White MSS., library of Stanford University.

[22] White to Henley, March 4, 1885. *Ibid.*

seemed to be in good standing. "You must remember," White wrote from Washington a few days later, "that the railroad people have at this moment considerable influence in Washington in California matters. Judge Field and Stanford are together, and I am on the other side." [23] "The 'Field' factionists are working like beavers," a friend wrote to White a month later.[24] White wrote a three thousand word letter to Secretary of Treasury Manning, attacking Field and his friends, and urging the appointment of W. D. English as collector of the port at San Francisco.[25] He enclosed copies of the Colton-Huntington letters which had been published in the *Chronicle,* and which seemed to show a disreputable connection between Field and the railroads.[26] The letter once written, he sent a copy to Henley, in Washington, and urged him to see that the original which was sent to Manning was read before it went into the waste basket.[27] President Cleveland seemed not greatly impressed by the claims of either faction of the party. He suggested that they settle their quarrels among themselves, and postponed the distribution of California patronage. A note of desperation crept into the letters of the liberals. White wrote to President Cleveland in defense of Barclay Henley, who was under fire from the conservatives, and attacking Field. The latter had not the confidence and good will of the Democracy in California, he said. No county committee, convention, or political assemblage had ever been willing to endorse him. Wherever the issue had been made Field had been repudiated. The collectorship appointment was anxiously looked for,

[23] White to L. J. Sacriste, March 10, 1885. *Ibid.*
[24] Seldon Hetzel to White, April 11, 1885. *Ibid.*
[25] White to Manning, April 23, 1885. *Ibid.*
[26] See pp. 247-48.
[27] White to Henley, April 30, 1885. *Ibid.*

White continued. It was regarded as the turning point upon which hinged the question whether the party could have its own officers, or whether the same corporate power which had foreclosed upon Republicanism had also a lien upon Democracy. "Justice Field is always on hand and we are aware that he is a man of talent. Under a democratic system of government he ought not to dictate to a state which will *not* trust or recognize him." [28]

C. W. Cross, of the California state senate, wrote an open letter to President Cleveland defending Field and attacking the "pirates on railroads" who were nominally at the head of the party, and who were responsible for the action of the Stockton convention.[29] Field wrote to Cross, thanking him for the letter and agreeing with his analysis. He denounced the treatment of certain members of the party by the convention. The party throughout the country was injured thereby, he said. Democrats outside of the state disapproved of such action, especially "when the object of such majority in so doing it is to commit the Democratic party to the lawlessness of confiscation and the chaos of communism, as was the case in California." He hoped that in the next convention the party would be represented by men who would remove the reproach cast upon it.

As for himself, he declared that he had no political ambition. "Of that my age is the best guarantee. My labors on the bench will be ended in a few years, and I shall then desire only repose and time for reflection, and possibly some literary recreation. The political strife in California will find in me no participant. I have no need to wrangle with defamers, nor any disposition to do so. They can not harm me, nor change any man's opinion of

[28] White to Cleveland, May 15, 1885. *Ibid.*
[29] *Argonaut,* July 18, 1885, reprinting from the San Francisco *Alta.*

the judicial work to which I have devoted nearly thirty
years of my life."

He declared that in spite of assertions to the contrary
he had urged very few appointments in Washington, and
most of these had been for officers of the Court over which
he presided, and for poor women in the departments.
"That which has given rise to such misrepresentations is
the fact that I have also expressed opinions against the
selection of any men whose appointments would seem to
commit the administration to an approval of the communistic railings of the Stockton convention mob. In
this way I have felt that, as a citizen, I could do our state
a service which ought not to be withheld, and perhaps
save it from further disgrace. Of course men who may
be thus interpreted in foisting themselves into places of
profit are much exercised lest I compromise my dignity
by interfering in politics, but I have yet to learn that
any office is so exalted that its incumbent may be deprived
of the privileges or released from the duties of citizenship. You and other friends may rest assured that no
dainty rules of propriety laid down for my conduct by
those who seek harm to our state will ever deter me from
such efforts as I may be able to make to thwart their
mischievous purposes. I shall never be prevented from
the discharge of this duty by any personal assaults upon
myself, however mendacious." [30]

In a similar letter to an old Marysville friend he said
that he had expressed opinions "against the appointment
of any men who entertain communistic or agrarian
views, thinking only those should hold office who believe
in order and law and property, and the great institutions
of society upon which progress and civilization depend." [31]

[30] Sacramento *Record-Union*, May 30, 1885.
[31] Field to Stephen Addington, in the *Record-Union*, June 24, 1885.

The struggle continued, with neither faction able to boast that its opponent was being vanquished. Field called on the President a number of times, with the results in doubt except that few appointments of any kind were made in California. Finally the President, without Field's approval, appointed Asa Ellis to the collectorship of internal revenue for the southern district in California, an office next in importance only to the collectorship of customs at San Francisco. Field was furious. Ellis, according to newspaper reports, had joined with White, English, and others in a typical attack upon Field, calling him a hireling of litigants, and otherwise picturing him in a quite unfavorable light. At a previous interview the President had promised to see Field again before the latter left for California for the summer. Field now wrote to Cleveland's secretary asking for an interview, and when he received no reply from this note, and none from a second one, he wrote a long letter to Cleveland.[32]

Almost the entire letter dealt with the Ellis appointment. Ellis was corrupt and unworthy, Field declared. "It is understood that his appointment was made upon the recommendation of Judge Wallace of California, a man utterly without principle, and who has attained a 'bad eminence' in that state for his extreme communistic views. More than any and all others in California has he contributed to divide and distract the party."

Field pasted in the body of the letter a newspaper clipping which told what Ellis, White, English, and others had said about him. The Ellis appointment would seem to Californians a justification of the attack made upon Field. He was sure that the President had not known of the attack, and that, hearing of it now, he would not retain Ellis in office. "I am not willing to think that you

---

[32] Field to Cleveland, June 7, 1885, with the Cleveland papers in the Manuscript Division of the Library of Congress.

will prefer to retain an officer, about whom you were misled and deceived, to doing an act of simple justice to one who has heretofore been your political friend and supporter."

When on the following day Field received a note from Cleveland's secretary saying that the President would be too busy to see him he again wrote to the President, saying that he would not have taken much time, that he had only wanted to ask him to do "a simple act of justice," and that "my private communication to you of yesterday, if read, will acquaint you of the serious character of the matters of which I complain." [33]

Field received small comfort from Cleveland in the matter at hand, but for the most part he was able to keep the Stockton convention leaders and their friends out of office throughout the period of the first Cleveland administration. In December, 1886, he prevented the appointment of White's law partner, John D. Bicknell, to a judgeship which White had helped to create. H. H. Markham, a representative in Congress from California, had worked hard for the appointment. "Stanford assured me over and over again that he could and would control Field," Markham declared. "Field was the only one I feared from the start, but after I had convinced Stanford that Bicknell was the proper man, and he manifested so much interest in that regard, I was sure that he could do what he thought he could." Markham thought Field demeaned himself by such activities. "Worse than all was to have him rear and pitch like a wild beast against Judge Bicknell simply because he happened to have a partner that did not agree with him upon political questions affecting our state." [34]

[33] Field to Cleveland, June 8, 1885. Cleveland papers.
[34] Markham to White, Dec. 23, 1886. White MSS.

White thought Markham would have succeeded in getting the appointment through had it not been for "that old scoundrel Field." "If he will come to California and run for justice of the peace in this county and I can not defeat him with an ex-member of the Los Angeles chain-gang I will pay his expenses."[35] English wrote to White that the appointments for southern California were "simply disgusting." Cleveland had treated the California Democrats like brutes, he said. "Field, Irish and Carr are running the administration, with Stanford in the background to approve their selections. Faithlessness is a passport to [appointment] by this mass of presidential fat."[36]

Notwithstanding his public protestations of freedom from political ambitions, Field admitted in private, after Cleveland was elected, that he wished he had entered the race himself.[37] His attitude revealed a yearning for power and prestige which it was not easy to satisfy. This fact may have had much to do with his attempts to advise and direct the administration in various ways. He, for example, urged President Cleveland to bring about the reorganization of the Supreme Court, increasing the number of justices to fourteen.[38] This would, as he said, have provided more men to perform the heavy tasks of the Court. In addition to that, however, it would probably have resulted in the appointment of five Democratic justices to be added to the one already on the bench. In the event of the death or resignation of two of the Republican justices then sitting, the Democrats would have acquired a majority of the positions on the bench. The plan was never worked out. Even if he had approved

[35] White to Markham, Dec. 17, 1886. *Ibid.*
[36] English to White, Dec. 24, 1886. *Ibid.*
[37] Statement of Irwin B. Linton in interview with author, Feb. 22, 1928.
[38] San Francisco *Call*, May 10, 1885.

it, the President would probably have had most serious difficulties in getting it through Congress, in the face of the charges of packing the bench which would have been made.

When Chief Justice Waite died, in 1888, Field was eager to be promoted to the head of the Court. It is said that friends and legal organizations all over the country, and other members of the Supreme Court itself, joined in urging his appointment. Since he was a Democrat and was recognized throughout the country as a judge of outstanding ability it did not seem improbable that he would get the coveted position. For some reason President Cleveland declined to make the appointment, however, using as an excuse the fact that he was unwilling to make an appointment from among the associate justices, and he finally selected Melville W. Fuller, of Illinois. There may have been good reason for going outside the existing membership of the Court for the new leader, but Field looked upon the action as a slight to himself, and never forgave Cleveland for it. When asked what had prompted it he replied that he had no personal knowledge of the President's mind in the matter, but that he had reliable information to the effect that Cleveland had appointed Fuller in order to get the support of the Middle West for another nomination.[39]

When it was assured that the place would not be his, Justices Bradley and Matthews wrote friendly letters to Field expressing their disappointment that he was not to sit as their chief.[40] To this extent, at least, he had consolation.

His varied political activities and aspirations played no small part in Field's life. When they are viewed at

[39] *Ibid.*, April 10, 1898.
[40] Gorham, *Biographical Notice*, pp. 107-9.

the distance of a succeeding century it seems a matter
for regret that this was true. He was not the type of
man to do effective work in the game of politics, while
he was a highly superior person as a judge. His participation in politics often obscured his more praiseworthy
judicial activities, and led to the suspicion that he used
his judicial position to advance the political and economic
interests of himself and his friends. There may even
have been some truth in the suspicion. At any rate, as a
not more than mediocre politician he severely damaged a
reputation which might have been, and indeed, in spite
of the scars, still is, that of a great judge. Because of his
political activities and his tragic encounter with Judge
Terry,[41] as well as because of the trend of his land title,
Chinese, and railroad decisions, he has been slow in receiving the approbation of his adopted state of California,
which might have been and ought to have been his.

[41] See Chap. XIII.

CHAPTER XIII
THE TERRY TRAGEDY

When the story has been told the reader will not be surprised that the tragic outcome of the clash between Justice Field and Judge Terry was for a time the object of nation-wide interest and attention. The unusual drama of the affair was enough to hold the interest of a public which had no real conception of what lay back of it all. The local public in California had gossiped for years over the events of which the shooting at Lathrop was the outcome, probably without any very deep understanding of the forces at play. Money, sex, Southern chivalry, pioneer coarseness, pride, malice, and stern devotion to principle were all mixed in the brew of controversy. It was a nasty situation in which the judicial ermine was not likely to remain unstained. While the legal points involved have provided endless conversations for lawyers, the story is told here chiefly for the clash of colorful personalities, for the conflict between people who were so different in background, training, interests, and habits of thought as to be virtually incapable of understanding each other. Field, of course, was one of these persons.

In the beginning the villain or the hero of the story, depending on the point of view of the observer, was William Sharon. Sharon was a wealthy mine owner and banker, with extensive business interests in both California and Nevada. He was prominent among the directors of the Bank of California, in San Francisco, in connection with which some of his activities had not been free from what seems to have been well warranted suspicion. He owned certain hotels in the city, among which were the Grand and the Palace. His Nevada mining interests gave basis for a claim of citizenship in that state. Nevada, politically, was little more than a "rotten borough" of the United States. Sharon, with his millions, was able to seat himself in the United States Senate for the term running from 1875 to 1881. His wife died in 1875, and after that time he made his home at the Palace Hotel, in San Francisco. His wealth, like that of other men in California at the time, made him the object of bitter envy and hatred on the part of persons who had been less fortunate in the great gamble of life in the pioneer West. He gained no popularity with these people by the fact that he was reputed to have quite a "way with the women."

Sarah Althea Hill, a colorful, ambitious, and head-strong young woman in her early twenties, came to California during the early part of Sharon's career as senator. She was supposed to be of good family, but she was poor at following family traditions, or traditions of any kind for that matter. In her native state she had had the·reputation of being a notorious flirt, but there were rumors that a bitter disappointment in love had made her what she was. She was unable to live in peace with her California relatives, and went to a hotel to reside. Her associates were often persons of doubtful "respecta-bility," and if she herself did not violate the canons of good morals her manners, at least, were very free indeed.[1]

In the summer of 1880 the amorous Sharon saw Miss Hill, was attracted to her, and arranged for an interview at his office, presumably to talk about investments in stocks. A short time afterward she moved to the Grand

[1] These facts are summarized from Gorham, G. C., *Attempted Assassina-tion of Justice Field*, pp. 8-14. See also Judge M. P. Deady's opinion in *Sharon* v. *Hill*, 11 Sawyer 290.

Hotel, which he owned, and which was connected by a bridge across the street to the Palace Hotel where he lived. For a period of more than a year she accepted invitations to visit him at his rooms. Then something happened. It is possible that the senator merely grew tired of the lady, but the ostensible cause of the break was the charge that she reported some of his business secrets to his competitors. At any rate, the manager of the Grand Hotel notified her that her room would be needed for other purposes. Wheedling letters protesting affection and innocence brought no reply from Sharon. After the door of her room had been taken from its hinges and the carpets removed from the floor she reluctantly departed. She gave Sharon a receipt for three thousand dollars in cash and four thousand five hundred in notes, as payment in full.[2]

After two years of efforts to win back the senator's affections she startled (and perhaps delighted) the general public by charging him with desertion and infidelity, and suing him for divorce, heavy alimony, and a division of his property. Her story was to the effect that on her first visit to Sharon's office he had offered her a thousand dollars a month to become his mistress. She had refused, whereupon the possibility of marriage had been mentioned. Subsequently they agreed to sign a marriage contract, but to keep it secret for two years. She offered this contract, or alleged contract, as evidence of the marriage. As further evidence she offered certain letters written to her by Sharon, most of them having to do with money matters, which addressed her as "Dear Wife," and which became popularly known as the "Dear Wife Letters."

As soon as the existence of the contract was made known, and before the case was started in the state court,

---

[2] Judge Deady's opinion in *Sharon* v. *Hill*, 11 Sawyer 290.

Sharon brought suit in the United States Circuit Court to have it canceled as a forgery and fraud. He urged that the federal Court had jurisdiction because of the fact of diversity of citizenship. The basis for the suit in equity lay in the fact that the title to property was endangered by the threatened use of the alleged contract. The divorce suit, which was started less than a month later, was removed to the Circuit Court, and then by consent of the parties taken back to the Superior Court to be tried before Judge Sullivan, without a jury.

The divorce suit was argued at great length, and huge amounts of evidence were offered which the public lapped up with avid interest. It seems evident that the sympathy of the masses was with the woman, and against the philandering millionaire. Many have thought that the judge was influenced by popular pressure. At any rate, he gave a decision awarding the woman twenty-five hundred dollars a month alimony, and apportioned sixty thousand dollars among her troop of lawyers. Soon afterward he entered a decree declaring that the plaintiff and defendant were husband and wife, that he had deserted her, and that she was entitled to a divorce, with half the common property accumulated since the marriage. She claimed that about ten million dollars had been added to the Sharon fortune during that time. Sharon carried two appeals to the state Supreme Court—one from the final judgment and one from the order for alimony.

In the meantime attorneys for the defendant sought in every way possible to delay progress in the suit brought in the United States Circuit Court by Sharon to compel the surrender of the marriage contract as a forged document. On March 3, 1884 Judge Sawyer, on a demurrer, ruled that there was equity jurisdiction for the case, since the title to millions of dollars in property was involved.

There was no adequate remedy at law, he declared, since the defendant could choose her own time for enforcing her claim under the alleged contract, even after the death of the other party. In that case there could be no testimony to defeat the fraud. She might do that, since she was a young woman, while Sharon was well up in his sixties.[3]

In another preliminary decision on October 16, 1884 Judge Sawyer denied the argument that the proceedings in the state Court might be pleaded in abatement of similar proceedings in the United States Circuit Court. The jurisdictions were separate. Anyway, he stated, the Circuit Court case was commenced first. At the same time he denied the plea of the defendant that Sharon was a citizen of California and not of Nevada, and hence had no right to appeal to the federal Court. In the three months which were allowed her the defendant had taken no testimony to prove her case, and had not even asked for an extension of time. The burden of proof was on her. In the absence of testimony the plea must be adjudged false and over-ruled.[4]

On March 19, 1885 Judge Sawyer ruled against a plea that an averment of diversity of citizenship stated only in the introductory part of a bill in equity was not sufficient.[5] On April 21 he had to go back to the authenticity of Sharon's claim to residence in Nevada. The defendant had taken testimony as to his residence and presented it to the Court. The judge declared that the matter had been settled once and could not be raised again. Furthermore, the evidence presented had to do with residence, which did not necessarily govern citizenship. The fact

[3] *Sharon v. Hill,* 10 Sawyer 48.
[4] *Sharon v. Hill,* 10 Sawyer 394.
[5] *Sharon v. Hill,* 10 Sawyer 634.

that Sharon had been a United States senator from
Nevada seemed to indicate that he was a citizen of that
state.[6]

During the summer of 1885 Sharon's counsel brought
about the taking of voluminous testimony on matters
relating to the validity of the marriage contract. Many
things were revealed or alleged which threw the character
of the woman involved into no favorable light. She was
present at the examination of many of the witnesses, and
enjoyed making trouble. Many times she burst forth
in violent language. She enjoyed playing with a gun
while she watched the scene malevolently. "I can hit a
four-bit piece nine times out of ten," she boasted to the
examiner as he tried to quiet her. She declared that
Senator William M. Stewart,[7] one of Sharon's counsel,
had put a woman up to lie about her. "I will shoot him
yet," she shrieked. "That very man sitting there. To
think he would put up a woman to come here and deliberately lie about me like that. I will shoot him." Unable
to prevent her interruptions the examiner adjourned and
appealed to the Circuit Court to enforce order.

Justice Field and Judge Sawyer heard the plea, and
gave their decision August 5. The marshal was ordered
to disarm the defendant whenever she came before the
examiner, and to appoint an officer to keep her under
strict surveillance. Said Field: "I myself have not, heretofore, sat in this case, and do not expect to participate in its
decision; I intend in a few days to leave for the East, but
I have been consulted by my associate, and have been
requested to take part in this side proceeding, for it is of the
utmost importance for the due administration of justice,
that such misbehavior as the examiner reports should

[6] *Sharon* v. *Hill,* 10 Sawyer 666.

[7] Senator Stewart was an old Marysville friend of Field's.

be stopped, and measures taken which will prevent its recurrence." [8]

After the opinions had been delivered Tyler, one of the counsel for Miss Hill, or Mrs. Sharon, wished to explain to the Court matters in connection with his own conduct. Apparently it was known that he had once gone into a state court armed, because of threats made against himself and his father. He desired to show the Circuit Court that his conduct had been justifiable. Field refused to hear him, and said that "any lawyer who so far forgets his professional duty as to come into a court of justice armed, ought to be disbarred from practice. . . . Any man, counsel or witness, who comes into a court of justice armed ought to be punished, and if he is a member of the bar, he ought to be suspended or removed permanently. That is the doctrine that ought to be inculcated from the bench everywhere. So far as I have the power, I will enforce it." This attitude is significant in the light of subsequent events.

On December 26, 1885 the Circuit Court, speaking through Judge Matthew P. Deady of the United States District Court of Oregon, gave its decision on the original action brought by Sharon.[9] The marriage contract was declared forged and fraudulent. The alleged signature of Sharon was declared to be a forgery, and evidence of many kinds was used to show that the relationship between the plaintiff and the defendant was not that of husband and wife. The salutations of the "Dear Wife Letters" were presumed to be false, and attention was called to the fact that the content of the letters related purely to business such as the payment of bills, and bore no evidence of family affection. Among other things, in order to show that the defendant had not shown a

[8] *Sharon* v. *Hill*, 11 Sawyer 122.
[9] *Sharon* v. *Hill*, 11 Sawyer 290.

wifely attitude toward the plaintiff Judge Deady called attention to evidence that on one occasion she had concealed herself in Sharon's room, and watched him and another woman undress and go to bed together, and then had mirthfully gone out and told her friends what she had seen. The judge was convinced that she would not have acted so had she been Sharon's wife. This, in his estimation, was evidence that the marriage contract was a forged document.

Sharon died about a month before the decision of the Court was given. This may account in part for the fact that the opinion of Judge Deady and the concurring opinion of Judge Sawyer echoed the deepest respect for the philandering millionaire, while vigorously condemning the woman involved. Without necessarily disagreeing with the judges as to the decision at which they arrived, the reader can not peruse the opinions without gaining the conviction that the woman was on trial, and was being condemned, for the multitude of ways in which she had violated the conventions of society. She was a tainted woman. Senator Sharon was but the victim of his own too generously affectionate nature.

A decree was entered as of a date prior to Sharon's death ordering that the marriage contract be surrendered to be canceled. Thus the state and federal courts were at odds with each other. The one granted a divorce, and the other declared that there had never been a marriage. The state Supreme Court had not yet spoken.

In the meantime another prominent character had come on the stage. David S. Terry, former Chief Justice of the state Supreme Court, had become attorney for Miss Hill. Terry was a giant of six feet three inches, and weighed two hundred and fifty pounds. He had great physical strength and agility. His jaw was firm; and cold, steel-gray eyes looked out from beneath heavy, dark brows. He was reserved and at times domineering in his relationships with people, except with his family where he was a model of gentleness, consideration, and Southern courtesy. He combined strict adherence to principles of personal integrity with an ungovernable temper which on rare occasions carried him into wild expressions of rage. He alienated himself from large groups when he killed Senator Broderick in a duel in 1859. His stern devotion to his own code of ethics cut him off from others who might have been his friends, yet there were some, especially in the vicinity of his home in Stockton, who were intensely loyal to him.

He fought for the Confederacy during the Civil War, and after the war spent some time in Mexico. Returning to Stockton he resumed the practice of law, appearing in many cases before the higher state and federal courts. He played a prominent part in the Constitutional Convention of 1878-79, working for a more equitable adjustment of the burden of taxation and for measures which would place restraint upon the powers of the great railroad corporations. He was prominent among those who worked to secure the adoption of the new constitution, but his popularity was not great enough to secure his election to any office. He had a number of severe misfortunes during the early eighties. His elder son, to whom he had given a ranch at Fresno, committed suicide. His younger son, a promising lawyer, died in April, 1885. Then his wife, a loyal comrade for many decades, also died. The home to which he had been devoted was gone.

What happened in the life of the man as the result of these tragedies remains for speculation. His demeanor continued in the same stern reserve which had long characterized it. The emotional outlet for his generous sympathies was no longer his. Perhaps it is not surprising that a yearning for emotional expression seems to have led him to see in his client, Sarah Althea Hill, traits of excellence which were not there, and blinded him to evil traits which he ought to have seen. Perhaps, on the other hand, he adjudged her more fairly than those who, in self-righteous manner, condemned her for her defiance of convention. At any rate, on January 7, 1886, less than two weeks after the Circuit Court declared her marriage contract with Senator Sharon to have been a forgery, he made her his wife.

"What do you think of Terry and Sarah A.," asked Stephen M. White of Barclay Henley. "Terry is just about old enough now to begin to get weak on the fair sex. These venerable mashes do funny things now and then." [10] Other people were more shocked and less philosophical about the matter. Terry and his first wife had been welcome in the most respectable society. With his new wife he was barred from the homes that once had welcomed him. Instead of making her respectable by marrying her he had been tainted by her, and had himself become an outcast. The result deepened his reserve, and any aspersion upon the character of his wife was all the more bitterly resented. No pure white lily of society could have been treated with more gentleness and courtesy by her husband than was the boisterous woman whom he had married.

If the Circuit Court decree were executed, compelling the surrender and cancellation of the marriage contract, it was evident that the Terrys would be hopelessly defeated. Terry took an action which he thought to be

[10] White to Henley, Jan. 11, 1886. White MSS.

the necessary step for an appeal from the decision of the Circuit Court, and then turned his attention to the state Supreme Court before which appeals were pending. On January 31, 1888 that Court, by a vote of four to three, affirmed the decision of the Superior Court that the marriage was valid, but reversed the order for counsel fees and reduced the alimony from twenty-five hundred to five hundred dollars a month. The Sharon heirs had fought for a new trial in the Superior Court, and had carried an appeal to the Supreme Court, which was still pending. Two years passed, however, before they tried to enforce the Circuit Court decree to bring about the cancellation of the marriage contract. There was undoubtedly a reason for this. Terry thought he had taken an appeal from the decision of the Court. The law provided, however, that since the action of the Court had been abated by the death of Sharon the case must be revived before an appeal could be taken. The time limit for an appeal was two years. The Sharon heirs, who were aware of this fact, were as quiet as mice for that period, and then it was too late for Terry to appeal. At the end of the two years they brought an action in the Circuit Court for the revival of the case, so that the decree could be enforced.

The action was brought against the Terrys by Frederick W. Sharon, a son of the senator, as executor, and Francis G. Newlands, a son-in-law, as trustee of the property. They were represented by some of the best attorneys in the state. Richard S. Mesick was noted for the huge fees which he was accustomed to win. Samuel M. Wilson was one of the shrewdest of the railroad lawyers. William L. Herrin was a brilliant young man who in later years was to appear at the head of the Southern Pacific organization. The case was argued before Justice Field and Judges

Sawyer and Sabin. Field, his colleagues concurring, gave the opinion of the Court September 3, 1888.[11]

The Circuit Court had consistently decided against the Hill-Terry interests. Both Terry and his wife had been bitter in their denunciation of the judges who had ruled against them. They had ruffled the dignity of Judge Sawyer beyond the point of forgiveness. On August 14 preceding the final Sharon-Terry decision he had taken a train from Los Angeles to San Francisco. The Terrys had taken the same train. They found it desirable to move from one end of the car to the other, in order to avoid the sun. Mrs. Terry strode up and down the aisle in a threatening manner and leered savagely at Judge Sawyer, who, by all accounts, was a bit uneasy as to the result of her performance. When she followed her husband to the other end of the car, she suddenly paused, seized the judge's gray hair, and gave his head a violent shake. Then, laughing gleefully, she went on to her seat. Terry later said that while he did not approve of what his wife did he couldn't help laughing. Judge Sawyer was enraged by the insult, and became uneasy as to what the Terrys might do if he brought about the irretrievable loss of their claim to the Sharon wealth. Hence, before the decision was given on September 3, he called United States Marshal Franks to his office and asked that he have a number of deputies in the court room to prevent violence.[12]

The case had achieved great notoriety, and when the court room opened on the appointed morning a crowd of expectant observers packed themselves into the seats, with deputy marshals and policemen arranged at strategic

[11] *Sharon* v. *Terry*, 13 Sawyer 387.

[12] Testimony of J. C. Franks, in transcript of record, p. 169, In re *Neagle*, 135 U. S. 1. The affidavits and testimony hereafter referred to are reprinted in this transcript, and are on file in the Law Division of the Library of Congress.

positions in the room. The Terrys came in and sat down at a table for attorneys, ten or twelve feet from the judges' bench. Marshal Franks stood over toward the west wall, a short distance from them, nearer to Terry than to his wife. Justice Field and Judges Sawyer and Sabin, who had heard the argument of the case, filed in, and with them came Judge Hoffman, who was interested in the events of the morning. They took their seats, and Field unrolled a huge manuscript, adjusted his spectacles, and began to read. As he read, in a low, even tone, the court room was quiet with expectancy. Presumably the only decision necessary was as to whether the previous decision, which had been abated by the death of Sharon, could be revived. For some reason, however, perhaps to give the decision the stamp of his own authority, Field went back and discussed at length the merits of the case, and again listeners were regaled with an appraisal of the character of Mrs. Terry.

As Field read on, C. W. Cross, a prominent lawyer and an admirer of Field, came into the room. Since no seats for spectators were vacant he walked up to the table for counsel and sat down beside Mrs. Terry. He noticed that she was nervously fingering the clasp of her satchel. Having heard that she carried a gun and that trouble was expected on this occasion, he determined to seize her arm if she made a move. After a long introduction Field came finally to the point where it was evident that the Court intended to compel the surrender of the marriage contract. Mrs. Terry suddenly released her satchel and started to her feet. "Judge," she cried, "are you going to take the responsibility of ordering me to deliver up that marriage contract?" [13] Field looked at her and said

[13] Statements as to the exact words used in the colloquies reported vary with each of the affidavits, but there is no important difference in their meaning.

in a stern, quiet manner, "Madam, sit down." "You have been paid for this decision," she shrieked. "How much did Newlands pay you?" "Mr. Marshal," said Field in his same manner, "remove that woman from the court room." Marshal Franks stepped toward her. She sprang at him and slapped him in the face. "You dirty scrub, you dare not remove me from this court room." Terry crowded between them, and his wife hurled herself into a seat. "Don't touch my wife," he said to the marshal. "Get a written order." Franks replied something to the effect that there was no time for that, and reached for Mrs. Terry's arm. "No God damn man shall touch my wife," Terry growled, and hit Marshal Franks a terrific blow in the mouth, breaking one of his teeth, and knocking him back across the room. A crowd of deputies helped throw Terry into a seat and hold him there, keeping his hand well away from his chest where he was thought to be trying to reach for his knife, and the marshal, with the assistance of others, dragged Mrs. Terry, screaming and scratching and kicking, out of the room, and into the marshal's office.

Terry's captors released him, and followed him down the aisle to the door. There the crowd was such that he found it hard to break through. He reached inside his coat and drew out a knife with a five-inch blade, as if to cut his way through. Again men leaped forward to restrain him, and a deputy faced him with a gun. As the knife was wrested from his hand an order was given to allow him to go into the marshal's office with his wife, and the crowd made way for him. Mrs. Terry demanded her bracelets and the satchel containing her money, which she proclaimed had been stolen from her. Marshal Franks brought her the broken bracelets, and went to Porter Ashe, a friend of hers, who held her satchel. Ashe was reluctant to give it up. Franks demanded it, opened it, and took out a gun, five of the six chambers of which were loaded. He then returned the satchel to Mrs. Terry.[14] So great was the excitement that few had any clear conception of what had happened. A newspaper reporter came out on the street prepared to swear that Mrs. Terry had fired a shot. Soon it was rumored that Field had been killed by Mrs. Terry, and that Terry had shot the marshal.[15] The judges remained relatively calm. "Justice Field sat with a page of the decision held suspended in his hand. Judge Sawyer surveyed the scene without moving a muscle. Judge Hoffman seemed to take a keen interest in it, as did Judge Sabin, who was in a half-rising attitude." [16] Most of the observers crowded into the corridor to see what happened there. When the tumult was stilled Field resumed the reading of the decision. When he had finished the judges withdrew for consultation, without saying anything about what had happened.

The Terrys continued to be held under guard in the marshal's office. Angry excitement was mixed with bitterness at the trouble they were in. Terry said Judge Sawyer was a "damned old scoundrel." [17] When they were held after the noon hour Terry exclaimed: "Tell that old bald-headed son of a bitch, Field, that I want to go to lunch." [18] Then he turned and gently placed his arm around his wife's shoulder. "My dear, you have made all this trouble," he said. "You have done all this." "My dear, I could not help it," she answered him. "I had to do it. I have got this now just where I wanted it. I want to keep this matter before the public. I don't want the public to lose sight of our case. I know

[14] Affidavit of J. C. Franks. Transcript, pp. 23-24.
[15] Wagstaff, *Life of David S. Terry*, p. 326.
[16] San Francisco *Call*, Sept. 4, 1888.
[17] Affidavit of N. R. Harris. Transcript, p. 29.
[18] Affidavit of J. C. Franks. *Ibid.*, p. 24.

they will send me to jail. I don't care. I want that old villain to send me to jail, and I have no doubt he will." [19] She could have killed Judge Field from where she stood in the court room, she said, but she "was not ready then to kill the old villain." [20] After lengthy deliberation the judges returned to the court room, and ordered Terry committed to the Alameda County jail for six months for contempt of court, and his wife for three months.[21] "Field thinks that when I get out he will be away," said Terry, "but I will meet him when he comes back next year, and it will not be a very pleasant meeting for him." [22]

About four o'clock the Terrys were taken from the marshal's office to the Lick House. Mrs. Terry was heard to say: "Don't it show that they were bought off when they come here and stop at Newlands' Palace Hotel? And there's Mrs. Field," with a sneer, "didn't she come down to the court room the first day of the case to see me, as though I was a prize elephant? I guess my husband has held as big positions as hers, and if she wants to see me she can call on me." [23] Later in the evening they were driven down to the ferry in a hack, to cross over to Oakland to the Alameda County jail. As they drove on the boat Mrs. Terry put her head out of the hack and called out to know if there were any members of the Laborers' Union present. Receiving no reply she asked again. A man dressed as a mechanic admitted that he was a member. She told him she had been sentenced to jail by that old villain, Judge Field, that she had always been a friend of the laborers, and that she wanted their support. She would make some speeches for them when she got out.

[19] Testimony of N. R. Harris. Transcript, p. 222.

[20] *Ibid.*, p. 223.

[21] See orders committing for contempt, In re *Terry Contempt*, 13 Sawyer 440.

[22] Affidavit of J. C. Franks. Transcript, p. 24.

[23] San Francisco *Call*, Sept. 4, 1888.

She continued to discuss the events of the day with her husband. She could have killed Field and Sawyer, and no jury would have convicted her, she boasted. "No," Terry replied, "you could not find a jury that would convict anyone for killing that old villain." [24] Judge Sawyer, Mrs. Terry said, remembered the wooling she had given him in the car. "I gave it to him good. I pulled his old hair good." [25]

It was seldom that the jail housed such a distinguished prisoner as a former Chief Justice of the Supreme Court. The sheriff and his wife tried in every way to make the prisoners comfortable and even gave up their own bed to them.[26]

Soon after his imprisonment Terry prepared a statement of facts as to the occurrences in the Circuit Court, intending to send it to the President in an application for a pardon. He sent a copy of it to John Stanly, who had been one of the counsel for Terry and his wife in the Sharon case. Some people thought that if Terry would send a conciliatory statement of his side of the case to the Circuit Court he would be set free. Stanly prepared a statement from that of Terry, and brought it to Terry for his signature. By it Terry was to declare that he had tried to calm his wife in the court room, and had arisen to take her out. He had not struck the marshal until assaulted by him. He had not drawn nor attempted to draw his knife in the court room, and had not assaulted the marshal with a deadly weapon, as he was charged in the order committing him to prison. Outside the court room he had drawn a small sheath-knife, in an attempt to get through the crowd to his wife. He had given up the knife, and had been admitted into the room where

---

[24] Testimony of N. R. Harris. Transcript, p. 223.
[25] *Ibid.*, p. 224.
[26] San Francisco *Call*, Sept. 4, 1888.

his wife was. He had intended no disrespect to the Court or the judges by what he said or did in the court or in the building in which the court was held. Under the circumstances it was only natural that he lost his temper.

Terry refused to sign the paper until Stanly had modified the sentence saying that he had intended no disrespect for the Court or the judges. He had intended no disrespect by what he did or said in the court room, he asserted, but in the building, outside that room, he had said things which he intended to reflect on the integrity of both Field and Sawyer. Terry declared that the judges were acting from malice, and that it would be no use to appeal to them. He finally agreed that Judge Heydenfeldt, who in the early days had sat on the bench of the state Supreme Court, might take the paper and talk it over with Field. If after this talk he thought it would be favorably received the paper was to be filed with the Court and the motion made.

Judge Heydenfeldt saw Field at the Palace Hotel on the evening of September 12, and in the course of conversation showed him the petition. Field put it in his pocket.[27] On the days that followed Field procured affidavits from a host of marshals, deputies, policemen, and others, as to the disturbances in court. Then, without a motion by any attorney for Terry, he himself filed the Terry petition in court, along with the affidavits which he had procured, and read an opinion denying the petition. Many of the affidavits declared, contrary to the statement of Terry, that he had not tried to restrain the actions of his wife. The testimony of other observers indicates that he may have made some efforts to do so, and have intended himself to take her from the room. He was convinced that the men who had provided the testimony which Field had taken were under Field's

[27] See Terry letter in the San Francisco *Examiner*, Oct. 23, 1888.

influence, and dared not antagonize him. The affidavits seem to show that the men making them had been questioned sharply on the points which differed from Terry's statement, as if to indicate that definite statements were desired on these points. In his opinion Justice Field declared that there were important mis-statements and omissions in the Terry petition. He continued:

"We can only account for his mis-statement of facts as they were seen by numerous witnesses, by supposing that he was in such a rage at the time that he lost command of himself, and does not well remember what he then did, or what he then said. Some judgment as to the weight this statement should receive, independently of the incontrovertible facts at variance with it, may be found from his speaking of the deadly bowie-knife he drew as a small sheath-knife, and of the shameless language and conduct of his wife as 'her acts of indiscretion.'

"No one can believe that he thrust his hand under his vest where his bowie-knife was carried without intending to draw it. To believe that he placed his right hand there for any other purpose—such as to rest it after the fatigue of his violent blow in the marshal's face, or to smooth down his ruffled linen—would be childish credulity.

"But even his own statement admits the assaulting of the marshal who was endeavoring to enforce the order of the Court, and his subsequently drawing a knife to force his way into the room where the marshal had removed his wife. Yet he offers no apology for his conduct, expresses no regret for what he did, and makes no reference to his violent and vituperative language against the judges and officers of the Court while under arrest, which is detailed in the affidavits filed. . . .

"Why did the petitioner come into court with a deadly weapon concealed on his person? He knew that as a citizen he was violating the law which forbids the carry-

ing of concealed weapons, and as an officer of the Court—
and all attorneys are such officers—was committing an
outrage upon professional propriety, and rendering himself liable to be disbarred." [28]

Terry appealed to the Supreme Court of the United
States for leave to file a petition for a writ of habeas
corpus. The Court, speaking through Justice Harlan,
denied the plea, because it appeared that on the basis of
the facts showed by the petitioner's own statement he
would be remanded to prison.[29] Field did not sit in this
case. An appeal to President Cleveland for a pardon was
similarly unsuccessful.

Terry had been regarded as an able judge and lawyer.
He knew law, and was skilled in applying it to new
cases. His efforts in his own behalf were not without
shrewdness, but the storms of emotion which had been
stirred up may have marred his usually accurate vision.
In addition to this he had against him some of the ablest
lawyers and judges in the state. A fair analysis of the
situation can not but lead to the conclusion that the
judges involved, in spite of their protestations that their
sole desire was to enforce the law, were partisans in opposition to Terry. None knew this better than Terry,
though he probably carried his belief in the fact beyond
all legitimate bounds, and conceived of himself as persecuted far more than he was. The order committing him
to jail stated among other things that he had assaulted the
marshal with a deadly weapon. This statement, technically, was untrue, and Terry made a great deal of it.
The judges had maliciously spread a falsehood upon the
record, he said. Field, in denying Terry's petition for
release, had stubbornly refused to admit the error. It
was perhaps natural that Terry minimized his own

[28] In re *Terry Contempt*, 13 Sawyer 440 (Sept. 17, 1888).
[29] Ex parte *Terry*, 128 U. S. 289 (Nov. 12, 1888).

offensive conduct and grew eloquent on the moral principle involved in committing him on a technically false charge.

He wanted, or thought he wanted, his day in court. He was resentful that Field himself had presented his petition for release instead of allowing Terry or his lawyers to present it, because he had hoped for a chance to show errors in the charges against him. When he was denied the opportunity it was a logical conclusion for one in his state of mind that Field had maliciously denied him the privilege he wanted, and had perhaps been afraid of the effect which his disclosures might have. In his effort to get vindication Terry brought an action against Marshal Franks in the Superior Court of San Francisco, and had an order made to examine Field as a witness. According to his account Field attempted to avoid the service of a subpena, and, failing in this, he got friendly attorneys to bring about the transfer of the case to the United States Circuit Court, where it was of course dropped.[30] Terry had hoped to make Justice Field swear on the witness stand that a part of the statement in the contempt order was false. It would have been excellent revenge to be able to charge Field with perjury.

Attempts were made to punish the Terrys on criminal charges, in addition to the sentences for contempt. The grand jury met before Field left California, and every effort was made to hurry the indictments through. Few witnesses for the defense were called, and those who were called were not allowed to testify. The grand jury agreed to bring the indictments. They were drawn up, and the district attorney asked the jury to approve them without their being read, saying that Justice Field was about to leave for the East, and wished the indictments found before he left. The jury, learning that the reading

[30] See Terry letter, San Francisco *Examiner*, Oct. 23, 1888.

would take about three hours, voted to dispense with it. Terry attacked these proceedings in the United States District Court, but to no avail.[31]

The sheriff of Alameda County, pursuant to a federal law providing for the commutation of sentences for good behavior, planned to release Terry before the expiration of six months. The United States district attorney, hearing of the plan, brought an action in the Circuit Court to compel the sheriff to show cause why he should not hold Terry for the full period of his sentence. The judges, Sawyer and Sabin, held that the commutation law did not apply to cases such as this.[32] On reference to the terms of law this seems fairly obviously to have been true. Nevertheless, the decision, together with the alleged fact that Field had written from Washington to urge the imprisonment of Terry for the full period of six months, heaped around the Terrys fuel for still hotter flames of hate.

During his imprisonment Terry wrote long letters to the *Political Record* of San Francisco, uncovering old gossip and scandal about Field. He told of the Turner affair in such a way as to make Field out as little more than a pompous coward. He revived the story of the trouble with Judge Barbour. He charged Field with visiting gambling dens in the early days and losing all his money. He reprinted from the *Gold Key Court* the accusations that Field, when on the bench of the state Supreme Court, had received specific sums, from persons who were named, for his court decisions.[33] It was a nasty series of charges to be brought against a man in Field's position. Terry declared that, having been in close con-

[31] *United States* v. *Terry*, 14 Sawyer 44 (May 24, 1889).

[32] In re *Terry*, 13 Sawyer 598 (Feb. 1, 1889).

[33] This material is compiled in *Character and Career of Stephen J. Field*.

tact with Field in the early days, he knew personally that many of the ugly things said about him were true. Prior to the date of the Sharon case, however, he seems to have given no publicity to these things if he knew them. The only charge which he had previously made was typically represented in his statement that "Field is an intellectual phenomenon. He can give the most plausible reasons for a wrong decision of any person I ever knew. He was never known to decide a case against a corporation. He has always been a corporation lawyer and a corporation judge, and as such no man can be honest." [34] The fact that he left many things unsaid until he was terribly provoked is of course no proof that they were untrue.

Both in and out of jail the Terrys continued to make threats of what they would do to Field when he returned to California. The possibilities were discussed in the press. Friends in California and the state representatives in Washington urged Field not to return to California in the summer of 1889. He had ample evidence of the probability of trouble, and he was not required to go, the law providing that the justices should visit their circuits once each two years. Nevertheless, he insisted upon going. His comment was characteristic: "I cannot and will not allow threats of personal violence to deter me from the regular performance of my judicial duties at the times and places fixed by law. As a judge of the highest court in the country, I should be ashamed to look any man in the face if I allowed a ruffian, by threats against my person, to keep me from holding the regular courts in my circuit." [35]

[34] Wagstaff, *Life of David S. Terry*, p. 294.
[35] Gorham, *Attempted Assassination of Justice Field*, pp. 74-75.

Pacific Coast senators and congressmen in Washington discussed the situation with Attorney-General W. H. H. Miller. He, having in mind the coming trial of the Terrys upon the indictments brought against them, wrote to Marshal Franks on April 27 saying:

"The proceedings which have heretofore been had in the case of Mr. and Mrs. Terry in your United States Circuit Court have become a matter of public notoriety, and I deem it my duty to call your attention to the propriety of exercising unusual precaution, in case further proceedings shall be had in that case, for the protection of His Honor Justice Field, or whoever may be called upon to hear and determine the matter. Of course, I do not know what may be the feeling or purpose of Mr. and Mrs. Terry in the premises, but many things which have happened indicate that violence on their part is not impossible. It is due to the dignity and independence of the Court and the character of its judges that no effort on the part of the government shall be spared to make them feel entirely safe and free from anxiety in the discharge of their duties.

"You will understand, of course, that this letter is not for the public, but to put you upon your guard. It will be proper for you to show it to the district attorney if deemed best."

On May 7 Franks replied to the letter, saying that ever since Judge Sawyer had told him of the disgraceful action of Mrs. Terry toward him in the cars he had resolved to watch the Terrys whenever they entered a court room, and be ready to suppress any indignities to the judges. When Field arrived, he, as well as the other federal judges, would be protected. He had consulted District Attorney Carey about asking for two or more detectives to assist in protecting Field when the Terrys were on trial upon criminal charges.

District Attorney Carey also wrote to the Attorney-General. He urged that the marshal be authorized to employ more deputies, and to use them in protecting the judges both in and out of court. "I verily believe," he said, "in view of the direful threats made against Justice Field, that he will be in great danger at all times while here." He advised complete secrecy in the matter. "Prudence dictates great caution on the part of the officials who may be called upon to have anything to do in the premises, and I deem it to be of the greatest importance that the suggestions back and forth be confidential." He thought that the deputies appointed to protect the judges should be strangers to the Terrys.

The Attorney-General replied in a letter to Franks on May 27: "Referring to former correspondence of the department relating to a possible disorder in the session of the approaching term of court, owing to the small number of bailiffs under your control to preserve order, you are directed to employ certain special deputies at a *per diem* of five dollars. . . ." [36] As a result Marshal Franks appointed David Neagle, a man small of stature but strong, left handed, and quick with a gun, to attend Field both in and out of court while in California, and protect him from any attack of the Terrys. Neagle had met Terry only once. He had been one of the men who helped to wrest Terry's knife from his hand just outside the court room the previous September.

The situation grew more and more tense. On January 22 Mrs. Terry had given notice of a motion in the Superior Court to have a receiver appointed to take charge of the Sharon estate. On January 29 the Circuit Court enjoined her and all others to desist from these proceedings. On June 3 the right to move for the appointment of a receiver was declared valid by Judge

[36] See these letters, In re *Neagle*, 135 U. S. 1.

Sullivan. He took issue with Field's Circuit Court opinion, although the Supreme Court of the United States had in the meantime refused to grant the appeal for a hearing of the case on its merits.[37] He set July 15 as the date for the hearing of the motion. On that date Mrs. Terry herself addressed the Court, moving for the appointment of a receiver. She said her lawyers were afraid that if they made the motion Justice Field, who had arrived in California June 20, would put them in jail. She preferred to go to jail and have her husband outside; hence he sat as a mere spectator.

The hearing was postponed for some days. On July 17 the state Supreme Court, which had undergone some change in personnel, reversed the order of Judge Sullivan denying a new trial in the Sharon case, thereby obliterating the judgment in favor of Sharon's alleged wife. Terry was in despair. "The Supreme Court has reversed its own decision in the Sharon case and made my wife out a strumpet," he exclaimed to a friend. "What can a person do in the face of Sharon's millions? It is infamous!" [38]

In the meantime the Terrys, by demurrers, were fighting the indictments against them. It was evident that now they were losers in the state courts as well as the federal courts. Nothing was left them but the struggle for protection from further punishment, and, possibly extra-legal revenge. Threats against Field continued to be heard, and some individuals and newspapers seemed eager to keep the matter stirred up.

David Neagle met Justice and Mrs. Field and the Condit-Smiths at Reno, and escorted them into San Francisco. He was taking no chance on early attempts at vengeance. Field was advised to go armed. His reply was: "No sir! I will not carry arms, for when it is known

[37] *Terry* v. *Sharon*, 131 U. S. 40 (May 13, 1889).
[38] Wagstaff, *Life of David S. Terry*, pp. 314-15.

that the judges of our courts are compelled to arm themselves against assaults in consequence of their judicial
action it will be time to dissolve the courts, consider
government a failure, and let society lapse into bar-
barism." [39] On August 8 he left for Los Angeles, to hold
court there. He objected to having a guard with him,
but Marshal Franks insisted that Neagle go along. They
left Los Angeles by train on August 13. Neagle occupied
a section in the sleeping car opposite Field. The Terrys
lived in Fresno. Neagle asked the porter to wake him
before the train arrived there. When the train stopped
at Fresno Neagle saw Mr. and Mrs. Terry get on board.
They were on their way to San Francisco to attend court
in connection with the charges against them. Neagle
went back and told Field that the Terrys were on board.
"I hope they will have a good sleep," [40] he answered.
Neagle asked the conductor to wire ahead and have the
constable at Lathrop present when the train arrived,
to assist in preventing violence if trouble occurred.

Field got up before the train reached Lathrop, and
told Neagle he intended to get breakfast there. Neagle
suggested that he eat at the buffet on board the train, but
Field insisted on going to the dining-room.[41] As soon as
the train stopped Field and Neagle left the train and
walked to the dining-room. Field, because a recent
injury had painfully irritated the old wound in his knee,
had to lean on Neagle's arm. They sat down at a table
near the center of the room. Shortly afterward the
Terrys entered and walked up the aisle which was across
the table from and in front of them. Mrs. Terry noticed
Field, and turned hurriedly and walked out of the room,
while her husband went on down the aisle to a seat at

[39] Gorham, *Attempted Assassination of Justice Field*, p. 86.
[40] Testimony of Field. Transcript, p. 313.
[41] *Ibid.*; also testimony of Neagle. Transcript, p. 333.

another table. The manager of the dining-room stood at the door, showing guests where to go. As Mrs. Terry hurried out his brother asked her where she was going. What business was it of his, she asked. A brakeman told the manager that Field was in the room. Suspecting that Mrs. Terry was about to make trouble the manager sent his brother to warn Terry. The brother returned to the manager and told him not to let Mrs. Terry enter when she returned.[42]

Terry remained seated for a time and then got up and walked down the aisle toward the door, this time taking the aisle immediately behind Field. Those who were watching him assumed that he was going to join his wife. When he arrived at a point just behind Field he turned suddenly and struck him twice on the side of the face or head. Succeeding events came too quickly for accurate observation. Neagle leaped to his feet and shouted "Stop, stop!" Neagle saw a terrible expression on the face of Terry, and thought that the latter reached for his knife.[43] With his right hand extended Neagle drew his gun with his left and fired twice in rapid succession, killing Terry instantly.[44]

The room was instantly in an uproar. Dazed, Field looked around, to see Terry slumped upon the floor, his eyes setting in death. "Of course it was a great shock to me," he said in his sworn testimony concerning the tragedy. "It is impossible for any one to see a man in the full vigor of life with all those faculties that constitute life instantly extinguished without being affected, and I was. I looked at him for a moment, then rose

[42] Testimony of Joseph Stackpoole. *Ibid.*, p. 295.

[43] Testimony of Neagle. *Ibid.*, p. 336.

[44] Neagle was left handed (his testimony, transcript, p. 339), a fact which would be disconcerting to an enemy who expected hostile action to come from the right hand.

. . . and looked at him again, and passed on." [45]   A traveling salesman who had sat near him cried, "What is this?" Field replied that he was a justice of the Supreme Court of the United States. Terry had threatened his life and attacked him, and the deputy had shot him.[46] Neagle hurried Field out to the train, while the salesman went back for his hat and cane. They entered their car and placed a guard at the door.[47]

At the sound of the shots Mrs. Terry had come running back to the dining-room. The manager tried to stop her, but she tore herself away from him, and with loud lamentation threw herself down upon her husband's body, crying that they had killed her only friend. She arose and begged those around her to search her husband to prove that he was unarmed. She had taken his arms from him in the car, she said, for she didn't want him to shoot Judge Field, though she didn't object to a fist fight.[48]   Perhaps it was true that he was not armed. Neither gun nor knife was found on him. Field's friends were convinced that as she had stooped over him she had taken his knife from his coat and secreted it under her dress.

Some one took a satchel containing a gun from the excited woman. It was apparently for the purpose of getting the satchel that she had returned to the car after first entering the dining-room. She insisted that Field had hired Neagle to shoot Terry. She wanted both Field and Neagle brought out and lynched. "If my husband had killed Justice Field the crowd would have lynched him," she cried, "and now, . . . you will not help me punish the murderers of my husband." [49]   Her father

[45] Testimony of Field. Transcript, p. 314.
[46] Ibid.
[47] Testimony of Neagle. Transcript, p. 341.
[48] Testimony of G. I. Lidgerwood. Ibid., p. 123.
[49] Ibid.

was a Mason, she said. She begged the Masons to stand by her. A man in the crowd asked for a gun. He would bring the two men out and help lynch them, he said. The salesman ordered him to sit down. If anybody talked of lynching there would be another big party there, and the result would be terrible. The man subsided.[50]

As the train pulled out the sheriff of Stanislaus County boarded it. He took Neagle in charge, in spite of the protests of Field, left the train at Tracy, and drove with him to the county jail at Stockton. Field rode on toward San Francisco alone. The sheriff of San Joaquin County wired to a detective in San Francisco to cross the bay at Oakland, meet Field, and arrest him. The detective crossed the bay, but so also did Marshal Franks. Franks ordered the detective to let Field alone, and threatened to arrest him if he did not obey. The marshal and a large group of Field's friends escorted him triumphantly to his quarters at the Palace Hotel.[51]

The news of the affair at Lathrop reached headlines in papers all over the country. Throughout California it stirred intense excitement. It was feared that Terry's friends, many of whom lived in the neighborhood of Stockton, would not rest until Neagle had paid for his deed at the end of a rope. Old scandals concerning Field were talked over. Stephen M. White wrote to a friend asking for copies of the Colton-Huntington letters that had seemed to reveal Field as a tool of the railroads. He was disgusted at the support which Field was getting from public opinion. "To be candid, it makes me tired to listen to the flunkey talk that is going on at this time about a man, who, in my judgment, is one of the most dishonest characters that has ever discharged the function

---

[50] *Ibid.*, pp. 123-24.
[51] Gorham, *Attempted Assassination of Justice Field*, p. 101.

of a judicial office." [52] To a friend who had a case headed for the Supreme Court of the United States, however, he wrote to be careful what he said about Field, lest he prejudice his chance of winning. White, himself, was making no public statement on the situation. "We all have opinions about men and persons of distinction some of which are decidedly unfavorable but if we were called upon to prove that our opinions are founded in fact it might be difficult to establish them." [53]

The drama of the situation was by no means at an end. Terry's body was taken to Stockton on the day of his death. That evening Mrs. Terry swore out a complaint charging Field and Neagle with the murder of her husband. On the following day the justice of the peace before whom she had appeared issued warrants for the arrest of the two men. Neagle was brought into court that day, August 15, and the date of his examination was set for August 21. Bail could not be given prior to the examination. He was assured of six more days in the Stockton jail. If the people chose to lynch him they had plenty of time. On that same evening Sheriff Cunningham, of San Joaquin County, went to San Francisco to arrest Field. Many believed that the arrest was planned so that the mob might have two victims instead of one. Field's friends were determined that the sheriff should not take him to Stockton.

Sheriff Cunningham realized that it was a serious matter to arrest a man in Field's position. When, on the evening of August 15, he visited the Palace Hotel he went in the company of the chief of police of San Francisco and Marshal Franks. They talked the matter over with Field, and it was arranged that the warrant should be

[52] White to George R. B. Hayes, of San Francisco, Aug. 16, 1889. White MSS.

[53] White to H. W. Head, of Garden Grove, Calif., Aug. 16, 1889. *Ibid.*

presented at one o'clock on the following day, at the building in which the federal courts were held. At the appointed hour Field, surrounded by a group of judges and prominent lawyers, awaited the sheriff in his Circuit Court chambers. The sheriff entered and somewhat diffidently presented his warrant. "Proceed with your duty," said Field. "I am ready. An officer should always do his duty." Looking at the warrant he continued, "I recognize your authority, sir, and submit to the arrest; I am, sir, in your custody." [54]

The fact that he was arrested did not mean that Field was to leave immediately to join Neagle in the jail at Stockton. He and his friends were much too versatile as lawyers to permit that. A petition for a writ of habeas corpus had already been made out, returnable before the United States Circuit Court. Immediately after the arrest it was signed and presented to Judge Sawyer, who ordered the writ to issue, returnable immediately. Marshal Franks walked to the sheriff and presented the writ to him. Field had in the meantime, in his courtly fashion, asked the sheriff to sit down with him. When the abashed officer began to mumble apologies for his action Field replied: "Not so, not so; you are but doing your plain duty, and I mine in submitting to arrest. It is the first duty of judges to obey the law." [55] When the writ was served they entered the court room, Field leaning on the sheriff's arm.

Field's petition for the writ set forth his official position and duties, and alleged that he had been illegally arrested while performing those duties, and that his illegal detention prevented his discharging them. The statement of facts included a summary of the Sharon case and of the events which had followed. It showed in detail that

[54] Gorham, *Attempted Assassination of Justice Field*, p. 106.
[55] *Ibid.*, p. 107.

Mrs. Terry had "been guilty of acts and conduct showing herself to be an abandoned woman, without veracity." Yet the charge against Field was based upon her affidavit, although she had not even been present, and had not seen the shooting. The petition declared that these facts were notorious in Stockton, as well as in other parts of California, and that they were believed to be well known to the district attorney of the county, and to the justice of the peace who issued the warrant. Had either of these officers taken any pains whatever to ascertain the truth in the case he would have learned that there was no pretext for the charge. The petition continued:

"Your petitioner further states that it is to him incomprehensible how any man, acting in a consideration of duty, could have listened to charges from such a source, and without having sought some confirmation from disinterested witnesses; and your petitioner believes and charges that the whole object of the proceeding is to subject your petitioner to the humiliation of arrest and confinement at Stockton, where the said Sarah Althea Terry may be able, by the aid of partisans of hers, to carry out her long-continued and repeated threats of personal violence upon your petitioner, and to prevent your petitioner from discharging the duties of his office in cases pending against her in the federal court at San Francisco."

The sheriff filed a formal return. To give time for traversing the return and producing witnesses the hearing was adjourned until August 22. Field was released on his own recognizance, with a bond fixed at five thousand dollars.

For the time being, at least, Field was safe. The next thing for him and his friends to do was to protect Neagle. On the same day Judge Sawyer granted a petition for a writ of habeas corpus in Neagle's case, which was served upon the sheriff immediately. At four thirty on the morning of August 17 the sheriff left Stockton with Neagle in a special car headed for San Francisco. Later in the day he appeared in court, and filed a return to the writ. The traverse to the writ which was then filed presented various grounds why Neagle should not be held, among which were the fact that he was an officer of the United States who had been arrested by state officials for duties performed under the laws of the United States. The Attorney-General of the state appeared with the district attorney of San Joaquin County and charged that only state tribunals could inquire into the crime against the state with which Neagle was charged. Further proceedings were scheduled for August 22.

The funeral of Terry had been held on the preceding day. The state Supreme Court refused to adjourn in respect for him. "The circumstances of Judge Terry's death are notorious," said Chief Justice Beatty, "and under these circumstances this Court has determined that it would be better to pass this matter in silence, and not to take any action upon it."

On August 22 United States Attorney Carey, Richard S. Mesick, Samuel M. Wilson, and W. F. Herrin appeared in court in defense of Justice Field. They filed a traverse to the return of the sheriff, to which the counsel for the sheriff filed a demurrer. Leave was given to counsel to file briefs at any time before August 27. Before that date the Governor of the state interfered, writing the following letter to Attorney-General A. G. Johnston:

"The arrest of Hon. Stephen J. Field, a justice of the Supreme Court of the United States, on the unsupported oath of a woman who, on the very day the oath was taken, and often before, threatened his life, will be a burning disgrace to the state unless disavowed. I therefore urged upon you the propriety of at once instructing the district attorney of San Joaquin County to dismiss the unwarranted proceedings against him.

"The question of the jurisdiction of the state courts in the case of the deputy United States marshal, Neagle, is one for argument. The unprecedented indignity on Justice Field does not admit of argument." [56]

The Attorney-General immediately put pressure upon the district attorney of San Joaquin County, and on August 26, on the motion of the latter, the case was dismissed by the justice of the peace who had issued the warrant. On the following day the sheriff announced that he had released Field from custody, and the case of habeas corpus was dismissed. Judge Sawyer denounced the "shameless proceeding" by which the application for the writ had been made necessary. "We are extremely gratified to find that, through the [action of the] chief magistrate, and the Attorney-General, a higher officer of the law, we shall be spared the necessity of further inquiry as to the extent of the remedy afforded the distinguished petitioner, by the Constitution and laws of the United States, or of enforcing such remedies as exist, and that the stigma cast upon the state of California by this hasty and, to call it by no harsher term, ill-advised arrest, will not be intensified by further prosecution." [57]

Popular sentiment had been for the most part against Field's arrest, but many people thought that Neagle should at least be brought to trial in the state courts. It was apparent that if he were tried at Stockton, where the jury would probably be in sympathy with Terry, he stood a good chance of being convicted of murder, if he were not lynched before the time came. Hence the interest of his friends in taking the case out of the state courts.

[56] See In re *Field*, 14 Sawyer 193.
[57] *Ibid.*

The prosecution had asked Stephen M. White to be present at the argument of the question of federal jurisdiction. White replied that he thought his absence would be of more benefit than his presence. "You know that ever since the Stockton convention Field has been bitter in the extreme towards me and his relations and mine are pretty well understood. Moreover other things have taken place—in the way of repeating conversations which has made that feeling all the more intense and my appearance in the Circuit Court would be the signal for some additional work against us. Field would use his very great influence on Sawyer whom he controls and upon Deady or Brewer or whoever might sit in the matter to prejudice them against me and my presentation under such circumstances would not merely be weakened but would also be embarrassed." [58] White wrote to the Attorney-General commending the dismissal of the case against Field, saying that on the evidence it was obviously due him, and that anyway his discharge would help the state case against Neagle.[59] In writing to a man in Washington White said:

"That Terry-Field episode was a most unfortunate affair. I think it is a grave mistake to assert federal control of the case. The United States judges are *personally bitterly* hostile to the Terry side and I believe they will take jurisdiction and discharge Neagle without a trial. The case is practically being tried by Field, though he is behind the scenes. When Field 'hates' he hates 'for keeps' and will do anything to win." [60]

Many who were well versed in law believed that both Field and Neagle were immune from state jurisdiction for anything they had done. Letters of congratulation and

---

[58] White to W. D. Grachy, Aug. 21, 1889. White MSS.
[59] White to G. A. Johnson, Aug. 26, 1889. *Ibid.*
[60] White to James McCreery, Sept. 11, 1889. *Ibid.*

approval poured in for Field from all over the country. They were varied in their nature, but the following extract from the letter of J. Proctor Knott, one of Field's admiring friends, may to some degree be taken as typical: "I had been troubled, ever since I saw you had gone to your circuit, with apprehensions that you would be assassinated, or at least be subjected to some gross outrage, and cannot express my admiration of the serene heroism with which you went to your post of duty, determined not to debase the dignity of your exalted position by wearing arms for your defense, notwithstanding you were fully conscious of the danger which menaced you. It didn't surprise me, however, for I knew the stuff you were made of had been tested before. But I *was* surprised and disgusted, too, that *you* should have been charged or even suspected of anything wrong in the matter. The magistrate who issued the warrant for your arrest may possibly have thought it his duty to do so, without looking beyond the 'railing accusation' of a baffled and infuriated murderess, which all the world instinctively knew to be false, yet I suppose there is not an intelligent man, woman or child on the continent who does not consider it an infamous and unmitigated outrage, or who is not thoroughly satisfied that the brave fellow who defended you so opportunely was legally and morally justifiable in what he did." [61]

The Neagle case was elaborately argued in the Circuit Court, both as to the merits and as to federal jurisdiction. The contention of the friends of Terry that there had been a conspiracy to provoke Terry to begin an attack, and then to do away with him for all time, had scant sympathy in the atmosphere which prevailed around the Court in which the case was tried. Scorn was aroused

[61] Reprinted from a copy of the letter in Gorham, *Attempted Assassination of Justice Field*, pp. 145-49.

by the plea that Terry had been unarmed and had only
slapped Field with his hand, possibly to provoke him to a
duel—an act which, however much to be condemned, did
not warrant Terry's being shot down on the spot. Elaborate testimony had been taken, to include the history of
all the violent expressions and activities of the Terrys in
connection with the Sharon case. Field testified at length
concerning the Lathop tragedy. He claimed that there
had been virtually no friction at any time between himself and Terry down to the time of the scene in the court
room. He declared that he would have committed the
best friend he had in the world for actions such as Terry's.
Others testified as to the scenes both in the court room
and at the final catastrophe in the dining-room at Lathrop.
Judge Sawyer included an account of the occasion on
which he had been grossly insulted by Mrs. Terry on the
train. Evidence was offered of innumerable occasions on
which the Terrys had threatened to attack Field.

Carey, Mesick, Wilson, and Herrin presented the case
for Neagle, arguing that in shooting Terry he had performed the duty of defending Field which had been laid
upon him as a federal officer, and that the performance
of such a duty could not be a violation of the laws of the
state. They argued, on the basis of the evidence submitted,
that the only step which Neagle could take to protect
Field's life was to shoot the man who had attacked
him. Judge Sawyer, in giving the opinion of the Court,
accepted their arguments. He approved of Neagle's
deed, and justified it under the laws of the federal
government. In closing he said:

"In our judgment he [Neagle] acted, under the trying
circumstances surrounding him, in good faith and with
consummate courage, judgment, and discretion. The
homicide was, in our opinion, clearly justifiable in law,
and in the forum of sound, practical common sense,

commendable. This being so, and the act having been 'done . . . in pursuance of a law of the United States,' as we have already seen, it cannot be an offense against, and the petitioner is not amenable to, the laws of the state. Let him be discharged." [62]

Neagle was immediately released, and received the congratulations of a host of friends and partisans. In the judges' chambers Field, after a few remarks, presented him with a massive gold watch and chain. It was inscribed, "Stephen J. Field to David Neagle, as a token of appreciation of his courage and fidelity to duty under circumstances of great peril at Lathrop, Cal., on the fourteenth day of August, 1889." [63]

The decision was appealed to the Supreme Court of the United States. Joseph H. Choate lent his magnificent abilities to the cause of Neagle, evidently at Field's request, and James C. Carter was with him on the brief. The Attorney-General of the United States also appeared for Neagle. Justice Miller gave the opinion of the Court, and, analyzing the case at great length, upheld the decision of Judge Sawyer. Justice Lamar and Chief Justice Fuller dissented, holding that the remedy of a writ of habeas corpus was not here available, since Neagle's deed was not done pursuant to a specific law of the United States.[64]

It would have been well if the enmities stirred by the whole affair could have been immediately done away with and forgotten. That was perhaps too much to expect. Articles, pamphlets, and books were written by partisans to bolster up particular versions of what had happened, and the controversy continued to be discussed with much feeling. Sarah Althea Terry remained an irritating misfit

---

[62] In re *Neagle*, 14 Sawyer 232 (Sept. 16, 1889).

[63] Wagstaff, *Life of David S. Terry*, p. 526.

[64] In re *Neagle*, 135 U. S. 1.

in the society in which she lived, and ultimately arrived at the place which harbors many others who fail to conform to convention, a hospital for the insane. There she spent the remaining years of her erratic existence.

Justice Field failed to forget things that he might well have allowed to pass from his mind. E. G. Waite, a California politician and journalist, wrote an article on the life and character of Terry which was published in the *Overland Monthly*. The article appears to have been an attempt at a dispassionate appraisal of the subject, but in the closing paragraph the writer referred to Terry as a man possessed of "sterling integrity of purpose." Later Waite was nominated by President Harrison to be register of the land office at San Francisco. Field heard about the nomination, and, because of the article, raised such strenuous objections that the nomination was withdrawn. Field's reported explanation was as follows:

"When Waite's nomination for register was made I handed to a senator an article written by Waite in the *Overland Monthly* of October, eulogistic of the late David S. Terry. Much surprise was expressed by the senator at the tone of the article, the senator stating that it was a reflection upon the administration in designating the marshal to protect Judge Sawyer and myself from murderous assault by Terry, for if he was, as represented by Waite, a 'man of sterling integrity of purpose,' it was meant, if it meant anything, that Terry was a man of high principles and pure character, having honorable principles of action. It was quite evident from what the senator to whom I gave the article and other senators said, that it would be impossible for the nomination of Waite to be confirmed. Quite certain I am that neither Governor Stanford, who was his friend, nor the whole delegation from California, could have secured his confirmation." [65]

This act of Justice Field's had an appearance of vindictiveness and cheapness of purpose which cast an unpleasant reflection upon him as the tragic affair drew to a close. At best the ugly complications of the Sharon case could have brought no special credit to the judiciary. At less than the best it brought disillusioned sneers at the reputed dignity of the judges and the courts. The enmities that were made and the hatreds that were stirred were destined to live until all the principal characters themselves were gone. Seen from any angle whatever, it was a sorry affair.

[65] *Themis* (Sacramento, Calif.) May 24, 1890.

CHAPTER XIV
THE PUBLIC INTEREST

None of Field's personal and judicial experiences threw more light on his disposition and character, and none showed more intimately the close relationship between the judicial process and his personal traits and characteristics, than those arising out of the turbulent life of California. He participated in the solution of other judicial controversies, however, which, though not essentially different from those which arose in California, were better known throughout the country, and had a wider significance. Outstanding among these were the cases having to do with the basic issue as to whether the states had the power to interfere with and regulate the management of great business and industrial projects, particularly the rapidly growing and increasingly powerful systems of railroads, networks of which now extended throughout the country.

In the more than half a century which has passed since the first important Supreme Court cases which had to do with the right of states to regulate the charges of grain elevators and railroads, such regulation has become commonplace, and is taken much as a matter of course, for these and many other types of enterprise. There are still critical problems in connection with it which the courts are called upon to solve, but the right to at least a minimum of regulation is no longer questioned. It is hard to realize, save by reference to concrete historical experience, such as that of California in dealing with her railroads,[1] that the power to regulate at all was once

[1] See Chap. IX.

resisted with all the energy of the business and industrial leaders of the country, and bitterly denounced by the host of doctrinaire exponents of laissez faire. This was true, however, during many of the years which Field spent on the bench, and cases dealing with this issue were among the most important of those which were heard by the Court. Something of Field's own position may be inferred from his decisions which had to do with the California railroads, already discussed. This series is significant not only because it has to do with the development of judicial doctrine but also because it provides an instance in which Field, by the force of economic and industrial circumstance throughout the country, was gradually compelled to change his position.

In these cases, as in those dealing with the constitutionality of the legal tender acts, the Court had to pass upon a type of situation about which the Constitution had nothing directly to say, and to make decisions for which there were no close precedents. The judges had to evaluate the elements of the problems before them and decide to the best of their judgments what the solutions ought to be, and then stretch some previously established legal principles to the point where they justified their decisions. The judges were specialists primarily in the field of law, but their decisions in these great policy-making cases inevitably grew more largely out of their conceptions of social and economic welfare than out of their knowledge of law. Their constructive legal work began after their decisions had been made, in their attempts to harmonize their decisions with the previously recognized dictates of law.

The judges, of course, in their official capacity, participated only at intervals in the control of the business and industrial life of the country. They had a voice only when particular problems, which were usually but minor segments of the great basic problems, were argued before them in the trial of particular cases. Nevertheless, for an understanding of the judicial process in these cases, and for an appraisal of the part which it played, it is necessary to have the general background well in mind. This is especially true if we are to understand the work of the Court in the period of business and industrial adolescence of the last third of the nineteenth century.

"We must follow out the era on which we have entered to its logical and ultimate conclusions," wrote Charles Francis Adams, Jr., at the beginning of the decade of the seventies, "for it is useless for men to stand in the way of steam engines. Change is usually ugly, and the whole world, both physical and moral, is now in a period of transition." [2] The steam engine, trackage for which was rapidly creating a network throughout the United States, was perhaps the dominant factor in this changing era. The new lines of railroads gave marketing outlets to new sections of the country, and, with outlets to markets provided, new settlements pushed farther and farther into the West. Isolated communities excitedly voted huge subsidies to induce the building of railroads which would give them connections with the outside world. Adventurers with organizing ability engaged in projects for building new roads, hoping to sell them at a profit or to gain wealth through the increased productivity of the country which resulted. It was a boom period, hopes ran high, and risks were freely taken.

Much of the ugliness which Adams deplored was the result of the cupidity of people in all walks of life who were fanatically trying to get rich by some sort of railroad manipulation. Construction contracts provided innumerable scandals. Even members of Congress were smirched with rather convincing accusations of having

[2] "Railroad System," *Chapters of Erie*, p. 354.

participated in filching money from the United States government in the Credit Mobilier, a construction company which members of the Union Pacific Railroad Company organized for their own benefit, and to which they let contracts at exorbitant figures. The Erie scandals were notorious, and David Dudley Field, through his manipulations of corrupt New York judges in the interests of the Erie managers, created a stench about himself that was not soon removed. So widespread were the piratical activities of business men and the corrupt practices of politicians that in 1873 a prominent editor brought an article to a cynical close by saying, "all being corrupt together, what is the use in our 'investigating' each other?" [3]

Citizens of communities which had subsidized the building of the railroads did not achieve wealth as rapidly as they had hoped. Many fraudulent companies carried construction just far enough to get control of the appropriated funds, and then stopped. When railroads were put in operation the companies tended to charge the highest rates the traffic would bear. Where other roads competed for the business, however, rates were frequently cut to very low figures, while communities having only one outlet were charged excessive rates to make up the deficit. The companies were animated by no spirit of service to the community. They were scheming for profit, and not for the welfare of the shippers. Furthermore, the managers and the employees of the railroads performed their services with an insolence toward patrons that rankled bitterly with the disillusioned aspirants for swiftly gathered wealth. Rumblings of discontent began to be heard. Farmers in the Middle West began to organize to discuss and remedy their ills—a thing hitherto almost unheard of. Farmers' clubs were organized, and then, a

[3] Godkin, E. L., in the *Nation*, May 22, 1873.

little later, a secret order called the Grange began to spread throughout the rural sections. The Grange itself was non-political, to be sure, but it provided social-center activities at which people came together and discussed their common problems. It was an effective agency for bringing about a sense of unity among people previously without a conception of common interest. Organization was followed by threats of activity against the common enemy, and in the early seventies the capitalists of the East began to look with uneasiness on the growing "prairie fire."

The numerous aspects of the situation provided food for discussion in newspapers and magazines throughout the country. The editorials of E. L. Godkin, in the *Nation*, except when they stooped to mere invective against the farmers, were among those showing the keenest insight into the problems. Writing of a convention of the Farmers' clubs in the spring of 1873 Godkin said that these clubs constituted an earnest, though inarticulate, protest against the whole present organization of the railroad system of the country—a protest more dangerous because both unintelligent and angry.[4]

The editorial continued: "In its essence, that which the farmers demand is just. They ask for an access to their markets which shall combine the three elements of certainty, economy, and impartiality. All these are reasonable demands, and yet these are just what the existing system of transportation can never afford. It is not the fault of the railroad corporations. It is nothing less than the breakdown of competition as applied to our railroad system. The cost of transportation cannot be certain where it is necessarily subject to periodical wars of rates, resulting in brief truces of extortions; it cannot be economical while performed by many agents dividing the

[4] The *Nation*, April 10, 1873.

traffic, which can only flow cheaply when concentrated in single broad, deep channels; it cannot be impartial while the results of ruinous competition at one point must necessarily be made good by double profits at another. In other words we are gradually realizing that this enormous interest has been built up on a false economic principle— that competition will regulate when it has free, full play, but where it has not such full, clear play, it must confound.

"A vague glimmering of this difficulty is beginning to dawn on our people. The remedy for it lies far beyond the verdict of any twelve men in a jury-box; however intelligent these may be they can hardly supplement defective laws of trade. The contest now going on in Illinois is one of the early skirmishes of the impending war, which, unless we greatly err, is destined to produce industrial, social, and, above all, political changes in this country of the most startling description. The locomotive is coming in contact with the framework of our institutions. In this country of simple government, the most powerful centralizing force which civilization has yet produced has, within the next score of years, yet to assume its relations to that political machinery which is to control and regulate it." [5]

The farmers undoubtedly displayed great varieties of fallacious reasoning in their attacks on the railroad corporations, and they were not ineptly likened to spoiled children. They frequently owed to the railroads the fact that their districts were settled at all, and if transportation rates were high they were no worse than no transportation at all. The farmers did not propose to destroy their enemy. It was essential that the trains be kept running, and apparently it was necessary that they be run by the companies with which the farmers were at war. In view

[5] *Ibid.*

of these difficulties it is not surprising that rural reasoning found difficulties in arriving at an adequate solution.

Many people, represented in the press by Godkin, Charles Francis Adams, Jr., and others, argued that the solution was in bringing about the combination of many railroad lines into a few, so that trade wars would no longer take place, and it would not be necessary for corporations to bleed communities where there were no competing lines in order to make up for the losses incurred in cut-throat competition elsewhere. They favored the establishment of fact-finding commissions which would serve as publicity agents, and by so doing would remedy abuses. There was to be no more government interference with the corporations than was absolutely necessary, for in the existing state of affairs the government was not in a position to be effective. The able men of the country were employed not by the government but by the corporations. Said Godkin:

"Contrast the array of counsel in the Credit Mobilier cases—Mr. Curtis, Mr. Evarts, Mr. Cushing, and Mr. Bartlett—with the Attorney-General and his two juniors. Contrast, too, the liberal fees that will be paid to these really leading counsel with the salaries of the Attorney- and Solicitor-Generals. Manifestly society, as represented by the government, is beaten whenever it comes in contact with the great corporations, because society has allowed these corporations to secure as agents men who can out-general, outwork, and in an ordinary fight overcome, the men who are the agents of the government. Corporations to a certain extent take the place in American society of the privileged classes in aristocratic Europe; for they constitute a feudal system which exacts service, if not homage, from an influential portion of every community, and which carries on a disguised warfare with the government, sometimes in Congress, sometimes in the state legislatures, in which warfare concentrated wealth and power are arrayed against the wishes and, in some cases, interests of society at large." [6]

But if some keen observers of the situation were willing to permit railroad corporations to govern themselves, subject only to such pressure as resulted from their being under the spotlight of publicity, the farmers were not. They had an abiding faith in the potency of legislation as a cure for their ills. Four states, Illinois, Wisconsin, Minnesota, and Iowa, passed laws providing for the limitation of freight and fare charges. The outcome of the election of a new judge to the Supreme Court of Illinois was said to have been determined by the candidates' attitudes toward the constitutionality of the "Granger" legislation. The masses of the people, for the time being, were giving full attention to the problem, and it looked as if extensive political control of the railroads, whether for better or worse, was sure to come.

The laws were venomously attacked by the friends of the railroads and of the investors. Newspapers and magazines advertised widely the alleged fact that further investments in the states involved would be unsafe. Whether or not they believed this to be true their warnings struck at a weak point in the armor of communities which were constantly seeking new capital. Cases having to do with the constitutionality of the laws were carried to the supreme courts of the states, but in most instances the laws were upheld. Friends of the applicants were hopeful that results would be different when the cases were presented in Washington. The *Nation* argued in 1874 that the Supreme Court of the United States "for the first time in its history, is out of politics. The judges are not Democrats or Republicans, nor are they politically divided as the country once was on the question of

[6] *Ibid.*, May 15, 1873.

internal improvements. Since the lamentable fiasco of the legal tender decision, the Court has shown a marked tendency to conservatism and self-respect." [7] In view of these facts it was hoped that the biased decisions of the state courts would be reversed. Appeals were argued before the Supreme Court in October and November, 1875, and January, 1876.

It was more than a year after the arguments were heard that decisions were given. In the meantime much had happened to change the situation in the states from which the appeals had come. The panic in the fall of 1873 resulted in the bankruptcy of approximately half the railroad mileage of the country. New construction almost ceased, and amid the depressed conditions which followed there was no question of exorbitant profits on the roads already built. The farmers failed to maintain their organization and their enthusiasm, and to follow through with the work which they had started. Presumably, although the charge is not easy to prove, the railroad interests took from the farmers the control of the state legislatures. At any rate, before any decision was given at Washington most of the objectionable laws either were repealed or were no longer enforced. The situation was summarized by Charles Francis Adams, Jr. as follows:

"In some respects the results produced by the movement have been most beneficial. The corporations owning the railroads have been made to realize that those roads were built for the West, and that, to be operated successfully, they must be operated in sympathy with the people of the West. The whole system of discriminations and local extortions has received a much needed investigation, the results of which cannot but mitigate or wholly remove its more abominable features; finally, certain great principles of justice and equality, heretofore too

[7] *Ibid.*, Sept. 24, 1874.

much ignored, have been driven by the sheer force of
discussion, backed by a rising public opinion, into the
very essence of the railroad policy. All this much is
gained. The burnt child dreads the fire, and the Granger
states may rest assured that, through an indefinite future,
the offensive spirit of absentee ownership will be far less
perceptible in the management of the railroads than it
was before and during the great railroad mania. Finally,
East and West, the good which has resulted and yet will
result from the Granger movement will be found greatly
to predominate over the evil; what is more, the good will
survive, while the evil will pass away." [8]

Although Adams' interpretation may not be a complete explanation of what had happened it indicates fairly
well the point at which the Supreme Court took a hand
in the problem of the control of this new and powerful
force in American social and economic life. The justices
had had little or nothing to do with the devious developments of earlier years, though they could not but know
and have opinions about them, but from now on they
were to exert a strategic influence. It was difficult to
forecast the results if the decision of the Court was either
for or against the state laws, but it was fairly easy to see
that a decision in either direction might have a great
influence on the whole future course of the control of
railroad corporations. It seems probable that the delay of
more than a year between the time of the arguments
and the date when the decisions were announced was
given not merely to a study of the relevant precedents at
law, but also to a careful observation of the situation in
the Middle West as it gradually worked itself out. It was
there, and not in legal precedents, that the data necessary

[8] "The Granger Movement," *North American Review*, April, 1875,
pp. 423-24.

for an understanding of the problems before the Court were to be acquired.[9]

On the first day of March, 1877, Chief Justice Waite gave the opinions of the Court in the Granger cases, upholding the constitutionality of the laws in question. Justices Field and Strong dissented. The Chief Justice established the legal basis of his opinions not in one of the five railroad cases [10] around which the bitter controversy had raged, but in *Munn* v. *Illinois*,[11] a case having to do with the regulation of the rates charged for the storing of grain in grain elevators, which had been argued before the Court after the railroad cases had been presented. Apparently his reason for reversing the order of the cases was that grain elevators seemed to him to provide a better analogy with which to tie into the relevant phase of English common law than did railroads. More than two hundred years before this time the regulation of the rates of warehouses under certain conditions had been justified in England by a doctrine of "public interest." There had of course been no railroads at that time. In order to make use of the doctrine he brought it down to his own period in the elevator case, and was then in a position to go a step further and apply it to railroads as well.

The facts of the elevator case were, briefly, as follows: Most of the grain produced in the West for sale in Eastern or European markets passed through Chicago, and much

[9] For accounts of the Granger movement see Buck, S. J., *The Granger Movement*, and *The Agrarian Crusade;* Adams, C. F., Jr., *Railroads, Their Origins and Problems* (1878); Hadley, A. T., *Railroad Transportation* (1886).

[10] *C. B. & Q. R. R.* v. *Iowa*, 94 U. S. 155; *Peik* v. *C. & N. W. R. R.*, 94 U. S. 164; *C. M. & St. P. Ry.* v. *Ackley*, 94 U. S. 179; *Winona & St. Peter R. R.* v. *Blake*, 94 U. S. 180; *Stone* v. *Wisconsin*, 94 U. S. 181.

[11] 94 U. S. 113.

of it had to be unloaded and reloaded there. To meet the needs of handling the grain fourteen warehouses, or elevators, had been constructed by the year 1874. They were owned by only thirty persons, and their control was chiefly in the hands of nine business firms. These firms agreed among themselves as to the charges which they would exact for their services. Since they had control of the business they were in position to take heavy toll from the principal products of seven or eight farming states of the West, if they chose to do so. The farmers had suffered enough from the cupidity of business men to make them fearful of such a situation. The new constitution which was adopted by Illinois in 1870 made it the duty of the legislature to pass laws for the protection of producers, shippers, and receivers of grain and produce, and the following year an act prescribing the maximum charges of grain elevators was passed. It was the constitutionality of this act which was contested before the Supreme Court.

Waite gave many illustrations to show that in the past the regulation of the use, or even of the price of the use of property, had not been regarded as contrary to due process of law. He therefore denied the arguments of counsel to the effect that they were protected against regulation by the provisions of the Fourteenth Amendment. For the principles upon which this power of regulation rested he looked to the common law, and quoted Lord Chief Justice Hale as saying that when property was "affected with a public interest, it ceases to be *juris privati* only." "This was said . . . more than two hundred years ago, . . . and has been accepted without objection as an essential element in the law of property ever since. Property does become clothed with a public interest when used in a manner to make it of public consequence, and affect the community at large. When, therefore, one devotes his property to a use in which the public has an interest, he, in effect, grants to the public an interest in that use, and must submit to be controlled by the public for the common good, to the extent of the interest he has thus created. He may withdraw his grant by discontinuing the use; but, so long as he maintains the use, he must submit to the control."

Having stated the principle and interpreted it thus broadly the Chief Justice showed how in early times it had been applied to ferries, to wharves, and to warehouses. To show that the Chicago grain elevators were affected with a public interest he quoted at length from the argument of one of the counsel for the owners of the elevators. The lawyer had used the material quoted for the purpose of showing that the work of the elevators played a strategic part in the flow of interstate commerce, and that hence they were subject only to federal, and not to state control. Waite used it to show the tremendous importance of the elevators in the life of the people, whereby they could not but be affected with a public interest, and, therefore, be subject to regulation by the state. He declared that the storing of grain was a local business, however, and was not a part of interstate commerce within the meaning of the Constitution.

He recognized that the situation was somewhat different from any hitherto passed upon, and that although the doctrine was old he was carrying it into new fields. He did not think this fact important. "Neither is it a matter of any moment that no precedent can be found for a statute precisely like this. It is conceded that the business is one of recent origin, that its growth has been rapid, and that it is already of great importance. And it must also be conceded that it is a business in which the whole public has a direct and positive interest. It presents, therefore, a case for the application of a long-known and well-established principle in social science, and this statute simply extends the law so as to meet this new development of commercial progress."

He had yet to answer the argument that "the owner of property is entitled to a reasonable compensation for its use, even though it be clothed with a public interest, and that what is reasonable is a judicial and not a legislative question." His answer was that the right of reasonable compensation was based on the common law, and that the legislature had the power to modify the common law. "The controlling fact is the power to regulate at all. If that exists, the right to establish the maximum of charge, as one of the means of regulation, is implied." Two further sentences promised small comfort to investors. Speaking of the power of regulation he said: "We know that this is a power which may be abused; but that is no argument against its existence. For protection against abuses by legislatures the people must resort to the polls, not to the courts."

This statement was peculiarly like that of Field, made nearly twenty years earlier, when he said: "It is to be supposed that the members of the legislature will exercise some wisdom in its acts; if they do not, the remedy is with the people. Frequent elections by the people furnish the only protection, under the Constitution, against the abuse of acknowledged legislative power." [12] Now, however, Field greeted the idea with scorn.

Although the Court had waited many months in silence after hearing the arguments in the Granger cases before giving any decision, the decision seems finally to have been announced with some suddenness. Justice Strong complained that he had had no time to prepare a dissenting opinion,[13] and Field completed and filed his dissenting

[12] Ex parte *Newman*, 9 Cal. 502. For discussion of this case see Chap. IV.
[13] 94 U. S. 154.

opinion at a later date.[14] During the preceding weeks
these two justices had been busy as members of the electoral commission. The people were watching this
controversy with such intentness that little attention was
paid to the decision of the Court. It is not improbable
that the decision was announced at this time because of
the fact that it would go on record with little attention
from the people. But however that may be, Field completed his dissenting opinion afterward at his leisure,
with the text of the opinion of the Chief Justice before
him, with full opportunity to analyze the points made
by his opponent.

Field argued the issues solely from the point of view
of the owners of the property which was made subject to
regulation. "The principle upon which the opinion of
the majority proceeds is, in my judgment, subversive of
the rights of private property, heretofore believed to be
protected by constitutional guaranties against legislative
interference, and is in conflict with the authorities cited
in its support." He analyzed the doctrine of public
interest as stated and applied by Sir Matthew Hale, and
argued that it did not apply to such situations as that
before the Court. It had been applied only where some
privilege had been granted by the king, or where the
owner had dedicated his property to a public use—a term
which Field did not attempt to define. That is to say,
the mere fact that the business of grain elevators was
such as vitally to affect the interests of the public did not
establish the fact that it was "affected with a public
interest" within the meaning of the law. It did not come
within the common law category as properly interpreted,
and must be treated as a private business for the regulation of the charges of which there was no established legal
precedent.

[14] Chicago *Tribune*, March 2, 1877.

The Chief Justice had recognized that the precedents did not completely cover the case at hand, but thought that the gap between the case and the precedents was not great, and that it was a part of the creative function of the Court to bridge it. Field saw the gap as a yawning chasm, the bridging of which would lead to the destruction of rights of private property. If legislatures might regulate the rates of grain elevators under the doctrine interpreted so broadly by the Court they might with equal facility determine rates in almost any conceivable kind of business. Private property would be at the mercy of the legislatures. For the protection of property Field placed more faith in the wise application of legal principles by learned judges than in the beneficent operations of political democracy. "Frequent elections by the people" was no longer the only remedy for legislative abuse.

He argued that justification for judicial interference to protect property against legislative control was to be found in the due process clause of the Fourteenth Amendment. "The doctrine of the state court, that no one is deprived of his property, within the meaning of the constitutional inhibition, so long as he retains its title and possession, and the doctrine of this Court, that, whenever one's property is used in such a manner as to affect the community at large, it becomes by that fact clothed with a public interest, and ceases to be *juris privati* only, appear to me to destroy, for all useful purposes, the efficacy of the constitutional guaranty. All that is beneficial in property arises from its use, and the fruits of that use; and whatever deprives a person of them deprives him of all that is desirable or valuable in the title and possession. If the constitutional guaranty extends no further than to prevent a deprivation of title and possession, and allows a deprivation of use, and the fruits of that use, it does not

merit the encomiums it has received. Unless I have
misread the history of the provision now incorporated
into all our state constitutions, and by the Fifth and
Fourteenth Amendments into our federal Constitution,
and have misunderstood the interpretation it has received,
it is not thus limited in its scope, and thus impotent for
good. It has a much more extended operation than either
court, state or federal has given to it. . . . The provision has been supposed to secure to every individual the
essential conditions for the pursuit of happiness; and for
that reason has not been heretofore, and should never be,
construed in any narrow or restricted sense."

The power of the state over the property of the citizen
was well defined, he said. The state might take property
for public uses, upon the payment of just compensation.
It could take a portion by taxation for the support of the
government. It could control the use and possession of
property so far as was necessary to secure protection to
the rights of others, and to secure to them the equal use
and enjoyment of their property. "The doctrine that
each one must so use his own as not to injure his neighbor
. . . is the rule by which every member of society must
possess and enjoy his property; and all legislation essential
to secure this common and equal enjoyment is a legitimate
exercise of state authority. Except in cases where property may be destroyed to arrest a conflagration or the
ravages of pestilence, or be taken under the pressure of
an immediate and overwhelming necessity to prevent a
public calamity, the power of the state over the property
of the citizen does not extend beyond such limits."

He admitted that innumerable regulations affecting the
use of property might be passed for the preservation of
the peace, good order, safety, and health of the community, but declared that in establishing these regulations
the control of prices for use and services was not a matter

of importance. There was nothing in the character of the business of the defendants as warehousemen, he declared, which called for interference for these purposes. "Their buildings are not nuisances; their occupation of receiving and storing grain infringes upon no rights of others, disturbs no neighborhood, infects not the air, and in no respect prevents others from using and enjoying their property as to them seems best."

He must have known, of course, that the rates at the elevators might, in the absence of regulation, suddenly be raised to such figures that the economic welfare of thousands of the people would be jeopardized. Nevertheless he continued with the declaration that "the legislation in question is nothing less than a bold assertion of absolute power by the state to control at its discretion the property and business of the citizen, and fix the compensation he shall receive. The will of the legislature is made the condition upon which the owner shall receive the fruits of his property and the just rewards of his labor, industry, and enterprise . . . . The decision of the Court in this case gives unrestrained license to legislative will."

The opinion showed Field a man of very different outlook from that which he claimed in 1858, when he saw clearly the menace to the rights and opportunities of men which grew out of the inequalities of economic positions and out of the fact that some were at the mercy of others who were in strategic positions of power.[15] "The exactions of avarice are not equally satisfied," he said then, and with approval he pointed out the fact that "the law steps in to restrain the power of capital." "To protect labor is the highest office of our laws," he said. Now his position seemed to be that the highest office of our laws was the protection of property, even against the enactments of the representatives of the people themselves.

[15] See discussion of Ex parte *Newman*, 9 Cal. 502, pp. 78-80.

His general shift in position was not occasioned by the fact that a due process clause had been enacted in the Fourteenth Amendment. The case of 1858 arose in a state court, under a state constitution which contained a due process clause which was capable of the same broad interpretation as that of the federal Constitution, yet it was not invoked. The real change was not in laws or constitutions, but in Field himself. It meant a shift of emphasis from the complex of relationships which determine human welfare, on the one hand, to the protection first of all of the rights of property on the other.

Taking Field's elevator case opinion in contrast with that of the Chief Justice, it stands the comparison well. The logic of his opinion stands in better form than that of his opponent. Field could always find apparently sound arguments for any position which he wanted to support while Waite was much less effective—an interesting bit of evidence of which is found in a note of thanks to Field for a suggested change in an opinion, in which he said humbly, "The difficulty with me is that I cannot give the *reasons* as I wish I could." [16] There were times, however, when decisions themselves were more important than the arguments by which they were justified, and this was certainly true of the elevator case.

Following the elevator case Waite read opinions giving the decisions of the Court in the five railroad cases. Railroad companies were carriers for hire, he said. They were incorporated as such, and were given extraordinary powers, in order that they might the better serve the public in that capacity. They were, therefore, engaged in a public employment affecting the public interest, and, under the decision in *Munn* v. *Illinois,* were subject to control as to their rates of fare and freight, unless pro-

[16] Waite to Field, April 28, 1882. In the library of the University of California.

tected by their charters. He held that as to the charters here involved the corporations were not so protected. He denied that it affected the case that before the power of regulation was exercised a company had pledged its income as security for the payment of debts incurred, and had leased its road to a tenant that relied upon the earnings for the means of paying the agreed rent. The company could not grant more than it had to give. After the pledge and after the lease the property remained within the jurisdiction of the state, and continued subject to the same governmental powers that existed before.[17] As for interference with interstate commerce, he insisted that until Congress acted a state might legislate concerning its domestic relations, even though it might indirectly affect commerce in other states at the same time.

Field dissented,[18] both from the judgments and from the reasoning upon which they were founded. Summarizing the arguments which railroad counsel had made before the Court he said: "The questions thus presented are of the gravest importance, and their solution must materially affect the value of property invested in railroads to the amount of many hundreds of millions, and will have a great influence in encouraging or repelling future investments in such property. They were ably and elaborately argued by eminent counsel, and nothing was omitted which could have informed or enlightened the Court. The opportunity was presented for the Court to define the limits of the power of the state over its corporations after they have expended money and incurred obligations upon the faith of the grants to them, and the rights of the corporators, so that, on the one hand, the property interests of the stockholder would be protected from practical confiscation, and, on the other hand, the

[17] *C. B. & Q. R. R.* v. *Iowa,* 94 U. S. 155.
[18] *Stone* v. *Wisconsin,* 94 U. S. 183.

people would be protected from arbitrary and extortionate charges. This has not been done; but the doctrine advanced in *Munn* v. *Illinois* . . . has been applied to all railroad companies and their business, and they are thus practically placed at the mercy of the legislature of every state."

The first question that should have been considered, he argued, was as to the rights and privileges conferred by the charters of the companies involved, and the restraints which they imposed upon legislative interference. "This question is not met by the Court in its opinion, the several cases being disposed of by the novel doctrine announced in *Munn* v. *Illinois,* that the legislature has a right to regulate the compensation for the use of all property, and for services in connection with it, the use of which affects the 'community at large'; and the further doctrine, equally novel, that although the charter of a company confers the power to make reasonable charges, the whole matter is reserved to be regulated by the state, in its discretion."

"So long as that decision remains," he said in closing, "it will be a waste of words to discuss the questions argued by counsel in these cases. That decision, in its wide sweep, practically destroys all the guaranties of the Constitution and of the common law invoked by counsel for the protection of the rights of the railroad companies. Of what avail is the constitutional provision that no state shall deprive any person of his property except by due process of law, if the state can, by fixing the compensation which he may receive for its use, take from him all that is valuable in the property? To what purpose can the constitutional prohibition upon the state against impairing the obligation of contracts be invoked, if the state can, in the face of a charter authorizing a company to charge reasonable rates, prescribe what rates shall be deemed reasonable for services rendered? That decision will justify the legislature in fixing the price of all articles and the compensation for all services. It sanctions intermeddling with all business and pursuits and property in the community, leaving the use and enjoyment of property and the compensation for its use to the discretion of the legislature. Having already expressed my objections to that decision in a dissenting opinion, I need not repeat them here."

It is only by implication that one can say whether Field was at all influenced in these cases by his horror of anything that bore the taint of socialism or communism, but it seems quite probable that this feeling played its part. The farmers of the Middle West had been charged with communism to such an extent that a state Supreme Court justice took occasion to deny the charge. One of the railroad counsel before the Supreme Court of the United States sought to turn that denial to his own advantage. The Wisconsin judge had said that the "statute had been denounced as an act of communism, but that he thanked God communism was a foreign abomination without recognition in Wisconsin, where the people were too intelligent, too staid, too just, too busy, too prosperous for any such horror of doctrine." "It is quite true," said the railroad lawyer, "that the theory of the statute is distinct from the doctrine of the communists. The latter divides property ratably between the plundered and the plunderers, while the former takes all for the Grangers." [19]

The tone of Field's opinion indicates that he may have accepted this view of the situation. At any rate, it is worth stating again that he had no faith in a political order which surrendered the powers of government

[19] Brief of E. W. Stoughton, p. 17, filed in *Peik* v. *Chicago & N. W. R. R.*, 94 U. S. 164.

to democratic expressions of popular desires. On matters of vital economic importance he would have had nine learned justices on the bench of the Supreme Court so use their powers of interpreting the Constitution as to make themselves the arbiters of the welfare of the people. It was a part of his own doctrine of economic welfare that business activities should have the greatest possible freedom of play.

It is perhaps useless to speculate as to what form of control of railroad charges would have evolved if the Court had held rate regulation to be unconstitutional. It did not so hold, and thereafter such regulation remained a potential weapon to be used by the states in preventing certain kinds of abuses. In the years which followed, business conditions changed for the better, and corporations began again to build new lines and compete strenuously for traffic, and in doing so gave impetus to some of the old abuses. Then the recognized instrument of control was again brought into use. State commissions were established with regulatory powers, although care was taken not to provoke again the cry of communism, and to frighten away investors. Using varied arguments and methods of approach, new cases testing the legality of regulation came from time to time for settlement before the Supreme Court.

In 1883 Chief Justice Waite gave the opinion of the Court in another case from Illinois, upholding a change in railroad rates by legislative act.[20] The charter had given the corporation power to make rules and by-laws, but they were not to be repugnant to the laws of the state. The Chief Justice declared that in view of this last provision the by-laws of a corporation fixng rates were

[20] *Ruggles* v. *Illinois*, 108 U. S. 526 (May 7, 1883).

subject to readjustment to harmonize with any state laws which might be enacted at any time. Justice Harlan, who had come to the bench after the decisions in the Granger cases were announced, concurred in the judgment here, believing that the rates established by the state were reasonable in this instance, or at least that they had not been shown to be unreasonable. He did not agree with the majority of the Court, however, that the subject of reasonableness was one into which the judiciary could not inqure.

Field expressed himself briefly, but, as usual, with considerable vigor: "I concur in the judgment in this case solely on the ground that no proof was made that the rate prescribed by the legislature was unreasonable. Under previous decisions of the Court the legislative rate is to be taken as presumptively reasonable.

"I do not give any weight to *Munn* v. *Illinois.* My objections to the decision in that case were expressed at the time it was rendered, and they have been strengthened by subsequent reflection. Besides, that case does not relate to corporations or to common carriers."

The last paragraph indicates that he was beginning to recognize either the necessity or the inevitability of some degree of state regulation of railroad charges, but that he was determined that regulation was to be kept within the limit of "reasonableness," a term the definition of which in particular instances was to be left with the Court. However, his position here differed from that taken in the Granger cases in that he concurred in regulation in a particular instance. For a man of his disposition even this concession is worthy of note.

Two years later Chief Justice Waite gave the opinion of the Court in another important case,[21] upholding the right of a state to limit the charges of a railroad the

[21] *Stone* v. *Farmers' Loan and Trust Co.,* 116 U. S. 307 (Jan. 4, 1886).

charter of which gave to the corporation the power to establish rates, but did not specifically deny to the state the power to interfere. "This power of regulation is a power of government, continuing in its nature, and if it can be bargained away at all it can only be by words of positive grant, or something which is in law equivalent. If there is a reasonable doubt, it must be resolved in favor of the existence of the power." Thus far the Chief Justice maintained the position which he, as spokesman for the Court, had taken in the Granger cases. Another paragraph, however, indicates that he felt the pressure exerted by Field and Harlan and by the friends of the great corporate interests who clamored for protection by the Court. Instead of reiterating his earlier statement that in case of legislative abuse in regulation the people must resort to the polls and not to the courts he now said:

"From what has thus been said, it is not to be inferred that this power of limitation or regulation is itself without limit. This power to regulate is not a power to destroy, and limitation is not the equivalent of confiscation. Under pretense of regulating fares and freights, the state cannot require a railroad corporation to carry persons or property without reward; neither can it do that which in law amounts to a taking of private property for public use without just compensation, or without due process of law."

This statement indicated that the earlier dire prophecies of Field as to the wholesale taking of private property by rapacious legislatures now seemed likely to go astray. Here was a hint that the supreme tribunal of the land would keep a watchful eye over the abuses which it had previously threatened to ignore, and, if the abuses became too great, would bring to bear the strong arm of the law.

Field and Harlan, in spite of Waite's concession, dissented in this case, declaring that under the law in question the obligation of contract was impaired. The decision turned in part upon the question of valuation, which thereafter was to be a perennial problem before the Court. According to Field's account the railroad in the controversy, in the state of Mississippi, had been a part of a proposed through line from the Gulf of Mexico to the Ohio River. "The road was to run, as thus seen, many hundred miles, part of which was in a country sparsely settled and in some places covered by almost irreclaimable swamps. It would require several years and the expenditure of many millions for its construction. The return for the heavy investment was to be in the distant future when the country should become more densely populated, and its resources better developed. It was a difficult matter to secure the necessary capital for an enterprise so costly in its character, so remote in its completion, and so uncertain in its returns. To effect this the several acts of incorporation authorized the president and directors of the company to adopt and establish such a tariff of charges for the transportation of persons and property as they might think proper, and to alter and change the same at pleasure."

"Certainly," Field continued, "no one will deny that the right to adopt a rate of charges, subject, as such rate always is, to the condition that they shall be reasonable, was of vital importance to the company. Without that concession no one acquainted with the difficulties, expenses, and hazards of the projected enterprise, can believe that it would have been undertaken. It was certainly the expectation of the constructors of the road that they should be allowed to receive compensation having some relaton to its cost. But the act of Mississippi allows only such compensation as parties appointed by the legislature, not interested in the property, nor required to possess any knowledge of the intricacies and difficulties of the business, shall determine to be a fair return upon the *value* of the road and its appurtenances, though that may be much less than the original cost. Within the last few years, such have been the improvements in machinery, and such the decline in the cost of materials, that it is probably less expensive by one-third to build and equip the road now than it was when the constructors completed it. Does anybody believe that they would have undertaken the work or proceeded with it, had they been informed that notwithstanding their vast outlays, they should only be allowed, when it was finished, to receive a fair return upon its value, however much less than cost that might be?"

Throughout the rate cases discussed thus far it has seemed that the Court, with Chief Justice Waite as spokesman, was chiefly interested in protecting the traveling and shipping public, while Field concentrated on the need of protecting investments in railroad property. In the last case he not only insisted that the corporations had a right to charge "reasonable" rates, whatever the enactments of legislatures, but that it was a part of "reasonableness" that they be allowed to use the total amount of the investment as the basis for rates, regardless of its relation to present value. It is an illuminating fact that years afterward the value of railroad property increased to such an extent that the present value was greater than the investment cost. Then the railroads and the representatives of the public changed positions with regard to the rate base to be used. The railroads wanted to use reproduction cost, while the public insisted that value was to be determined by determining the amount invested. It is interesting to speculate on the question as to whether Field would have changed his position along with the reversal of the interests of the railroads and of the public.

Field's persistent repetition of his ideas on the subject of rate regulation probably had its effect in bringing about the slow change toward conservatism, even as, in the face of changing conditions, he made some adjustments in his own position. In October, 1888, a few months after the death of Chief Justice Waite, the Court voted unanimously to uphold the act of the Georgia legislature conferring certain powers upon a commission, among them being that of fixing railroad rates.[22] Field wrote the opinion of the Court. He attempted to establish the consistency of his position by the following statement:

"The incorporation of the company . . .; the grant to it of special privileges to carry out the object of its incorporation, particularly the authority to exercise the state's rights of eminent domain that it may appropriate needed property,—a right which can be exercised only for public purposes; and the obligation, assumed by the acceptance of its charter, to transport all persons and merchandise, upon like conditions and upon reasonable rates, affect the property and employment with a public use; and where property is thus affected, the business in which it is used is subject to legislative control. So long as the use continues, the power of regulation remains, and the regulation may extend not merely to provisions for the security of passengers and freight against accidents, and for the convenience of the public, but also to prevent extortion by unreasonable charges, and favoritism by unjust discriminations. This is not new doctrine, but old

[22] *Georgia Railroad & Banking Co.* v. *Smith*, 128 U. S. 174 (Oct. 29, 1888).

doctrine, always asserted whenever property or business is, by reason of special privileges received from the government, the better to secure the purposes to which the property is dedicated or devoted, affected with a public use."

"There have been differences of opinion," he continued, "among the judges of this Court in some cases as to the circumstances or conditions under which some kinds of property or business may be properly held to be thus affected, as in *Munn* v. *Illinois,* 94 U. S. 113, 126, 139, 146; but none as to the doctrine that when such use exists the business becomes subject to legislative control in all respects necessary to protect the public against danger, injustice, and oppression. In almost every case which has been before this Court, where the power of the state to regulate the rates of charges of railroad companies for the transportation of persons and freight within its jurisdiction has been under consideration, the question discussed has not been the original power of the state over the subject, but whether that power had not been, by stipulations of the charter, or other legislation, amounting to a contract, surrendered to the company, or been in some manner qualified. It is only upon the latter point that there have been differences of opinion."

Thus, in disregarding the category of "public interest," which Chief Justice Waite had resurrected from seventeenth century English common law, and employing that of public use, Field endeavored to show that there had really been no change at all in his position. Credit must be given him for the superb strategy of his argument. As a matter of fact both he and the majority of the Court had changed a great deal since the announcement of the decisions in the Granger cases.

The direction in which the Court was moving was shown by a case which was decided in March, 1890, Justice Blatchford giving the opinion of the Court.[23] The decision held unconstitutional a Minnesota act which provided that the ruling of a state commission should be final as to the reasonableness of the rates which it established. "It deprives the company of its right to a judicial investigation, by due process of law, under the forms and with the machinery provided by the wisdom of successive ages for the investigation judicially of the truth of a matter in controversy, and substitutes therefor, as an absolute finality, the action of a railroad commission which, in view of the powers conceded to it by the state court, cannot be regarded as clothed with judicial functions or possessing the machinery of a court of justice."

The significance of the decision was pointed out by Justice Bradley in his dissenting opinion: "I cannot agree to the decision of the Court in this case. It practically over-rules *Munn* v. *Illinois*, . . . and the several railroad cases that were decided at that time." "By the decision now made we declare, in effect, that the judiciary, and not the legislature, is the final arbiter in the regulation of fares and freights of railroads and the charges of other public accommodations. It is an assumption of authority on the part of the judiciary which, it seems to me, with all due deference to the judgment of my brethren, it has no right to make."

With the right of the judiciary to review rate regulation thus firmly established in constitutional law it is not greatly surprising to find Field, in January, 1892, giving the opinion of the Court upholding an act requiring railroad companies to pay the expenses of a state railroad commission, a part of whose function was to regulate the charges of the roads.[24] He restated at length his reasons for holding that the rates charged by the roads were

---

[23] *C. M. & St. P. Ry.* v. *Minnesota*, 134 U. S. 418 (March 24, 1890).
[24] *Railroad Co.* v. *Gibbs*, 142 U. S. 386 (Jan. 4, 1892).

subject to regulation. "Being the recipients of special privileges from the state, to be exercised in the interest of the public, and assuming the obligations thus mentioned, their business is deemed affected with a public use, and to the extent of that use is subject to legislative regulation." Since all railroads in the state were treated alike, and since the work of the commission was limited to the supervision of railroads, there was no discrimination on the basis of which the railroads could object to paying the bills.

This was the last of the railroad rate regulation cases in which Field wrote an opinion. Before summarizing the story it is of interest to see what happened in connection with the problem of regulating the rates of grain elevators. Field never changed his position far enough to agree to such regulation. In a case decided in February, 1892, Justice Blatchford said, speaking for the Court, "The main question involved in these cases is whether this Court will adhere to its decision in *Munn* v. *Illinois.* . . ." [25] The power of regulation was upheld. Field dissented. He did not submit an opinion of his own, but concurred in one sponsored by his nephew, Justice Brewer. The style of the opinion is such as to suggest that the two justices may have worked together in its preparation.

"I dissent from the opinion and judgment in these cases," Brewer began. "The main proposition upon which they rest is, in my judgment, radically unsound. It is the doctrine of *Munn* v. *Illinois* . . . reaffirmed." "The vice of the doctrine is, that it places a public interest in the use of property upon the same basis as a public use of property. Property is devoted to a public use when, and only when, the use is one which the public in its organized

[25] *Budd* v. *New York*, 143 U. S. 517 (Feb. 29, 1892).

capacity, to wit, the state, has a right to create and maintain, and, therefore, one which all the public have a right
to demand and share in. The use is public, because the
public may create it, and the individual creating it is
doing thereby and *pro tanto* the work of the state. The
creation of all highways is a public duty. Railroads are
highways. The state may build them. If an individual
does that work, he is *pro tanto* doing the work of the
state. He devotes his property to a public use. The state
doing the work fixes the price for the use. It does not
lose the right to fix the price, because an individual voluntarily undertakes to do the work. But this public use is
very different from a public interest in the use. There
is scarcely any property in whose use the public has no
interest."

He illustrated at length his conception of the difference
between "public interest" and "public use." Like his
uncle he believed that men had a natural right to be let
alone in the use of their proprty so long as they did not
interfere with the rights of others, or did not devote it to
a "public use." He argued that the existence of a
monopoly did not necessarily justify legislative interference. "There are two kinds of monopoly," he declared;
"one of law, the other of fact. The one exists when
exclusive privileges are granted. Such a monopoly, the
law which creates alone can break; and being the creation
of law justifies legislative control. A monopoly of fact
anyone can break, and there is no necessity for legislative
interference."

Brewer continued with a statement of his political
philosophy, a statement which might as easily have been
made by Field himself: "The paternal theory of government is to me odious. The utmost possible liberty to the
individual, and the fullest possible protection to him and
his property, is both the limitation and the duty of

government. If it may regulate the price of one service, which is not a public service, or the compensation for the use of one kind of property which is not devoted to a public use, why may not it with equal reason regulate the price of all service, and the compensation to be paid for the use of all property? And if so, 'Looking Backward' [26] is nearer than a dream."

In still another elevator case [27] Field concurred in a similar dissent written by Brewer. "Public use" gave a legitimate basis for regulation, he maintained, but "public interest," as interpreted by the Court, did not. These two concepts, indeed, were at the core of most of Field's expressions on the subject of rate regulation. "Public use" was relatively narrow, and confined regulation to a limited field, while the concept of "public interest" was broad enough to permit legislative interference with much that Field looked upon as purely private enterprise.

It is a significant part of the story of his connection with the subject of rate regulation that the Court, which at first ignored his plea that the due process clause be used as a basis for judicial examination of the regulative work of legislators, slowly came around to his point of view. He himself moved from his dissenting position to one in which he justified regulation within a limited field, but only after the Court had decided that "due process of law" was involved, and that in order to discover whether due process had been followed it must pass upon the "reasonableness" of the acts of the state legislatures and commissions. Field had a great deal to do, undoubtedly, with leading the Court to make itself the master hand in

[26] Edward Bellamy's Utopia, *Looking Backward*, was written in 1887. It was a dream of an ideal socialized world as seen in the year 2087. In it private enterprise had completely disappeared.

[27] *Brass* v. *North Dakota*, 153 U. S. 391 (May 14, 1894).

the business of rate control. Whether for better or for worse, it was another instance where a function of great responsibility was taken out of the hands of the representatives of the people by an irresponsible body, or by a body responsible only to its own interpretation of the law, which is much the same thing.

CHAPTER XV

THE INCOME TAX

A great many of Field's Supreme Court opinions reveal not only his knowledge of law but also his ideas as to what was good and what was bad in the economic life of the country. Again and again he stressed the importance of great corporations in the achievement of things that were worth while. Because of their importance he insisted upon their being protected to the full extent of the law. Nothing stirred his ire more quickly than short-sighted efforts to restrict corporate activities. Such efforts were, in his estimation, of a piece with the dictates of the vicious doctrines of socialism and communism, and it was the duty of the courts to bring about their frustration. Yet his interest seems not to have been in corporations as such, but rather in the achievements of men of vision and energy who used corporations as tools. His opposition, with but occasional exceptions, was to government interference with freedom of action anywhere in the business world. When business and industrial leaders garnered rich rewards for their labors, Field was ready to use the machinery of the law to protect them against the resentment and cupidity of the masses.

The contest over the constitutionality of the federal income tax law, in the last decade of the nineteenth century, offers a good illustration of the way in which he came to the defense of the larger propertied interests of the country. The first half of that decade was a period of falling prices, of hard times, particularly for debtors, and of widespread discontent. The populist movement in politics, which to a large extent was sponsored by distressed farmers, was one of the manifestations of this discontent. One subject of populist agitation, and of agitation by other people who did not align themselves with the movement politically, was the demand for a scheme of taxation which would result in the collection of taxes from the wealthy and prosperous men of the country in proportion to the amounts of their possessions. It was believed that the excises, imposts, and duties levied by the federal government upon consumption goods were passed on to ultimate consumers in the form of higher prices, so that men of wealth paid relatively little more in federal taxes than those who had but little property. The plan of the populists was to remedy the situation by levying a tax upon large incomes. It was their belief that income taxes could not be shifted, as other taxes were, and that they would come solely out of the pockets of the persons against whom they were assessed.

The subject provided a prominent plank for the populist platform in the presidential campaign of 1892. The party showed such strength in the election that President Cleveland and Congress chose to give some attention to its program. In 1893 the President recommended the enactment of an income tax law, and in August, 1894 an act was passed which, with certain exceptions, placed a tax of two per cent on incomes above four thousand dollars. The act was hailed as a boon to civilization by the masses of the people, but the rich minority flew to arms to defend themselves against its operation.

The act was to go into effect January 1, 1895. Previous decisions of the Supreme Court had held that the collection of taxes levied by the federal government would not be restrained by the courts. Taxes could be paid under protest, and then suit could be brought for their return. A host of eminent lawyers, however, set out to prevent the original collection from being made.

A number of suits were brought, prominent among which was *Pollock* v. *Farmers' Loan & Trust Company.*[1] This was not a suit against the government to prevent the collection of a tax, but an equity suit brought against a corporation by a stockholder to prevent a threatened breach of trust by the making of illegal payments from the treasury of the corporation.

The arguments in this and other similar cases were delivered in the Supreme Court March 7 to 13, 1895. William D. Guthrie, Clarence A. Seward, George F. Edmunds, and Joseph H. Choate argued against the constitutionality of the tax, and with them on briefs were Benjamin F. Bristow, David Wilcox, Charles Steele, Samuel Shellabarger, Jeremiah M. Wilson, and Charles Southmayd. Attorney-General Olney, Assistant Attorney-General Whitney, and James C. Carter spoke in defense of the tax, while Herbert B. Turner, William Jay, Flamen B. Candler, and William C. Gulliver appeared on briefs. It was an imposing array of counsel, with the preponderance of weight on the side of the opposition to the income tax. The so-called briefs ran to large volumes, delving deep into historical and legal lore and abounding in sharp logical distinctions which were set up to guide learned judges to the chosen solutions of the problem. So voluminous and intricate were the arguments that a general summary and appraisal can not be presented here. Suffice it to say, at this point, that the principal legal charges made against the tax were that it was a direct tax but was not apportioned among the states according to population as the Constitution prescribed, and that it was not levied in such a way as to meet the requirements of uniformity. In so far as there were precedents in the decisions of the Supreme Court they indicated that the tax was constitutional.

[1] 157 U. S. 429 (April 8, 1895).

More, perhaps, than any of the others, the arguments of Joseph H. Choate and James C. Carter showed what was behind the controversy. Choate pointed out that the income tax law which had been in force during the Civil War and thereafter until 1873, with an exemption of incomes up to two thousand dollars, had resulted in a tax four-fifths of which, during the last year of its operation, was collected in New York, Pennsylvania, Massachusetts, and New Jersey. The present law, with its exemption of four thousand dollars, would bring about the "most iniquitous result" that even a larger proportion of the tax would be collected from these four states. Furthermore, if the courts approved of this tax with a four thousand dollar exemption, and "this communistic march" went on, five years later the exemption might be raised to twenty thousand dollars, and the rate raised to twenty per cent. The right to acquire property above certain amounts might be virtually taken away. "I have thought," Choate continued, "that one of the fundamental objects of all civilized government was the preservation of the rights of private property. I have thought that it was the very keystone of the arch upon which all civilized government rests, and that this once abandoned, everything was at stake and in danger. . . . I supposed that all educated, civilized men believed in that. According to the doctrines that have been propounded here this morning, even that great fundamental principle has been scattered to the winds." [2] Although he declared that "we are deciding this as a question of law, not of political economy," the implication back of his argument was that somewhere in the Constitution provisions were to be found embodying political princi-

[2] Choate's brief, *Pollock* v. *Farmers' Loan & Trust Company,* 157 U. S. 429, 534.

ples which were in harmony with fundamental principles
of economics.

In his closing paragraph he reasserted his opinion as
to the importance of the case. He had never before
felt such responsibility in a case, and never expected to
again. He believed that no member of the Court had
ever sat or ever would sit in another case of such far-
reaching consequences as this—"not even the venerable
member who survives from the early days of the Civil
War, and has sat upon every question of reconstruction,
of national destiny, of state destiny that has come up
during the last thirty years." [3] No member of the Court,
he declared, would live long enough to hear a case involving a question of greater importance than this, "the
preservation of the fundamental rights of private property and equality before the law, and the ability of the
people of these United States to rely upon the guaranties
of the Constitution." If, as opposing counsel claimed,
it was true that the passions of people were aroused on
this subject and that a mighty army of sixty million
citizens was likely to be incensed by the decision, "it is
more vital to the future welfare of this country that this
Court again resolutely and courageously declare, as
Marshall did, that it *has* the power to set aside an act of
Congress violative of the Constitution, and that it will
not hesitate in executing that power, no matter what the
threatened consequences of popular or populistic wrath
may be." [4]

Choate's able argument revealed no awareness of the
fact stressed by the Attorney-General, that the plan for
an income tax grew out of a desire to distribute the
burden of taxation according to capacity to pay. He
laid all his emphasis upon what he called a fundamental

[3] The reference is to Field.
[4] Choate's brief, 157 U. S. 553.

principle of government, a principle which, if carried to its proper length, would result in the destruction of the act which was being contested before the Court.

James C. Carter, who, like Choate, was one of the most eminent lawyers in the country, presented the other side of the situation. He admitted that the law had been enacted as a result of conditions in which the rich had succeeded in getting from under the burden of taxation and in leaving it upon the poor. He admitted that the tax would fall only upon about two per cent of the population of the country, but he reminded the Court that without the income tax this two per cent of the population, which was probably receiving more than fifty per cent of the national income, was paying little more than two per cent of the nation's taxes. The rapid concentration of wealth in the hands of the few had resulted in the splitting of the old political parties by a reform party, and the income tax was a part of the reform party remedy. He admitted that the act was both class and sectional legislation, but declared it to be so because wealth had become class and sectional. He reminded the Court that its powers were limited, and that it transgressed these limits if it sought to invalidate an act of Congress because the judges disagreed with the economic theories involved. The situation was serious, he declared, and it would be dangerous to attempt to baffle and defeat a popular determination by a judgment in a law suit. He concluded:

"When the opposing forces of sixty millions of people have become arrayed in hostile political ranks upon a question which all men feel is not a question of law, but of legislation, the only path of safety is to accept the voice of the majority as final. The American people can be trusted not to commit permanent injustice; nor has history yet recorded an instance in which governments have been destroyed by the attempts of the many to lay undue burdens of taxation on the few. The teachings of history have all been in the other direction." [5]

The decision of the Court was given on April 8, 1895, Chief Justice Fuller reading the majority opinion.[6] The decision held that a tax upon income from land, like a tax upon land itself, was a direct tax, and must be apportioned among the states according to population. Since the act in question did not provide for such apportionment of the tax, it was unconstitutional. It held, likewise, that a tax upon income from municipal bonds was unconstitutional, being a tax on the powers of the state. As to whether the void provisions of the act invalidated the whole act, whether a tax on income from personal property was a direct tax, and whether the act was invalid for want of uniformity, the court was evenly divided and expressed no opinion. Owing to illness, Justice Jackson had not heard the arguments nor participated in the decision.

Field concurred in the decision as far as it went, and vigorously attacked the constitutionality of the law in all its aspects. Gossip has it that long before the decision was given he wrathfully declared that Congress could not get away with the iniquitous law—which, it is well to remember, was sponsored by President Cleveland, whom Field no longer looked upon as his friend. In any case, his sanction could hardly have been expected. Warnings of the danger of violent measures which might be taken against the government, such as those given by Carter, never affected him pleasantly, and usually led him to do the opposite of what he was advised. He refused to be frightened. The populist movement, amid which the

[5] Carter's brief, *Pollock* v. *Farmers' Loan & Trust Company*, 157 U. S. 531-32.

[6] *Pollock* v. *Farmers' Loan & Trust Company*, 157 U. S. 429.

agitation for the income tax law had been begun, smacked too strongly of the nature of the hated Kearneyism in California. Again it was a case where the masses of the people were threatening the winnings of the men who had planned and carried through the major business and industrial achievements of the day. Such attacks had always stirred him to wrath, and it is not surprising that they did so again. Perhaps he was to be criticised for not realizing that in the increasingly complex conditions of living the rapidly growing burden of supporting the federal government was falling chiefly upon those who were least able to pay. Possibly he did realize it, even though he failed to admit the fact. Anyway, although the possession of far-sightedness and the ability to change his position in the face of changing conditions would have merited praise, it is not surprising that, as he approached his eightieth year of life and his fortieth on the bench, he was unable to modify his conception of one of the fundamental principles of government far enough to justify a movement that had been branded as communism.

Gossip further has it that while the case was being argued Field began to show signs of a failing mind, and that his mutterings on the bench indicated that in thought he was far from the Capitol in Washington. This may or may not have been true. In other cases, in later years, his mind did wander far from the scenes around him. It may be questioned whether this matter is as important as it at first seems. His virile opinion bears no mark of senility. Although his mind had for many years been made up on the question of the sanctity of private property to such an extent that the arguments delivered by Joseph H. Choate might well have been his own, he nevertheless corresponded at length with David A. Wells, a prominent writer in economics at the time, on the theory and practice of income taxation. Perhaps he merely wanted justification for his own beliefs, but the fact remains that he turned to an economist for aid. It has been asserted that Field's opinion contained a number of paragraphs which were almost word for word reproductions of other paragraphs in a letter written to him by Wells.[7] Further evidence is to be found in the fact that in Wells' *Theory and Practice of Taxation,* which was published a few years later, certain paragraphs are cited as quoted from Field's opinion, but upon examination they prove to be somewhat different in wording and arrangement from the version carried in the *United States Reports.* Other paragraphs which are not reported as quotations at all follow almost word for word the text of Field's opinion. The inference seems to be that in most instances Wells was using his own material in his text, and only cited portions as from Field when he wished to lend a tone of added authority on certain points. However, if Wells was the author of certain paragraphs in Field's opinion, their import was such that they might well have been written by the justice himself, and they fit well into the context of the lengthy dissertation. Wells was himself too much enamored of the traditional principles of economic theory to be sympathetic with any proposed change.

Like counsel on both sides, and like the other justices who gave opinions, Field went back to the Constitutional Convention of 1787 to discover whether an income tax was a direct tax in the meaning of the founders, and had to be apportioned among the states according to population. Suffice it to say, he discovered that it was. He found that the act did not apply uniformly to all persons

[7] Bullock, C. J., "Purpose and Effect of the Direct-Tax Clause of the Federal Constitution," *Political Science Quarterly,* Vol. XV, p. 454, note 1 (1900).

and corporations, and declared it to be void because of this fact. It was class legislation. Class legislation led "inevitably to oppression and abuses, and to general unrest and disturbance in society." His comment was typical of those which he had made time and again: "Under wise and constitutional legislation every citizen should contribute his proportion, however small the sum, to the support of the government, and it is no kindness to urge any of our citizens to escape from that obligation. If he contributes the smallest mite of his earnings to that purpose he will have a greater regard for the government and more self-respect for himself, feeling that though he is poor in fact, he is not a pauper of his government. And it is to be hoped that, whatever woes and embarrassments may betide our people, they may never lose their manliness and self-respect. Those qualities preserved, they will ultimately triumph over all reverses of fortune."

On all other legal points that were raised he was equally convinced that the law was unconstitutional. Having discussed them emphatically and at length he said:

"Here I close my opinion. I could not say less in view of questions of such gravity that go down to the very foundation of the government. If the provisions of the Constitution can be set aside by an act of Congress, where is the course of usurpation to end? The present assault upon capital is but the beginning. It will be but the stepping-stone to others, larger and more sweeping, till our political contests will become a war of the poor against the rich; a war constantly growing in intensity and bitterness.

" 'If the Court sanctions the power of discriminating taxation, and nullifies the uniformity mandate of the Constitution,' as said by one who has been all his life a student of our institutions, 'it will mark the hour when the sure decadence of our government will commence.' If the purely arbitrary limitation of $4000 in the present law can be sustained, none having less than that amount of income being assessed or taxed for the support of the government, the limitation of future congresses may be fixed at a much larger sum, at five or ten or twenty thousand dollars, parties possessing an income of that amount alone being bound to bear the burdens of government; or the limitation may be designated at such an amount as a board of 'walking delegates' may deem necessary. There is no safety in allowing the limitation to be adjusted except in strict compliance with the mandates of the Constitution which require its taxation, if imposed by direct taxes, to be apportioned among the states according to their representation, and if imposed by indirect taxes, to be uniform in operation and, so far as practicable, in proportion to their property, equal upon all citizens. Unless the rule of the Constitution governs, a majority may fix the limitation at such rate as will not include any of their own number."

Field's opinion covered forty-one pages. Justice White, Justice Harlan concurring, wrote forty-seven pages dissenting from the decision of the Court except as to the taxing of income from municipal bonds. Justice White was the youngest member of the Court in point of service, a Cleveland appointee. He declared that his brief judicial experience had convinced him that the custom of filing long dissenting opinions would be better if unobserved, since the effect, if any, was to weaken the result of the opinion of the majority. In this case, however, he felt that the Court was overthrowing a long line of consistent decisions upholding the principle of the tax; and he must protest against it. His analysis of these decisions was, to say the least, impressive. It was a mistake at this late date, he declared, to go back to the founders to discover what they had meant by a direct tax. "If we are to go back to the original sources of our political system, or are to appeal to the writings of economists in order to unsettle all these great principles, everything is lost and nothing saved to the people." The value of the Court to the government and to the people lay in the consistency and orderliness with which it pursued its work of interpretation, he continued. "The fundamental conception of a judicial body is that of one hedged about by precedents which are binding on the Court without regard to the personality of its members. Break down this belief in judicial continuity, and let it be felt that on great constitutional questions this Court is to depart from the settled conclusions of its predecessors, and to determine them according to the mere opinion of those who temporarily fill its bench, and our Constitution will, in my judgment, be bereft of value and become a most dangerous instrument to the rights and liberties of the people."

No one was able to deny that the Court had in the past upheld the constitutionality of various forms of income taxation. This had been done, however, before the rumblings of popular discontent were apparent, and before the menace of populism and communism began to be vigorously paraded before the justices. Perhaps the larger consistency of giving protection to the existing order seemed of greater worth to them than the meticulous pursuit of the line of their own decisions.

The press gave prominent notice to the decision. The New York *Sun* praised the opinion of Justice Field, "the oldest and in some respects the ablest member of the Court," saying that it was on the same vigorous lines as the speeches made in Congress by Senator Hill and other lawyers at the time the populist element of the Democratic party was clamoring for the passage of the law.

The failure to decide the main question of constitution-ality was deplored. "It was not democracy against republicanism . . . ., but populism and Clevelandism against democracy, and the vote was four to four." Justice White was bitterly denounced. "He not only withheld the vote that would have overthrown in its entirety this abominable, undemocratic tax, but also delivered from the bench something very like a stump eulogy of the administration measure." [8]

"Thank God the voice of a Democrat was heard also!" the *Sun* continued. "The Democrat was there in the person of Stephen J. Field, and the democracy he repre-sents, and has represented for thirty-two years on this same bench, is not the democracy of Cleveland, or Gresham, but the democracy of the Constitution and of the founders. This time the scourge is applied by the hands of a member of the Supreme Court, and the prophetic warning and rebuke proceed from the bench itself. Comparable only with Judge Black's memorable denunciation nineteen years ago are the remarks delivered yesterday by Mr. Justice Field in the presence of his spineless associates." [9]

Field's rebuke, the same paper declared, was intended for those who, like James C. Carter in arguing before the Court, urged the Court to yield before the threat of the majority and the possibility of a revolution. [10]

The New York *World* was pleased with the fact that the principle of the law was still unshaken. [11] The New York *Times* was apparently pleased with the "wreck of the populist law." [12] The Washington *Post* regretted that

[8] New York *Sun*, April 9, 1895.
[9] *Ibid.*
[10] *Ibid.*, April 10, 1895.
[11] New York *World*, April 9, 1895.
[12] New York *Times*, April 10, 1895.

the Court had not disposed of the entire law. It disagreed
with the justices who insisted on following precedent.
"If the Supreme Court be not here to make instead of
follow precedents, then it is not half so important an
institution as we had supposed." [13] In spite of the fact
that the law had not been wholly done away with, however, the *Post* thought it pretty well wrecked, and
remarked that the Supreme Court was a great sticking
point for populist legislation, and that the income tax
law would be almost as effective as the Interstate Commerce Act [14]—the whittling down of which had already
been begun.

The opponents of the tax were eager to have the case
re-argued before a full Court, in the hope that it would
be declared unconstitutional in all its provisions. Justice
Jackson returned to Washington, and the arguments were
heard May 6 to 8, 1895. The court room was packed
with observers. A young reporter for the New York
World, Arthur Brisbane, noted descriptions of the justices
as they sat in their places. He was much impressed by
Field. "Justice Field, who sits immediately on the right
of the Chief Justice, looks exactly as a judge of the
Supreme Court ought to look. If he was not on the
bench he would deserve to be put there simply for his
looks. His appearance is awe-inspiring and dignified. He
looks like a statue of one of the old prophets. In fact,
he might have been the model for Raphael's picture of
the Creator in his great vision of the Ascension. Justice
Field has long grey hair, and a long, grey beard. Both
are curly. His forehead is very high. His cheek bones
are just prominent enough to give strength to his face.

[13] Washington *Post*, April 10, 1895.
[14] *Ibid.*, April 12, 1895.

He has a fine nose, prominent and thin. His hands are delicate. His voice is deep, and he uses it with theatrical effect in reading a decision."[15] Brisbane thought Justice Harlan looked like a great man, but not such an intellectually great man as Justice Field.[16]

Twelve days after the close of the second argument the decision of the Court was announced.[17] A week earlier the New York *Sun* had declared that in the consultation of the justices Justice Jackson had voted to uphold the constitutionality of the income tax law, thereby giving a majority in its favor.[18] The *Sun* proved to be only partly right. Justice Jackson did support the law, but another of the justices changed from his earlier position, and by a vote of five to four the law was declared unconstitutional, Chief Justice Fuller giving the opinion of the Court. Justices Harlan, Brown, Jackson, and White wrote dissenting opinions. Field had nothing more to say.

The delivery of the opinions, contrary to custom, was at times highly dramatic. Justice Harlan found it difficult to restrain his emotion. As the scene was described: "He displayed a personal excitement during his speech for the populist income tax which is even described as passionate. He pounded the desk, shook his finger under the noses of the Chief Justice and Mr. Justice Field, turned more than once almost angrily upon his colleagues of the majority, and expressed his dissent from their conclusions in a tone and language more appropriate to a stump address at a populist barbecue than to an opinion on a question of law before the Supreme Court of the United States."[19] "At times he turned deliberately

[15] New York *World*, May 7, 1895.
[16] *Ibid.*
[17] *Pollock* v. *Farmers' Loan & Trust Co.*, 158 U. S. 601.
[18] New York *Sun*, May 13, 1895.
[19] *Ibid.*, May 22, 1895.

around and faced the Chief Justice and Justice Field, as
if his remarks were particularly addressed to them, while
at another moment, when he intimated that the majority
opinion was influenced by the argument that the law
had been enacted by the votes of senators and members
from states that would least bear the burdens of the tax,
he seemed to ignore every one in the chamber except
Justice Gray." [20]

The decision was received jubilantly by the moneyed
interests, while popularly it was vigorously condemned.
The undignified shifting of its position brought the Court
into bad repute, and particular justices were the objects
of attack by one side or the other. Field did not escape.
His opinion in the first case, which was highly praised by
some, was by others condemned for its unnecessary force
and venom, and has been called his "tirade against the
legislators who passed the income tax law." [21]

Without any attempt either to justify or to condemn
the Court, it may be said that an appearance of siding
with great moneyed interests and against the people in
other cases as well as in the income tax cases added to its
unpopularity. In January of the same year it had refused
to bring the great sugar trust within the provisions of
the anti-trust act,[22] and one week after the second income
tax decision it placed its stamp of approval on "government by injunction" through the opinion of Justice
Brewer in the Debs case.[23] It looked as if great corporations were still to bleed the country through the
extraction of exorbitant profits, as if their incomes were
to be practically untouchable, and as if labor was to be

[20] Washington *Post*, May 21, 1895.
[21] Bullock, "Origin and Effect of the Direct-Tax Clause," *Political
Science Quarterly*, Vol. XV, p. 453.
[22] *United States* v. *E. C. Knight Co.*, 156 U. S. 1 (Jan. 21, 1895).
[23] In re *Debs*, 158 U. S. 564 (May 27, 1895).

enjoined from acting in its own defense. Hence it is not surprising that many were bitterly hostile to the Court.

On the other hand, in view of the legal, political, and economic principles with which the justices had been indoctrinated by years of study and association, it is not surprising that they took the positions which they did. Least of all, in view of the habits of thought which he had revealed over the long period of his judicial life, is it surprising that Field declaimed against evidences of change which in his mind bore the stamp of communism. Perhaps his knowledge of the deep conservatism of the American people should have assured him that no violent and drastic changes would come about even without the guardianship of the Supreme Court. Nevertheless, it was true of him as he grew older that he took more and more seriously the guardianship of the courts over the welfare of the country, and carried in his own mind a burden from which a broad sense of humor might have saved him. The judicial dignity which Arthur Brisbane so much admired may have had its drawbacks.

But whatever the influences that lay back of the income tax decision, it prevented federal income taxes from being collected in the United States for nearly two decades.

CHAPTER XVI

WELLSPRINGS OF JUSTICE

The opinions summarized or cited in previous chapters are but a small percentage of the more than one thousand which Field wrote in the forty years of his judicial activities. Scores of others might be fruitfully analyzed for a knowledge of the political, economic, social, and legal conditions amid which he worked, and for an understanding of the philosophy in terms of which he dealt with the problems which came before him. In a general summary of the factors which loomed large in his decisions, however, it seems best to draw upon particular opinions only in an incidental fashion, as they illustrate conclusions which seem to flow from the records when thoughtfully surveyed. A number of elements, whether as ideas, beliefs, dogmas, or prejudices, appear again and again as seemingly determining components in his decisions. These factors appear usually in combination or in conflict with each other or with other forces, so that the apportionment of the exact influence of any one or more of them is quite impossible. For all that, however, they are highly significant, and for the space of a chapter are worthy of a position under the spotlight.

Primarily worthy of note are his belief in the existence of natural and inalienable rights, the protection of which was one of the principal functions of government, and the use which he attempted to make of the doctrine in particular cases. It will be recalled that in preceding chapters the doctrine has either openly or implicitly played an important rôle. In the early part of his term as Supreme Court judge there had been logical difficulties about the treatment of a conception of inalienable rights as a basis for judicial decisions. Inalienable rights were mentioned in the Declaration of Independence, but the Constitution which was subsequently adopted was altogether silent concerning them. In spite of some difficulties of linkage Field used the doctrine in his opinions in the test oath cases, introducing it by calling it the "theory upon which our political institutions rest." That theory was, he said, that among the inalienable rights were "life, liberty, and the pursuit of happiness; and that in the pursuit of happiness all avocations, all honors, all positions, are alike open to everyone, and that in the protection of these rights all are equal before the law." [1]

Although he used the doctrine to good effect in this case it is evident that he was not altogether satisfied with its basis. When the Fourteenth Amendment was adopted, therefore, including certain general phrases which were left to definition by the Court, he seized upon these phrases and quite openly attempted to read the doctrine into them. The first and most important section of the amendment read as follows:

All persons born or naturalized in the United States, and subject to the jurisdiction thereof are citizens of the United States, and of the state wherein they reside. No state shall make or enforce any law which shall abridge the privileges or immunities of citizens of the United States; nor shall any state deprive any person of life, liberty, or property, without due process of law; nor deny to any person within its jurisdiction the equal protection of the laws.

The motives and ideas of those who participated in the enactment of the amendment were much confused, and it was not easy to determine what had been intended by

[1] *Cummings* v. *Missouri*, 71 U. S. 277. For discussion of this case see Chap. VI.

certain of the general phrases. According to many contemporary newspapers and magazines the chief purpose of the amendment was the protection of the newly emancipated negroes. A civil rights bill had previously been enacted prescribing in detail ways in which negroes in the South were to have exactly the same treatment as white people. There had been serious doubts as to the constitutionality of the act, and in the debates on the proposed constitutional amendment it was admitted that the first section was the civil rights bill incorporated into the Constitution.[2]

Quite a different purpose was indicated some years later by Roscoe Conkling, who had been a member of the drafting committee: "At the time when the Fourteenth Amendment was ratified, as the records of the two houses will show, individuals and joint stock companies were appealing for congressional and administrative protection against invidious and discriminating state and local taxes. One instance was that of an express company, whose stock was owned largely by citizens of the State of New York, who came with petitions and bills seeking acts of Congress to aid them in resisting what they deemed oppressive taxation in two states, and oppressive and ruinous rules of damages applied under state laws.

"That complaints of oppression, in respect of property and other rights, made by citizens of the Northern states who took up residence in the South, were rife in and out of Congress, none of us can forget.

"The war and its results, the condition of the freedmen, and the manifest duty owed to them, no doubt brought on the occasion for constitutional amendment, but when the occasion came, and men set themselves to the task, the accumulated evils falling within the purview of the work, were the surrounding circumstances in the light of

[2] Flack, H. E., *The Adoption of the Fourteenth Amendment*, p. 54.

which they strove to increase the safeguards of the Constitution and the laws."

Conkling made this statement in his argument before the Supreme Court in the San Mateo case,[3] in which he appeared for the defense of the Southern Pacific Railroad. He was known as a corporation lawyer, and was employed by clients who repeatedly invoked the protection of the federal government against state legislation which was hostile to their interests. His interpretation of the facts concerning the framing of the amendment may conceivably have been biased by a desire to influence the Court in favor of his clients, but thorough students of the history of the period are convinced that his interpretation was correct.[4] Says one, the purpose of the radical leaders in Congress in proposing the first section of the amendment was "to increase the power of the federal government very much, but to do it in such a way that the people would not understand the great changes intended to be wrought in the fundamental law of the land."[5]

The amendment became a part of the Constitution in 1868, and received its first interpretation by the Supreme Court in the Slaughterhouse cases[6] in 1873. The cases came up from Louisiana. The "carpet-bag" legislature of 1869, apparently from corrupt motives,[7] had passed an act to regulate the slaughtering business in New Orleans. It restricted slaughtering activities throughout a territory of 1,154 square miles to one

[3] *County of San Mateo v. Southern Pacific*, 116 U. S. 138 (p. 18 of brief filed Dec. 19, 1882). For the history of the case see Chap. IX.

[4] See Beard, Charles A., *Contemporary American History*, pp. 54 ff; and Beard, Charles A. and Mary R., *The Rise of American Civilization*, Vol. II, pp. 112 ff.

[5] Flack, *Adoption of the Fourteenth Amendment*, p. 69.

[6] 83 U. S. 36.

[7] See Lonn, Ella, *Reconstruction in Louisiana after 1868*, pp. 42-43.

small area below the city of New Orleans, and provided that all slaughtering should be done in the houses of one corporation. This corporation was required to permit other butchers to unload stock at their yards and to allow the butchering of stock there for certain fixed sums. The effect was virtually a monopoly grant of the business. The butchers of the city who were being deprived of their callings appealed to the courts on a number of grounds. The chief of these, and the one of greatest importance in a study of Field's judicial methods, was that when many butchers in the prescribed section were deprived of their calling by the legislative act they were divested of their "privileges and immunities" as citizens of the United States, which were guaranteed to them by the Fourteenth Amendment.

Cases growing out of this controversy were argued before the Supreme Court in January, 1872. Justice Nelson was absent at the time, due to illness, and his eight colleagues were equally divided on the issues. The cases were put back on the calendar for argument before a full bench and were again presented in February of the following year, when Nelson had been succeeded by Justice Hunt. A five to four decision resulted. Justice Miller gave the opinion of the Court, speaking for himself and for Justices Clifford, Davis, Strong, and Hunt. Chief Justice Chase and Justices Swayne, Field, and Bradley dissented, the last three writing opinions. Miller held that "privileges and immunities of citizens of the United States" did not refer to the great body of undefined rights which belonged to men as citizens of the states, such as the right of pursuing one's own vocation undisturbed by interference from others. The purpose of the amendment, he said, had been chiefly to protect the recently acquired rights of the negroes. If certain persons had been deprived of their civil rights by the act of the Louisiana legislature their recourse was to the state government, and not to the federal courts.

The basis of Field's disagreement with the majority of the Court was in this limited interpretation of the privileges and immunities clause. "No one will deny the abstract justice which lies in the position of the plaintiffs in error," he declared; "and I shall endeavor to show that the position has some support in the fundamental law of the country." Under the pretense of prescribing a police regulation a state could not "be permitted to encroach upon any of the just rights of the citizen, which the Constitution intended to secure against abridgment." There were, he said, only two provisions in the law in question which could be called police regulations. One of them required the landing and slaughtering of animals below the city, and the other provided for their inspection before they were slaughtered. The other provisions of the act were "a mere grant to a corporation created by it of special and exclusive privileges by which the health of the city is in no way promoted." "The health of the city might require the removal from its limits and suburbs of all buildings for keeping and slaughtering cattle, but no such object could possibly justify legislation removing such buildings from a large part of the state for the benefit of a single corporation. The pretense of sanitary regulations for the grant of the exclusive privileges is a shallow one, which merits only this passing notice."

The real question to be decided, as he saw it, was "whether the recent amendments to the federal Constitution protect the citizens of the United States against the deprivation of their common rights by state legislation. In my judgment the Fourteenth Amendment does afford such protection, and was so intended by the Congress which framed and the states which adopted it."

"The amendment was adopted to obviate objections which had been raised and pressed with great force to the validity of the civil rights act, and to place the common rights of American citizens under the protection of the national government." It recognized citizenship of the United States, and made it dependent upon birth or adoption, and not upon the constitution or laws of any state, or upon conditions of ancestry. "A citizen of a state is now only a citizen of the United States residing in that state. The fundamental rights, privileges, and immunities which belong to him as a free man and a free citizen, now belong to him as a citizen of the United States, and are not dependent upon his citizenship of any state. The exercise of these rights and privileges, and the degree of enjoyment received from such exercise, are always more or less affected by the condition and the local institutions of the state, or city, or town where he resides. . . . They do not derive their existence from its legislation, and cannot be destroyed by its power."

Field declared that the granting of monopolies had long been illegal under the common law of England, and that when the colonies separated from the mother country "no privilege was more fully recognized or more completely incorporated into the fundamental law of the country than that every free subject in the British Empire was entitled to pursue his happiness by following any of the known established trades and occupations of the country, subject only to such restraints as equally affected all others. The immortal document which proclaimed the independence of the country declared as self-evident truths that the Creator had endowed all men 'with certain inalienable rights, and that among these are life, liberty, and the pursuit of happiness; and that to secure these rights governments are instituted among men.' "
The Fourteenth Amendment secured the protection of

these rights to all citizens of the United States. "That amendment was intended to give practical effect to the declaration of 1776 of inalienable rights, rights which are the gift of the Creator, which the law does not confer, but only recognizes."

It seems evident that if the Supreme Court had recognized that the federal government could legislate for the protection of the undefined body of "rights which are the gift of the Creator" the whole theory of the relations between the state and federal governments would have been changed. If these rights were interpreted broadly enough there were few activities of the states with which the federal government could not interfere. Justice Miller recognized this fact, and declared that the state governments would be degraded by being subjected to the control of Congress. Field, a Democrat, who was opposed to the scheme of reconstruction which Congress employed in the South, could hardly have been desirous of increasing the powers of that body. Apparently he kept in mind the fact that the courts, and not Congress, were the interpreters of the rights in question. The Supreme Court, of which he was a member, was to have the final word in the definition of the boundaries of the inalienable gifts of God.

Another case decided at the same time as the Slaughter-house cases illustrated the manner in which the social and economic conceptions and philosophies of the judges would have determined decisions had Field's interpretation of the privileges and immunities clause been adopted.[8] Justice Miller, speaking for the Court, held that the Fourteenth Amendment did not confer upon a woman the right to practice law in state courts, and used his opinion in the Slaughterhouse cases as the basis for

[8] *Bradwell* v. *Illinois*, 83 U. S. 130.

the decision. Justices Field, Bradley, and Swayne concurred in the judgment, but could not consistently accept the opinion by which Miller justified it. Bradley therefore wrote a concurring opinion for the three justices.[9] In view of the position which the minority had previously taken he had to determine whether the right to practice law was one of the many "privileges and immunities of citizens of the United States" when claimed by a woman. He based his argument on his conception of the place of women in society:

"In my opinion, in view of the peculiar characteristics, destiny, and mission of woman, it is within the province of the legislature to ordain what offices, positions, and callings shall be filled and discharged by men, and shall receive the benefit of those energies and responsibilities, and that decision and firmness which are presumed to predominate in the sterner sex.

"For these reasons I think that the laws of Illinois now complained of are not obnoxious to the charge of abridging any of the privileges and immunities of citizens of the United States."

In the following year in a concurring opinion in a case which was likewise decided on the basis of the Slaughterhouse cases Field took occasion to reiterate his argument for a broad interpretation of the privileges and immunities clause.[10] The purpose of the Fourteenth Amendment, he said, had not been merely to confer citizenship upon the negro race. "It was intended to make it possible for *all* persons, which necessarily included those of every race

[9] Chief Justice Chase did not join with the three. Being unable to appear in court he wrote to Field as follows: "Will you please say for me that I dissent from the opinion in *Myra Bradwell* v. *Illinois*. I think it better to dissent generally than to dissent from the reasoning of the opinion." Chase to Field, April 13, 1873, in the library of the University of California.

[10] *Bartemeyer* v. *Iowa*, 85 U. S. 129.

and color, to live in peace and security wherever the jurisdiction of the nation reached. It, therefore, recognized, if it did not create, a national citizenship, and made all persons citizens except those who preferred to remain under the protection of a foreign government; and declared that their privileges and immunities, which embraced the fundamental rights belonging to citizens of all free governments, should not be abridged by any state. This national citizenship is primary, and not secondary. It clothes its possessor, or would do so if not shorn of its efficiency by construction, with the right, when his privileges and immunities are invaded by partial and discriminating legislation, to appeal from his state to his nation, and gives him the assurance that, for his protection, he can invoke the whole power of government."

Another case arising out of the slaughterhouse controversy came before the Supreme Court some years later, giving Field another opportunity to reiterate his argument that the privileges and immunities clause of the Fourteenth Amendment gave the federal government power to protect all the "inalienable rights" of citizens.[11] He repeated that the federal government could not interfere with the states in the exercise of their police powers. "When such regulations do not conflict with any constitutional inhibition or natural right," he declared, "their validity cannot be successfully controverted." The exception which he noted, however, left open many problems for judicial controversy, for it meant that the Court could pass upon any exercise of the police power to decide whether it transgressed any "natural right." Again he explained his doctrine of rights:

[11] *Butchers' Union Slaughter-House and Live-Stock Landing Co.* v. *Crescent City Live-Stock Landing and Slaughter-House Co.,* 111 U. S. 746 (May 5, 1884).

"As in our intercourse with our fellow men certain principles of morality are assumed to exist, without which society would be impossible, so certain inherent rights lie at the foundation of all action, and upon a recognition of them alone can free institutions be maintained. These inherent rights have never been more happily expressed than in the Declaration of Independence, that new evangel of liberty to the people: 'We hold these truths to be self-evident'—that is so plain that their truth is recognized upon their mere statement—'that all men are endowed'—not by edicts of emperors, or decrees of parliament, or acts of Congress, but 'by their Creator with certain inalienable rights'—that is, rights which cannot be bartered away, or given away, or taken away except in punishment of crime—'and that among these are life, liberty, and the pursuit of happiness, and to secure these'—not grant them but secure them—'governments are instituted among men, deriving their just powers from the consent of the governed.' "

Even the Declaration of Independence did not declare the right of acquiring property to be inalienable. It did so list the pursuit of happiness, however, and Field declared that this meant "the right to pursue any lawful business or vocation, in any manner not inconsistent with the equal rights of others, which may increase their prosperity or develop their faculties, so as to give to them their highest enjoyment." The common business and callings of life, the ordinary trades and pursuits, which were innocuous in themselves, were to be free to all alike upon the same conditions. In support of this contention he quoted at length from Adam Smith.[12]

Thus from extremely general statements in the Constitution he moved through almost equally general

[12] Smith, Adam, *Wealth of Nations*, Book I, Chap. X.

statements in the Declaration of Independence, and
through his own individualistic philosophy via the *Wealth
of Nations,* to the conclusion that the right to butcher
livestock in Louisiana was an inalienable right, which
could not be prohibited by the state. "I cannot believe,"
he said, "that what is termed in the Declaration of Independence a God-given and an inalienable right can be
thus ruthlessly taken from the citizen, or that there can
be any abridgment of that right except by regulations
alike affecting all persons of the same age, sex, and
condition."

Field and his minority colleagues never succeeded in
persuading the Court to broaden its interpretation of the
privileges and immunities clause. Their efforts were not
in vain, however, for the Court gradually permitted new
meaning to be read into the due process clause of the
same amendment, and ultimately embodied in the constitutional law of the country much of the same material
which Field had endeavored to introduce by way of the
privileges and immunities clause. Natural rights decisions were made in terms of "due process of law," and,
as might be expected, the social and economic conceptions of the judges determined the legal boundaries of
these rights. It has been said that as the new protection
of the Fourteenth Amendment was persistently invoked
by counsel against the growing efforts of the states to
regulate economic enterprise, the rejected dissents of Mr.
Justice Field gradually established themselves as the view
of the Court. "Though speaking the language of abstrac-
tions, the opinions of Mr. Justice Field reflected ade-
quately enough the vital elements of the social and
economic order in which he grew up. But his society
was in process of drastic transformation, and indeed had
largely passed, certainly when Mr. Justice Peckham wrote

Mr. Justice Field's dissents into the opinions of the Court." [13]

The minority justices in the Slaughterhouse cases were not the only believers in natural law and natural rights. It has been rightly said that Field was "the pioneer and prophet of our modern constitutional law, but this is not so because his natural law creed was his own peculiar possession, but on the contrary because, though none of them was so ready to proclaim the faith that was in him both in season and out, it was shared none the less by almost all of his associates on the supreme bench." [14] In *Loan Association* v. *Topeka*,[15] Justice Miller, the spokesman of the majority in the Slaughterhouse cases, justified a decision in such a way as to illustrate admirably what might be called the natural law habit of mind. Being unable to find any constitutional principle upon which to declare invalid an objectionable act of a state legislature he based his decision on what he called "the essential nature of all free governments." Of the entire personnel of the bench at that time, only Justice Clifford dissented against this type of judicial settlement. Field's distinction lay in the persistent force with which he stated and restated his conceptions of the content of natural or inalienable rights, with such effectiveness that they were gradually accepted as a part of the content of American constitutional law.

* * *

[13] Frankfurter, Felix, "Mr. Justice Holmes and the Constitution," *Harvard Law Review*, Vol. XLI, pp. 141-42. See opinions of Justice Peckham particularly in *Allgeyer* v. *Louisiana*, 165 U. S. 578, and *Lochner* v. *New York*, 198 U. S. 45. On this point see also Pound, Roscoe, "Liberty of Contract," in *Trade Unionism and Labor Problems*, Series 2, ed. by John R. Commons.

[14] Corwin, E. S., "The Supreme Court and the Fourteenth Amendment," *Michigan Law Review*, Vol. VII, pp. 653-54.

[15] 87 U. S. 655.

His attitude toward so-called inalienable rights is a matter of prime importance in an appraisal of Field's judicial work. Since the content of these rights which he endeavored to protect through his judicial decisions was largely made up of his own ideas as to what was good in the life around him a study of his conception of the good society is also important. The nature of that society is to be inferred from the story of his life and from the texts of his judicial decisions. It was eminently on the one hand an orderly society, and on the other it was a society where few regulations were necessary. The desire for orderliness weighed so heavily with him as to be almost a fetish, yet he bitterly opposed more than the minimum of government interference with the doings of individuals. Perhaps a maximum of freedom and a minimum of government interference is of supreme value only in very simple organizations of society or in society in its pioneer stage, but Field did not think so. To him it was a condition of universal excellence, applicable to the new business and industrial order that was dawning as well as to the pioneer era which was drawing to a close.

Field took deep delight in the outstanding economic achievements of his time—in the network of railroads that covered the country, in the towns that sprang up and grew speedily larger, in the factories that were built, in the business that was carried on. He keenly admired the men who were turning sun-scorched deserts and wind-swept prairies into scenes of human residence and activity. He made friends of men of this type, and, whether inevitably or not, he shared their way of thinking about economic welfare and the relations of government to economic problems. When, with the growing complexity of economic life in the United States, people demanded some measure of control over the industries built up by the daring leaders of the times, such as rail-roads and grain elevators, Field was one of those who stood out most firmly against that control. It was but slowly and with great reluctance that he finally conceded a minimum of regulatory power.

His emphasis, almost constantly, was on rights of property. He quoted with approval the statement that "the moment the idea is admitted into society that prop-erty is not as sacred as the laws of God, and that there is not a force of law and public justice to protect it, anarchy and tyranny commence." [16] It is true that back in the early days, when he was a state judge in California, he had recognized that it was the function of the state to protect those who had little property from the cupidity of those who had superior power through the possession of more property.[17] In the years which followed, how-ever, he almost never emphasized the need for protecting the masses against the superior strength of the few. Instead he stressed the need for protecting the strong, who were bringing about superior achievements in the business and industrial world, against the restraining activities of the public. Perhaps he reasoned that ulti-mately the public at large was immeasurably benefited by the achievements of the few, and, on the whole, had no cause for complaint. At any rate, with regard to the right of business men to carry on their activities undis-turbed by government interference, he was more of an individualist in his later years than in his early life as a judge.

Although they are little more than food for specula-tion there are certain possible influences upon his philosophy which are worthy of mention. Among the personal enemies whom Field made during his lifetime,

[16] *Sinking Fund Cases*, 99 U. S. 700, 767.
[17] See Chap. IV.

such as Judge Turner, Harvey Lee, and Judge Terry, there were few whom he ever forgave. It was not merely outstanding individuals, however, who provoked his hostility. Great numbers of what must have been to him undifferentiated citizens poured out scathing criticisms upon him after many of his judicial decisions. They humiliated him by refusing to help advance his political aspirations, and they threatened even by violence to interfere with the property and activities of his friends. It is not at all improbable that the masses finally came to symbolize an enemy almost if not quite as clearly as Judge Terry, for instance, had done. If this was true it is not surprising that there is little in his judicial decisions to indicate friendship and sympathy for the masses of the people when they acted in their organized capacity.

Field was not necessarily unfriendly to men of no more than average intelligence, ability, or fortune when he met them as individuals. On the contrary he was sympathetic with the ills of even the most lowly, and he was always ready to contribute to the needs of those who were in distress. The plight of the Chinese undoubtedly stirred his sympathy, and there is no suggestion of hypocracy in his exhortations that the Californians, in their treatment of the Chinese, should conduct themselves as a "brave and manly people." Other evidence of his sympathy for individuals is to be found in his efforts to limit the application of the fellow servant doctrine. Instead of freeing employers from responsibility for injuries to employees caused by the actions or negligence of their fellow workmen, or "fellow servants," he sought to establish distinctions between workmen employed at slightly different tasks, or in slightly different capacities, denying that the fellow servant relationship existed, and holding that employers must make recompense for injuries done. For a time the majority of the Court was with him.[18] Then, with changes in the personnel of the Court, he fought in dissenting opinions against the extent of the rule, clashing hotly with his nephew, Justice Brewer.[19] He felt that if employers were held responsible for injuries to their workmen they would be much more careful whom they employed and under what conditions, so that workmen would on the whole be much safer than otherwise. This attitude bore some resemblance to that of his earlier years, when he had supported legislation securing large exemptions from sale for debt, and upheld laws which were designed to prevent laborers from having to work on Sunday.

It is no easier to account with certainty for these exceptional instances than for those which seemed more nearly to follow the rule of his life. However, it is evident that in these instances there was no principle involved which could easily be carried to such extremes as to work any great changes in the existing social and economic order. On the other hand, if in one instance the masses were given the power of interference with the property of wealthy individuals and great corporations, there was no possibility of knowing where the interference might stop. The violation of the sacred rights of property might lead to the destruction of the good society. The menace of communism was no idle threat. Field's letters and judicial opinions bear evidence that, however courageous he may have been in his personal relations with people, he was thoroughly fearful of attacks upon what were to him fundamental principles of the organization of society.

With these facts, suggestions, and hypotheses in mind, it is of interest to turn to a study of his conception of

[18] See *C. M. & St. P. Ry.* v. *Ross*, 112 U. S. 377.
[19] See *B. & O. R. R.* v. *Baugh*, 149 U. S. 368.

judicial duty. It will be recalled that in connection with some of the highly controversial issues that came before him in court, such as those of anti-Chinese legislation, the regulation of the rates of grain elevators and railroads, and the issuing of legal tender notes, he declared in deeply prophetic tones what was and what was not to be. Arthur Brisbane likened him to a Hebrew prophet, or to Raphael's picture of the Creator. A judge who long ago heard him deliver an opinion and saw him sit back in quiet but powerful repose likened him to Michelangelo's great representation of Moses. Again and again, in one way or another, we get the suggestion of his resemblance to a prophet. His utterances had the authority of "Thus saith the Lord." Intense conviction, phrased with cutting precision, marked his pronouncements. He believed firmly in the correctness of his judgment and the righteousness of his point of view.

He conceived it to be his function, as a member of the Court, to declare the law, for the purpose of preserving order. He conceived the task of the Court to be chiefly the prevention of dangerous changes in the good society. "It possesses the power of declaring the law," he said in his letter informing his colleagues of his resignation, "and in that is found the safeguard which keeps the whole mighty fabric of government from rushing to destruction. This negative power, the power of resistance, is the only safety of a popular government." [20] Such an attitude inevitably resulted in a limitation of the influence of the man who held it, for changes were to come, and with a fair degree of rapidity. They brought parallel changes among people in society, different types of relationships from those which had existed in the pioneer order. Consequently there was need for other changes in legal relationships than those which merely gave pro-

[20] See letter in appendix, 168 *United States Reports*.

tection to the achievements of business and industry. Field, however, and for the most part the Court as a whole, labored stubbornly to keep the country chained to the old order of legal relationships, in spite of the new social and economic conditions which had already come, and others which were to follow.

Thus we might summarize these analyses of Field's judicial activities. People will not all react alike to the beliefs, attitudes, and situations which played a part in guiding the course of his decisions. Neither will they react in the same way to the principles of our constitutional law which he helped to develop. That he played a prominent part in his more than a third of a century on the bench no one will deny. If in spite of his prophetic mien he was at times lacking in foresight, and if he was motivated too much by fear and not enough by faith, it must yet be said that he backed his convictions with tireless energy and a keen mind, and that, as in his work on the state bench in California, he helped to drive a scheme of logical order through the principles used by the Court in rationalizing its decisions. If his colleagues were at times more liberal than he it was only in isolated cases. They more easily gave way before the force of social and economic circumstance, as for example most of them did in the Granger cases and some of them in the income tax cases, but seldom did they reveal outstanding capacity for predicting or bringing about new schemes of social and economic relationships.

Furthermore, had one searched in other places than the courts for men of high vision and socially inventive capacity he would usually have found the same blindness, blundering, and conservatism that characterized the judges. Men were feeling their way along step by step without any adequate conception of where they were going. Few tried harder to understand the path which civilization was following or to keep it in the right path than did Field. He did his best, and in so doing he placed his stamp upon the institutions of the country for years to come. If some of his work has proved a bar to social and economic adjustments which are now widely regarded as desirable, condemnation should not be directed chiefly at him, but rather at the social and economic order which he represented and helped to build. The legal structure upon which he exercised his craftsmanship was one in which capable, energetic, and venturesome men in business and industry could have the greatest freedom in their work, with full protection for the fruits of their endeavors. It was a legal structure desired by and adapted to the needs of such men as Rockefeller in his kingdom of oil; Carnegie, Frick, and Morgan in the domain of steel; and Stanford, Huntington, Gould, Harriman, and Hill in the realm of railroads. Field helped to pave the way for the business and industrial order which sprang from the genius of a comparatively few men. Whether that order is justified by its gifts to society, or is to be condemned by the inequities which it produced, or whether it is one which merely needs to be gradually remodelled amid the complex conditions of another century, are questions which need to be kept in mind when a deep and thoughtful appraisal of Field's life is made.

Certainly Field's place in American history is alongside that of these outstanding leaders in business and industrial life, rather than with the mediocre men who were the statesmen of his time, and who played the game of politics in an unimaginative and ignoble fashion. As a man of energy, courage, vision, and insight he sits well in Stanford's banquet hall. With Grant, Seymour, Tilden, Hayes, Garfield, Blaine, Arthur, Cleveland, Harrison, and McKinley, he seems much less at home. Indeed, it is in his relationships with politicians, and in his attempts to play their game as they played it, rather than in his association with business and industrial leaders, that his reputation has been cheapened a bit for posterity. His contribution to society was made through his labors as a judge. As a justice of the Supreme Court of the United States he must be classified as one of the great men of the country—great as one of the master-builders of the legal structure needed for the housing of a particular economic order through a dramatic era of our history.

All this we can say in an appraisal of the part which he played in the life of his time. While an appraisal of the heritage which he and his colleagues and contemporaries left for future generations must be left to other discussions, one ironic commentary is worthy of record. A niece of Mrs. Field, whom the Justice loved as his own and who shared in the property left by the couple, became in after years an exponent of a social and economic philosophy the very thought of which had brought horror to Field's mind. She was a woman of keen mind and superior academic training. She had no cause for worry about the means wherewith she was to live. Yet experience in social service work and contact with the warped lives of thousands in city slums, the apparent victims of the present economic system, convinced her that something must be done to remold the order to the building of which her uncle had given his life. As if by a religious conversion she became a radical, aligned herself with the torchbearers of communism, and fell afoul of a criminal syndicalism law which was an outgrowth of World War frenzy in Field's beloved state of California. It would be beside the point here either to praise or to blame her. To the student who attempts to analyze the situation without bias it may appear that both she and her uncle have carried banners representative of untoward extremes in the building of the social and economic order, and that somewhere between the two positions are the makings of the system which should prevail. Yet those who have carefully studied the life of Justice Field know that he was not one to pursue a middle path where his convictions were involved. On this subject his convictions were profound. His position is not hard to understand, even by those who disapprove.

CHAPTER XVII

THE CLOSING YEARS

The decade of the nineties, the last which Field was destined to see, brought to him a mixture of joys and tragedies. Members of the New York bar pleased him greatly in 1894 by urging him to transfer his circuit from the West to the territory which included New York, Connecticut, and Vermont. Justice Blatchford, who had been assigned to that circuit, had died, and Justice White took his place on the supreme bench. Since none of the justices resided in New York, Connecticut, or Vermont, it was necessary to assign one of the non-resident justices to the circuit. The Chief Justice offered the assignment to Field. Joseph H. Choate, of New York, wrote warmly urging him to accept the position, saying that the bar wanted him, that New York needed him, and that he would thereby be saved the strenuous trips to the Pacific Coast.[1]

The United States senators from California and Oregon, and one senator each from Nevada and Idaho, joined in a letter to him urging him not to desert the Pacific Coast. After summarizing his services and achievements on the California supreme bench and in the Circuit Court the letter continued: "The people of the Pacific states and territories are justly proud of the great services you have rendered to the whole country by your learning, ability and judicial wisdom in expounding the Constitution and laws of the United States, and they

[1] See Choate's letter and other letters relating to the proposed change of circuits in *Some Account of the Work of Stephen J. Field*, 511 ff.

appreciate the compliment which a desire of the bar of New York for your assignment to that circuit implies. Your contributions to the jurisprudence of the United States during your long, useful and conspicuous career as a justice of the highest court in the land make your name and fame the common property of all the people of the United States, and entitle you to the love, honor, and respect of every section of our country. But the love and respect of the people of the Pacific Coast, where your greatest triumphs have been and where your judicial labors have been most beneficial, although mingled with regret at your departure, would remain with you wherever you might go." In view of these sentiments they urged him to continue to serve them if possible, and to continue to make his home in California.

A similar memorial was presented to him with the signatures of the United States circuit and district judges of California and Oregon, the supreme judges of California, and an imposing list of members of the California bar.

Field replied warmly to both letters. There had been a sentimental charm about returning to the scenes of his youth. In addition, in view of his age and his lameness, it might seem wise for him to transfer to the eastern circuit, and render long trips unnecessary. Nevertheless, he was pleased that the people of California still wanted him. "I have done a great deal of work, the value of which it is not for me to discuss," he said. "It has not been of a kind to bring popularity, and that no judge should seek. I have done the best I could, and, mindful of the obligations of the great trust confided to me, I have discharged my duty at all times, as I understood it, without fear, favor, affection, or hope of reward." He had considered the matter carefully, and had decided that the ties of his western home were too strong to be broken.

"I respond heartily to all your good words, and assure you that California, the state I helped to build, will continue to be my home, and that my circuit work will continue on the Pacific Coast."

His home life in Washington continued happily, save for such ills as inevitably came with old age. Sarah Swearingen, one of Mrs. Field's sisters, had lived with the Fields for many years. Rather late in life she married General Condit-Smith, a friend of Field, and a widower with several daughters. The General died a few months after he was married, and his widow, with her step-daughters, returned to Washington. She purchased an apartment next to that of the Fields, in the Old Capitol building, and the families were much together from that time on. The daughters of Mrs. Whitney, another of Mrs. Field's sisters, were often in the home. Field was extremely fond of the group of vivacious young people around him, who affectionately called him "Uncle Judge." He seemed, indeed, to become something of a head of the clan of his wife's relatives, and to take pride in the overlordship. He seems to have regretted that he had no children of his own. Perhaps as a recompense, he always took a deep interest in the children of others, whoever they might be. When an expected child of one of his wife's sisters turned out to be a girl, and so could not be called Stephen as he had hoped, he compromised by persuading the family to call her Stephenie.

Mrs. Field, even in her later years, was a beautiful and regal woman. She was fond of society to an extent which her husband found onerous, and he complained about the necessity of attending parties and keeping late hours. Nevertheless he was fond of her in a very fine way, and continued to treat her with the same courtly respect and affection which had characterized their early life together. She continued to be "my beautiful Sue."

At the approach of the time when the light of his keen intellect began to flicker, and when, perhaps under the influence of the pain caused by his lameness, he became extremely nervously irritable, she shielded him more and more from the embarrassments which came from evidences of his weakness. She could soothe and calm him when others only stirred him to angry excitement.

The close relationship with his brothers continued as long as they lived, but one by one they passed away, until only Henry, the youngest, was left. The children of the brothers were not of the caliber of the sons of the old minister of Stockbridge, and gave little promise of lending distinction to the family name. The brilliant son of David Dudley Field died at a youthful age. A daughter of Cyrus Field became insane; and it is said that a son involved himself in speculation in such a way that it took most of his father's fortune and a finding of insanity to save him. The tragedy was a rough shock to family pride. "It broke Judge Field," said one who was in position to know.

David Brewer, son of Emelia Field Brewer, with whom Stephen Field had made his boyhood trip to Greece and Turkey, did better by the family traditions. From his legal training in David Dudley Field's office he passed through a successful practice of his own and through a federal judgeship in Kansas to a position on the bench of the Supreme Court of the United States. It is said that Justice Field tried to induct his nephew into the proper way of arriving at decisions in the Court. Brewer, however, although of a much more mellow disposition than most of the Fields, was averse to being led. On more than one occasion the two men clashed heavily in their decisions—in spite of the fact that they were much alike in their political, economic, and legal philosophy. On the whole the relationship was probably pleasant, but some say that Field never quite forgave Brewer for some of his differences.

Men who worked for or with Field have left varied reports concerning him. Some, although they found him hot tempered and unreasonable at times and always insistent that work be done on schedule, have remembered with pleasure the days spent in his service. Others resented his lack of consideration for them, and some declared they would not work for him for his salary. Certain of the boys working around the court room feared and perhaps hated him, and one man has recalled Field's outbursts of profanity when the temperature in the office of the clerk of the Court did not suit him. On this occasion and many others it seems evident that his irritability was due in large part to the constant pain which he suffered and to the strain which his vocation threw upon him. On one occasion he mistreated one of the pages to such an extent that his colleagues insisted that he go to the boy and apologize. Field thought it over. "No," he replied. "You say I insulted him. I'll make the apology as good as the insult." He therefore had the boy called into the consultation room, where the other justices were, and there apologized for his unkindness.

He never ceased to put in long and arduous hours at his tasks. In San Francisco, when working in the chambers of the Circuit Court, he often sent the court copyist out to bring him a whisky punch when he grew weary. The drink was ordinarily carried in under a paper sack. One day the copyist was absent, and a more venturesome employee was sent to get the punch. Thinking to have some fun out of the Justice he brought in the glass, covered as usual, but filled with water. A roar of invective half paralyzed the man with fright. The trick was not tried again.

In the court room he was always courteous and keenly attentive to the arguments of counsel. He asked questions at times, but always for the purpose of getting at the heart of the situations. He never maliciously attempted to confuse counsel, as others in his position have been known to do. To young attorneys who were perhaps embarrassed and confused by their first appearances in the august presence of the Court he was without exception kind and considerate, and found ways to put them at their ease. Indeed, one of his great pleasures was in helping young men of promise to get on their way as lawyers. He never became a teacher in the academic world, as he had planned in his youth, but he exercised admirably the teaching function in his attempts to help young men with whom he came in contact. It was due in large part to these efforts that he left among the younger generation of lawyers a group of hero worshipers such as those which often surround great teachers. He at times regretted, in his later years, that he had not accepted the invitation to lecture at the Columbian Law School, in Washington, in order to keep in touch with more of the young men in his profession.

As he sat on the bench he looked always the same, save for the fact that over a period of years his hair grew thinner and whiter, and his long, heavy beard turned gray. He dressed in the very finest of black broadcloth and spotless linen, and always wore a black tie. Indeed, there was something clean cut about Field in everything, from the clothes which he wore to the conciseness of his opinions.

His friends grew solicitous about his increasing lameness, which came at length to make it difficult for him to get to his position on the bench. "I don't write my opinions with my leg," he once protested. Nevertheless, it was extremely difficult for him to go to California and travel his circuit. On his last trip he realized that he must never attempt to make the rounds again. Even in San Francisco a clerk of the Court used to make regular visits to the Palace Hotel to assure him that there was no business which required his attention. Mrs. Field would join in pleading with him to remain in his rooms. It was never suggested that he was unable to go, however, lest he stubbornly attempt to show his capacity by limping off toward the court room. None of his pride had deserted him.

Over a long period of years there were persistent rumors in the press and in political circles that Justice Field was about to resign. It was said in 1885 that he planned to resign in 1888 and devote the ensuing years to writing the memoirs of his unusually dramatic life. This would have given Grover Cleveland an opportunity to appoint a Democrat in his place. That he did not resign was attributed to the hostility that developed between him and the President. He remained on the bench and his memoirs remained unpublished, save as he circulated fragments of them among his friends through new editions of his *Personal Reminiscences* and of the compilation, *Some Account of the Work of Stephen J. Field*. Gossip has it that a quarrel with President Harrison led him to decide to remain on the bench during another presidential term; and then Grover Cleveland was elected again, with the result that Field determined to sit still another four years. People conversant with social life in Washington believed that Mrs. Field was reluctant to give up the life there, and that she played a part in preventing her husband's resignation. It is evident that another prominent influence was the fact that he was now to be numbered among those who had served longest on the bench. John Marshall held the record up to that time, but Field had served almost as long. He coveted the record for himself. As people went to him for confirmation of the ever-increasing number of rumors that he was about to resign they were told flatly that he had no such intention.

"I regard it as entirely improbable that there will be any successor to Judge Field during the present administration," wrote Senator Stephen M. White, in July, 1896. "I was in San Francisco a few days ago and made special inquiry, but failed to find any justification for the very positive statements of the newspapers. Judge Field is, no doubt, weak physically, and perhaps, is not as active mentally as was once the case, though his mind is still clear and he can write as strong opinions as ever, though I do not think he can do as much work as formerly. Indeed, his vitality and intellectuality are astonishing when we take his age into consideration. The comments made by the newspapers will not tend to accelerate his retirement." [2]

During the winter of 1896-97 Field's mind became noticeably feeble. His questions in the court room at times indicated that he had no conception of the arguments that were being made before him. It was reported that he voted on cases and then forgot how he had voted. Periods of clear perception were followed by others of dull stupor. His colleagues at times found it wise to coach him on cases before them. Something of his condition is indicated by the following account:

Chief Justice Fuller sent two of his colleagues over to the Old Capitol home to present the materials which they had gathered on a case then before the Court, and to show how they arrived at the decision which they were about to adopt. They found Field in an unusually lethargic condition. He sat in a great arm chair, his head dropped forward on his breast, and his eyes closed. He

[2] S. M. White to W. H. Grant, July 22, 1896. White MSS.

stirred for a moment as he recognized his visitors, then again dropped his head and closed his eyes. Uncertain what to do, his colleagues hesitantly took out their papers and asked if they might read them to him. Their host gave no assent nor denial, nor sign that he was any longer aware of the presence of his colleagues. Nevertheless one of them began to read the opinion which he had written. For some time Field gave no evidence that he heard. Then suddenly he raised his right hand. "Read that again," he commanded. The passage was read again. "That is not good law," he exclaimed. "You err when you say—" and here he launched into a clear and forceful argument which finally convinced his listeners that he was right. His argument completed, he lapsed into his former comatose condition. He showed no sign that he was aware when the two justices gathered up their papers and left the room.

They remained convinced that Field was right in his contention, and upon presenting his argument to their colleagues they brought about a change in the proposed decision of the Court. Yet it remained an open question with them whether Field had been fully conscious when he delivered his argument. It was as if the legal phrases read in his presence had stimulated his mind to a sort of automatic activity. Once set going, the mind, apparently without effort, passed through the accustomed logical channels to the decision which must follow. At any rate, it appears to have been evident that at this time no other kind of stimulus could have aroused coherent response in his mind.[3]

His colleagues continued to be worried about the situation. In the words of Chief Justice Hughes: "I heard Justice Harlan tell of the anxiety which the Court had

[3] This account, by Walter Wellman in the Chicago *Times-Herald,* was reprinted in the San Francisco *Argonaut,* Nov. 1, 1897.

felt because of the condition of Justice Field. It occurred
to other members of the Court that Justice Field had
served on a committee which waited upon Justice Grier
to suggest his retirement and it was thought that recalling
the incident to his memory might aid him to decide to
retire. Justice Harlan was deputed to make the suggestion. He went over to Justice Field, who was sitting
alone on a settee in the robing room apparently oblivious
of his surroundings, and after arousing him gradually
approached the question, asking if he did not recall how
anxious the Court had been with respect to Justice Grier's
condition and the feeling of the other justices that in his
own interest and in that of the Court he should give up
his work. Justice Harlan asked if Justice Field did not
remember what had been said to Justice Grier on that
occasion. The old man listened, gradually became alert
and finally, with his eyes blazing with the old fire of
youth, he burst out:

" 'Yes! And a dirtier day's work I never did in my
life!'

"That was the end of that effort of the brethren of the
Court to induce Justice Field's retirement; . . ." [4]

When Grover Cleveland was due to leave the White
House a second time, President-elect McKinley chose
Judge Joseph McKenna, of California, to be his Attorney-
General, with the understanding that he was later to
have Field's place on the bench. Field is said to have had
some part in the agreement, which was managed mainly
by Justice Brewer.[5] In April, 1897, without the knowledge of the public, Field sent his letter of resignation to
President McKinley. It was to take effect December 1,
and thus bring to a close a term of thirty-four years, eight

[4] Hughes, Charles E., *The Supreme Court of the United States*, pp. 75-76.
[5] S. M. White to S. C. Houghton. White MSS. White thus failed to
control the appointment.

months and twenty days, the longest served by any man on the supreme bench. He made public the fact of his resignation on October 12 by a letter to his colleagues.

"When my resignation takes effect," he said, "my period of service on this bench will have exceeded that of any of my predecessors, while my entire judicial life will have embraced more than forty years. I may be pardoned for saying that during all this period, long in comparison with the brevity of human life, though in retrospect it has gone with the swiftness of a tale that is told, I have not shunned to declare in every case coming before me for decision the conclusions, which my deliberate convictions compelled me to arrive at, by the conscientious exercise of such abilities and acquirements as I possessed." [6]

He had written six hundred and twenty opinions for the Supreme Court, he declared, fifty-seven for the Circuit Court, and three hundred and sixty-five for the state Supreme Court in California, making a total of one thousand and forty-two. He had come to Washington as the first judicial representative of the new empire which had arisen on the Pacific Coast. The supreme bench had needed a man who understood the condition of the confused land titles in California, and he had been selected at the wish of the senators and representatives of the state. The period following the war had been one of marvelous material development. Gigantic enterprises had been undertaken. The conditions of life had greatly changed from those prevailing before the war. Out of changed social and economic conditions had arisen cases of vital importance to the future prosperity and safety of the country. He congratulated the American people that although they had not always approved of the decisions of the Court they had nevertheless rendered unfaltering obedience, thereby demon-

[a] See letter in appendix, 168 *United States Reports*.

strating their capacity for popular government. The Supreme Court, he declared, was a truly democratic institution, one which kept the "whole mighty fabric of government from rushing to destruction."

"With this I give place to my successor," he concluded. "But I can never cease to linger on the memories of the past. Among the compensations for all the hard work that a seat on this bench imposes, have been the intimacies and friendships that have been formed between its members. Though we have often differed in our opinions, it has always been an honest difference, which did not affect our mutual regard and respect. These many years have been years of labor and toil, but they have brought their own reward; and we can all join in thanksgiving to the Author of our being that we have been permitted to spend so much of our lives in the service of our country."

So he brought his long period of service to a close, leaving Justice Harlan, appointed fourteen years later than he, as the senior member of the Court. Three chief justices and eighteen associate justices had passed away during his incumbency.

Although his health seemed to improve after the cessation of his labors he was still feeble.[7] He read a great deal. He saw only a few visitors, but enjoyed talking with

[7] Justice Field had made his will in May, 1897, about a month after he had sent in his letter of resignation from the bench. With the exception of a few specified articles all of his property was to go to his wife. If her death occurred before his, the property was to go to certain of her relatives. One special bequest in the will was a gift of five hundred dollars to William Joice, the negro servant who had attended him for a quarter of a century, and who, if reports be not exaggerated, was the survivor of many stormy scenes. An appraisal of the property, made shortly after Justice Field's death two years later, disclosed that he had approximately sixty-five thousand dollars in cash, stocks, bonds, and other personal property, in addition to the home in the Old Capitol building. His long and strenuous life had not brought him wealth, and the charges that he had used his office for personal aggrandizement were shown to have been quite without justification.

friends. He continued to be interested in California. However, because of the Terry affair and the railroad situation much of the press was still unfriendly to him, and his family found it wise to withhold California newspapers from him to keep him from being continually wrought up by the controversies. He was fond of driving, and in the last years of his life rarely failed to take a daily trip around the Capitol grounds and out toward the Soldier's Home.

For a long time, perhaps during most of his life, the validity of the dogmas of religion had given him little concern. He rented a pew in the Epiphany Church, and attended occasionally, but he was not commonly regarded as a religious man. Some years prior to his retirement, however, he turned his attention to theological reading and inquiry. He went into the question of revealed religion, attempting to analyze it without reference to any preconceptions, as if it were a case which he was trying in court. For two years he kept his library filled with books on all phases of the subject. As a result, while he retained his belief in a supreme being and a future life he discarded the Trinitarian and atonement dogmas, and failed to find any evidence that made miracles credible to him.[8]

This interest was perhaps for the most part intellectual. In his last years, however, an emotional interest was evident. His mind turned often to the religious aspects of the life which he had known in his boyhood home, to the time when the family had gathered around the hearth for worship and his sister Mary had led the hymns and his father had led in prayer. One morning as his secretary went out Field asked if he were going to church. "Yes," the secretary replied. "Pray for me," he said soberly.

[8] Hopkins, Archibald, "The Late Mr. Justice Field," *Green Bag*, June, 1899, pp. 245-51.

Later he spoke of wanting to be baptized—though some thought that he was confused in his mind, and that what he wanted was to make a public confession.

Early in April, 1899, he came in chilled by his drive. He became ill, and grew steadily worse. His mind wandered at times; he heard music and asked the nurse if she could hear it. She replied that she could not. "It must be the angels then," he said. At one time a vision came to him. "There's Father. There's Mother. There's Mary," he cried. At another time he seemed much distressed; he prayed for forgiveness; then came quiet and a sense of peace. One morning he had the colored servants in the household called to his bedside; there he asked their forgiveness for his harshness with them. He pulled his colored valet down to him and kissed him.

On Sunday evening, April 9, with Mrs. Field, Mrs. Condit-Smith, Justice Brewer, and others at his side, and while Reverend Edward Mott, son of Judge Mott of Marysville, read prayers, Justice Field died.

The Supreme Court adjourned for a day, as a mark of respect to his memory. It was planned to have the funeral on Wednesday, but it was discovered that a daughter of Chief Justice Fuller was to be married on that day. Since Mrs. Field wished the justices of the Supreme Court to act as honorary pall-bearers, the funeral gave way to the wedding, and was postponed until Thursday morning. Some wanted to arrange for a public funeral in the Supreme Court chamber but the family objected, insisting that the ceremony be as simple and private as the ritual of the Episcopal church would permit.

On Thursday morning the family, including Henry Field, the last of the brothers, gathered in the house for a service of prayer, which was conducted by Reverend Mott. Then the funeral procession set out for the Church of the Epiphany. The rector of the church and the bishop of the diocese met the casket at the head of the aisle, and led the procession to the chancel. Following the casket were the justices of the Supreme Court, acting as honorary pall-bearers, and then came the members of the family. In the church were President McKinley; Secretaries Wilson and Long; Attorney-General Griggs; Sir Julian Pauncefote from England, Baron von Hollebon from Germany, and other ambassadors, ministers and diplomatic officers from Russia, France, China, and many other countries. There were large delegations from the Senate and the House of Representatives, and many members of the bar.

The services were as brief as possible and wholly unostentatious, though marked by deep feeling. The assembled congregation, representatives from all parts of the Occidental world, joined with the choir in singing "Nearer, My God, to Thee," while the Chinese Minister reverently beat time with his hand. At the close of the ceremony the remains of Justice Field were taken to Rock Creek cemetery, in Washington. There he lies buried, his grave marked with a simple monument inscribed, "Justice of the Supreme Court of the United States for over thirty-four years."

INDEXES

INDEX TO CASES CITED

Ableman v. Booth, 111
Ah Fong, In re, 211-13
Ah Kee, In re, 233
Ah Lung, In re, 232
Ah Moy, In re, 232
Ah Sing, In re, 230
Ah Tie, In re, 230
Allgeyer v. Louisiana, 426
Andrews, Ex parte, 81
Archy, Ex parte, 74

Baltimore & Ohio R. R. v. Baugh, 429
Bank v. Supervisors, 174
Barbier v. Connolly, 226-27
Bartmeyer v. Iowa, 421
Benham v. Rowe, 60
Biddle Boggs v. Merced Mining Company, 83 ff.
Blair v. Thompson and Ridgely, 154
Bradwell v. Illinois, 420-21
Brass v. North Dakota, 394
Broderick's Executor v. Magraw, 175
Bronson v. Rodes, 174-75
Budd v. New York, 392-94
Butchers' Union Slaughter-House and Live-Stock Landing
    Co. v. Crescent City Live-Stock Landing and Slaughter-
    House Co., 422-23.
Butler v. Horwitz, 174
Bybee v. Oregon & California R. R. Co., 267

California v. Central Pacific R. R. (127 U. S. 1), 261-62
California v. Central Pacific R. R. (162 U. S. 91), 262-63
Central Pacific R. R. v. California, 249
Chae Chan Ping v. United States, 237

Cheen Heong, *In re*, 234
Chew Heong *v.* United States, 234-36
Chicago, Burlington & Quincy R. R. *v.* Iowa, 372, 381
Chicago, Milwaukee & St. Paul Ry. *v.* Ackley, 372
Chicago, Milwaukee & St. Paul Ry. *v.* Minnesota, 391
Chicago, Milwaukee & St. Paul Ry. *v.* Ross, 429
Civil Rights Cases, 165
Colton *v.* Stanford, 248
Cornwall *v.* Culver, 89
Coryell *v.* Cain, 55, 91
Cummings *v.* Missouri, 138 ff.

Debs, *In re*, 411
Deming *v.* United States, 182 ff.
Dooley *v.* Smith, 195
Dred Scott *v.* Sanford, 111

Ex parte Andrews, 81
Ex parte Archy, 74
Ex parte Garland, 138 ff.
Ex parte McCardle (73 U. S. 318), 159-61
Ex parte McCardle (74 U. S. 506), 161
Ex parte Merryman, 112
Ex parte Milligan, 135-37
Ex parte Newman, 77 ff., 103, 375
Ex parte Stephen J. Field, 41
Ex parte Terry, 340
Ex parte Vallandigham, 134-35, 138
Ex parte Virginia, 165, 285

Ferris *v.* Coover, 89, 90
Field, *In re*, 355
Fong Yue Ting *v.* United States, 238

Garland, *Ex parte*, 138 ff.
Georgia R. R. & Banking Co. *v.* Smith, 389-90
Georgia *v.* Stanton, 158

Granger Cases. *See* Munn *v.* Illinois and cases discussed therewith

Grogan *v.* San Francisco, 93

Hart *v.* Burnett, 76, 97
Hepburn *v.* Griswold, 174 ff.
Hicks *v.* Bell, 82
Ho Ah Kow *v.* Nunan, 206, 216 ff.
Holland *v.* San Francisco, 93
Houston *v.* Williams, 106-7

Income Tax Case. *See* Pollock *v.* Farmers' Loan and Trust Co.
In re Ah Fong, 211-13
In re Ah Kee, 233
In re Ah Lung, 232
In re Ah Moy, 232
In re Ah Sing, 230
In re Ah Tie, 230
In re Cheen Heong, 234
In re Debs, 411
In re Field, 355
In re Kew Ock, 233
In re Look Tin Sing, 233
In re Low Yam Chow, 231
In re Neagle (14 Sawyer 232), 358-59
In re Neagle (135 U. S. 1), 332 ff., 359
In re Pacific Railway Commission, 264
In re Quong Woo, 224-25
In re Terry, 342
In re Terry Contempt, 336, 338-39

Jennison *v.* Kirk, 57
Juilliard *v.* Greenman, 198 ff.

Kew Ock, *In re*, 233
Knox *v.* Lee, 176, 187 ff.

Lane County *v.* Oregon, 174
Latham *v.* United States, 182 ff.

Lin Sing *v.* Washburn, 207-9
Loan Association *v.* Topeka, 425
Lochner *v.* New York, 425
Look Tin Sing, *In re,* 233
Low Yam Chow, *In re,* 231

McCardle, *Ex parte* (73 U. S. 318), 159-61
McCardle, *Ex parte* (74 U. S. 506), 161
McCracken *v.* San Francisco, 92-93
Mahoney *v.* Van Winkle, 89
Maryland *v.* Railroad Co., 197
Merryman, *Ex parte,* 112
Miller *v.* United States, 164
Milligan, *Ex parte,* 135-37
Mississippi *v.* Johnson, 156-57
Missouri Cases. *See* Cummings *v.* Missouri
Moore *v.* Smaw, 87
Moore *v.* Wilkinson, 89
Munn *v.* Illinois, 80, 214-15, 372 ff.

Neagle, *In re* (14 Sawyer 232), 358-59
Neagle, *In re* (135 U. S. 1), 332 ff., 359
Newman, *Ex parte,* 77 ff., 103, 375

Pacific Railway Commission, *In re,* 264
Parker *v.* Davis, 187 ff.
Passenger Cases, 207
Peik *v.* Chicago & Northwestern R. R., 372, 383
People *ex rel.* Barbour *v.* Mott, 62
People *ex rel.* Field *v.* Turner (1 Cal. 188), 44
People *ex rel.* Field *v.* Turner (1 Cal. 190), 44
People *ex rel.* Mulford *et al. v.* Turner, 41
People *ex rel.* Stephen J. Field *v.* Turner, 41
People *v.* Downer, 207
Perry *v.* Washburn, 170-71
Pierce *v.* Carskadon, 154
Pimental *v.* San Francisco, 94

Pollock *v.* Farmers' Loan and Trust Co. (157 U. S. 429), 398 ff.

Pollock *v.* Farmers' Loan and Trust Co. (158 U. S. 601), 410-11

Prize Cases, 114-15

Queen *v.* Earl of Northumberland, 82
Queue Case. *See* Ho Ah Kow *v.* Nunan
Quong Ting *v.* United States, 238
Quong Woo, *In re*, 224-25

Railroad Co. *v.* Gibbs, 391-92
Railroad Co. *v.* Johnson, 196-97
Railroad Co. *v.* Mississippi, 252
Riley *v.* Heisch, 89
Ruggles *v.* Illinois, 384-85

San Francisco & Northern Pacific R. R. *v.* Board of Equalization, 252
San Francisco *v.* Hazen, 92
San Francisco *v.* United States, 99
San Mateo *v.* Southern Pacific R. R. (13 Fed. 145), 252-53
San Mateo *v.* Southern Pacific R. R. (13 Fed. 722), 254-56
San Mateo *v.* Southern Pacific R. R. (116 U. S. 138), 260, 416
Santa Clara *v.* Southern Pacific R. R. (18 Fed. 385), 258
Santa Clara *v.* Southern Pacific R. R. (118 U. S. 394), 260, 416
Saunders *v.* Haynes, 49
Sharon *v.* Hill (10 Sawyer 48), 325
Sharon *v.* Hill (10 Sawyer 394), 325
Sharon *v.* Hill (10 Sawyer 634), 325
Sharon *v.* Hill (10 Sawyer 666), 326
Sharon *v.* Hill (11 Sawyer 122), 326-27
Sharon *v.* Hill (11 Sawyer 290), 322-23, 327-28
Sharon *v.* Terry, 332 ff.
Sinking Fund Cases, 248-49, 285, 427
Slaughterhouse Cases, 416 ff.
Soon Hing *v.* Crowley, 227 ff., 234
Southern Pacific R. R. *v.* California, 262-63

Stephen J. Field, *Ex parte,* 41
Stoakes *v.* Barrett, 92
Stone *v.* Farmers' Loan and Trust Co., 385-88
Stone *v.* Wisconsin, 372, 381 ff.

Terry Contempt, *In re,* 336, 338-39
Terry, *Ex parte,* 340
Terry, *In re,* 342
Terry *v.* Sharon, 346
Teschmacher *v.* Thompson, 90
Test Oath Cases. *See Ex parte* Garland *and* Cummings *v.* Missouri
Townsend *v.* Greeley, 100
Trebilcock *v.* Wilson, 195

United States *v.* Circuit Judges, 100
United States *v.* E. C. Knight Co., 411
United States *v.* Greathouse, 131-32
United States *v.* Stanford, 245
United States *v.* Sutter, 89
United States *v.* Terry, 342
United States *v.* Union Pacific R. R., 246

Vallandigham, *Ex parte,* 134-35, 138
Vaughan and Telegraph, The, 196
Veazie Bank *v.* Fenno, 175
Virginia, *Ex parte,* 165, 285
Virginia *v.* Rives, 285

Winona & St. Peter R. R. *v.* Blake, 372
Wong Wing *v.* United States, 238

GENERAL INDEX

Abbott, Josiah G., writes Democratic minority protest against Electoral Commission decision and opposes publication before his death, 279-81

Adams, Charles Francis, Jr.: on era of change, 364; on railroad problems, 368, 370-71

Adams, Henry, on legal tender question, 186-87

Alcalde. See Marysville

Alvarado, Juan B., 84

American Knights or Sons of Liberty, 135

Appointment of Field to federal supreme bench: urged by California senators, 116; made and confirmed, 116; purpose of Congress in, 117; popular reception of, 117-18; oath of office, 1-2, 118

Argonaut: denounces Field's Queue case decision, 220; jubilant over San Mateo railroad decision, 256-57. See also Pixley, F. M.

Ashe, Porter, 334-35

Asper, J. F., 144

Athens, Field's life in, 14

Attorneys and counselors, 47-48, 139, 149-50

Baldwin, Jos. G.: attorney for Biddle Boggs, 85; in "City Slip" controversy, 93; accused of corruption, 85-86, 93; capacity of as judge, 74; advises Field's retraction of statements about Harvey Lee, 109; opinion of in Ex parte Andrews, 81

Barbour, Wm. T., 62-64

Barnard, Judge Geo. G., and Erie scandals, 173

Beatty, Chief Justice W. H., refuses adjournment of California Supreme Court for Terry's funeral, 354

Bennett, Nathaniel, 70

Bicknell, John D., 317-18

Bills of attainder, 148-49

Black, Jeremiah S.: counsel in Ex parte McCardle, 159; "objector" before Electoral Commission, 274

Black Friday, 173

Blatchford, Justice Samuel: opinion in Budd v. New York, 392; C. M. & St. P. Ry. v. Minnesota, 391; death, 435

Blockade of Southern ports, 114-15

Board of Land Commissioners, 98

Boggs, Biddle, 84

Boruck, M. D., denounces Field's enemies, 308, 310-11

Boutwell, Geo. S., 182

Bradley, Justice Jos. P.: appointed, 181; opinion in California v. Central Pacific R. R., 262; concurring opinion in Bradwell v. Illinois, 421; in Knox v. Lee, 189; dissent in C. M. & St. P. Ry. v. Minnesota, 391; in Slaughterhouse cases, 417; opposes withdrawal of Latham and Deming cases, 185; chosen member of Electoral Commission, 272; votes with Republicans, 276-77; hanged in effigy, 278; explains his vote, 279; regrets Field not chosen to be Chief Justice, 319

Brewer, Justice David J.: opinion in B. & O. R. R. *v.* Baugh, 429; dissent in Brass *v.* North Dakota, 394; in Budd *v.* New York, 392-94; in Quong Ting *v.* United States, 235; relationship with Field, 438; arranges selection of Field's successor, 444; present at Field's death, 448

Brewer, Rev. Josiah, takes Stephen Field to Smyrna, 13-14

Bribery. *See* Corruption *and* Property, Field's

Brisbane, Arthur, description of Field, 409-10

Broderick, David C.: carries Field's challenge to B. F. Moore, 53; wins Field's friendship and political support, 53; forces his own nomination to U. S. Senate, 69; loses patronage to Wm. M. Gwin, 70; refuses to support Field for Supreme Court judgeship, 70; killed by David S. Terry in duel, 74

Brown, of Colorado, seconds Field's nomination for Democratic candidate for presidency, 296

Burlingame, Anson, and treaty with China, 209

Burnett, Justice Peter H.: elected to the California Supreme Court, 72; capacity as judge, 73; opinion in Biddle Boggs *v.* Merced Mining Co., 84-85; in *Ex parte* Archy, 73-74; in Holland *v.* San Francisco, 93

California: beginning of gold rush, 24; Field helps keep state loyal, 110-11; problems peculiar to state, 111. *See also* Chinese; Marysville; Railroads of California; San Francisco

Cannon, Jock, 65

Cardozo, Judge Albert, and Erie scandals, 173

Carey, District Attorney John T.: warns U. S. Attorney-General of Field's danger from Terrys, 345; defends Field in Circuit Court, 354; defends Neagle in Circuit Court, 358

Carpenter, Matthew H.: counsel in *Ex parte* Garland, 139-40; in *Ex parte* McCardle, 159

Carr, Jesse D., 312

Carter, Jas. C.: on brief, *In re* Neagle, 359; counsel in Pollock *v.* Farmers' Loan and Trust Co., 398

Catron, Justice John, death of, 133

Central Pacific R. R. *See* Railroads of California

Chase, Chief Justice Salmon P.: as Secretary of the Treasury, dislike of state bank notes, 168; sponsors issue of greenbacks, 169; has Treasury represented in state cases where constitutionality of legal tender acts is argued, 170; sees legal tender acts as temporary measures, 171; as Chief Justice tells Secretary of Treasury Boutwell Supreme Court will hold legal tender acts unconstitutional, 182; objects to reopening legal tender question, 182-83; publishes his ideas through Henry Adams, 187; writes account of legal tender disagreement in Court, 185; discouraged at his defeat, 194-95; opinion in Bank *v.* Supervisors, 174; in Bronson *v.* Rodes, 174; in Butler *v.* Horwitz, 174; in Hepburn *v.* Griswold, 176 ff.; in Lane County *v.* Oregon, 174;

in Mississippi *v.* Johnson, 157; in Veazie Bank *v.* Fenno, 175; dissent in Bradwell *v.* Illinois, 421; in *Ex parte* Milligan, 136; in Knox *v.* Lee and Parker *v.* Davis, 189; in The Vaughan and Telegraph, 196; political interests, 125, 133, 269; death, 196-97

China, value of commerce with, 209, 231

Chinese: early reception in California, 205; taxation of, 207-9; Burlingame treaty, 209; as laborers, 209; Field's exhortation against hostile treatment, 210-11; Field opposes discriminating legislation, 212-13; his decision in Queue case, 217-19; Field helps to get confirmation of new treaty, 223-24; laundries, 224-29; federal restriction of immigration, 230-39; decisions regarding hurt Field politically, 300, 302, 305-6

Choate, Jos. H.: counsel, *In re* Neagle, 359; in Pollock *v.* Farmers' Loan and Trust Co., 398 ff.; urges Field to accept circuit in East, 435

Cholera: in Smyrna, 14; in Paris, 23; Field suffers from in Panama, 25

Circuit Court of United States for Tenth Circuit: Field begins work in, 119; serves until his retirement, 435-37

City Slip property. *See* San Francisco

Civil Practice Act. *See* Legislature

Classification for legislation, 226-27

Clay, Henry, 48

Cleveland, Grover: elected President, 310; delays filling offices in California, 313; gives office to enemy of Field and refuses to discuss it with him, 316-17; appoints Melville W. Fuller to be Chief Justice, 319; recommends enactment of income tax law, 397; hostility between him and Field, 441

Clifford, Justice Nathan: pronounced Democrat, 271-82; chairman of Electoral Commission, 273; absent from Hayes inauguration, 281; hopes for Democratic successor, 282

Codification of law: David Dudley Field engaged in, 22, 283; Stephen Field uses brother's codes in drafting California practice acts, 54

Colleagues of Justice Field, 3, 125-26

Colton, David D.: resents sinking fund enactment, 247; plans that Field shall pass upon sinking fund act in U. S. Supreme Court, 247

Communism: Field accuses his enemies of committing Democratic party to, 314, 316; his San Mateo decision proclaimed a victory over, 256-57; his hostility to socialism and, 396; Grangers compared with Communists, 383; income tax law branded as communistic, 399; Field's niece joins Communist party, 433

Condit-Smith, Mrs. Sarah S.: goes East with Fields, 119; marries General Condit-Smith, 437; present at Field's death, 448

Confiscation of Southern property: demanded in North, 134; Field objects to, 164-65

Congress: creates position for tenth justice of Supreme Court, 116;

radical character, 154 ff.; prevents new appointments to Supreme Court, 155; withdraws jurisdiction of Supreme Court in McCardle case, 160; investigates Field's statements on reconstruction, 163; restores Supreme Court membership to nine, 180

Conkling, Roscoe: counsel in San Mateo case, 257; on purpose of Fourteenth Amendment, 415-16

Conness, John, 99, 100

Constitutional convention in California: attempts to limit Chinese immigration, 214-16; plans for railroad regulation, 250-51; on taxation, 251

Contracts, obligation of, 191, 200, 201-2

Cooke, Jay, 197

Cope, Justice W. W.: capacity as judge, 74; opinion in Lin Sing v. Washburn, 207; dissent in Hart v. Burnett, 97; administers oath to Field, 118

Corporations: entitled to equality of treatment with individuals, 255-56; need of defining limits of state control over, 381-82; security of title to property, 248-49

Corruption, charges of: against Field and Baldwin, 85-86; against San Francisco City Council, 91-92; against Field of speculating on basis of court decisions, 95; against Field of accepting bribes, 97-98; Field's comment on, 97

Covillaud, Chas., 30

Covillaud, Mary, 31

Criminal Practice Act. See Legislature

Crocker, Chas., 241

Crosby, E. O., 32

Cross, C. W., 314, 333

Cruel and unusual punishment, 218

Cunningham, Thos., 351-52

Currency. See Greenbacks

Curtis, Geo. Ticknor, 170

Dana, Chas. Henry, on legal status of war, 114-15

Davis, Garrett, 117

Davis, Justice David: appointment, 113; opinion in Ex parte Milligan, 136; resigns to become U. S. senator, 125-272; declines membership in Electoral Commission, 272; at Hayes inauguration, 281

Deady, Judge Matthew P., opinion in Sharon case, 327-28

Delmas, D. M.: attacks Field before Stockton convention, 306-7; denounced by M. D. Boruck, 308

Democratic conventions. See Political activities

De Tocqueville, Alexis, on position of lawyers in American life, 20-21

Dueling: Field challenges B. F. Moore, 52-53; accepts challenge of W. T. Barbour, 62; Broderick killed by Terry, 74

Due process of law: in taxing of railroads, 255; as limitation upon rate regulation, 386, 391; as basis for natural rights decisions, 424. See also Fourteenth Amendment

Dwight, Timothy, president of Yale and teacher of Field's father, 9-10

Edmunds, Geo. F.: counsel in San Mateo case, 257; in income tax case, 398

Education, Field's: in school at Stockbridge, 9; through home life, 11-12; trip to Smyrna, 13 ff.; Williams College, 16 ff.; study of law, 20-21

Electoral Commission: personnel, 271-72; decision of, 276-77; Democratic protest against decision of, 279-81

Ellis, Asa, 316

English, W. D., chairman of Democratic executive committee in California, 312

Equal protection of the laws guaranteed to corporations, 254-55, 261. See also Fourteenth Amendment

Europe, Field's year in, 23

Evarts, Wm. M., "objector" before the Electoral Commission, 274

Ex post facto laws, and test oath cases, 149-51

Fairfax, Chas. S., 64, 107

"Fellow servant" doctrine. See Labor

Felton, Chas. N., 64, 66

Field, Cyrus W.: boyhood, 8; travel in Europe, 23; owns part of Old Capitol property, 122; energetic character, 245, 284; reputation, 287; hostility to Tilden, 284; back of Justice Field's presidential campaign, 284 ff.; family, 438

Field, David Dudley (Sr.): training for the ministry, 9; marries Submit Dickinson, 10; takes church at Haddam, 10; moves to Stockbridge, 5-6; leads devotions in home, 7-8; character of preaching, 10-11; theological beliefs, 11; influence over Stephen Field, 11-12

Field, David Dudley (Jr.): at Williams College, 12-13; studies law, 20; takes Stephen Field as partner, 21; works on codification of law, 22, 283; dominating character, 22; becomes an Abolitionist, 45, 268; his codes of procedure used by Stephen Field in California legislature, 54; aids in nomination of Abraham Lincoln, 116; deeds Old Capitol home to Justice Field, 122-23; influence over Justice Field, 122, 151-52; counsel in Cummings v. Missouri, 142; in Ex parte McCardle, 159; in Ex parte Milligan, 135-36; in support of legal tender acts, 170; reputation and appearance, 274-75, 287, 365; "objector" before Electoral Commission, 274; cross-examination of J. Madison Wells, 277; in Justice Field's presidential campaign, 284 ff.; death of son of, 438

Field, Emelia: marries Rev. Josiah Brewer, 13; takes Stephen to Smyrna, 13-14

Field family: ancestry of, 9; characteristics of boys of, 6; religious practices of, 7-8; education in home of, 8-9, 11-12; financial prosperity of, 23; golden wedding in, 61; next generation of, 438

Field, Henry M.: account of home life, 7-8; travel in Europe, 23; comment on Stephen Field's absence from parents' golden wedding, 61; account of brother's appointment to supreme bench, 116-17; at Justice Field's funeral, 448

Field, Jonathan Edwards: named for evangelist, 10; enters Williams College, 13; graduates, 16

Field, Mary: at family devotions, 7; travels in Europe, 23

Field, Matthew Dickinson, engineer in Tennessee, 45

Field, Submit Dickinson: marries Rev. David Dudley Field, 10; cares for large family, 5

Field, Sue Virginia Swearingen: marries Stephen J. Field, 110; influence over husband, 110, 437-38, 441; inherits husband's property, 446; asks Supreme Court justices to be honorary pallbearers for husband, 448

Field, Zachariah, first Field to settle in America, 9

Fiske, James, Jr., and Erie scandals, 173

Flower, Roswell P., 309

Foote, S. A., 170

Fourteenth Amendment: basis for invalidating taxing provisions of California constitution, 255-58; Field urges as limitation upon state interference with business, 377-78, 381; purpose of adoption, 414-16; Field's attempt to read "inalienable rights" into, 418-25

Franks, J. C.: asked by Judge Sawyer to have deputies guard court room, 332; encounter with Terry in court room, 334; appoints David Neagle to protect Field, 345; prevents Field's arrest, 350

Fremont, John C., 84

Fuller, Chief Justice Melville W.: appointment, 319; opinion in Central Pacific R. R. v. California and Southern Pacific R. R.

v. California, 262; in income tax case, 402, 410; sends colleagues to coach Field on decision, 442

Gallatin, Albert, 247

Gambling. See Property, Field's

Garland, A. H., and federal test oath act, 139

Gates, I. E., 265, 266

Godkin, E. L., on railroad problems, 365-70

Goodwin, J. O., 40, 43

Gould, Jay, and Erie scandals, 173

Grain elevators, regulation of, 372 ff., 392-94

Grant, Ulysses S., accused of appointing judges to reverse legal tender decision, 181

Gray, John A. C., 116

Gray, Justice Horace, opinion in Juilliard v. Greenman, 199

Greenbacks: issued, 169; constitutionality of tested in state courts, 170; reception of in California, 170; Field declines to pass on constitutionality of, 171; opposition to withdrawal of, 172; evils of inflation of, 172-73; Supreme Court decisions bearing on, 174-75; legal tender acts authorizing declared unconstitutional, 176-77; decision on reversed, 188-92; increase of issue of prevented by veto, 197; provisions for redemption and reissue of, 198; constitutionality of reissue of upheld, 198-99; Field's final dissent on reissue of, 199-202

Grier, Justice Robt. C.: opinion of in Prize cases, 115; delays decision in Missouri case, 143; protests at disposal of McCardle case, 160-61; confused on legal tender question, 174-75; resigns at request of colleagues, 176; attends funeral of intended successor, 181

Guthrie, Wm. D., counsel in income tax case, 398

Gwin, Wm. M.: political contest with Broderick, 69-70; aids Field's presidential campaign, 287

Habeas corpus: for Field's release in Marysville, 39; in *Ex parte* McCardle, 158-60; in *Ex parte* Merryman, 112-13; in *Ex parte* Milligan, 135-37; for Field's release after death of Terry, 352-53; for release of David Neagle, 353-54, 357-59

Haddam, Conn., birthplace of Field, 5

Hale, Sir Matthew, and "public interest" doctrine, 373 ff.

Hancock, Winfield S., nominated for presidency, 297

Harlan, Justice John M.: opinion in Chew Heong v. United States, 235; in *Ex parte* Terry, 340; concurring opinion of in Ruggles v. Illinois, 385; dissent in income tax case, 410-11; attempts to persuade Field to retire, 444; becomes senior member of Court, 446

Haun, Judge Henry, 39

Hayes, Rutherford B., takes presidential oath, 281

Hayes-Tilden controversy, 269-82. *See also* Electoral Commission

Haymond, Creed: close to Leland Stanford, 244; counsel in San Mateo case, 252

Hendricks, Thos. A., 304

Henley, Barclay, 311-13

Herrin, Wm. L.: counsel for Sharon interests, 331; defends Field in Circuit Court, 354; defends Neagle in Circuit Court, 358

Heydenfeldt, Justice Solomon: opinion in Hicks v. Bell, 82; in Stoakes v. Barrett, 83; counsel in Biddle Boggs v. Merced Mining Co., 84; leaves Terry's petition with Field, 338

Hill, Sarah A.: biographical sketch of, 322; her relationship with William Sharon, 322-23, 328; begins divorce suit, 323; threatens Senator Stewart, 326; denounced by Judge Deady, 328; marries David S. Terry, 330; pulls Judge Sawyer's hair, 332, 337; creates uproar in court room, 333-35; sentenced to jail, 336; appears in own interest in Superior Court, 346; sees Field at Lathrop, 347; grieves over death of Terry, 349; wants Field and Neagle lynched, 349-50; swears out warrants for Field and Neagle, 351; goes to hospital for insane, 359-60

Hoar, Ebenezer R.: appointment to Supreme Court not confirmed, 181; urges re-argument of the legal tender question, 182-84

Hoffman, Judge Ogden, 335

Holmes, Justice Oliver Wendell, comment on U. S. Supreme Court, 127

Hopkins, Albert, 17

Hopkins, Mark: becomes president of Williams College, 18; as teacher, 18-19; influence over Stephen Field, 19-20

Hopkins, Mark, prominent in Central Pacific R. R. Co., 241

Humanitarian legislation, Field's interest in, 57

Huntington, Collis P.: as leader in Central Pacific R. R. Co., 241; lobbies in Congress, 243; tries to control provisions of sinking fund act, and approves Field's passing on it in Supreme Court rather than in Circuit Court, 246-48; becomes unfriendly to Stanford, 267

Immigration. *See* Chinese
Inalienable rights. *See* Judicial process
Income tax. *See* Taxation
Inflation. *See* Greenbacks

Jackson, Justice Howell E., and income tax law, 402, 409, 410
Johnson, A. G., 354-55
Johnson, Andrew, 154, 155, 159
Johnson, Jas. A., offers Field support of his newspaper, 301
Johnson, Reverdy: counsel in *Ex parte* Garland, 139; tells what Supreme Court will do in Missouri case, 142; Field recommends his rebuke, 145
Joice, Wm., 446
Juanita, lynched in spite of Field's efforts, 64-66
Judicial notice, and anti-Chinese legislation, 208, 218, 227, 229
Judicial process: as Field participated in it, 3-4; as he used it in Marysville, 36-37; in shaping California constitutional law, 75; nature of law, 81; conceptions of welfare as determining decisions, 87-88; irregular methods in, 100-101; analysis of Field's use of in California, 101-4; inalienable rights as basis of decision, 148; training of judges, 167; economic ideas and legal

tender decisions, 179; judicial legislation in legal tender cases, 192-94; nature of Field's judicial arguments, 202-4; law as progressive science, 214-16; construction of laws, 230; judicial method and regulation of business, 362-64, 380, 389-90; considerations in income tax decision, 412; reading "inalienable rights" into Fourteenth Amendment, 418-25; summary of judicial process as Field participated in it, 426-34

Kearney, Dennis: leads attack on Chinese, 213; Field dislikes his followers, 250
Knott, J. Proctor, 357

Labor: its need for protection against capital, 78-79; Chinese competition with white, 209-10; unemployment and race riots, 213; workingmen's party organized, 213; Field's dislike for radical labor groups, 250; his efforts to limit "fellow servant" doctrine, 428-29
Lake, Delos, 120, 252, 254
Lamar, Justice L. Q. C., dissent, *In re* Neagle, 359
Land grants, Mexican: to private proprietors, 88-91; Field attempts to settle problems of ownership of, 90-91. *See also* San Francisco
Lathrop, scene of Terry tragedy, 377 ff.
Law. *See* Judicial process
Law practice of Stephen J. Field: partnership with David Dudley Field, 21-22; attempt at in San Francisco, 29; courage in, 66-67;

success before state Supreme
Court, 67
Lee, Harvey, 106-8
Legal tender acts. *See* Greenbacks
Legislature of California: Field's
campaign for membership, 44-47;
rough character of, 52-53; bills
sponsored by Field in, 47-48;
Turner controversy in, 49; Field's
work on practice acts in, 54 ff.
Liberty: of contract, 78-79; personal, 264
Lieber, Francis, 156-57
Lincoln, Abraham: reluctant to fill
all Supreme Court vacancies
with Northern men, 113; appoints Swayne, Miller, and Davis,
113; appoints Field, 1, 116-17;
appoints Chase as Chief Justice,
133; assassinated, 134
Low, of Marysville, said to have
bribed California Supreme Court
judges, 97-98
Lynching: Field saves man from
lynch jury, 46; fails to save
woman, 65-66

McCulloch, Hugh, Secretary of
Treasury, begins withdrawal of
greenbacks, 171-72
McElrath, J. E., nominates Field
as Democratic candidate for pres-
idency, 295
McKenna, Justice Joseph, chosen as
Field's successor, 444
McKip, Rev. Wm., 68
McRuer, Donald C.: sponsors bill
for Field, 100; unpopular in Cali-
fornia, 153
Markham, H. H., 317
Marriage of Field to Sue Virginia
Swearingen, 110
Marysville: Field's arrival and pur-
chase of lots, 30; government

organized, 30-31; establishment
of police force, 33; Field's
achievements as alcalde, 33-37;
Turner controversy, 38 ff.; incorporation, 58; Field and civic
life in, 68
Matthews, Justice Stanley, regrets
Field not chosen to be Chief Justice, 319
Memorials, with regard to Field's
retaining position on ninth circuit, 435-36
Mesick, Richard S.: counsel for
Sharon interests, 331; defends
Field in Circuit Court, 354; defends Neagle in Circuit Court,
358
Mexican land grants. *See* Land
grants; Supreme Court of California
Military tribunals: set up by authority of President, 134; Supreme Court refuses to pass upon
them during war, 134-35; later
declares their use unconstitutional, 136
Miller, John F., 221-22
Miller, Justice Samuel F.: appointment, 113; character sketch,
125-26; opinion in Bradwell *v.*
Illinois, 420-21; in Dooley *v.*
Smith, 195; in *In re* Neagle, 359;
in Loan Association *v.* Topeka,
425; in Slaughterhouse cases,
417; dissent in Bronson *v.* Rodes,
174-75; in Butler *v.* Horwitz,
174; in Hepburn *v.* Griswold,
178-79; in test oath cases, 150-
51; in Trebilcock *v.* Wilson, 195;
protest against vote in Hepburn
case, 176; wants legal tender
question re-argued, 182-85;
writes account of legal tender
disagreement in Court, 185-86;

member of Electoral Commission, 271

Miller, W. H. H., Attorney-General, 345

Milligan, Lamdin P., 135

Mining claims: legislation concerning, 55-56; legal right to minerals on, 82-87

Monopoly, kinds of, 393

Moore, B. F., 52-53

Motives of legislators, judicial notice of, 229

Mott, Rev. Edw., 448

Mott, Judge Gordon N.: Field defends his rights to continue as district judge, 62; wants to see Field President, 309

Mulford, S. B., 40, 43

Murray, Chief Justice Hugh C.: opinion in San Francisco *v.* Hazen, 92; dissent in Holland *v.* San Francisco, 93; loses books loaned to Harvey Lee, 106; death, 72

Neagle, David: appointed to protect Field from Terrys, 345; meets Field on way to California, 346; attends Field to and from Los Angeles, 347; shoots Terry when he attacks Field, 348; taken to jail, 350; exonerated by Circuit Court, 358-59; exonerated by U. S. Supreme Court, 359; rewarded by Field, 359

Nelson, Justice Samuel: opinion in United States *v.* Circuit Judges, 100; dissent in Prize cases, 115; dissent in Veazie Bank *v.* Fenno, 175; Field suggests that he may have told what court decision was to be, 145; Seward claimed to control him, 161-62; illness, 188

New Helvetia, 89

Newlands, Francis G.: defends Field before Stockton convention, 305-6; brings suit against Terrys, 331

O'Conor, Chas., 274-75

Old Capitol building: history, 121-22; as Field's home, 122-23

Panama, Field's experiences in, 25

Personal traits of Field: as employer, 123-24, 339; as shown by demeanor in court room, 440; irritability in old age, 339

Philosophies. *See* Judicial process

Pixley, Frank M.: discusses Chinese situation with Field, 221; praises Field's dissent in sinking fund cases, 250; denounces Kearney crowd, 250; denounces treatment of Field by Stockton convention, 307-8

Plague, in Smyrna, 13-14

Police power, nature of, 378-79

Political activities of Field: secures own election as alcalde of Marysville, 31; successful candidate for legislature, 45-47; campaigns for David C. Broderick, 53; fails to get nomination to state senate, 61-62; candidate for U. S. Senate, 69; elected to California supreme bench, 69-71; appointed to U. S. Supreme Court, 116; suggested as Democratic candidate for presidency in 1868, 268-69; serves on Electoral Commission, 271-82; candidate for Democratic nomination for presidency in 1880, 285 ff.; campaign methods, 290-92; nominating speeches, 295-96; defeat, 296-97; urged by conservative California Democrats to be candidate in 1884, 300 ff.; denounced by California Democratic convention at Stockton, 305; defends himself, 302, 308-9, 314-15; tries to keep his enemies out of office, 312-17; 360-61; failure to get chief justiceship, 319; ineffectiveness as politician, 320

Pomeroy, John Norton: appraises Field as judge, 101-2; counsel in San Mateo case, 254

Populist movement, support of income tax law, 396-97, 408

Price, Rodman M., 162

Privileges and immunities, 419 ff. See also Fourteenth Amendment

Property, Field's: accumulates little in New York, 22; buys Marysville lots on credit, 30; rents his property, 32; prospers as alcalde, realtor, and landlord, 37; fined by Judge Turner, 38; expenses of campaign for legislature, 47; in debt, as result of loss of practice and "speculations," 58-59; pays all debts, with heavy interest, 60; alleged loss of money through gambling, 61; earnings from law practice and salary as judge, 72; alleged speculations on basis of court decisions, 95; alleged acceptance of bribes, 97-98; purchase of Old Capitol home, 121-22; property at death in 1899, 446

Property rights. See Rights of property; Fourteenth Amendment; Communism; Judicial process

Public interest, as basis for regulation of business, 373 ff.

Public use, as basis for regulation of business, 389 ff.

Pueblo land. See San Francisco

Purdy, Samuel, 26

Railroads: conditions leading to state regulation of, 362-69; Field's protest at regulation on basis of "public interest," 381-83; Field urges use of total investment as base for rate making, 387-89; "reasonableness" of rates, 391. See also Railroads of California

Railroads of California: building of Central Pacific R. R., 240-43; early attempts at state regulation, 243-44; Field's relations with builders, 244-46; sinking fund act, 246-49; new constitutional provisions for taxing, 251; these provisions before courts, 252-63; Field's railroad decisions injure him politically, 305-7. See also Railroads

Ralston, Jas. H., 70

Reconstruction: clash between Congress and President, 154-55; reconstruction acts, 156; Supreme Court refuses to pass on reconstruction acts, 157-61

Regulation. See Grain elevators; Railroads; Railroads of California

Reid, Whitelaw, 221

Religion: Sunday services, 7; religious life in Field home, 7-8; decadence of religion in New England, 10-11; Field's experiences with Turks and Greek Catholics, 15-16; Field helps found church in Marysville, 68; his comment on source of religion, 77; religion as sanction for law, 79-80; religious appeal in Field's legal tender opinion, 192-93; in opinion concerning

Chinese, 212; Field investigates evidence of revealed religion, 447; Field's emotional interest in religion shortly before death, 447-48

Residences, Field's: garret of Marysville office, 59; Dawson House in Sacramento, 105; St. George Hotel in Sacramento, 105; San Francisco, 119; Washington, 121-23

Resignation, Field's: colleagues desire it, 444; his reasons for continuing, 441-42; letter to colleagues announcing resignation, 444-46

Rhodes, Jas. Ford, on Supreme Court and reconstruction acts, 158

Rights of property, sanctity of, 87, 427

Sabin, Judge Geo. M., 335

Sanderson, S. W., counsel in San Mateo case, 257

San Francisco: life in 1849-50, 26-29; "City Slip" property, 91-95; pueblo land, 96-101; stock market slump, 213

Sawyer, Judge Lorenzo: opinions in Sharon-Hill cases, 325-26; hears pleas to enforce good conduct on part of Sarah A. Hill, 326; his hair pulled by Sarah A. Hill (now Mrs. Terry), 332, 337; asks that deputies guard court room, 332; looks on at Terry court room disturbance, 335; requires Terry to serve full jail sentence, 342; issues writ of habeas corpus for Field, 352; grants petition for writ of habeas corpus for Neagle, 353; opinion, In re Field, 355; In re Neagle, 358-59

Scofield, G. W., 163

Sectionalism, 130 ff.

Sedgwick, Robt., 21

Seward, Wm. H.: declares blockade of Southern ports, 114; claims he controls Judge Nelson, 161-62

Sharon, Frederick W., brings suit against Terrys, 331

Sharon, Sarah A. See Sarah A. Hill

Sharon, Wm.: biographical sketch, 321-22; relationship with Sarah A. Hill, 322-23, 327; brings suit to cancel marriage contract, 324; death, 328

Smith, Samuel B.: becomes Field's law partner, 61; aids his campaign for presidency, 286

Smyrna, Field's life in, 13 ff.

Southern Pacific R. R. See Railroads of California

Sovereignty: as affecting title to valuable minerals, 84-85, 87; its residence, 201

Specie payment. See Greenbacks

Squatters: Field expels from property in Marysville, 35; oppose Field's election to state supreme bench, 70; Field rules against, 89-90; their rights in court, 90-91

Stanford, Leland: supports Field for U. S. Supreme Court justice, 116, 243; says Field is repudiated in California because of test oath opinions, 153-54; leader in Central Pacific R. R. Co., 241; lobbies in California legislature, 243; associates with lawyers and judges, 244; causes criticism of Field, 257; quizzed on his lobbying activities, 263-64; protected through Field's decision, In re Pacific Railway Commission, 264-65; elected to U. S. Senate, 311;

fails to control Field in matter of appointment, 317

Stanford, Mrs. Leland, close friend of Justice and Mrs. Field, 245

Stanly, John, 337-38

Stanton, Edwin M., 181

States' rights, doctrine stated by Field, 285

Stephenson, Colonel, 22, 28

Stevens, Thaddeus, 154

Stewart, Wm. M.: with Field at Downieville July 5, 1851, 64; as counsel for Wm. Sharon, threatened by Sarah A. Hill, 326

Stockbridge, Field family moves to, 5-6; golden wedding there, 61

Stockton Convention, 303 ff. See also Political activities.

Strong, Justice Wm.: appointed, 181; opinion in Knox v. Lee and Parker v. Davis, 188-89; member of Electoral Commission, 271; hanged in effigy, 278

Sullivan, Judge, 324, 345-46

Sumner, Chas., 154

Sunday laws, 77-82

Supreme Court of California: orders Judge Turner to reinstate Field at bar, 41; second reinstatement ordered, 44; decides against Field's client in Barbour-Mott controversy, 62; personnel, 73-74; nature of its tasks, 75-76; Sunday law cases, 77-88; Mexican land grant cases, 88-91; San Francisco land title cases, 91-101; publication of court opinions, 105-7; refusal to adjourn for Terry's funeral, 354

Supreme Court of the United States: formal procedure, 1, 127-28; unpopularity before war, 111-12; effect of war upon personnel, 113, 116; court room,

126-28; membership limited by Congress, 155; restored to nine, 180; court room dispute on legal tender question, 183-84. See also Sectionalism; Greenbacks; Public interest; Taxation

Sutter, John A., 30, 38, 89

Swayne, Justice Noah H.: appointment, 113; statement on legal tender question, 188; dissent in Slaughterhouse cases, 417

Swearingen, Mrs. Isabel, 109-10

Swearingen, Sarah. See Condit-Smith, Mrs. Sarah S.

Swearingen, Sue Virginia. See Field, Sue Virginia Swearingen

Swift, John F., 223-24

Tammany Hall: friendly to Field, 288; hostile to Tilden, 294

Taney, Chief Justice Roger B.: unpopularity, 112; clash with President Lincoln, 112-13; death, 132

Taxation: of Chinese, 207-9; California constitution and taxing of railroads, 251; Field and taxing of California railroads, 252-63; income tax movement, 397; income tax and Supreme Court, 398 ff.; Field's income tax opinion, 402-6

Terry, David S.: biographical sketch, 74, 328-30; opinion in Ex parte Newman, 77; disgusted at Field's retraction to Harvey Lee, 109; becomes attorney for Sarah A. Hill, 328; marries her, 330; attacks Marshal Franks in court room, 334; sentenced to jail, 336; petitions court for release, 338; appeals to U. S. Supreme Court and to President Cleveland, 340; brings action against Marshal Franks, 341;

threatens Field, 336-43; attacks
Field, shot by Neagle, 348; funeral, 354

Terry, Sarah A. *See* Hill, Sarah A.

Test oaths: required of attorneys
and counselors in federal courts,
139; required of citizens in Missouri, 140; Supreme Court decision on postponed, 141-42;
Court controversy over, 142-45;
politicians eager to know Court
decision on, 143-44; decision of
Court, 146-51; political value
of Field's opinions, 153-54, 287

Tevis, Lloyd, 289

Thurman, Allan G.: sponsors sinking fund bill, 247; California
Democrats favor for presidency,
288, 304

Tilden, Samuel J.: defeated in Electoral Commission, 277; incurs
hostility of David Dudley and
Cyrus W. Field, 283-84; declines
to be presidential candidate, 293;
choice of California Democrats,
304

Torpedo, sent to Field through mail,
119-20

Treason, 130-32

Tucker, Beverly, aids Field's campaign for presidency, 290

Turks, Field's experience with, 15-
16

Turner, Judge Wm. R.: comes to
Marysville, 37; punishes Field for
misconduct, 38; burned in effigy,
39; dismisses Field and others
from bar, 39-40, 43; suspension
urged, 41-42; opposes Field's
candidacy for legislature, 46-47;
Field sponsors bill which trans-
fers Turner to another district,
47; Henry Clay expresses confidence in Turner, 48; Field fails

to get Turner tried on impeachment charge, 49; tries to make
peace with Field, 50

Tyler, attorney for Sarah A. Hill,
in altercation with Field, 327

Union party, Field loses prestige
with, 154

United States notes. *See* Greenbacks

Van Buren, John, 21

Van Ness Ordinance, 97

Waite, Chief Justice Morrison R.:
lack of political aspirations, 125;
opinion in Munn *v.* Illinois,
372 ff.; in other Granger cases,
380 ff.; in San Mateo *v.* Southern Pacific R. R., 260; in Santa
Clara *v.* Southern Pacific R. R.,
260; in Sinking Fund cases, 248;
point of view in Granger cases,
388; death, 319, 389

Waite, E. G., 360

Walker, Wm., 64-65

Wallace, Judge Wm. T., 316

Ward, Samuel, 162

Washington, Field's life in, 124-26

Washington, L. Q., 286

Wayne, Justice Jas. M., death of,
174

Weapons: Field learns to shoot from
pockets, 40; guns carried in legislature, 52; Field agrees to begin
duel with guns and finish with
bowie-knives, 62; Field carries
pistol and knife, 66; Field declares attorneys who enter court
room armed should be disbarred,
327

Welles, Gideon, on Supreme Court
in McCardle case, 161-62

Wells, David A., consulted by Field on income tax question, 403-4

White, Justice Edw. D.: appointment, 406-7, 410; dissent in income tax case, 435

White, Stephen Mallory: ridicules Field's protection of Chinese laundries, 225-26; leads Stockton convention Democrats against Field faction in struggle for patronage, 311 ff.; denounces Cleveland, 318; disgusted at support given Field in Terry controversy, 350-51; declines to aid in prosecution of Neagle, 356; on possibility of Field's retirement, 442; fails to control appointment of Field's successor, 444

Whitney, Mrs. Geo. E., 119, 437

Williams College: faculty, 17; entrance requirements, 17; curriculum, 17-18

Williams, John B., 99-100

Wilson, Samuel M.: says federal government should control Chinese immigration, 214; closely associated with Leland Stanford, 244; supports Field for presidency, 288-89; counsel for Sharon interests, 331; defends Field in Circuit Court, 354; defends Neagle in Circuit Court, 358

Wilson, Henry, introduces Senate bill to increase membership of Supreme Court, 180

Workingmen's party. See Labor

Yale, Gregory, 26, 41